W9-BLL-095

THE INSIDERS' GUIDE® TO GREATER Indianapolis

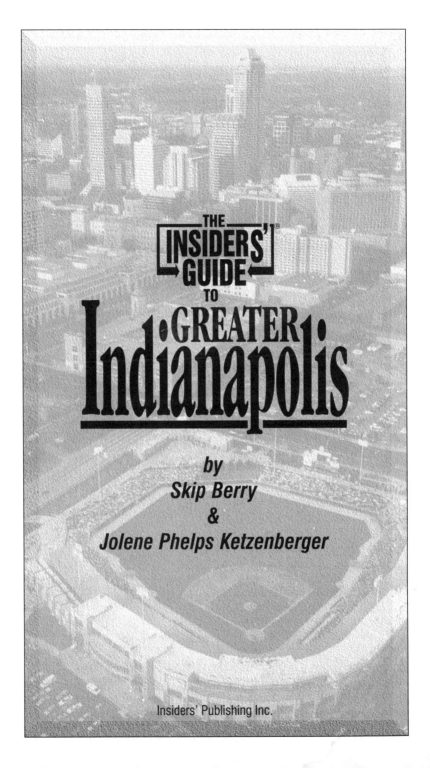

THE INSIDERS' GUIDE TO
GREATER
Indianapolis

by
Skip Berry
&
Jolene Phelps Ketzenberger

Insiders' Publishing Inc.

Co-published and marketed by:
Indianapolis Newspapers Inc.
307 N. Pennsylvania Street
Indianapolis, Indiana
(317) 633-1240

Co-published and distributed by:
Insiders' Publishing Inc.
105 Budleigh St.
P.O. Box 2057
Manteo, NC 27954
(919) 473-6100

•

SECOND EDITION
1st printing

•

Copyright ©1997
by Indianapolis Newspapers Inc.

•

Printed in the United States
of America

•

Publications from The Insiders' Guide®
series are available at special discounts
for bulk purchases for sales promotions,
premiums or fundraisings. Special
editions, including personalized covers,
can be created in large quantities for
special needs. For more information,
please write to Insiders' Publishing Inc.,
P.O. Box 2057, Manteo, NC 27954 or
call (919) 473-6100 x 233.

ISBN 1-57380-015-5

Indianapolis Newspapers Inc. Supplemental Publications

Advertising Director
Kimberly Parker

Project Manager
Laura Bridgewater

Sales Manager
Jim O'Donnell

Account Executives
**Darrin Gray, Pam Ballard,
Annette Rainbolt, Darlene Shaw
and Patrick Bates**

Advertising Artist
Joe Thom

Project Editor
Jeff Hauersperger

Assistant Editors
Patty Deely and Terri Mackney

Insiders' Publishing Inc.

Publisher/Editor-in-Chief
Beth P. Storie

President/General Manager
Michael McOwen

Affiliate Sales and Training Director
Rosanne Cheeseman

Partner Services Director
Giles MacMillan

Sales and Marketing Director
Jennifer Risko

Creative Services Director
Mike Lay

Online Services Director
David Haynes

Managing Editor
Theresa Shea Chavez

Fulfillment Director
Gina Twiford

Project Editor
Theresa Shea Chavez

Project Artist
Mel Dorsey

Preface

Welcome to Indianapolis! Whatever brings you here, it won't take long for you to realize that you're genuinely welcome. It's called Hoosier hospitality, but that isn't all our city has to offer.

Indianapolis is the 12th-largest city in the United States. It has a metropolitan population in excess of a million people. It's one of the most affordable cities of its size in the country, making it attractive to businesses and individuals looking to relocate. It's one of the key manufacturing, warehousing and distribution sites in the country. It's a vital center for medical research and amateur athletics. And, of course, it's the home of the Indianapolis 500, the largest one-day professional sporting event in the world.

Once dismissed as "Naptown" and "Indiano-place," this city revived and renewed itself in the 1980s, becoming what *Newsweek* called "the Cinderella of the Rustbelt." Now, midway through the '90s, Indianapolis continues to polish its image with such projects as Circle Centre, the long-awaited mall that has revitalized retail in the downtown district, and such nationally admired efforts as the privatization of many municipal services.

A book like this, which confirms the city's significance as a destination for travelers, conventioneers and relocators, is long overdue. By providing information about an array of area organizations and services, it offers access to those organizations and services — and makes clear the city's complexity and variety.

Writing any guidebook is a daunting task; writing one that provides a comprehensive, inside look at a metropolitan area the size of Greater Indianapolis is even more so. We've done our best to guide you to the best and brightest of Greater Indianapolis. We hope you'll enjoy our favorite shops, restaurants, attractions, parks, weekend getaways, etc. that we've included in this book. We've covered a wide range of topics. But we know things have been omitted, often inadvertently. If you don't find your favorite cafe in our Restaurants chapter, or if you discovered some intriguing nooks and crannies while exploring the city, please let us know. Write to us in care of:

Editor
Insiders' Publishing Inc.
P.O. Box 2057
Manteo, North Carolina 27954

We'll be updating this book annually, so we'll have the opportunity to correct oversights and mistakes and ensure the continued accuracy of existing entries.

That said, *The Insiders' Guide® to Greater Indianapolis* is the most comprehensive guidebook to Indiana's capital city yet developed. That's not to say there aren't other good guides available — there are. But the book you're holding is the only one to assemble such a large volume and variety of information under one cover.

Don't let this book gather dust on a bookshelf. Use it! Stick it in your car's glovebox. Toss it in your briefcase or backpack. Scribble in the margins. Circle things that interest you. Think of it as your personal tour guide.

Use it and enjoy. We're glad you're here or are planning a trip or move to Greater Indianapolis. We look forward to hearing from you.

Charles L'Enfant, who assisted in the planning of Washington, D.C., modeled Indianapolis after the nation's capitol.

About the Authors

S. L. (Skip) Berry has lived in Indianapolis for 13 years. During that time he has freelanced for such publications as *The New York Times*, *Travel & Leisure* and *USAir Magazine* in addition to a number of local and regional newspapers and magazines. Currently, he is a feature writer for *The Indianapolis Star* and *The Indianapolis News*.

Berry is the author of more than a dozen nonfiction books for children and adults, including one on Indianapolis. His biography of photographer Gordon Parks was designated one of 1991's outstanding books for teens by the New York Public Library. Among his other books for young readers are biographies of poets Emily Dickinson, Langston Hughes and E. E. Cummings and books on Little League baseball and the Tour de France bicycle race.

Berry has provided freelance writing services to a variety of corporations and nonprofit organizations. He's led writing workshops for children and adults in schools, universities, libraries and museums throughout Indiana.

He lives with his wife, Margo, and their son, Tyler, in one of Indianapolis' comfortable older neighborhoods. When not writing, he enjoys walking, bicycling and gardening. He's also an avid reader, movie lover, music buff and closet musician.

Jolene Phelps Ketzenberger

Born and raised in Central Indiana, Jolene Phelps Ketzenberger has spent much of her writing career focusing on the Indianapolis area, first as an editor with *Indianapolis Monthly*, then as restaurant critic for *NUVO Newsweekly*. Her writing has earned numerous awards, including honors from the Hoosier State Press Association and the Society of Professional Journalists. She also teaches writing at Indiana University-Purdue University at Indianapolis.

Ketzenberger began her exploration of the city at age 18 when she lived on campus as a student at IUPUI. While there, she discovered the City Market, the Children's Museum, the Central Library and Broad Ripple — she was hooked. After finishing her journalism degree at Ball State University, Ketzenberger and her husband, John, a newspaper reporter, lived in Columbus, Indiana. They settled in Indianapolis in 1987 and have been enjoying city life while renovating their 1920s-era home. They also are raising three active young children, Aaron, Adam and Jane Ann, with whom they enjoy watching Indians games, playing at Holliday Park and hanging out in the backyard.

Though busy with writing and with her children, Ketzenberger enjoys cooking, reading and traveling around the state. And although she's never been to the 500, she does know all the words to "Back Home Again in Indiana."

For those living in the fast lane, we present high-speed banking.

Your time is too precious to waste in bank lines. That's why KeyBank has so many ways to speed up your banking. Like automatic bill paying. Phone banking. And enough ATMs to keep you from having to see the inside of a bank until well into the next millennium. For more time-saving ideas, enter our phone number, 1-800-539-2968. Preferably, in your speed dial.

1·800·KEY2YOU®

Member FDIC

Key. For a new America.℠

Table of Contents

Directory of Maps

Acknowledgments

Skip . . .

Scores of people are responsible for this book — all the people who took time to talk with me in person or on the phone, all the people who sent me information I requested, all the people who verified facts I was trying to check. I can't thank each of you by name, but I can thank all of you collectively. You helped make this book possible.

Beyond that, I offer special thanks to the following people and organizations for their help with this project: Tom Aikens, Laura Bridgewater, Brad Carlson and the Indiana Sports Corporation, Greg Charleston and The Arts Council of Indianapolis, Indiana University, the Indianapolis Chamber of Commerce, the Indianapolis City Center, Indianapolis Downtown Inc., the Indianapolis-Marion County Public Library, the Indianapolis Project, Pat Miles and CIOCA The Access Network, the POLIS Research Center at IUPUI, and Judy Wade and her colleagues at Indy Parks.

I also want to thank my colleagues at *The Indianapolis Star* and *The Indianapolis News* for their understanding, especially Jim Lindgren who put off assigning me big sprawling articles while I was in the midst of this big sprawling project. You're a gentleman, Jim, and I appreciate it.

But most of all I want to thank Margo and Tyler, who put up with the time and energy demands that this project made on me. I know it was hard on you both, and I appreciate your love and support. You're the best.

Jolene . . .

I offer many, many thanks to my husband, John, for all the love, support and time; to my sons, Aaron and Adam, for trying to understand; to Sara Kendall, for her interest and enthusiasm for this project and for her unflagging willingness to try yet another restaurant; to Lisa Montgomery, for listening; to my sister, Judith Bastin, for her encouragement; and to my parents, Ed and Betty Phelps, and my in-laws, Denny and Mary Ann Ketzenberger, for their love and moral support.

I'd also like to thank all the groups, businesses and individuals who answered questions and provided information for this book; *The Indianapolis Star*, *The Indianapolis News* and *Indianapolis Monthly* for all the background information; and the authors of *The Encyclopedia of Indianapolis* for their excellent reference book.

I also owe a big thank you to editor Theresa Chavez for her patience and to Debbie Paul, for the chance to write about Indianapolis in the first place.

Greater Indianapolis

Regional Indianapolis

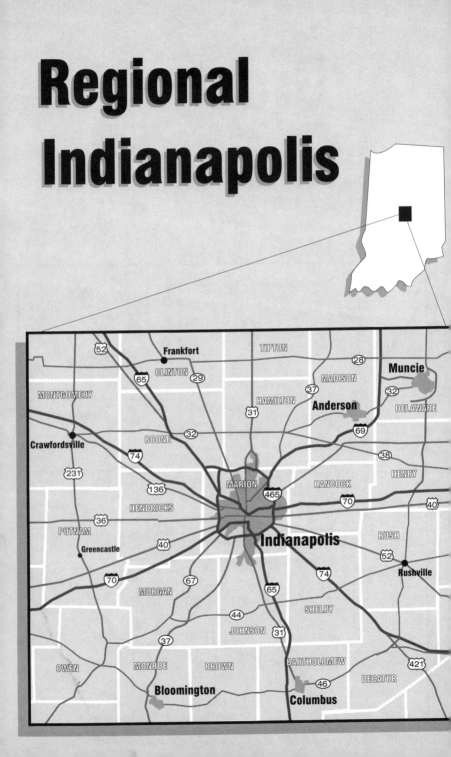

History

Novelist Kurt Vonnegut Jr. once observed that his hometown of Indianapolis is the world's largest city not on a navigable waterway. The irony of that observation lies in the fact that Indianapolis was purposely situated on the banks of Central Indiana's White River because its founders believed the river would meet their transportation and development needs.

But it didn't. Then as now, the White River is too shallow most of the year for anything other than small boats to navigate safely. From the start, Indianapolis was landlocked.

The trick, it turned out, was not to focus on such an obvious liability but to capitalize on an equally obvious asset — Indianapolis's central geographic location. As roads and highways — and later railways and air routes — were mapped out, Indianapolis became a logical connecting point for east-west and north-south traffic. By virtue of a shallow river, Indianapolis became the self-proclaimed Crossroads of America.

So it goes.

Prehistory

During the last Ice Age, glaciers crept southward across what would later be Indiana, covering the top two-thirds of the state. When they finally began their retreat, they left behind a landscape with few wrinkles but plenty of lakes and rivers, streams and ponds, creeks and wetlands. And deep, rich, fertile soil, from which sprang magnificent hardwood forests.

The earliest known inhabitants of this region date to some 8,000 years ago, according to *The Indiana Way, A State History* by Indiana University History Department Chair James H. Madison. From that point on, archeologists believe, various indigenous peoples populated Indiana, congregating mostly near bodies of wa-

ter — Lake Michigan to the northwest, the upper Wabash and Maumee rivers to the northeast, the lower Wabash and Ohio rivers to the south, and in Central Indiana along the White River.

By the time European and early American explorers began venturing into the Midwest in the 17th and 18th centuries, the prehistoric Indians who had once called Indiana home had vanished. Living here in their stead were many Native Americans, most prominently the Miami and Potawatomi.

The New Purchase

Central Indiana's modern history began with the New Purchase Treaty of 1818 in which William Henry Harrison, former governor of the Indiana Territory, negotiated the acquisition of several million acres of Indian lands, primarily from the Miamis and the Potawatomis. It wasn't much of a deal from the Indians' perspective.

In return for promises of annual payments, as well as token gifts, they gave up claim to land that had been their home for generations. And they agreed to either settle on plots that Harrison and his cohorts magnanimously agreed to reserve for them or to move westward — out of the way of the ever-advancing wave of white settlers.

On the other hand, Indiana, which literally (and ironically) means "land of Indians," made out like a bandit. Confined at the time to a handful of counties bordering the Ohio and the lower Wabash rivers, the fledgling state (it had attained statehood only two years earlier) gained so much territory that it more than doubled in size.

By spring of 1820, settlers started trickling into the new territory. Among them were the

McCormicks: John, James and Samuel. Heading northwest out of Connersville into the New Purchase region, the McCormicks chopped a path through forests so dense that midday seemed like twilight.

When they reached the confluence of the White River and Fall Creek, the McCormicks stopped. There, John McCormick staked claim to a piece of land. The heavily forested terrain offered plentiful supplies of firewood and logs; the soil was rich and perfect for farming. James and Samuel settled close-by.

While the McCormicks busied themselves clearing their new land, Indiana's first governor, Jonathan Jennings, plotted Indiana's future. In late 1820, he sent 10 commissioners out into the New Purchase to select a site for a new state capital. At the time, the town of Corydon, in the southeast part of the newly expanded state, was the capital. Jennings and many members of the state Legislature, known officially as the Indiana General Assembly, wanted a site nearer the center of Indiana so the capital would be equally accessible to residents throughout the state. The commissioners looked at three potential locations before agreeing on the area surrounding John McCormick's cabin. Realizing the economic potential of that choice, the enterprising McCormick opened a tavern, which became one of the new state capital's earliest business success stories.

Once the site for Indiana's new capital had been chosen, the state Legislature had to give it a name. Several people suggested Indian names, but those and other suggestions were voted down. Then, in the first of what has become an Indiana tradition of choosing the obvious when it comes to naming public places, Judge Jeremiah Sullivan scribbled "Indiana" on a slip of paper. Then he added the Greek suffix "polis," which means "city." The result — "Indianapolis"— won legislative approval more by default than by delight. No one was particularly thrilled with the name, but no one had a better idea, either. Hence, the new state capital was officially dubbed Indianapolis.

Designing a State Capital

Even with a name, Indianapolis was still more of an idea than an actuality. So state officials hired surveyors Alexander Ralston and Elias P. Fordham to draw up a plan for the capital city. Ralston, who had assisted Charles L'Enfant in the planning of Washington, D.C., took one look at the heavily wooded site and said, "It will be a beautiful city — if it is ever built."

Then he designed a city modeled after Washington. He plotted a square with mile-long sides, which was as large as he envisioned Indianapolis ever becoming. In the center of the square, Ralston put a wooded knoll encircled by a wide street; four diagonal streets radiated out from it like spokes on a wagon wheel.

The plan called for the governor's house to sit atop the knoll. And between 1827 and 1839, it did, though no governor ever lived there. The idea of being on constant display in the center of the city wasn't something any governor relished. The house on the circle was torn down in 1857.

However, Ralston's legacy is still amply evident in Indianapolis today. The downtown district is known as the Mile Square, and its heart is Ralston's central circle with streets radiating outward. But the wooded knoll long ago gave way to the Soldiers and Sailors Monument, which memorializes Indiana's Civil War veterans. One of the city's best known landmarks, the monument earned the city's center the official designation of Monument Circle — though most residents today just refer to it as "the Circle."

At first, Ralston's doubts about the city's future seemed prophetic. The lack of decent roads and passable waterways hampered development. The lure of building a city from scratch attracted only the most rugged settlers to the site. And those who came suffered not only primitive living conditions, but disease as well — the settlement's proximity to swampy river floodplains led to the out-

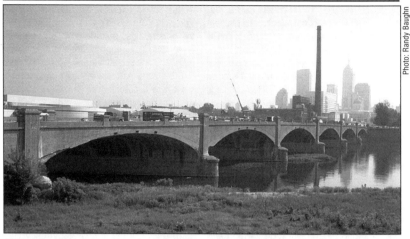

White River, which proved useless as a large-scale transportation route, plays a key role in city development plans.

break of malaria in the summers of 1821 and 1822.

Despite the problems, the Indiana General Assembly decided to move government operations there permanently in 1824. In November of that year, Samuel Merrill, the state treasurer, loaded Indiana's stockpile of silver, official documents, a printing press and his family and furniture, onto four wagons and headed north out of Corydon. Merrill's daughter, Priscilla, later described the 160-mile trip over rutted, muddy roads as frightening, especially when the horses and wagons would sink into the deep water that covered much of the route. When the frazzled travelers finally straggled into Indianapolis, they found a village populated by fewer than 500 people.

But while Indianapolis wasn't quite the bustling capital city that Governor Jennings and the General Assembly had envisioned, neither was it a disaster. By 1825, it had such touches of civilization as a post office, a school building, some small shops and a courthouse. The courthouse also served as the home of the state Legislature until the first capitol building was constructed in 1835. But it wasn't until government officials and local businesspeople tackled the problem of limited accessibility that Indianapolis really took shape. The key to the city's growth and prosperity, then as now, was transportation.

Transportation Hub

When the White River proved useless as a large-scale transportation route, it forced legislators and settlers alike to develop alternatives. In 1836, the Indiana General Assembly passed a piece of legislation whose title left no doubt about its intention — "The Mammoth Improvement Bill." It called for the development of roads, canals and railways throughout the state. By the mid-1830s, two major roads under development crossed in Indianapolis. The National Highway, which is now known as U.S. Highway 40, started in Cumberland, Maryland, and ran west. The Michigan Road, which is now U.S. Highway 421, started at the Ohio River and ran north toward Lake Michigan. The intersection of these two highways put Indianapolis on the road to its future. Over the next few years, more roads were cut through the wilderness; many of them started in, ended at or passed through Indianapolis.

Started in 1836, the Central Canal project was designed to link Indianapolis with the Wabash and Erie canals. The Central Canal began north of the city in the village of Broad Ripple. However, after only 8.8 miles of the canal had been dug, the money to pay for it dried up. Today that portion of the canal remains, running from Broad Ripple, where it's home to hundreds of well-fed ducks and geese, to downtown Indianapolis. The dirt path once trod by mules tugging canal boats is now trod by families, anglers, runners, artists and nature lovers. In recent years, the downtown stretch of the canal got a face-lift, complete with new apartment and office buildings perched along its banks.

Work on the Madison-to-Indianapolis rail line began in 1839, but it wasn't until eight years later that the first steam train chugged into Indianapolis. Within a short time after that, railroad tracks crisscrossed the city. By 1855, Indianapolis was home to eight rail lines. The Indianapolis Union Depot was the first central railroad station in the United States: With a train shed and passenger depot that measured 420 feet long by 200 feet wide, railroad employees could service five trains and their passengers at the same time. It wasn't long before every passenger train passing through the Indianapolis region was routed through Union Depot. And the residents of Indianapolis began referring to their town as the Crossroads of America.

From Settlement to City

Indianapolis was incorporated as a town in 1832, but it wasn't until 1847, with the adoption of a city charter, that it officially became a city. That same year, residents elected their first mayor — Whig Party candidate Samuel Henderson. They also voted to establish a tax to support free public schools.

Since the first school's creation in 1821, Indianapolis parents had paid for their children's lessons, sometimes using coonskins as currency. From coonskins to school taxes was a big step, and it took several years after the 1847 vote to actually establish a public school system. The first free public school in Indianapolis opened its doors in 1853, a precursor to the development of the Indianapolis Public Schools system, which now operates more than 80 schools, serving more than 45,000 students.

As transportation routes improved, the population of Indianapolis expanded. By 1850, more than 8,000 people called Indianapolis home. Many came from the bordering states of Ohio and Kentucky; others moved from

Pennsylvania, North Carolina and Virginia. European immigrants also came looking for the opportunities that the new settlement offered. Two immigrant groups that had an immediate impact on life in the young city were the Germans and the Irish. As members of these two groups settled in, neighborhoods with names such as Germantown and Irish Hill evolved.

So did churches. The importance of religion to the town's immigrant residents gradually made Indianapolis a city of churches: Lutheran, Catholic, Presbyterian, Episcopal, Baptist and Methodist congregations were housed in buildings ranging from simple wooden structures to elaborate brick and stone edifices.

The love of music shared by many German and Irish residents resulted in choirs, orchestras and community bands. And their passion for politics resulted in community newspapers, public debates and political rallies.

There were only about 500 African Americans living in Indianapolis in 1850, and they were barred both by law and prejudice from participating in much of community life. As a result, they developed their own vital community, including fraternal organizations and churches. Two of the latter — the Bethel African Methodist Episcopal Church, founded in 1836, and the Second Baptist Church, founded a decade later — continue today.

Despite the General Assembly's passage in 1851 of a constitutional article prohibiting blacks from taking up residence in Indiana, fugitive slaves regularly found refuge in and around Indianapolis. And the Civil War increased still further the black population in Central Indiana.

The Civil War

By the time the Civil War broke out, Indianapolis had become a bustling railway center, which in turn made it an important center of Union Army activity. Trainloads of Union soldiers on their way to or from battle stopped in Indianapolis. Restaurants, hotels and saloons were filled with bluecoats, traders, farmers, merchants and gamblers.

The city thrived as its stockyards, meat packing plants, granaries, wagon makers, clothing manufacturers and munitions factories supplied the Union forces. In 1862, Indianapolis resident Dr. Richard Gatling unveiled a hand-cranked, ten-barrel gun that fired more than 250 shots a minute. The Gatling gun became the first widely used machine gun and permanently affected both offensive and defensive battlefield strategies.

Indiana's governor during this time, Oliver P. Morton, single-handedly directed many of the state's war efforts, including mustering up thousands of volunteers for the Union Army. Men from around the state poured into Indianapolis for training at Camp Morton, while the governor pulled strings and twisted arms to ensure that Indiana's soldiers were well-armed, well-clothed and well-fed.

One of Morton's most audacious actions was the creation of an arsenal that initially supplied munitions only to Indiana troops but later became one of the leading suppliers to the entire Union Army. That arsenal and its munitions manufacturing plant became so important to the war effort that the federal government moved it from the State House grounds to a 76-acre site just east of the Mile Square. Today, that site is home to Arsenal Technical High School, one of the city's best-known public schools.

Because of its central geographic location, Indianapolis was a hotbed of pro-North and pro-South sentiments. Heated debates flared on street corners, fueled by newspapers that cheered for one side and jeered at the other. Abolitionists such as Ovid Butler argued passionately against slavery, while pro-slavery advocates tried to use the Fugitive Slave Law to enslave local resident John Freeman, a respected black house painter. When local attorneys and businesspeople rallied to support Freeman, he won his battle to remain a free man.

Meanwhile, east of the city, Hiram Bacon's dairy farm served as a way-station for the Underground Railroad. Bacon hid runaway slaves in his barn as they made their way north from Confederate states to Canada. At the same time, on the northeastern edge of the Mile Square, Camp Morton was converted into a prison camp for Confederate soldiers.

In spite of contrasting viewpoints, Indianapolis prospered during the Civil War and continued to prosper following the war's end. Ex-soldiers, freed slaves, European immigrants and newcomers from the East Coast jostled through city streets. Mule-drawn streetcars, freight wagons, farm carts and fringe-topped carriages clattered over cobblestones and crowded intersections. Business was booming.

Industrial Growth

Because it was a railway center, Indianapolis also became an industrial center in the latter part of the 19th century. Much of the credit for the city's industrial development belongs to mayor John Craven, who, during a walk one afternoon in 1876, came up with the idea of a system of railroad tracks that would encircle the city and connect with all the rail lines already in place. By 1878, a system of tracks known as the Belt Line surrounded Indianapolis, giving all freight trains coming into the city access to the stockyards, factories and warehouses that sprang up along the tracks.

The same year that mayor Craven conceived the Belt Line, a former Union Army colonel named Eli Lilly founded what would become one of the city's best-known companies — Eli Lilly and Company. Known initially as Eli Lilly, Chemist, the small pharmaceutical manufacturing operation quickly became a success, making Lilly and his heirs wealthy. Today, Eli Lilly and Company is an international corporation; its corporate headquarters, research laboratories and production facilities cover hundreds of acres of land both southeast and southwest of the Mile Square.

While Lilly became one of the industrial giants in Indianapolis, the city didn't pin all its hopes on pills and potions. The fertile soil of Central Indiana had made agriculture and such related activities as meat packing, grain milling and blacksmithing important industries from the beginning. By the late 19th century, the Kingan Brothers meat packing plant was the world's largest. Van Camp Company was a leading producer of canned pork and beans. And National Starch turned corn from the surrounding farmlands into the starch that stiffened many a banker's shirt.

In addition to agricultural industries, Indianapolis was home to foundries and machine shops, carriage and wagon manufacturers, bicycle makers, distilleries, publishing companies and printing plants.

Between 1870 and 1900, immigrants continued to make their way to Indianapolis. Among their numbers were Italian tailors, shoemakers, barbers, fruit and vegetable dealers and musicians, as well as Greek mechanics and merchants. By 1910, Armenians, Hungarians, Poles, Macedonians and other eastern Europeans also had arrived, finding jobs in factories or setting up small shops.

With the growth of industry came the trade union movement. In the late 19th and early 20th century, Indianapolis became a center of union activities when organizers such as Eugene Debs, who founded the International Workers of the World, and John L. Lewis, who founded the United Mine Workers, set up offices in the city and held rallies on the Circle. Other unions followed suit. In all, Indianapolis was home to the national headquarters of a dozen unions, though all eventually decamped for the higher profile of Washington, D.C.

Presidential Campaigning, Harrison Style

In 1888, Indianapolis attorney and U.S. Senator Benjamin Harrison (grandson of William Henry Harrison, the New Purchase Treaty negotiator and later the ninth President of the United States) became the Republican Party's challenger to unseat then-President Grover Cleveland. A reserved man, Harrison refused to take to the campaign trail, preferring instead to campaign from the front porch of his house and a platform in University Square (now University Park). Newspaper reporters then telegraphed his speeches and statements around the country.

Harrison's unorthodox tactic worked. He was elected President, serving from 1889 to 1893. During his term, he signed into law such memorable pieces of legislation as the McKinley Tarriff Act and the Sherman Anti-Trust Act. When his bid for a second term was unsuccessful, Harrison returned to Indianapolis where he lived out his life, dying in 1901. He's buried in Crown Hill Cemetery. Harrison's memory is preserved in two separate sites. His former residence at 1230 N. Delaware Street now serves as his memorial and is open to the public. On the northeast side of the city is Fort Harrison State Park, formerly a U.S. Army base known as Fort Benjamin Harrison. Though historians don't rate Harrison among the countries finest chief executives, Indianapolis continues to remember him fondly. Unfortunately, Fort Ben, as the base is affectionately known, officially closed in January 1996. The state of Indiana now leases the 1,700-acre facility and is gradually converting it into a park. When completed, the park will include 1,100 acres of wood, two lakes, an 18-hole golf course, hiking trails, horseback trails, a biking trail, three nature preserves, a nature center, a museum, a swimming pool, playgrounds and picnic areas. The park will open in stages beginning in late 1996 and early 1997 but will not be fully operational until 1999.

Soldiers and Sailors Monument

When the original governor's house was torn down in 1857, the Circle became a local eyesore: Livestock grazed there, and the ground was littered with trash. With the end of the Civil War came a move to make better use of the city's most visible piece of land — it was turned into a park. But in 1887, the Indiana General Assembly created a commission that was given the task of creating a monument, which was to be erected on the Circle to honor the state's Civil War veterans. Out of 70 designs submitted by architects from throughout the world, commissioners chose the work of German architect Bruno Schmitz. Work on Schmitz's monument began in 1888 and lasted until 1901. The finished monument included not only Schmitz's original concepts but also incorporated works from three sculptors, including George T. Brewster who created *Victory*, a.k.a. "Miss Indiana," which tops the monument. Soldiers and Sailors Monument quickly became (and remains) one of the city's best known landmarks, and it led to its site being officially designated Monument Circle. Flanked to the north and south by curved banks of steps and to the east and west by tiered fountains and reflecting pools, the 284-foot-tall monument is a popular lunchtime gathering place for downtown workers in the summer. Festooned with strands of lights every December, it's the city's best-known Christmas symbol — the self-proclaimed "world's largest Christmas tree." The monument's observation tower, which is accessible by elevator or 32 flights of stairs, offers a panoramic view of the Indianapolis skyline.

Madame Walker and Indiana Avenue

While Eli Lilly's medicines were making him a household name, Madame C.J. Walker's hair care products for African Americans were doing the same for her. A former washer woman with limited education, Madame Walker turned her homemade hair ointment into one of the most visible black-owned companies in America. In the process, she became the country's first black female millionaire.

From humble beginnings in Walker's homes in St. Louis and Denver, the Walker System of hair care grew into a thriving enterprise, with a variety of products and services. Walker employed more than 20,000 people nationwide. In 1910, Walker moved her company to Indianapolis where she built a factory and became a well-respected local philanthropist. Six years later, Walker left for Harlem, but her company continued to operate successfully in Indianapolis.

As the local African-American population began to increase after the Civil War, a neighborhood and business district took shape northwest of the Mile Square. Indiana Avenue became the main artery in what was a thriving community of schools, churches and black-owned businesses. The rise of jazz in the 1920s, which local musicians helped create and foster, brought national prominence to Indiana Avenue. The clubs lining the Avenue booked some of the best-known jazz musicians of the day, and Indianapolis became a jazz capital known throughout the country.

To commemorate Madame Walker's success, her daughter Lelia commissioned the construction of the Madame C.J. Walker Center in 1928. A block-long office and theater complex on Indiana Avenue, the Center became the centerpiece of the community and remained so until hard times hit the Avenue in the 1950s and '60s. Renovated in the late '80s, the Walker Center, which is listed on the National Register of Historic Places, is once again a vital part of African-American cultural activities in Indianapolis.

The Auto Industry

By the late 19th century, there were several carriage and bicycle manufacturers in Indianapolis; when the automobile rolled onto the nation's streets, many of those manufacturers turned their tools and attention to making cars. In 1899, carriage-maker Charles Black became the first to do so, but he was far from the last. Between 1900 and 1936, Indianapolis was home to at least 60 different auto makers, including makers of such elegant speedsters as the Stutz, the Marmon and the Duesenberg. But when Henry Ford perfected assembly-line production in his Detroit-based factory, Indianapolis lost the race to become the country's auto manufacturing center. Ironically, however, between 1914 and 1933, Ford operated a branch manufacturing plant in Indianapolis.

As the auto industry evolved, Indianapolis retained its importance by becoming the site of factories making essential auto and truck components. And by becoming the home of the world's best-known auto racing facilities — the Indianapolis Motor Speedway.

Indianapolis Motor Speedway

Developed in 1909 by car salesman and entrepreneur Carl Graham Fisher and partners Arthur Newby, Frank Wheeler and James A. Allison, the Indianapolis Motor Speedway is actually in the town of Speedway, a couple of miles west of the Mile Square. After sponsoring several poorly attended racing events, the Speedway partners decided to host a 500-mile, $25,000-purse race on May 30, 1911. It was a gamble that paid off handsomely.

Forty cars qualified for the race, including a locally built black and yellow Marmon Wasp

Famous Indiana Faces

A wide variety of famous faces have been seen around these parts at one time or another. Many well-known celebrities and historical figures can claim a Hoosier heritage. Some such celebrities may return regularly, such as Indianapolis-born David Letterman, who makes an annual pilgrimage to the 500.

Others barely acknowledge their Indiana roots, such Guns 'N Roses rocker and Lafayette native Axl Rose (a.k.a. Bill Bailey). Read on for a quick roundup of more than 50 famous Hoosiers.

- Former Boston Celtics star Larry Bird, "the hick from French Lick"
- Fashion designer and Fort Wayne native Bill Blass
- Presidents Nixon and Ford's secretary of agriculture Earl Butz
- Bloomington-born songwriter Hoagy Carmichael
- Singer and actor Scatman Crothers, born in Terre Haute
- Garfield creator and Marion native Jim Davis
- 1950s movie idol James Dean, born in Marion
- Labor leader Eugene V. Debs
- *Three's Company* star Joyce DeWitt, from Indianapolis
- Bank robber John Dillinger, who grew up in Mooresville
- Music biz whiz and singer "Baby Face" Edmonds, graduate of North Central High School in Indianapolis
- Chad Everett, *Medical Center's* Dr. Joe Gannon, who was born in South Bend
- Fort Wayne-area native Janie Fricke, who hit it big in Country music
- Actor and Frankfort native Will Geer who played Grandpa Zeb Walton on *The Waltons*
- Evansville native and *Barney Miller* star Ron Glass
- Architect Michael Graves, from Indianapolis
- Football Hall of Famer Bob Griese, an Evansville native
- Astronaut Gus Grissom, of Mitchell, who was killed during a simulation flight on Apollo 1
- John Gruelle, newspaper cartoonist and creator of the enduring Raggedy Ann character, who grew up in Indianapolis
- Bobby Helms of "Jingle Bell Rock" fame from Martinsville
- Florence Henderson, of Dale, played Carol Brady on *The Brady Bunch*
- "Artless Dodger" Gil Hodges, a native of Princeton
- The Jackson 5 began singing together in Gary in 1966
- Indianapolis native and jazz musician J.J. Johnson
- Boxing champ (and TV pitchman) Marvin Johnson
- All-American tackle Alex Karras, who played for Emerson High School in Gary
- Wolcottville native Ken Kercheval who played Cliff Barnes on TV's *Dallas*
- New York Yankee Don Larsen, from Michigan City
- Indianapolis native and former weekend weatherman David Letterman
- Actress Carole Lombard, born Jane Alice Peters in Fort Wayne
- Actress Shelley Long, from Fort Wayne
- Evansville's Don Mattingly, who was pulled from the New York Yankee lineup in 1991 for having long hair
- Basketball player George McGinnis, from Indianapolis
- *The Magnificent Seven* tough guy Steve McQueen, born in Beech Grove
- Seymour-born singer/songwriter John Mellencamp
- Jazz great Wes Montgomery, born in Indianapolis

CBS funny man David Letterman (center) grew up in Broad Ripple
and was once a local TV weatherman.

- Noblesville native and fashion designer Norman Norell
- Indianapolis native Jane Pauley got her start on local TV
- Lafayette-born film director Sydney Pollack, who won an Oscar for *Out of Africa*, one of his many successful movies
- Songwriter Cole Porter, from Peru
- Gene Stratton Porter, who lived in Geneva and wrote The Girl of the Limberlost
- Dana native Ernie Pyle, a well-respected war correspondent during WWII
- Former vice president Dan Quayle
- Brazil native and popcorn king Orville Redenbacher
- Oscar Robertson began his basketball career in Indianapolis and played for Crispus Attucks High School
- Bloomington native, singer David Lee Roth, formerly of the group Van Halen
- Though he made his name with Kentucky Fried Chicken, Col. Harlan Sanders was born near Henryville
- Classic clown Red Skelton, born in Vicennes in 1913
- Malden Sukilovich, who changed his name to Karl Malden and starred in *The Streets of San Francisco* before becoming an American Express pitchman, hails from Gary
- Pulitzer Prize-winner Booth Tarkington
- Chuck Taylor played for Columbus High School long before he developed his famous high-top sneakers
- Ballet dancer and choreographer Twyla Tharp, born in Portland
- Forest Tucker, actor on "F Troop" TV show, who is from Plainfield
- Indianapolis native and bestselling author Kurt Vonnegut Jr.
- *Going All the Way* author Dan Wakefield
- Country music star Steve Wariner, from Noblesville
- Singer Deniece Williams, from Gary
- Elwood native Wendell Wilkie carried Indiana but lost to Franklin Roosevelt in 1940
- *Laugh In* regular Jo Anne Worley, born in Lowell
- Golfer and native Hoosier Fuzzy Zoeller of New Albany.

(This information was culled from a book called *Awesome Almanac Indiana*.)

that Ray Harroun drove to victory in six hours and 42 minutes at an average speed of 74.9 miles an hour. So well-received was that first 500-mile race that it became a tradition.

In 1927, a group of investors, headed by former race car driver and World War I ace aviator Eddie Rickenbacker, bought the track. Under Rickenbacker's guidance, the track continued to thrive until World War II, when gas rationing and manufacturing limitations brought auto racing to a standstill. For four years, the Speedway sat empty.

In 1945, Terre Haute businessman Anton "Tony" Hulman bought the facility. By that time, disuse had led to decline — the track was in terrible shape. Hulman spearheaded a renovation effort that restored the Speedway to its former glory and updated it as racing needs and spectator demands dictated.

Today, the Indianapolis Motor Speedway, still privately owned by the Hulman family, hosts not only the annual Indianapolis 500, which is billed as the world's largest one-day sporting event, but also the annual Brickyard 400 stock-car race. And the track is used year-round by automakers and racing teams to test tires and engines. See our Auto Racing chapter for more information.

World War I and the American Legion

When the United States entered World War I in 1917, Indianapolis played an important role. Soldiers from throughout Indiana trained at Fort Benjamin Harrison, while local factories manufactured munitions, engines for aircraft, trucks and tanks. And as in the Civil War, it was a connecting point for trains carrying troops and freight.

Following the Armistice of 1918, which officially ended the war, the American Legion was founded. In 1919, the new organization announced its national headquarters would be in Indianapolis. A year later, the Indiana General Assembly agreed to appropriate funds for the construction of a building to house the Legion and for the creation of a Memorial Plaza to honor the soldiers who had served in WWI.

Today, the American Legion's national headquarters and the Indiana War Memorial stand at opposite ends of a five-block-long plaza on the northern edge of the Mile Square.

D. C. Stephenson and the Ku Klux Klan

The Roaring '20s were a dark time in Indiana and Indianapolis — it was a time defined by the presence and influence of the Ku Klux Klan. The Klan openly supported political candidates, effectively controlling congressional seats, the governor's office and the state Legislature. In Indianapolis, there were Klan-backed politicians in the mayor's office and on both the city council and the school board.

Wielding its white-supremacist beliefs like a club and using racial and religious bigotry as a rallying call, the Klan became one of the strongest political and social movements in Indiana during the 1920s. In Indianapolis, whites from all walks of life — white collar and blue collar, devout Protestants and agnostics, educated and uneducated — joined the Klan.

Not everyone joined, however. The Klan met resistance from the city's powerful Catholic and Jewish communities and from substantial numbers of Protestants who didn't see God's love being manifested in cross burnings and intimidation. Black residents also resisted — most who had long supported the Republican Party became Democrats when the Klan began to dictate the Republican agenda.

One of the most powerful people in the Klan during this time was Grand Dragon D. C. Stephenson, who lived in the Irvington area on the east side of Indianapolis. Stephenson was responsible for recruiting and managing Klan members in 23 states, including Indiana. As a result of selling memberships and Klan paraphernalia, he became wealthy — and egocentric. Thinking himself beyond reproach, Stephenson did what he wanted, including raping and poisoning a young woman named Madge Oberholtzer. But Oberholtzer lived long enough to identify Stephenson. Despite his many political ties, Stephenson was not only charged but convicted of second-degree murder.

That was the beginning of the end of the Klan in Indiana. Within a very short time, thanks in part to a Pulitzer Prize-winning series of newspaper articles about the Klan in *The Indianapolis Times*, membership plummeted. By 1930, the Klan's reign in Indiana was over.

Lockefield Gardens

During the 1930s, Indianapolis suffered through the Great Depression along with the rest of the nation. Still, there were bright spots, most notably the development of Lockefield Gardens, one of the first and finest public housing developments in the nation. Created by the federal Public Works Administration, Lockefield Gardens contained 24 apartment buildings, two- to four-stories tall, with a total of 748 low-cost, high-quality housing units. The complex was on 22 acres on the near-northwest side along Indiana Avenue and included large, open, green spaces, shops, playgrounds and a school. It became one of the centerpieces for the African-American community in Indianapolis.

But in the 1950s and '60s new housing opportunities led to more black families moving out to the suburbs, which in turn led to the decline of Lockefield Gardens. Buildings fell into disrepair, and the complex was finally closed in the 1970s. In 1983, all but seven of the original buildings were demolished to make way for the expansion of the campus of nearby Indiana University-Purdue University at Indianapolis (IUPUI). The remaining buildings were renovated and are now part of a smaller upscale apartment complex.

World War II and Beyond

When the United States became involved in World War II, the rail system again proved important to Indianapolis. The city's central geographic location made it a logical connecting point for troops heading to bases around the country. At the same time, all of its rail lines made Indianapolis a logical place for manufacturing and shipping essential war materials.

The city became "Toolmaker to the Nation." Everyone who was old enough to hold down a job went to work. Factories ran 24 hours a day, seven days a week, turning out transportation equipment, weapons parts and aircraft equipment. General Motors' Allison Division in Speedway manufactured America's first jet engine in 1945.

A healthy economy and plentiful labor supply made Indianapolis attractive to an array of companies during and after the war. Ford, Chrysler, RCA and Western Electric opened plants. Shadeland Avenue north of Washington Street (U.S. 40) became an industrial corridor and an employment haven for job seekers.

However, as manufacturing boomed in Indianapolis in the 1950s and '60s, railroad traffic fizzled. More cars than ever before took to the nation's blossoming interstate highway system, and more people took to traveling cross-country by air. And Indianapolis' stature as the Crossroads of America shrank.

While the business climate was healthy and life was comfortable, Indianapolis began to slow down in comparison to other cities around the country. The hustle and bustle of its railroad heydays dwindled. It got a reputation as a city that woke up every May for the annual running of the Indianapolis 500 then drowsily drifted through the rest of the year. Indianapolis became known as Naptown.

Unigov

Between 1890 and 1960, the population of Indianapolis expanded nearly fivefold, from 100,000 to 476,000. With that expansion came a number of governance issues, not the least of which were the confusing (and sometimes conflicting) regulatory roles of the various city, township and county boards and agencies. While attempts to reorganize local government had been made several times throughout the city's history, it wasn't until 1969 that anything substantial happened.

Limestone from Lawrence County is used for landmarks throughout the state and nation.

Under the leadership of Republican mayor Richard Lugar (now the senior U.S. senator from Indiana), and with the support of Republican majorities on the city council, in county offices and in both chambers of the Indiana General Assembly, reorganization legislation was drafted and voted into law. Known as Unigov (for "unified government"), that legislation consolidated some of the elected positions and administrative functions of Indianapolis and Marion County government. It also made several smaller communities in the county part of greater Indianapolis.

Unigov made Indianapolis the state's only Consolidated City and created a joint City-County Council and six joint administrative departments. It also extended the city's boundaries to match those of Marion County, a move that greatly increased both the city's territorial size and population. In the process, the Crossroads of America became one of America's largest metropolitan districts (the 12th largest as of 1994).

How effective Unigov has been in improving life in Indianapolis is a matter of opinion. Proponents say it has done wonders for the city's growth and development. Opponents say that rather than simplifying local government, it has complicated it. Regardless of opinions, there's no denying that Unigov set the stage for further transformation of the city.

The Business of Sports

Size isn't everything. City officials knew that having more land and more people wasn't enough to make post-Unigov Indianapolis a major player on the national scene. What they needed was an angle, something they could use to help the city shed its Naptown image. Then they hit upon sports.

It began with the Indiana Pacers. In 1973, Mayor Lugar met with a group of developers who wanted to build a new arena on the north side of the city to house the Pacers, then an American Basketball Association team. They'd been playing at the State Fairgrounds' Coliseum, and the developers felt it was time that they had a new, state-of-the-art sports venue. Lugar agreed. But he insisted that the new arena be built downtown. He saw it as the first step in what he hoped would be the revitaliza-

tion of a decaying district. Market Square Arena, at the corner of Market and Alabama streets, three blocks east of Monument Circle, opened in 1974. It has been the home of the Indiana Pacers ever since.

When Lugar left the mayor's office to run for the U.S. senate in 1976, William H. Hudnut was elected to the office. And under Hudnut, who was mayor for an unprecedented 16 years, sports became the focal point of the city's downtown redevelopment efforts. Between 1979 and 1989, the city, with the help of local philanthropic giant Lilly Endowment and other foundation and corporate investors, spent more than $126 million in the creation of world-class athletic facilities.

As a result, Indianapolis attracted an array of national and international sporting events, including the 1982 National Sports Festival, the 1987 Pan American Games, NCAA basketball and track and field championships, ice skating competitions and 1988 Olympic trials in track and field and rowing. Impressed by the city's commitment, a number of amateur sports organizations established their headquarters here. The result of all this was a new self-proclaimed title: "The Amateur Sports Capital of the World."

But interest didn't stop with amateur sports. The city also went after professional events — and teams. In March, 1984, the NFL's Baltimore Colts moved west to become the Indianapolis Colts, playing in the newly constructed Hoosier (now RCA) Dome. The city also became an annual stop for professional golf and tennis tournaments. And in August 1994, the Indianapolis Motor Speedway hosted the first annual NASCAR Brickyard 400.

Sports have become a well-established part of Indianapolis's economic foundation and recreational scene. Naptown is once again wide-awake.

The 1990s Onward

Downtown revitalization efforts didn't stop with the construction of sports facilities. Millions of dollars have also been poured into reviving rundown buildings throughout the Mile Square, converting former warehouses and factories into apartments, condominiums and offices. Millions more have been spent erecting office towers. In the process, the Indianapolis skyline has been dramatically altered.

The latest (and one of the most controversial) downtown projects is an urban mall known as Circle Centre. Circle Centre, which opened in September 1995, is a $300 million effort to resurrect downtown shopping. More than a decade in the planning, it contains more than 100 stores, movie theaters and restaurants.

All the attention and money lavished on downtown projects attracted plenty of criticism. Critics argued some of those resources should have been directed at more pressing concerns: education, homelessness, low-income housing, healthcare for the uninsured and neighborhood redevelopment. These and other community concerns are now helping shape a new agenda for city officials. Under current mayor Stephen Goldsmith, efforts are being made to address some concerns by allocating more economic development resources to neighborhoods and by privatizing many government services.

The Crossroads of America is at a crossroads of its own. Figuring out how to balance ongoing development efforts with social needs and economic realities is the challenge facing city officials in the 1990s and beyond.

But at least they don't have to carve a city out of the wilderness. That part's done. And, as Alexander Ralston predicted, Indianapolis is a beautiful city. It's the trees. The city has a lot of trees. No navigable waterway, but a lot of trees. They're a legacy from the wild, wooded past. You should see this place in the autumn.

As you might expect from a city that bills itself as the Crossroads of America, getting around Indianapolis is fairly easy.

Getting Around

As you might expect from a city that bills itself as the Crossroads of America, getting around Indianapolis is fairly easy — unless you rely on mass transit . . . then it's a challenge.

Developing mass transit alternatives to auto travel hasn't been a priority — the only form of public transportation available is the Metro Bus System. (See entry in this chapter.)

However, if you've got a car, you're in luck.

Surface Streets

The surface street pattern in Indianapolis is pretty straightforward. Essentially, the entire city is laid out on a grid of north-south and east-west streets, with a few diagonals thrown in for good measure.

The downtown district, which is known as the **Mile Square**, originally established the street grid. Laid out by surveyor Alexander Ralston in 1821, the Mile Square's boundaries are defined by four 1-mile-long streets: **North Street**, **South Street**, **East Street** and **West Street**. In the center of the Mile Square is **Monument Circle**, which is bisected by **Meridian Street**, the city's primary north-south street. It's also the dividing line between east and west addresses. A block south of the Circle is **Washington Street**, the primary east-west street — and the dividing line between north and south addresses. Washington Street is also **U.S. 40**, the old **National Road**.

Four diagonal avenues — **Massachusetts**, **Indiana**, **Virginia** and **Kentucky** — radiate out from the Square. Massachusetts and Indiana begin (or end, depending on your perspective) at **New York Street**, a block north of the Circle; Virginia does the same at Washington Street and Kentucky at South Street.

For nine blocks north of the Circle, all east-west streets have names. From that point on, they're numbered, starting with **9th Street**. Some essential numbered streets to acquaint yourself with are **16th** (home of the Indianapolis Motor Speedway), **30th** (home of the Children's Museum of Indianapolis), **38th** (home of the Indiana State Fairgrounds and the Indianapolis Museum of Art) and **82nd** (home of myriad restaurants and Castleton Mall, two of the city's most upscale shopping malls).

A couple of cautionary notes: West of White River, **82nd Street** becomes **86th**; it confuses even the locals. And in addition to **East** and **West Washington Street**, there is **North Washington Boulevard**. Fortunately, the two Washingtons never intersect.

Highways

When it still bore the name the **National Road**, **U.S. Highway 40** was the first highway to link Indianapolis with the East Coast. It's still a vital road, though its importance was diminished with the arrival of such east-west interstates as **Interstate 74**, which connects Indianapolis with Cincinnati to the east and Danville, Illinois, to the west, and **Interstate 70**, which links Indianapolis with Columbus, Ohio, to the east and St. Louis, Missouri, to the west.

As for north-south interstates, **I-65** runs north to Chicago and south to Louisville, Kentucky, while **I-69** (which, depending on the direction you're heading, starts or ends at Indianapolis, though there is talk of extending it south to Evansville) runs north. There's also **U.S. Highway 31**, which runs north to South Bend, Indiana (home of University of Notre Dame), and south to Columbus, Indiana (home of some of the most splendid contemporary architecture in the country). **U.S. 37** runs south

General and Visitor Information

Indiana State Information Center	302 W. Washington St. • 232-3140
Indiana Chamber of Commerce	1 N. Capitol Ave. • 264-3110
Indianapolis Chamber of Commerce	320 N. Meridian St. • 464-2200
Indianapolis City Center	201 S. Capitol Ave. • 237-5200
Indianapolis Convention & Visitors Assn.	One RCA Dome • 639-4282
Indianapolis Downtown Inc.	201 N. Illinois St. • 237-2222
Indianapolis Tourism Hotline	(800) 824-INDY

to Bloomington (home of Indiana University) and north to Marion.

The city's bypass, **Interstate 465**, connects with all the major surface streets and highways. While traffic usually flows smoothly, key on- and off-ramps do back up during morning and afternoon rush hours. This is especially true for ramps at 82nd and 96th streets to the north, 38th Street to the west and Emerson and Shadeland avenues to the east. Generally, traffic peaks between 6:30 and 8:30 AM and 4:30 and 6:30 PM.

To get downtown from I-465, you have to use either inbound I-65 or I-70, or exit onto a surface street.

Parking

There are parking meters throughout downtown Indianapolis. They accept a maximum of two hours' worth of change, and they're patrolled regularly. The fine for parking at an expired meter is $12.50 if paid within 72 hours, $17.50 thereafter.

Parking garages and lots abound throughout downtown, at least until you need a space. Then, of course, every place is full. Prices are all over the map. For example, there's a sur-

face lot on the southeast corner of Washington Street and Alabama Street that only charges $2 for an entire day, but it's far enough from most downtown buildings that you'll have to walk a ways to get to where you're going. And there are the Circle Centre parking garages, which charge only $1 for up to three hours. Then there are the office building garages that charge five or six times that for a few hours.

Indianapolis International Airport

Twelve minutes west of the Mile Square via I-70, Indianapolis International Airport serves nearly 6 million passengers a year and handles some 591,000 tons of cargo.

Designed to minimize problems for passengers and their guests, the two-story terminal is easy to get around, with all arrival services on the lower level and all departure services on the upper. To meet travelers' various needs, there are rental car counters, a travel agency, a visitors information center, bank machines and restaurants.

The terminal is also designed to efficiently accommodate physically challenged individu-

INSIDERS' TIP

On weekends between Thanksgiving and New Year's Day, avoid East 82nd Street between Allisonville Road and I-465 (the Castleton Mall area) — traffic is bumper-to-bumper during the pre- and post-Christmas shopping frenzy.

als. There are sloped curb cuts and elevators, motion activated doors and volume-controlled telephones, enclosed walkways, wheelchair-accessible restrooms, lift-equipped buses and van-accessible parking spaces. Wheelchairs and telecommunications devices for the deaf (TDDs) are also available. The airport's TDD number is 487-5151.

There is garage and surface lot parking for short-term stays and a remote lot with free shuttle service for multi-day parking needs. A ground transportation center provides easy access to a variety of services, including buses, hotel courtesy vehicles, taxis, and limousines. To arrange for transportation, call 487-7243.

Seventeen airlines, including major carriers and their regional partners, offer passenger services at the airport. They are:

Air Canada, (800) 776-3000

America West, (800) 235-9292

American Airlines/American Eagle, (800) 433-7300

American Trans Air, (800) 225-2995

Continental Airlines, (800) 525-0280

Delta Airlines, (800) 221-1212

Execujet Inc., 247-7773

Midwest Express Airlines, (800) 452-2022

Northwest Airlines, (800) 225-2525

Skyway Airlines, (800) 452-2022

Southwest Airlines, (800) 435-9792

TWA, (800) 221-2000

United Airlines, (800) 241-6522

USAir/USAir Express, (800) 428-4322

ValuJet, (800) 825-8538

For general information and paging services, call 487-7243.

In addition to being home to the nation's largest charter airline, American Trans Air, the airport also serves as a hub for both Federal Express and the U.S. Postal Service. Both American Trans Air and United Airlines have airplane maintenance operations at the airport.

FYI

Unless otherwise noted, the area code for all phone numbers in this guide is 317.

Trains and Buses

For a city that once was one of the largest passenger railway centers in the country, Indianapolis now has very limited train service. Amtrak operates the city's only existing interstate passenger train line, an Indianapolis-to-Chicago route that departs from Union Station downtown. As of this writing, trains depart Indianapolis for Chicago twice on Monday, Thursday and Saturday mornings and once on Sunday, Tuesday, Wednesday and Friday mornings. For a current schedule, call (800) 872-7245.

Greyhound and Trailways provide interstate bus services, with a total of some 50 buses arriving from or leaving for cities throughout the country. The **Greyhound** terminal is downtown at 127 N. Capitol, 267-3057. The **American Trailways** terminal is a few blocks farther south, 350 S. Illinois Street, 687-1111.

Mass Transit

In Indianapolis, mass transit means one thing — Metro Bus.

The **Metro Bus** system shuttles passengers throughout the metropolitan area. Fares are $1.25 on express buses, which cover longer distances with fewer stops than their non-express counterparts, $1 at peak-usage times and 75¢ off-peak for non-express buses. Transfers cost 25¢. Exact change is required at all times. For route and schedule information, call 635-3344.

Special bus services are available for physically challenged passengers. For information about Metro's open-door service for the disabled, call 635-2100, extension 242.

INSIDERS' TIP

Parking is prohibited on key downtown streets during peak rush hours. Signs warn cars of times during which cars will be towed. Heed these signs. Towing is done regularly and within minutes of the beginning of the no-parking time period.

Taxis

Unlike in many cities, taxis in Indianapolis don't usually cruise in search of fares. The best places to hail a cab are the airport, in front of major downtown hotels or at downtown taxi stands. Otherwise, you're better off calling for a taxi by phone.

Local taxi companies include **Yellow Cab**, 487-7777; **Hoosier Cab**, 243-8800; **Metro Cab**, 634-1111; **Quality Cabs**, 244-8294; **Five Star Taxi**, 381-1111; and **Indy Taxi Service**, 243-2424.

Limousines

If you're in the mood for a mode of transportation with a bit more panache, try a limousine. Among local limo operators are **Indy Connection Limousines**, 241-6700; **Carey Limousines**, 226-9499; **Dynasty Limousines**, 241-9900; **Carte Blanche Limousines**, 867-0440; **Personal Touch Limousine Service**, 254-0415; and **Perfection Limousine**, 921-8708.

Carriages

For a downtown ride that's romantic and leisurely, it's hard to beat a horse-drawn carriage. The clip-clop of hooves on pavement and the gentle sway of the carriage cab take you back in time. Board a carriage outside of Union Station or at the Capitol Street entrance to the Hyatt Regency. Or hire one for an evening interlude with someone special. Then settle into a different form of getting around.

For information about rates and availability of carriages, contact **Yellow Rose Carriages**, 634-3400; **Metropolitan Carriages Inc.**, 631-4169; **Colonial Carriages Inc.**, 637-2004; or **Blue Ribbon Carriages**, 631-4169.

The Indianapolis Heliport: Another Intersection at the Crossroads of America

One mode of transportation that might not come to mind when you hear the phrase "Crossroads of America" is helicopters. But Indianapolis is home to the most successful urban heliport in the United States.

The Indianapolis Heliport, on the southeastern edge of the Mile Square, consists of a three-story, 26,000-square-foot building with lighted touchdown pad, taxiway and a 2½-acre tie-down area. In addition to serving as a landing and fueling facility for helicopters passing through the region, the heliport provides maintenance and repair services for helicopters owned by area TV stations, hospitals, law enforcement agencies, corporations and individuals — a vital service when you realize that one definition of a helicopter is "7,000 parts flying in close formation."

Close-up

A joint venture between the Indianapolis Airport Authority and the privately owned Indianapolis Heliport Corporation, the heliport opened in 1985. It was the first such facility developed under the auspices of an urban heliport program developed by the Federal Aviation Administration.

In its 1983 Rotorcraft Master Plan, the FAA projected that in the 21st century, helicopters will play an important role in interurban travel, supplanting (or at least supplementing) the current reliance on jet airliners to make short regional trips. The FAA's long-range purpose is the creation of a network of heliports throughout the country, linking the downtown business districts of cities within 300 to 400 miles of one another. For example, within a 300-mile radius of the Indianapolis facility are the downtown districts of Chicago, Cincinnati, St. Louis, Louisville, Cleveland and Detroit.

Photo: Rich Miller

Methodist Hospital's Lifeline helicopter lands at the Indianapolis Heliport.

While it remains to be seen whether the FAA's forecast of a network of urban heliports will come to pass (there are others in New York, New Orleans and the Dallas suburb of Garland), it's clear that the Indianapolis Heliport is another instance of the value of the transportation industry to the vitality of the Crossroads of America.

For more information, call the Indianapolis Heliport, 51 S. New Jersey Street, 262-3000.

Just about everyone who's lived here a while will tell you the Indianapolis area is indeed a great place to raise a family.

Area Overviews

Fifty Fabulous Places to Raise Your Family lauds the Indianapolis area for its rapidly growing economy, affordable housing, low crime rate, great sports and overall family atmosphere. And it's all true. Visitors and newcomers are often surprised at how much house their money will buy and that we walk around downtown or in the popular Broad Ripple neighborhood at night and enjoy solitary morning jogs at Eagle Creek Park, a huge park on the northwest side. We're not foolhardy about personal safety, of course, but we do feel a level of confidence here that residents of bigger cities cannot claim.

Just about everyone who's lived here awhile will tell you the Indianapolis area is indeed a great place to raise a family. And the area offers such a wide range of places to call home. With the creation of Unigov, Indianapolis and Marion County merged (see our History and Government chapters for details) and have been considered one entity as far as population goes. Still, the county includes the towns of Speedway, Lawrence, Beech Grove and Southport, all of which were excluded from Unigov and retain their own individual personalities. The central city too features numerous historic neighborhoods, each with a colorful history or ethnic heritage. Across the city and county, neighborhoods such as Broad Ripple, Irvington and Woodruff Place preserve and promote their own distinct characters. (See our Neighborhoods chapter for details.)

In general, Indianapolis offers big-city amenities and a hometown ambiance, a combination that residents find hard to beat and that visitors remark upon. *American Demographics* magazine ranked the city 10th in the nation in kindness toward strangers, a helpfulness rating based on such criteria as willingness to make change for a quarter and to help a blind person cross the street. Out-of-

towners, especially those from either coast, may find it odd that we actually obey the "walk" and "don't walk" traffic signals. But they appreciate our friendliness and hospitality.

If they find the city friendly, wait till they visit the surrounding counties, where life often moves at a slower pace and people still wave when they pass one another driving down a county road. Basketball hoops really do hang on the sides of barns, and high school gymnasiums are packed to the rafters for Friday night games. Farms and fruit stands offer the best the land has to offer, including incredible tomatoes, cantaloupe, watermelon and sweet corn.

But if you can't see the beauty in a freshly plowed field or in gently rolling acres of corn, you'll have a tough time appreciating the scenery. In most of our surrounding counties, farming remains an ever-present fact of life. In fact, if you drive along our state and county roads in the spring and summer, you'll eventually get stuck behind slow-moving farm equipment — until the tractor or combine driver politely pulls to the side of the road to let traffic pass.

Agriculture remains the state's No. 1 industry, and Indiana ranks among the top-five states in the nation in the production of corn, soybeans, tomatoes, cantaloupe, popcorn and, in the northern part of the state, spearmint and peppermint. Though many families nationwide lost their farms during the 1980s, 85 percent of Indiana farms remain individual operations; corporations own just 4 percent.

Central Indiana and the seven counties that surround Indianapolis — Hamilton, Johnson, Boone, Hendricks, Hancock, Shelby and Morgan — reflect these statewide agricultural trends. Farming remains vital to many of these counties; farmland accounts for 70 to 80 percent of land mass in several counties.

These Indianapolis-area counties are easy

to reach, thanks to the state's excellent highway network. Seven interstates crisscross Indiana, more than in any other state, providing easy access to most Central Indiana locations.

Two major U.S. highways also intersect at Indianapolis. U.S. 40, the old National Road (known as Washington Street within the city) runs east and west through Central Indiana. Though still a busy route, the historic highway doesn't see as much of the cross-country traffic as it once did; I-70 now handles most of that. Still, vestiges of its traffic-laden past can be seen in the numerous small motels scattered along the route. In Central Indiana, U.S. 40 cuts through downtown Greenfield, the Hancock County seat, continues through the middle of Indianapolis, then on into Hendricks County's Plainfield.

Extending north and south through Central Indiana is U.S. Highway 31. It cuts through Franklin and Greenwood in Johnson County, then becomes Meridian Street as it runs through the heart of Indianapolis. It continues on through Hamilton County, where Indianapolis gives way to Carmel.

Many well-maintained state roads also provide popular routes through the counties. And, of course, the I-465 loop provides quick access around the city's periphery. Visitors can pick just about any state road exit and within minutes find themselves out in the country, driving past churches established in the 1800s, well-kept Princess Anne-style farmhouses and countless front-yard fruit stands. (Stop and buy some of those fresh tomatoes. You'll never settle for the grocery-store variety again.)

In some areas, primarily in Hamilton and Johnson counties, it's tough to tell where Indianapolis ends and Carmel (to the north) and Greenwood (to the south) begin. Still, even in the more urban areas, once you turn off the main roads and get away from the upscale housing developments and strip malls, you'll find those fruit stands and antiques shops.

Prop your feet up and read on for an introduction to Indianapolis' seven surrounding counties, where residents and visitors enjoy easy city access and the best in suburban, small-town and country life. (Here we give just an overview. For more information about specific restaurants, shops, festivals, etc., see our corresponding chapters throughout the book.)

Hamilton County

Just to the north of Indianapolis is Hamilton County, the state's fastest growing county in terms of population. The county experienced a 32.8 percent gain in the number of residents in the decade between 1980 and 1990, and the group with the largest increase in population was the 35- to 44-year-olds; yes, Hamilton County is home to a great many baby boomers. Restaurants, specialty shops and upscale housing developments abound.

Carmel (pronounced like the candy, with the emphasis on the "Car"), is the county's largest city and has seen plenty of growth, especially since the mid-1980s. **Fishers**, by some estimates the fast-growing town in the Midwest, continues to expand. In 1970, the population of Fishers hovered around 500; a special census in 1988 counted more than 4,500 residents. By the 1990s, the numbers had reached more than 14,000. Its convenient location (close to many northside businesses and corporations) and a well-regarded school system continue to attract young families. Though town officials have had to hustle to provide services to all these new residents, they have been determined to manage the growth. Its open space ordinance, for example, requires developers to incorporate green spaces in any new subdivision.

And there are plenty of subdivisions in Hamilton County. The median price of new homes is more than $100,000, and many go for several times that figure.

Despite its yuppie reputation, Hamilton County is more than just image. It's home to those who like its easy access to Indianapolis as well as its emphasis on top-quality education and high school athletics.

Though Hamilton County can boast plenty of amenities, once outside Carmel, the pricey subdivisions give way to farmland. And though Hamilton County offers shopping, sushi and such unique restaurants as Illusions, where magicians perform tableside, it's also home to Stonycreek Farm, where visitors can feed animals, pick a pumpkin or browse through the herbs and specialty items at the Buggy Barn gift shop. The county also offers at least 20 antiques shops and three options for purchasing handmade pottery: Bastine Pottery and Strawtown Pottery studios and Conner Prairie, a living history village where it's always 1836.

The Transportation Museum in **Noblesville**, the county seat, provides a glimpse into Indiana's railroad past. The museum also offers train rides each August to the Indiana State Fair and summertime train ride/dinner packages to such restaurants as Fletcher's of Atlanta, in a tiny town in the northern part of the county where local chef Fletcher Boyd serves up top-notch regional cuisine. Noblesville, with its busy, revitalized downtown area, also offers plenty of antiques and specialty shops.

Hamilton County boasts top-notch recreational facilities as well. It is home to the 1,478-acre Geist Reservoir and the 1,800-acre Morse Reservoir, both of which are surrounded by beautiful waterfront dwellings, many costing half a million or more. The area hosts a number of special events throughout the year, including the Deer Creek Fair and Music Festival and the Amish Country Market in Noblesville.

For more Hamilton County info, contact the Carmel-Clay Chamber of Commerce, P.O. Box 1, Carmel, Indiana 46032, 846-1049; Cicero Area Chamber of Commerce, 73 W. Jackson Street, Cicero, Indiana, 984-4079; Fishers Chamber of Commerce, 8710 E. 116th Street, Fishers, 578-0700; Noblesville Area Chamber of Commerce, 159 N. Ninth Street, Noblesville, Indiana 773-0086; and Westfield-Washington Chamber of Commerce, Westfield, Indiana 896-2378.

Johnson County

South of Indianapolis lies Johnson County, whose population of more than 93,000 ranks it 15th out of 92 counties in the state. The number of Johnson County residents increased by more than 26 percent in the 1970s and by more than 14 percent in the '80s. Growth has slowed somewhat in the '90s, but, like Hamilton County to the north, the age group in Johnson County with the greatest increase in numbers in the last 10 to 15 years was the 35- to 44-year-old baby boomers.

Hamilton County's Carmel and Johnson County's Greenwood have had a long-running

but good-natured feud about which boasts the best in suburban living, but the same things attract young families to the south side as to the north: low crime, convenient shopping and excellent schools. Some would say the north side is more upscale and the south side more casual, but one thing is certain: Each area has much to recommend it.

Driving south from downtown Indianapolis on U.S. 31 or I-65, the commute to **Greenwood** takes about 20 minutes, depending on traffic or road construction (disgruntled commuters observe we only have two seasons around here: winter and construction). Many residents make the commute each day; the city of Greenwood is home to nearly 30,000 people. Though the Greenwood Park megamall, which vies with Fort Wayne's Glenbrook Square for designation as the state's largest, dominates the area's shopping scene, Old Towne Greenwood offers unique shopping in the old business district as well. Check out Making Thyme for a variety of herbs and gift items and the Cornerstone Gallery for interior design ideas; both are located on West Main Street.

Franklin, the county seat, boasts a population of about 15,000 and can claim a gem in Franklin College. The small, four-year institution provides a cultural focal point for the town. Franklin also features the traditional courthouse square, Main Street's Artcraft Theatre and Heiskell's Restaurant, which specializes in seafood, steaks and prime rib in its charming turn-of-the-century Victorian setting.

Recreational activities in Johnson County focus a great deal on the outdoors. The nearby Atterbury Fish and Wildlife Area near **Edinburgh** covers 6,400 acres and offers hunting, fishing and a wildlife viewing area. Sixteen lakes, ranging in size from 3 acres to 309 acres, provide even more outdoor options. Bass, bluegill and catfish are usually biting in Sugar Creek, Stone Arch and Pisgah lakes within the Atterbury area. Deer, upland game, dove and waterfowl hunting is also allowed.

Those who'd rather hunt for bargains have much territory to cover in Horizon Outlet Center near Edinburgh. Though actually in Bartholomew County, this outlet mall provides plenty of options for Johnson County shoppers.

For more information on Johnson County, contact the Greater Franklin Chamber of Commerce, P.O. Box 264, Franklin 46131, 736-6334; and the Greater Greenwood Chamber of Commerce, 300 S. Madison Avenue, Suite 420, Greenwood, 888-4856.

Boone County

Northwest of Indianapolis, Boone County remains more rural than either Hamilton or Johnson counties, though I-65 runs through the county, providing quick access to downtown Indianapolis. Despite growth in the number of high-end housing developments in recent years, the comparatively unspoiled natural beauty is a Boone County draw. More than 80 percent of the county land is farmed.

But they raise more than corn in Boone County. This is also horse country, or as near to horse country as you get in Central Indiana. OK, so it isn't Lexington, but you'll still find small horse farms dotting the county. One of the area's best-known annual events (and which wins the longest name award) is the Traders Point Hunt Club Charity Horse Show and Country Fair each August.

Lebanon, with its impressive domed courthouse and 12,000-plus residents, is the county seat, but when Indianapolis residents think of Boone County, **Zionsville** comes to mind. This charming village of about 5,500 boasts brick streets lined with Victorian cottages, many with the requisite picket fences and flower gardens. Known for its historic ambiance, Zionsville also features numerous top-notch restaurants, including Gisella's, Z'Bistro and Panache. Antique and specialty shops abound, but one establishment proves especially unique: Albers Rolls-Royce — America's oldest exclusive Rolls Royce dealer.

Zionsville hosts a number of community festivals, including its Country Market art, antiques and craft show and annual Fall Festival and Christmas in the Village. For a different take on tradition, Lebanon hosts the American Indian Council Annual Traditional Pow Wow each August, as well as a spring pow wow in April or May each year.

For more information on the area, contact the Boone County Chamber of Commerce, 221 N. Lebanon Street, Lebanon, 46052, 482-1320; and the Greater Zionsville Chamber of Commerce, P.O. Box 148, Zionsville, Indiana 46077, (765) 873-3836.

Hendricks County

Hendricks County sits to the west of Indianapolis, an area that saw heavy growth from the 1960s through the '80s, as new residents sought the county's slower pace and more rural atmosphere. Even now about 70 percent of the county remains farmland. However, county residents can quickly reach Indianapolis via I-70 and U.S. 36.

Communities within the county retain a small-town feel, though the area continues to grow. **Plainfield** is the county's largest with more than 10,000 residents and is situated on U.S. 40, the old National Road. Though considerably smaller, Danville, with its 5,000 or so residents, is the county seat.

A picture-perfect Midwestern small town, **Danville** boasts tidy streets, big houses and lots of red brick. The town square, where you'll find the Mockingbird Cafe (specializing in prime rib) and the Royal cinema, surrounds the handsome courthouse. For the news of the area, pick up a *Hendricks County Flyer* from a box outside the Mayberry Cafe. Have a seat on the bench, or head inside and peruse the paper over a cup of coffee.

In nearby **Brownsburg**, check out Harley's restaurant, a longtime favorite of westsiders and, in May, of Indianapolis Motor Speedway regulars. Like most area small towns, Brownsburg features a number of places to browse for antiques.

Hendricks County is also seeing more business development and is benefiting from its proximity to the Indianapolis International Airport and that area's industrial growth. A proposed amusement park featuring Garfield the cartoon cat is also generating a great deal of interest in the county.

Hendricks County hosts a number of special events throughout the year that highlight

---

FYI

Unless otherwise noted, the area code for all phone numbers in this guide is 317.

its country ambiance, including the Hendricks County 4-H Fair in July and Danville's Heartland AppleFest in October, from which come the wonderful aromas of the Great Apple Pie Bake-off. (See our Close-up in this chapter.)

For more Hendricks County information, contact the Brownsburg Chamber of Commerce, P.O. Box 82, Brownsburg, Indiana 46112, 852-7885; the Greater Danville Chamber of Commerce, P.O. Box 273, Danville, Indiana 46122, 745-0670; and the Plainfield Chamber of Commerce, P.O. Box 14, Plainfield, Indiana 46168, 839-7222.

Hancock County

Just east of Indianapolis, Hancock County is home to approximately 50,000 residents. Hancock County remains primarily rural, with more than 80 percent of the land in farms that grow corn, soybeans and winter wheat and plenty of gardens producing those luscious tomatoes. I-70 cuts through much of the farmland, but you'll find more roadside vegetable stands along U.S. highways 40 and 52.

Just off I-70, **Greenfield**, the county seat, is home to more than 12,500 residents, many of whom are drawn by the easygoing lifestyle and the city's emphasis on historic preservation. The birthplace of famed Hoosier poet James Whitcomb Riley, who wrote such childhood favorites as "Little Orphant Annie" and "The Raggedy Man," the city takes pride in its historic heritage. James Whitcomb Riley Days, held each October, includes art, antiques and, of course, a poetry contest. Don't miss touring the Riley birthplace and the Old Log Jail Museum.

Even without a festival, antiques buffs love this part of the area. Those browsing Greenfield's many shops are likely to keep on driving east on U.S. 40 to Knightstown, actually located in southeast Henry County; numerous small towns situated along U.S. 40 make up Antique Alley (see our Shopping chapter).

Other Hancock County towns include **Cumberland** (which straddles the Marion/Hendricks County line) with more than 4,700 residents, **Fortville** with 3,000-plus residents and **New Palestine**, home to about 750 people. The Hancock County 4-H Fair in July draws residents from across the county for its traditional fair food, animal judging, games and amusements.

For more information about Hancock County, contact the Greater Greenfield Chamber of Commerce, 110 S. State Street, Greenfield, Indiana 462-4188; or the New Palestine Area Chamber of Commerce, P.O. Box 541, New Palestine, Indiana 46163.

Shelby County

Southeast of Indianapolis is Shelby County, a primarily rural area that is home to more than 40,000 people. Like Hancock County to its north, Shelby County retains strong ties to agriculture; more than 80 percent of its area is in farmland. I-74 provides quick access to Indianapolis, though you'll see more of the county if you head out along U.S. 421 or 52. In fact, Frank's Orchard & Farm Market, which offers a variety of fruits and vegetables throughout the season, is located at the intersection of U.S. 52 and Ind. 9.

While on Ind. 9, pull the car to the side of the road, and take a look at the ostriches and emus that wander around a farm located just past County Road 350 N. Oddly enough, more ostriches can be spotted from I-74 around the Acton exit near the Shelby-Marion county line; you'll get a better view of this flock if you get off at Acton and drive along Southeastern Avenue.

I-74 takes you right to **Shelbyville**, the county seat, home to about 16,000 residents. Many smaller towns, such as **Morristown** and **St. Paul**, with about 1,000 residents each, offer an easygoing, rural atmosphere where family and community remain the focal points.

Though some of these tiny burgs may seem frozen in time, one town capitalizes on a bygone era. The popular Boggstown Inn and Cabaret offers hearty food and a ragtime atmosphere. Daily shows feature banjos, dueling pianos and plenty of audience participation. People from all over the world have signed the guest book. Not as elaborate but still worth the drive (if you like freshly made ice cream, that is) is Compton's Cow Palace in Shelbyville. Morristown's Kopper Kettle is well-known for its family-style meals, especially its fried chicken dinners.

Special events in the area include the Shelby County Fair in July, one of only a few in the state that still offers harness racing, and Shelbyville's Bears of Blue River Festival in late August, which celebrates the county's historic heritage as the setting for Charles Major's book *The Bears of Blue River*. The Blue River Valley Pioneer Fair in October, held at the county fairgrounds, spotlights historic arts and crafts (don't miss the traditional funnel cakes and just-pressed apple cider).

For more information about Shelby County, contact the Shelby County Chamber of Commerce, 33 E. Washington Street, Shelbyville, Indiana 46176, 398-6647; or the Morristown Chamber of Commerce, P.O. Box 476, Morristown, Indiana 46161, (765)763-6830.

Morgan County

Southwest of Indianapolis, Morgan County is known for its rugged, forested scenery as well as its ultraconservative heritage (in its un-

seemly past, Morgan County was a hotbed of Ku Klux Klan activity).

Today, more than 58,000 people call Morgan County home, many of whom moved to the county in the high-growth 1970s. Ind. 37 and Ind. 67 provide direct routes through the county for those who work in Indianapolis; I-70 cuts through the area as well. Many of the county's residents live in **Martinsville**, the county seat, which boasts a population of more than 12,000. **Mooresville** is home to more than 5,800 people, and a number of smaller communities dot the scenic countryside. Residents enjoy the laid-back pace and small-town atmosphere characteristic of Morgan County.

They're also fond of all the outdoor recreation opportunities. The Morgan-Monroe State Forest covers more than 23,000 acres in Morgan, Brown and Monroe counties where picnicking, hiking, camping, hunting and fishing abound. Twenty area lakes also provide an abundance of fishing. Those who really like to rough it can contact the state

Helen Ellis' Apple Pie

For a real taste of Central Indiana, try this prize-winning recipe, fresh from the Heartland Apple Fest's Great Apple Pie Bake-off, our favorite part of the early October festival held at Beasley's Orchard in Danville. (See our Annual Events and Festivals chapter for more information.)

Crust

(makes enough for two pies)
4 cups unsifted all-purpose flour
11/2 tablespoons sugar
11/2 teaspoons baking powder
1 teaspoon salt
12/3 cups lard
1 large egg, slightly beaten
1 tablespoon white vinegar
1/2 cup ice water, divided

Filling

(makes enough for one pie)
3 cups Jonathan apples, quartered
1 teaspoon lemon juice
1 cup sugar, divided into thirds
2 tablespoons flour, divided
1/2 teaspoon cinnamon
1/4 cup water
5 to 6 thin slices butter

For crust, in a large bowl, stir together flour, sugar, baking powder and salt, mixing well. Using a pastry blender, cut in lard until mixture is crumbly. Stir together egg, vinegar and water and combine with flour mixture. After the dough is mixed, divide dough in half and chill (work only with half; reserve half for another pie). Roll out bottom crust and place in deep 8-inch pie pan.

For filling, peel, core and quarter apples and sprinkle with lemon juice. Stir together 1/3 cup sugar, 1 tablespoon flour and the cinnamon and sprinkle over apples. Stir together another 1/3 cup sugar and 1 tablespoon flour and sprinkle evenly over bottom of unbaked pastry in pie pan. Arrange apples in pie pan. Sprinkle last 1/3 cup sugar on apples and dot with butter slices. Roll out and arrange top crust over apples.

Bake in preheated 400-degree oven for 15 minutes. Reduce heat to 350 degrees and continue baking until apples are tender when pierced with a fork, about 45 minutes.

forest at (765) 342-4026 and inquire about reserving Draper's Cabin, a cottage in the middle of the forest without electricity or running water. Visitors are welcome to gather wood and build a fire in the cabin's stone fireplace, but they'd better bring along a sleeping bag if they want to curl up in front of the fire — there are no beds or other furniture.

Morgan County's scenic beauty draws foliage watchers from across Central Indiana who monitor the forest for the peak color in the fall. In fact, the Morgan County Fall Foliage Festival in October draws residents and visitors alike to take in the brilliant reds and yellows of an Indiana autumn. While in the county, stop by the Sugar Grove Vineyard and Winery, 611 Newlin Road, in Mooresville; it offers tours and wine tastings daily.

For more information about Morgan County, contact the Greater Martinsville Chamber of Commerce, P.O. Box 1378, Martinsville, Indiana 46151, (765) 342-8110; or the Mooresville Chamber of Commerce, P.O. Box 62, Mooresville, Indiana 46158, (765) 831-6509.

Whether you're looking for a quiet little bed and breakfast or a hotel large enough to host hundreds of conventioneers, Indianapolis is very accommodating.

Accommodations

Indianapolis has plenty of room for you. In fact, it has plenty of rooms — more than 16,000 of them. Whether you're looking for a quiet little bed and breakfast or a hotel large enough to host hundreds of conventioneers, Indianapolis is very accommodating.

Hoosier hospitality isn't just a phrase — it's a fact. Enjoy your stay.

Using This Chapter

This chapter is divided into two major sections: "Hotels and Motels" and "Bed and Breakfasts." In turn, each of these sections are arranged geographically. This was done to help you find a place to stay that will be convenient to specific business districts and local attractions. For places that offer toll-free phone numbers, those numbers are included along with local numbers.

Each facility's entry includes a dollar-sign symbol indicating the approximate price range for a one-night stay, midweek, double-occupancy. The price ranges are:

$50 or less	**$**
$51 to $100	**$$**
$101 to $150	**$$$**
$150 and more	**$$$$**

Please note that prices were quoted by a reservationist at each facility, and were current as of September 1, 1995. As always, prices are subject to change without notice. Rates are higher during times of heavy demand — major conventions and annual events (the Indianapolis 500, Indiana Black Expo, Brickyard 400, Circle City Classic, etc.).

Also, regardless of the rate, a 5 percent local hotel tax combined with a 5 percent state sales tax will add 10 percent to your room bill. Unless otherwise noted, all establishments accept major credit cards.

In this chapter, we've tried to present you with a fairly comprehensive overview of area lodgings. But by no means is this a complete list. For other options call the Indianapolis Convention & Visitors Association (see contact information below).

Indianapolis Convention & Visitors Association

One RCA Dome, Ste. 100 • 639-4282, (800) 824-INDY

For help finding the right accommodations for your next stay in Indianapolis, this is the place to start. The Association is a central source of information about a variety of places to stay, from the plush and expensive to efficient and economical.

Hotels and Motels

Downtown

The Canterbury Hotel

$$$ • 123 S. Illinois St. • 634-3000

Listed on the National Register of Historic Places, this 99-room, European-style hotel is one of Indiana's best facilities. Just a block from the Indiana Convention Center and the RCA Dome, it's well situated for well-heeled business travelers, conventioneers and sports fans; it's also the choice of many celebrities: Elton John, The Rolling Stones and the Rev. Jesse Jackson have all stayed there. The Canterbury has a cozy cocktail lounge and an elegant dining facility known disarmingly as The Restaurant. The hotel offers limousine service to and from Indianapolis International Airport.

Photo: Randy Baughn

The Hyatt Regency Indianapolis is a 500-room facility that includes a 20-story atrium, glass elevators and a revolving rooftop restaurant and lounge.

The Columbia Club
$$$ • 121 Monument Cir. • 635-1361

Those who don't stay at The Canterbury probably stay here. In fact, author Tom Wolfe, in search of perfect accommodations, once moved from The Canterbury to this 86-room private club on the Circle. Honoring club memberships from around the country, the Columbia Club provides guests with Euro-small rooms in an old-money atmosphere. As it should, given its roots.

Founded in 1889 by the Harrison Marching Society, a group of wealthy, enthusiastic supporters of local attorney Benjamin Harrison who they helped elect President of the United States in 1888, the Columbia Club has traditionally been a bastion of white, male Republican Party stalwarts. While that has gradually changed (Democrats, women and other minorities can now become members) it still retains its position as one of the city's centers of economic and political power. (Every Republican President from Harrison to George Bush has stayed here.)

Now listed on the National Register of Historic Places, the Columbia Club has four floors of guest rooms, a library, a billiards room, a

barbershop, a fitness center, a lounge and dining facilities.

Courtyard by Marriott
$$$ • 501 W. Washington St. • 635-4443

This 233-room facility is across the street from the Eiteljorg Museum of American Indians and Western Art, a block from the Indiana Convention Center and the RCA Dome and two blocks from the Indianapolis Zoo. Other downtown attractions, Circle Centre, the Artsgarden, Union Station, the Indiana Repertory Theatre and the Circle Theatre, are an easy walk or a brief cab ride away.

Amenities include free parking, free airport shuttle service, facilities for the disabled, a playground and an outdoor pool. The on-site restaurant, T.G.I. Friday's, was 1994's Franchise Restaurant of the Year; it's also a popular lunch and after-work watering hole.

Crowne Plaza Union Station
$$$ • 123 Louisiana St. • 631-2221

Attached to the west end of Union Station, this 276-room hotel includes 26 rooms inside refurbished Pullman train cars. If you've ever wondered what it would have been like to travel by rail while ensconced in a private, furnished Pullman, this is your chance to find out — minus the rattles and jolts of actual train travel.

The hotel also contains an indoor pool, a whirlpool, an exercise room and concierge and airport shuttle services. The on-site Louisiana Street Restaurant and Bar serves breakfast, lunch and dinner.

Across the street from the Indiana Convention Center and the RCA Dome, the Crowne Plaza is within walking distance of Circle Centre and most other downtown attractions. It's also a short drive from the Indianapolis Zoo, the IUPUI campus and the Children's Museum.

Days Inn Downtown

$$ • 401 E. Washington St. • 637-6464, (800) 325-2525

A 100-room facility adjacent to Market Square Arena, Days Inn Downtown is an easy walk from Circle Centre, the Indiana Convention Center and RCA Dome, Union Station, Monument Circle and other downtown attractions. The hotel offers free parking and airport transportation. Complimentary continental breakfast is provided to all guests; there's also an on-site restaurant, Tommy's Fine Food & Spirits, which serves breakfast, lunch and dinner in a casual atmosphere.

Embassy Suites Downtown

$$$ • 110 W. Washington St. • 236-1800, (800) 362-2779

This 360 all-suites hotel is right in the center of the action downtown. Diagonally across Washington Street from Circle Centre and the Artsgarden, between Claypool Courts and the Indiana Repertory Theatre and just two blocks from the Indiana Convention Center and the RCA Dome, Embassy Suites is perfectly situated for both business and pleasure. A parking garage is attached to the hotel (parking is extra; valet services are available).

The hotel's suites each contain a pair of TVs, two phones, a microwave oven, a refrigerator, a coffeemaker and a foldout sleeper couch in the living room. There are also facilities for disabled persons. Every guest receives a full cooked-to-order breakfast each morning

and access to the two-hour "manager's reception" (re: happy hour) with complimentary beverages and snacks each afternoon. Also on-site is the cozy, elegant Ellington's restaurant. Work off the extra calories in the hotel's exercise room and indoor pool.

Hyatt Regency Indianapolis

$$$$ • One S. Capitol Ave. • 632-1234

Directly across Washington Street from the Embassy Suites and across Illinois Street from Circle Centre, this 500-room facility includes a 20-story atrium, glass elevators and a waterfall. It also includes 23 grand suites, 16 shops, seven restaurants (including the Eagle's Nest, a revolving rooftop restaurant and lounge), a full-service bank and a variety of meeting and business-plan rooms with phone and fax capabilities.

And because all work and no play is bad for you, the Hyatt contains the largest on-site fitness club of any downtown hotel.

Because it's less than a block from the Indiana Convention Center and the RCA Dome and only a few blocks from Market Square Arena, the Hyatt is a favorite of NFL and NBA teams, as well as of meeting planners and conventioneers. What's more, its central location makes getting most anywhere else — Eli Lilly and Company, Indianapolis International Airport, the Indianapolis Tennis Center, the I.U. Medical Center, the IUPUI campus, the Indianapolis Zoo, the Indianapolis Art Museum or the Children's Museum — a snap.

Howard Johnson's

$$ • 1530 N. Meridian St. • 634-6100, (800) 233-4639

Just minutes from Monument Circle, this 160-room hotel offers convenience to all downtown sites and to such attractions as The Children's Museum, the Indianapolis Museum of Art, the Indianapolis Motor Speedway and the Indiana State Fairgrounds. Amenities include a pool. The on-site restaurant, Rumor's Cafe, serves breakfast, lunch and dinner and boasts of having a menu with the city's largest selection of heart-healthy foods.

FYI

Unless otherwise noted, the area code for all phone numbers in this guide is 317.

Omni Severin Hotel

$$$$ • 40 W. Jackson Pl. • 634-6664,
(800) 843-6664

This 423-room, highly rated facility adjacent to Union Station is a block south of Circle Centre and a block east of the Indiana Convention Center and the RCA Dome. It's also within easy walking distance of other downtown attractions. Amenities include 38 suites and a fitness club complete with indoor pool. Dining options include the 40 West Coffee Cafe (espresso, pastries and salads) and the Hot Tuna (fish, steaks and pastas).

Ramada Plaza Hotel

$$ • 31 W. Ohio St. • 635-2000,
(800) 272-6232

A block from Monument Circle, this 371-room hotel has such amenities as a rooftop pool and an on-site health club. Just a short jaunt away are Market Square Arena, Circle Centre, the Convention Center and RCA Dome. For casual downtown dining, the Ramada Plaza offers English's Cafe, serving breakfast, lunch and dinner.

Renaissance Tower Historic Inn

$$ • 230 E. Ninth St. • 261-1652,
(800) 676-7786

This elegant brick inn on the northeast side of the downtown district is listed on the National Register of Historic Places. It contains 80 studio suites available for both short- and long-term stays; among the amenities are free local phone service, voice mail, cable TV and on-site parking. The suites have fully equipped kitchens, including cooking and eating utensils, and there's an on-site laundry facility. All major downtown sites are just a short drive (or a healthy walk) away.

The Tower Inn

$$ • 1633 N. Capitol Ave. • 925-9831

Just across the street from Methodist Hospital and 16 blocks north of the Indiana Convention Center and the RCA Dome, this facility contains 62 rooms, all nonsmoking. There's an attached parking garage.

The inn offers easy access to all downtown sites and to the Indianapolis Motor Speedway and the Children's Museum.

University Place Conference Center and Hotel at IUPUI

$$ • 850 W. Michigan St. • 269-9000,
(800) 627-2700

This highly rated facility combines a 278-room hotel with a 30-room high-tech conference center. Guests have access to such amenities as a fitness facility and pool, The Bistro (for breakfast) and Chancellor's Restaurant (for lunch and dinner). Covered walkways link University Place with the I.U. Medical center facilities and the I.U. Natatorium and Track and Field Stadium. Other area attractions — the Eiteljorg Museum of American Indians and Western Art, the Indianapolis Zoo, the Indiana Repertory Theatre, Circle Theatre, the Artsgarden and Circle Centre — are easily accessible by car or on foot.

The Westin Hotel, Indianapolis

$$$$ • 50 S. Capitol Ave. • 262-8100,
(800) 228-3000

Connected by a covered skybridge to the Indiana Convention Center and RCA Dome complex, this 573-room, highly rated hotel is in the heart of downtown Indianapolis' convention, sports, shopping and entertainment district. Its amenities include a fitness facility and indoor pool.

Airport

Adam's Mark Hotel

$$$ • 2544 Executive Dr. • 248-2481,
(800) 444-ADAM

For luxury accommodations with easy airport access, this is it. With 407 rooms, including 44 elegant suites, this full-service hotel can accommodate everything from a couple on a

weekend getaway to a banquet hall full of conventioneers. On-site facilities include 28,000 square feet of meeting space, two restaurants (Applebees's for casual dining, The Marker for more sophisticated occasions) and a lounge (Marker Lounge) and a nightclub (Quincy's). The hotel offers free airport shuttle service, free parking, indoor and outdoor pools and a fitness facility. Downtown Indianapolis is minutes away via I-70.

Budgetel Inn
$$ • 2650 Executive Dr. • 244-8100, (800) 428-3438

Near the airport, this 102-room facility offers easy access to west-side businesses; the downtown district is a short drive east on I-70. Rooms are handicapped-accessible. All guests receive continental breakfast delivered to their rooms.

Courtyard by Marriott
$$$ • 5525 Fortune Cir. E. • 248-0300, (800) 321-2211

This quiet, residential-style facility has an indoor pool and whirlpool, a fitness facility and 151 handicapped-accessible rooms. There's free shuttle service to the nearby airport, and there's an on-site restaurant and lounge.

Days Inn Airport
$$ • 5860 Fortune Cir. W. • 248-0621, (800) 325-2525

A 238-room hotel offers guests free airport shuttle service, an outdoor pool and exercise facilities. Also on-site is P.K.'s Dining & Diversions, a restaurant and lounge serving breakfast, lunch and dinner. Each room includes cable TV and free local telephone service.

Hampton Inn Hotel
$$ • 5601 Fortune Cir. W. • 244-1221, (800) HAMPTON

At this 131-room hotel guests can choose among two types of rooms: those with king-size beds and those with double beds; non-smoking rooms are available, and rooms are handicapped-accessible. Among the amenities are free airport shuttle and local phone service, complimentary continental breakfast and satellite TV.

Holiday Inn Airport
$$$ • 2501 S. High School Rd. • 244-6861, (800) HOLIDAY

With a 22,000-square-foot conference center and more than 20 meeting/banquet rooms, this 274-room, full-service hotel at Indianapolis International Airport is more than a place to stay — it's also a place to work and play. Also among its offerings are airport shuttle service, free parking, an indoor pool and whirlpool and an exercise room. Guest accommodations are handicapped-accessible. On-site attractions include Chantéclair, an elegant French restaurant; The Gallery, an atrium lounge; and Benchwarmers, a sports bar.

LaQuinta Inn West
$$ • 5316 W. Southern Ave. • 247-4281, (800) 531-5900

Only a mile from the airport, this 122-room facility offers free local phone service, satellite TV, continental breakfast, an outdoor pool and airport shuttle service. Rooms are handicapped-accessible. Downtown Indianapolis is about a 10-minute drive east.

Ramada Indianapolis Airport
$$$ • 2500 S. High School Rd. • 244-3361, (800) 228-2828

This 288-room facility on the airport grounds includes some 14,000 square feet of meeting space and offers easy access, via I-70 and I-465, to downtown Indianapolis, the Motor Speedway and other areas of the city. Among the hotel's amenities are an indoor pool, free parking and shuttle service and an on-site restaurant (Alexander's) and a lounge (Amelia's).

Northeast

Amerisuites
$$ • 9104 Keystone Crossing • 843-0064, (800) 833-1516

Situated in the upscale commercial and retail bustle of the Keystone Crossing area, this facility contains 126 two-room suites, each of which includes a refrigerator, microwave and coffeemaker. Handicapped-accessible accommodations are available. Among Amerisuites's amenities are deluxe continental breakfasts, newspapers, free local phone service and an on-site fitness club and pool.

Best Western Luxbury Inn Castleton
$$ • 8300 Craig St. • 842-9190, (800) 252-7748

This 114-room facility is near Community Hospital North and the Castleton commercial and retail district. In addition to having a pool, it offers handicapped accessibility and easy access to a variety of area restaurants, movie theaters and nightclubs.

Hampton Inn Northeast
$$ • 6817 E. 82nd St., 576-0220, (800) HAMPTON

A 130-room facility at the I-69 and I-465 junction offers handicapped-accessible rooms, an indoor pool and convenient access to the Castleton commercial and retail district. Included with each room is free cable TV and local phone service.

Holiday Inn Express Northeast
$$ • 9790 North by Northeast Blvd. •578-2000, (800) HOLIDAY

This two-story, 76-room hotel includes some rooms with whirlpool tubs and as well as handicapped accommodations. Enjoy a free continental breakfast.

Homewood Suites at the Crossing
$$ • 2501 E. 86th St. • 253-1919, (800) 225-5466

Just west of the Keystone Crossing commercial and retail area, this 116-suite hotel is nestled in a neighborhood-like setting. Designed for both short and long-term stays, Homewood Suites offers elegantly comfortable accommodations, complete with facilities for physically disabled guests. On-site amenities include an outdoor pool and a fitness club.

Knights Inn North
$ • 9402 Haver Way • 848-2423, (800) 843-5644

Just off Keystone Avenue north of I-465, this 110-room facility is near both the Keystone Crossing and the Carmel commercial and retail districts. Rooms are handicapped-accessible, and some include kitchenettes.

There's an outdoor pool available and ample parking.

Omni Indianapolis North Hotel
$$$ • 8181 N. Shadeland Ave. • 849-6668, (800) THE-OMNI

A deluxe, full-service, high-rise hotel near the Castleton and Keystone Crossing commercial and retail districts, the Omni contains 222 rooms, a health club, an indoor pool and sauna and Abruzzi's Cafe and Grill. Rooms are handicapped-accessible.

Quality Inn Castleton Suites
$$ • 8275 Craig St. • 841-9700, (800) 228-5151

North of 82nd Street, just west of I-69, this facility includes 163 suites, each of which contains a wet bar and refrigerator, a conference table and chairs. Room rate includes free local phone service, cable TV and daily newspaper.

You'll enjoy easy access to Castleton, Fishers and Keystone office parks, nearby Castleton Square mall and an array of other area stores, movie theaters, restaurants and nightspots. Suites include handicapped-accessible facilities. The hotel offers free airport shuttle service.

Radisson Plaza and Suite Hotel
$$ • 8787 Keystone Crossing • 846-2700, (800) 333-3333

Twelve miles from the downtown district, this 561-room hotel is right in the heart of the Keystone Crossing commercial and retail district. It also offers easy access to the Castleton and Carmel areas. Among its amenities are an indoor pool, a fitness club, two restaurants (Keystone Cafe and Waterson's), a lounge (the Lobby Bar) and a nightclub (Whirligig's). Rooms are handicapped-accessible.

Signature Inn Castleton
$$ • 8380 Kelly Ln. • 849-8555, (800) 822-5252

A two-story, 123-room facility at the intersection of I-465 and Allisonville Road, this hotel is near the Castleton and Keystone Crossing commercial and retail districts. Among its amenities are meeting rooms, guest offices, free local phone service, cable TV, free breakfast express, daily newspaper and an outdoor pool. Guest accommodations are handicapped-accessible.

Studio Plus
$$ • 9750 E. Lakeshore Dr. • 843-1181

A 71-room extended-stay facility in the Keystone Crossing area, Studio Plus provides lodging that includes fully equipped kitchens, free local phone service and cable TV and an on-site laundry. There's also a pool, sauna and exercise room. Rooms are handicapped-accessible.

Northwest

Best Western Waterfront Plaza Hotel
$$ • 2930 Waterfront Pkwy. W. Dr. • 299-8400, (800) 528-1234

Nestled beside a small lake, this 140-room hotel at I-465 and Crawfordsville Road combines business and pleasure. There's 17,500 square feet of on-site meeting space and easy access to the airport and west-side commercial and industrial parks. There's also an indoor pool, whirlpool, sauna dining (The Waterfront Cafe) and entertainment (The Excalibur II Lounge). Rooms are handicapped-accessible.

Comfort Inn North
$$ • 3880 W. 92nd St. • 872-3100, (800) 228-5150

This 58-room, three-story inn at the junction of I-465 and Michigan Road offers 22 non-smoking rooms and an indoor pool. Rooms are handicapped-accessible and include free cable TV and local phone calls.

Days Inn Northwest
$$ • 3740 N. High School Rd. • 293-6550, (800) 329-7466

This facility's 155 rooms are spread among four buildings, arranged around a central courtyard containing an Olympic-size pool. The

hotel also provides free airport shuttle service, free cable TV and local phone calls. Rooms are handicapped-accessible.

Embassy Suites Hotel
$$$ • 3912 Vincennes Rd. • 872-7700, (800) EMBASSY

This gleaming white, eight-story, 222-suite hotel looks like a transplant from southern Spain. In keeping with its setting amid the Park 100 office park area (I-465 and Michigan Road), there are meeting and banquet rooms and catering services available. Amenities include complimentary breakfast and an indoor pool and fitness club. A variety of restaurants are nearby, as is Beef & Boards Dinner Theatre. Suites are handicapped-accessible.

Hampton Inn Northwest
$$ • 7220 Woodland Dr. • 290-1212, (800) HAMPTON

This 124-room inn near the I-465 and 71st Street junction features an indoor pool and whirlpool, a workout area, and handicapped-accessible facilities. Continental breakfast is on the house. Enjoy easy access to the surrounding Park 100 area and to other northside commercial and retail sites; the downtown district is minutes away via I-465.

Holiday Inn North
$$$ • 3850 DePauw Blvd. • 872-9790, (800) HOLIDAY

Near the I-465 and Michigan Road interchange, this 351-room Holidome facility offers an indoor pool, saunas, Jacuzzi, fitness equipment and putting green. Airport transportation is available, as are weekend packages. On-site restaurants and lounges include Cafe St. Paul (breakfast, lunch and dinner), San Remo Grill (dinner), and Benchwarmers Sports Food & Spirits (sports bar). Situated amidst the Park 100/Pyramids business district, the hotel also offers easy access via I-465 to other north-side commercial and retail areas and to downtown. Rooms are handicapped-accessible.

INSIDERS' TIP

For news and feature stories about the people and places that make up the Greater Indianapolis area, check the city and state sections in *The Indianapolis Star* and *The Indianapolis News*.

Lees Inn Indianapolis

$$ • 5011 N. Lafayette Rd. • 297-8880, (800) 733-5337

A 75-room facility at I-65 and Lafayette Road, Lees Inn offers free HBO and a complimentary continental breakfast. Some rooms have Jacuzzis; all are handicapped accessible. It's just minutes from downtown via I-65.

New England Suites Hotel

$$ • 3871 W. 92nd St. • 879-1700

The 40 two-room suites in this hotel all contain microwave ovens, refrigerators and TVs with VCRs (videotapes are available).

Amenities include free local phone service and breakfast. Suites are handicapped-accessible. This hotel is near northwest-side office parks.

Pickwick Farms
Short-Term Furnished Apartments

$$ • 9300 N. Ditch Rd. • 872-6506, (800) 869-RENT

By the day, week or month, this apartment complex offers guests their choice of studio, one-, two- or three-bedroom furnished quarters, each with a dishwasher, microwave, stove, refrigerator, toaster and coffeemaker.

The Big Business of Conventions

Because Indianapolis is easily accessible from throughout the country, it has become a popular site for regional and national conventions, trade shows, corporate meetings and special events. According to the Indianapolis Convention & Visitors Association, between 1984 and 1994 convention business increased from 30 events to 231, and the number of people attending those events jumped from 147,000 to more than 858,000.

In addition to location, Indianapolis has equipped itself well to handle expanding convention traffic. The Indiana Convention Center and RCA Dome complex contains a combined 127,595 square feet of meeting space and more than 301,500 square feet of exhibit space. The complex has hosted the NCAA Final Four, the nation's largest

Photo: The Indianapolis Star and The Indianapolis News

The RCA Dome is home to the NFL Colts and numerous other events — including NCAA Final Four games in 1997.

African-American exhibition (Indiana Black Expo), the North American Christian Convention and the Fire Department Instructors Conference.

At the same time, there are a number of hotels within easy walking distance of the Center and Dome, as are a variety of restaurants, nightclubs, theaters and sports facilities.

And in September 1995, the missing link — downtown shopping — was forged with the opening of Circle Centre, an 800,000-square-foot retail and entertainment complex. Containing department stores (Nordstrom and Parisian), 100 speciality stores, a multi-screen cinema and restaurants, Circle Centre offers a refuge for meeting-weary conventioneers.

For more information, contact the Indianapolis Convention & Visitors Association, 639-4282.

Rates include all utilities, local phone service, voicemail and cable TV. Amenities include tennis and racquetball courts, a workout room, indoor volleyball, bowling, a play area for children and an outdoor pool. There's also an on-site laundry.

Pickwick Farms offers convenient access to Park 100, College Park and the Pyramids, as well as other north-side business districts. Downtown is minutes away via I-465.

Red Roof Inn North
$$ • 9520 Valparaiso Ct. • 872-3030

With 108 handicapped-accessible rooms in two buildings, this facility offers economical lodgings in a location convenient to the Park 100/Pyramids business district. Like other budget accommodations, the inn provides guests with free cable TV and local telephone service.

Residence Inn by Marriott
$$$ • 3553 Founders Rd. • 872-0462, (800) 331-3131

This facility at 86th Street and Michigan Road has 88 suites each of which has a fully equipped kitchen (stove, refrigerator, microwave, cooking and eating utensils) and a furnished living room complete with a desk. All suites are available for either short- or long-term stays. Amenities include an outdoor pool, exercise equipment, valet service and an on-site coin-operated laundry. Suites are handicapped-accessible.

St. Vincent Marten House Hotel & Conference Center
$$ • 1801 W. 86th St. • 872-4111

Adjacent to St. Vincent Hospital, the Marten House has meeting and banquet facilities in addition to 173 handicapped-accessible guest rooms. Amenities include an indoor pool and fitness club, free parking and a host of personal guest services. The on-site restaurant, Piccard's Restaurant, serves breakfast, lunch and dinner from a menu offering an array of heart-healthy selections.

Signature Inn North
$$ • 3910 Payne Branch Rd. • 875-5656

This 143-room inn at I-465 and Michigan Road offers free local phone service, cable TV, daily newspaper, meeting rooms and offices for business travelers. There's an outdoor pool and free breakfast.

Studio Plus
$ • 9030 Wesleyan Rd. • 872-3090

This 71-room extended-stay hotel in the College Park area provides quarters with fully equipped kitchens, free local phone service and cable TV. Amenities include an outdoor pool

INSIDERS' TIP

Check out the Sugar Grove Winery, 611 Newlin Road, in Mooresville. The area's newest winery makes a terrific stop when on a drive through Morgan County to admire the fall foliage.

and exercise facility. Daily, weekly or monthly rates are available. Rooms are handicapped-accessible.

Super 8 Motel North
$$ • 9090 Wesleyan Rd. • 875-7676, (800) 800-8000

In College Park west of the Pyramids, this 116-room motel at Michigan Road and Wesleyan Road provides complimentary breakfast. There's an outdoor pool. Rooms are handicapped-accessible.

East

Best Western Indianapolis East
$$ • 2141 N. Post Rd. • 897-2000, (800) 528-1234

Convenient to both the east-side commercial district and the northeast-side commercial and retail district, this 156-room hotel at the intersection of I-70 and Post Road has an on-site fitness club and pool, a restaurant and lounge.

Budget Inn
$ • 6850 E. 21st St.
• 353-9781

Recently renovated, this 139-room facility near the intersection of I-70 and Shadeland Avenue offers access to the east-side commercial and industrial corridor. It has rooms equipped for people with disabilities. Amenities include VCRs and on-site video rentals.

Budgetel Indianapolis East
$ • 2349 N. Post Rd. • 897-2300

This inn, which is 12 miles from the city's downtown district, contains 106 rooms. Among its amenities are free parking and valet service, nonsmoking rooms, free local phone service and complimentary continental breakfast.

Fairgrounds Inn
$ • 1501 E. 38th St. • 926-4401

Across the street from the Indiana State Fairgounds, this 147-room hotel has on-site parking, meeting rooms, an outdoor pool and a play area for children. The facility has handicapped-accessible rooms and offers free air-

port shuttle service. There's also a restaurant and lounge.

Hampton Inn East
$$ • 2311 N. Shadeland Ave. • 359-9900, (800) HAMPTON

Less than 10 minutes east of downtown Indianapolis via I-70, this 125-room inn includes an indoor pool, whirlpool and fitness area. Rooms are accessible to people with disabilities.

Howard Johnson's East
$ • 7050 E. 21st St. • 352-0481, (800) 446-4656

This facility at I-70 and Shadeland Avenue contains 124 rooms and offers handicapped accessibility. Amenities include an outdoor pool and restaurant/lounge facilities.

Holiday Inn I-70 East
$$ • 6990 E. 21st St., 359-5341, (800) HOLIDAY

Eight miles east of downtown on I-70, this 184-room hotel has an indoor pool and whirlpool, a fitness facility, guest laundry, game room and in-room movies. Also available are Nintendo (say it's for the kids), free local phone service and in-room coffeemakers. Rooms are handicapped-accessible. Also on-site is Damon's Restaurant (famous for barbecued ribs and chicken).

LaQuinta Inn East
$$ • 7304 E. 21st St. • 359-1021, (800) 531-5900

A highly rated facility, this 122-room inn adjacent to the intersection of I-70 and Shadeland Avenue offers easy access to the east-side commercial and industrial area. Comfortable, handicapped-accessible rooms include a continental breakfast. There's an outdoor pool, an exercise facility and an on-site guest laundry.

Marriott Hotel
$$$ • 7202 E. 21st St. • 352-1231, (800) 228-9290

Indoor and outdoor pools and a fitness facility are just some of the amenities avail-

FYI
Unless otherwise noted, the area code for all phone numbers in this guide is 317.

Photo: The Indianapolis Star and The Indianapolis News

The Metro Bus system shuttles passengers throughout the metropolitan area.

able at this 252-room, highly rated hotel at I-70 and Shadeland Avenue. Rooms are accessible to the physically disabled. Durbin's Restaurant and Lounge offer dining and entertainment.

Quality Inn East
$$ • 3525 N. Shadeland Ave. • 549-2222, (800) 228-5151

This full-service, 123-room inn includes Jacuzzi tubs, an indoor pool and fitness room, a game room and meeting rooms. There are also 12 honeymoon and executive suites with king-size waterbeds, wet bars and stereo systems. Rooms are handicapped-accessible. The on-site restaurant is Rafferty's, which serves breakfast, lunch and dinner; the lounge is the Ritz Nightclub, which offers a variety of live entertainment.

Ramada Inn Indianapolis
$$ • 7701 E. 42nd St., 897-4000, (800) 228-2828

Just off I-465 at the Pendleton Pike Exit, this 192-room facility also includes 11 meeting rooms, a large ballroom, indoor and outdoor pools and an exercise room. Rooms are handicapped-accessible. The Ramada offers

easy access to the east-side commercial and industrial area and to downtown Indianapolis.

Signature Inn East
$$ • 7610 Old Trails Rd. • 353-6966, (800) 822-5252

Primarily designed to serve business travelers, this 102-room hotel at I-465 and E. Washington Street offers free guest offices, meeting rooms, local phone service, breakfast and daily newspaper. Rooms, which are handicapped-accessible, include free cable TV; there's an outdoor pool available as well. Enjoy easy access to the east-side commercial and industrial area and to the downtown district.

West

HoJo Inn Speedway
$$ • 2602 N. High School Rd. • 291-8800, (800) 446-4656

Conveniently sandwiched between the Indianapolis Motor Speedway (2 miles east) and Indianapolis Raceway Park (4 miles west), this 125-room facility is ideal for race fans. There's an outdoor pool and an on-site restaurant. Adjacent to the intersection of I-465 and

Crawfordsville Road, the hotel offers easy access to the downtown area and the airport. Included in the price of each single or double room are cable TV and free local phone calls.

Brickyard Crossing Golf Resort & Inn
$$ • 440 W. 16th St. • 241-2500

This 108-room inn on the grounds of the Indianapolis Motor Speedway offers easy access to the Speedway, the Hall of Fame Museum and to the 18-hole, Pete Dye-designed Brickyard Crossing golf course. Other amenities include an outdoor pool, free airport shuttle service and an on-site restaurant (Brickyard Restaurant) and lounge (Flagroom Lounge). Rooms are handicapped-accessible.

Red Roof Inn Speedway
$$ • 6415 Debonair Ln. • 293-6881, (800) THE-ROOF

This 108-room facility at the Clermont Exit off I-465 is close to both the Indianapolis Motor Speedway and Indianapolis Raceway Park. The airport and downtown Indianapolis are also easily accessible. Rooms are handicapped-accessible.

Signature Inn West
$$ • 3850 Eagle View Dr. • 299-6165, (800) 822-5252

At the intersection of 38th Street and I-465, this 99-room hotel features spacious, handicapped-accessible rooms, airport shuttle service and an outdoor pool. Other amenities include free local phone service, cable TV, breakfast express, and daily newspaper. Meeting rooms and offices are available to business travelers. Signature Inn West is convenient to the Indianapolis Motor Speedway and the airport (via I-465), the Indianapolis Museum of Art (via 38th Street E.), and downtown (via I-65).

South

Econo Lodge South
$$ • 4505 S. Harding St. • 788-9361, (800) 553-2666

Convenient to southwest-side businesses, downtown and the airport, this 150-room motel at I-465 and Harding Street offers free airport shuttle service. There's an outdoor pool, an on-site restaurant and lounge. Rooms are handicapped-accessible.

Comfort Inn South
$$ • 5040 S. East St. • 783-6711

Ten minutes from the downtown area and the airport, this 104-room facility has both single rooms and suites; handicapped-accessible and nonsmoking accommodations are available. Amenities include free satellite TV, free continental breakfast, 24-hour hot coffee service, an outdoor pool and free parking.

Days Inn South
$ • 450 Bixler Rd. • 788-0811, (800) 325-2525

Five miles south of downtown, at the junction of I-465 S. and U.S. 31, this facility has a meeting room with kitchen, a guest laundry and an outdoor pool and play area for children. Room rates include continental breakfast and cable TV. Rooms are handicapped-accessible.

Days Inn Southeast
$ • 5151 Elmwood Dr. • 783-5555, (800) 325-2525

At the intersection of I-465 and Emerson Avenue, this 119-room inn offers easy access to south-side businesses and downtown sites. Amenities include an outdoor pool. Rooms are handicapped-accessible.

Hampton Inn South
$$ • 7045 McFarland Blvd. • 889-0722, (800) HAMPTON

This 113-room inn provides free local phone service and cable TV, an indoor pool and complimentary continental breakfast. For small groups in need of meeting space, Hampton Inn has a board room and hospitality suite available.

Holiday Inn Express
$$ • 3514 S. Keystone Ave. • 788-3100, (800) HOLIDAY

This 62-room facility has suites with kitchenettes and whirlpools, free HBO and ESPN, free local phone service and a free breakfast bar. There are on-site meeting rooms. Guest quarters are handicapped-accessible.

Quality Inn South
$$ • 520 E. Thompson Rd. • 787-8341, (800) 228-5151

This 182-room room facility at the junction of I-465 and U.S. 31 S. is a 10-minute drive from downtown and the Greenwood Park Mall. On-site amenities include indoor and outdoor pools, a whirlpool and sauna, a health club and a play area for children. Enjoy dining at the Garden Park Restaurant and music and dancing in the Celebration Lounge. Free airport shuttle service is available. Also available are meeting/banquet rooms. Accommodations are handicapped-accessible.

Holiday Inn Southeast
$$ • 5120 Victory Dr. • 783-7751, (800) HOLIDAY

This six-story high-rise at I-465 and S. Emerson Avenue is just minutes from downtown and the airport. Amenities include an outdoor pool, shuttle service, free parking, a guest laundry and a game room. Enjoy on-site dining at Grenadyne's and cocktails at The Rusty Locker. Rooms are handicapped-accessible.

Ramada Inn South
$$ • 4514 S. Emerson Ave. • 787-3344, (800) 2-RAMADA

This 193-room facility at the intersection of I-465 and Emerson Avenue (that translates to 8 miles southeast of the downtown district) has suites with fireplaces available for those chilly nights. Other amenities include an outdoor pool and a play area for children. Dining choices include Damon's (for ribs) and the Clubhouse (a sports bar and grill). Rooms are handicapped- accessible.

Signature Inn South
$$ • 4402 E. Creekview Dr. • 784-7006, (800) 822-5252

This 101-room hotel at I-65 and Southport Road offers large, comfortable rooms with free local phone service, free cable TV (including HBO) and in-room recliners (when it's time to kick back and relax). Other amenities include a pool, fitness club access and on-site offices for business travelers. Rooms are handicapped-accessible. The hotel's location makes for easy access to Southport, Greenwood and downtown Indianapolis.

Super 8 Motel
$ • 4502 S. Harding St. • 788-4774, (800) 800-8000

This 69-room motel at the intersection of I-465 and State Road 37 S. offers free local phone service and cable TV, free shuttle service to the airport and downtown and free continental breakfast. Rooms are handicapped-accessible.

Carmel

Courtyard by Marriott
$$ • 10290 N. Meridian St. • 571-1110, (800) 321-2211

For busy business travelers, this 149-room facility features meeting rooms, laundry and valet services and daily newspapers. When it's time to unwind, take advantage of an indoor pool, whirlpool and fitness equipment. Other amenities include nonsmoking rooms, cable TV and free parking for cars and motorcoaches. There's an on-site restaurant/lounge and easy access to all north-side commercial and retail districts.

Guest Quarters Suite Hotel
$$$ • 11355 N. Meridian St. •844-7994, (800) 424-2900

This facility at the junction of I-465 and Meridian Street contains 138 suites, many of which are handicapped-accessible. Amenities include both indoor and outdoor pools, fitness equipment and (for carb-loading) an on-site restaurant.

INSIDERS' TIP

Stop by the Goethe Link Memorial Daffodil Gardens, 5 miles south of Mooresville on Ind. 67, in early spring for a visual treat: 15 acres of brilliant yellow blooms.

Wyndham Garden Hotel
$$ • 251 Pennsylvania Pkwy. • 574-4600

A 171-room hotel with lap pool, Jacuzzi and workout room, the Wyndham also offers such amenities as coffeemakers and blow dryers in every room. Six rooms are specially designed to accommodate handicapped guests. There is a full-service restaurant and lounge on-site.

Greenwood

Greenwood Inn FantaSuite Hotel
$ for standard rooms, $$$ for fantasy suites • 1117 E. Main St., Greenwood • 882-2211, (800) 444-STAY

This 92-room suite hotel includes 24 fantasy suites as well as standard guest rooms. The fantasy suites bear names that reflect their theme and decor: Jungle Safari, complete with a bed enclosed in mosquito netting; Northern Lights, where you can sleep inside an igloo; Sherwood Forest, with a bed tucked amid trees and a whirlpool with a waterfall; and Alien Invasion, where you'll sleep in a flying saucer. Suites are more expensive than standard rooms, but then who among us wouldn't pay a little extra to live out our fantasies? There's also an outdoor pool.

Bed and Breakfasts

The Hoffman House
$$ • 545 E. 11th St. • 635-1701

An American Four-Square-style structure (c.1903), this facility offers two second-floor guest rooms furnished with antique double beds and handmade quilts. Continental plus breakfasts are served on china with silver utensils. The Hoffman House is convenient to the downtown business and entertainment district.

The Old Northside Bed & Breakfast
$$-$$$ • 1340 N. Alabama St. • 635-9123, (800) 635-9127

Housed in a brick Romanesque Revival house (c. 1885) in the near-downtown Old Northside neighborhood, this bed and breakfast features original handcarved woodwork and handpainted murals on the ceilings and

walls. Guests have their choice of a variety of themed rooms. The Literary Room includes memorabilia from the Golden Age of Indiana literature as well as such romantic touches as a fireplace and an extra-large Jacuzzi tub. The Theatre Room contains a large bed on a curtained stage with spotlights surrounding it, posters and playbills on the walls and a Jacuzzi tub. The Bridal Room has a specially designed shower and Jacuzzi as well as a fireplace. The 500 Room has auto racing mementos galore: For racing fans this is the ideal room to spend a night. Come prepared to eat — breakfasts here are scrumptious.

Downtown

Le Chateau Delaware
$$-$$$ • 1456 N. Delaware St. • 636-9156

Just up the street from former President Benjamin Harrison's house, this Italian villa-like manor offers guests a choice of eight rooms, some with private baths, all furnished with either brass or poster beds and antiques. Amenities include fresh flowers in each room, daily newspapers and breakfast (homemade rolls and muffins, fresh fruit, juices and coffee). The 1,200-square-foot living room can be reserved for meetings, receptions, seminars, conferences or weddings. Le Chateau Delaware offers easy access to the downtown business district, Circle Centre, Market Square Arena and other downtown attractions.

Stone Soup Inn
$$-$$$ • 1304 N. Central Ave. • 639-9550

This lovely old home on a wooded lot in the historic Old Northside neighborhood is within walking distance of downtown Indianapolis. Because proprietors Jeneane Life and Jordan Rifkin speak Japanese (and Jeneane speaks German too), the inn caters to an international clientele. It contains four large guest rooms, all furnished with Victorian or Mission-style antiques. Two of the rooms have fireplaces, two have bay windows, one has a two-person Jacuzzi, one a steam shower. All four share a common second-floor sitting room and balcony. There is also a second-floor butler's pantry with complimentary beverages and popcorn in addition to a stock of brochures on downtown attractions and menus from downtown restaurants.

On the first floor, the living room has a fireplace and a baby grand piano. There is also a library and a dining room large enough to accommodate a house full of guests. On weekdays, breakfast is continental, with fresh breads and fruits, juices, coffee and tea. Weekends mean full breakfasts with egg dishes or cinnamon apple pancakes.

The Tranquil Cherub
$$ • 2164 N. Capitol Ave. • 923-9036

In this 90-year-old Greek Revival-style house there are three rooms and a three-room attic suite, each with its own personality. Rogers' room includes a king-size bed with a headboard designed by innkeepers Thom and Barb Feit. The Gatsby Room features a foster-poster cannonball bed (queen size), and art deco furnishings. The Victorian Room contains an antique iron and brass double bed and white wicker furniture. Grannie's Attic, which consists of a sitting room, bath and bedroom, is furnished with an eclectic variety of antiques including a steamer trunk, a wicker baby buggy and a Victorian fainting sofa.

Breakfast consists of juice, freshly made coffee and homemade muffins or breads. This adults-only bed and breakfast offers easy access to the downtown area, the Children's Museum, the Indianapolis Art Museum and the Speedway.

North

Boone Docks on the River
$$ • 7159 Edgewater Pl. • 257-3671

Tucked alongside the White River in a 1920s English Tudor that many people consider a storybook house, this bed and breakfast contains a garden-level suite with private entrance and white wicker furnishings. Guests also have access to the Common Room where they can relax around a piano or beside a fireplace. There are two outside decks: the Main Deck, shaded by a huge ancient oak tree, is where breakfast is served when weather permits; the Riverside Deck, shaded by a weeping willow, is a good place to contem-

plate or simply watch the heron and geese that fish the river.

Boone Docks is run by Lynne and Michael Boone. Michael is the great, great, great, great grandson of legendary pioneer Daniel Boone.

As far as credit cards go, Boone Docks on the River only accepts American Express.

The Brick Street Inn
$$ • 175 S. Main St., Zionsville • 873-9177

In the heart of Zionsville's quaint village district, this romantic inn pampers guests with down comforters and gourmet breakfasts and is furnished with antiques and reproductions. There are five rooms. There's also a hot tub available. Cozy up to the fireplace, stroll the streets or take a twilight carriage ride.

The Nuthatch
$$ • 7161 Edgewater Pl. • 257-2660

This 1920s French country cottage overlooks the White River and contains two guest rooms. There's an attached greenhouse and a private terrace – the latter is a great place to have your morning coffee or tea. The Wren's Nest is an intimate downstairs hideaway complete with private entrance. It contains a queen-size bed, a cozy sitting area and a bath with a claw-footed tub; the decor includes stained glass and antique lighting fixtures. There's a small deck in the herb garden outside.

Breakfast choices range from Hoosier home cooking to heart-smart, vegetarian, herbal or exotic — all prepared by Joan Morris, a gourmet cook and culinary instructor who operates The Nuthatch with her husband Bernie.

The Frederick-Talbott Inn
$$-$$$ • 13805 Allisonville Rd., Fishers • 578-3600

Tastefully appointed in English Country decor, this inn offers guests a choice of 12 rooms complete with private baths and antique furnishings. Luxury and comfort abound throughout — gracious 19th-century hospitality with a contemporary flair. Set in a lovely country landscape, the inn is just up the road from Conner Prairie, one of the country's premier living history museums. There's a full buffet breakfast served each morning.

South

The Richardson House
$$ • 2422 E. Southport Rd., Southport
• 781-1119

Just 7 miles south of downtown Indianapolis, the Richardson House is a Queen Anne house (c. 1900) with three extended-stay, adults-only guest rooms, each with kitchen and bath facilities. Rental is on a weekly or monthly basis. Amenities include all cooking and eating utensils, toaster, coffeemaker, cable TV and free local phone service. The Richardson House does not accept credit cards.

Persimmon Tree Bed & Breakfast
$$ • One N. Madison Ave., Greenwood
• 889-0849

Built in the 1880s, this bed and breakfast in Greenwood's Old Town district offers rooms decorated with antiques. A wraparound veranda, beveled glass windows, claw-foot tubs, and lace curtains lend an air of old-fashioned elegance.

East

Friendliness With a Flair
$ • 5214 E. 20th Pl. • 356-3149

Offering two lovely nonsmoking rooms, this bed and breakfast is in a residential area. Weather permitting, guests can have breakfast in a Florida room. Hostess Loretta Whitten goes out of her way to make you feel at home. Staying here is like staying in the home of an old friend.

Friendliness With a Flair does not accept credit cards.

If you take the time to look, you're bound to discover lots of great food and enjoyable ambiance.

Restaurants

As you peruse this chapter devoted to one of our favorite activities — dining out — you'll find plenty of possibilities, putting to rest once and for all that old saw about there being no place to eat in Indianapolis.

In fact, the choices prove so enticing that our favorite thing to make for dinner is reservations. Downtown and the Broad Ripple neighborhood offer an abundance of dining possibilities, and we've dedicated ourselves to trying them.

Though the choices here have traditionally been heavy on American, Italian and Chinese, within the last 10 or so years the city has seen a wider variety of ethnic cuisines, including Indian, Ethiopian and Russian. Fine dining opportunities have expanded as well. In other words, if you take the time to look, you're bound to discover lots of great food and enjoyable ambiance.

And you'll probably turn up some excellent eateries that we haven't even mentioned here. In fact, we're sure you will. We haven't included every commendable restaurant in Indianapolis for the simple reason that we haven't been to them all, at least not yet. One of our goals for the next edition is to expand this chapter with even more suggestions. And if you run across a great little place we should know about, drop us a line. We'll be sure to check it out.

Though we've included brief introductions to the city's main restaurant districts, individual listings are arranged by food category, so your favorite specialties should be easy to find. Indianapolis is such a drivable city — you can get just about anywhere in a half-hour or less. So, if you have a passion for pepperoni pizza, you'll quickly find a place to satisfy your taste in the pizza category. We have, however, excluded most chain restaurants, primarily because you probably already know all about

them. Here we've tried to spotlight some of our best local eateries in a wide variety of categories.

When you head out for a taste of Indianapolis, be sure to call ahead for current hours or to make reservations. Though often not needed, or even accepted, at many casual eateries, fine dining often calls for a little advance planning.

To help with planning, we've included a handy price guide, though remember it is only a guide — menus change, and prices often fluctuate. Prices are based on dinner for two, excluding cocktails and wine, appetizers and desserts, tax and tip.

$	$12 or less
$$	$13 to $22
$$$	$23 to $39
$$$$	More than $40

Restaurants mentioned here accept major credit cards, at least Mastercard and Visa, unless otherwise noted.

Keep in mind a check total jumps considerably when you add on appetizers, drinks and desserts. Likewise, you can hold down costs at a pricier place by passing on the extras or by splurging only on dessert (our favorite ploy). And prices may prove significantly lower at lunch.

So grab a friend or go alone, but be sure to explore the terrific restaurants around here. Sample the specialties, try something new and report your discoveries back to us. We're always looking for a favorite new restaurant.

Enjoy.

Restaurant districts

With the opening of Circle Centre, the new downtown mall, Indianapolis has witnessed a new emphasis on downtown dining. In addi-

Dick Clark's American Bandstand Grill is a popular eatery on the city's north side.

tion to longtime favorites such as St. Elmo for steaks, Bazbeaux for pizza and The Old Spaghetti Factory for pasta, downtown now offers the Euro-bistro Palomino, the new American cuisine of California Cafe, two brew pubs — Alcatraz and Rock Bottom — and a new location of Ruth's Chris steakhouse. And there's the promise of more to come. You'll also find a Houlihan's bar and grill and such casual fare as a new Steak 'n Shake and a varied food court in the mall itself.

Broad Ripple of course has long been considered our city's main restaurant and nightlife district, and clustered in this little neighborhood you'll find eateries to please just about every taste. Along Broad Ripple Avenue and the surrounding streets, restaurant-goers can sample Indian, Greek, Italian and Mexican cuisine; favorites include Star of India, the Parthenon, Ambrosia and La Jolla. Check out Mezza Luna too, and don't miss the country French fare (and delicious desserts) at Renee's.

And there are enough bars and nightclubs to fill anyone's evening. On the north side of the city along 86th and 82nd streets (which despite the changing address as you pass Keystone at the Crossing, are really the same street), you'll find strip mall after strip mall.

Though they may look generic, these shopping centers house plenty of top-notch eateries, many with an ethnic flair. You'll find Moscow Nights and Russia House, Taj of India, Afghani fare at Kabul, Italian at Bacco and a range of specialties at A Taste of New York. And of course there's plenty of shopping.

Farther north in Boone County (turn north on Zionsville Road from W. 86th Street) lies the charming village of Zionsville. Bricked streets and quaint shops provide ambiance, but you'll also find a number of excellent dining options, from German at Gisela's and Greek at Zorba's to country French at Z'Bistro and regional American at Panache. And if you've ever pondered what lion or alligator tastes like, try Adam's Rib (it has great steaks and seafood too). Be sure to browse the following listings for more enticing options.

Afghani

Kabul
$$ • 1355 W. 86th St. • 257-1213

Check out the deliciously different Afghani fare (don't miss the aush soup) at this comfortable, casual north-side restaurant that opened in new quarters just across the parking lot from its former location in early 1996. Reminiscent of both Middle Eastern and Indian fare, Afghani food includes such seasonings as dill and yogurt. You'll find a variety of dishes, including lamb, beef and vegetarian options.

American

Adam's Rib
$$$ • 40 S. Main St., Zionsville • 873-3301
While this place may be known for its exotic appetizers (roasted lion and black bear, deep-fried alligator, African antelope), you'll also find excellent steaks, seafood and prime rib served in a casual atmosphere.

Bobby Joe's Beef and Brew
$$ • 4425 Southport Crossings Way • 882-BEEF
While you might expect traditional bar fare from this south-side establishment, be ready to be surprised. The restaurant, full of sports reporting memorabilia from namesake Bob Collins' long career, offers excellent French onion soup, an herbed salmon filet and a delicious steak with brandy sauce. Note that there is no family dining, meaning no kids are allowed.

Bombay Bicycle Club
$$ • 9111 N. Michigan Rd. • 872-3446
Those who work at the nearby Pyramids office complex have made the BBC a popular spot for after-work drinks and dinner. The casual restaurant, which attracts plenty of northwestsiders on the weekends, features a varied menu with chicken, pasta, fresh seafood, steaks and daily specials.

Brickyard Restaurant
$$ • 4400 W. 16th St. • 241-2500
A trip to the Indianapolis Motor Speedway wouldn't be complete without stopping in at the Brickyard Restaurant. You're likely to see some famous faces in May; look for car owners and drivers such as A.J. Foyt. But be sure to try the specialty prime rib at this casual eatery anytime.

California Cafe
$$$ • Circle Centre, 49 W. Maryland St. • 488-8686
Make reservations at this terrific Circle Centre restaurant, and enjoy a wide range of seasonal specialties, excellent service and a good variety of premium California wines. The salads are excellent. Bread is served with olive oil for dipping, and we love the Thai curried duck with fusilli.

Cork and Cuisine
$$$ • 3316 E. 86th St. • 846-7300
Chef Ray Pichetti, formerly of the Provincial Kitchen, now creates his seasonally changing specialties at the Cork and Cuisine. (The Provincial Kitchen has, to our regret, closed.) You'll find menu icons denoting heart-healthy choices, large portions and vegetarian dishes, a carry over from the PK. The quality and creativity also remain; Chef Pichetti has a knack for combining flavors, such as the pancetta bacon, fresh basil and sweet onions in the bucatini amatriciana. Try the steak-and-potato soup, Nonna's bistecca or the delicious Marco Polo (sauteed scallops and tiger shrimp with pasta).

Dalts
$$ • 8702 Keystone Crossing • 846-7226
You may have to wait for a table at this popular Keystone at the Crossing eatery, especially at lunchtime. But once seated, you'll enjoy the varied menu. The seasoned fries are always a hit, and we especially like the chicken salad quesadilla. A favorite among Fashion Mall shoppers and office workers, Dalts is also a good place to take the kids (they'll love the milk shakes).

Del Frisco's
$$$ • 3 E. Market St. • 687-8888
Overlooking Monument Circle, this second-floor restaurant occupies a prime location. Don't miss its prime cuts, but the pasta dishes rate highly too. Reservations are a must, even at lunch, and remember it has a formal atmosphere: nice linens on well-set tables amid a power-broker ambiance. Be sure to notice Monument Tower's Art Deco flourishes.

Graffiti's

$$ • 50 S. Capitol Ave. • 231-3970

So named for the paper-topped tables with crayons for doodling, this restaurant's food is hardly trivial. The Westin Hotel's second-floor eatery features American cuisine in an upscale yet casual atmosphere; you'll see diners dressed in everything from jeans to suits. Downtown power-lunchers like the convenient and tasty buffet.

Dick Clark's American Bandstand Grill

$$ • 3550 E. 86th St. • 848-2002

A chain, yes, but it's so popular we couldn't overlook it. Diners enjoy great burgers, ribs, fajitas and pasta amid the high-energy American Bandstand-themed decor. You can also purchase souvenir T-shirts, sweatshirts, jackets, CDs and other Bandstand merchandise.

The Diner

$ • 9762 W. Washington St. • 839-9464

If you're looking for a slice of Americana, look no further. This '50s-era dining-car-style restaurant serves up a great breakfast as well as short order specialties such as burgers, fries and tenderloins. Such aluminium-clad landmarks once dotted U.S. 40 (a.k.a. the old National Road or, near the city, Washington Street), and The Diner is a reminder of a time when the route saw lots of cross-country traffic. The very reasonable prices (the $7 rib-eye dinner ranks as the most expensive) will remind you of an earlier era.

Dodd's Town House

$$$ • 5694 N. Meridian St. • 257-1872

This N. Meridian Street landmark, wedged in among the beautiful homes in this historic neighborhood, has operated here under different names for 150 years. Originally the Seven-Mile Inn (because, you guessed it, the place is 7 miles from the Circle), Dodd's specializes in real American cooking. You just can't

go wrong with their steaks and fried chicken. And don't miss dessert. Have a cup of coffee and enjoy a slice of blackberry or chocolate cream pie.

Durbin's at the Marriott

$$ • 7202 E. 71st St. • 352-1231

Though this hotel restaurant is a fine choice in its own right, a pleasant if typical hotel dining room with nicely set tables and tasteful decor, what we find special are the recipes, such as chicken velvet soup from what used to be the old downtown L.S. Ayres restaurant.

Hollyhock Hill

$$$ • 8110 N. College Ave. • 251-2294

Like Dodd's and the Iron Skillet, the popular Hollyhock Hill offers family-style dining and plates full of fried chicken. Be sure to try the house salad dressing. Tucked into a residential area between Broad Ripple and Nora, this comfortable restaurant boasts a homey ambiance.

Houlihan's

$$ • 111 W. Maryland St. • 266-8711

A mall restaurant without the mall look, Houlihan's fine food, including burgers, steaks, chicken and pasta, also belies its location. But be prepared for less than speedy service. Quick, can you find the old Chesterfield Kings advertisement among the memorabilia that fills the walls?

Illusions

$$$ • 969 Keystone Way • 575-8312

Magic is the theme at this Carmel restaurant where magicians perform tableside at dinner (and also in the lounge). The food's great too, and the menu offers a wide enough variety that just about everyone can find a favorite amid the offerings of fresh fish, chicken, steaks and duck. School-age kids enjoy Illusions as a special-occasion treat; adults like to catch the magic acts in the bar.

INSIDERS' TIP

Those who like to dine alfresco need only walk through the popular Broad Ripple neighborhood, where they'll find nearly a dozen restaurants that offer sidewalk cafe-style dining.

Iron Skillet
$$$ • 2489 W. 30th St. • 923-6353

Comfort food, such as well-seasoned fried chicken, pan-fried walleyed pike, New York strip and all the sides, fills the menu at this restaurant set between two golf courses and across from the city's Soapbox Derby Hill. A courteous staff, which also happens to know many of the patrons, serves it all family style.

Johnson County Line
$$ • 1265 N. Madison Ave., Greenwood • 887-0404

Straightforward American fare is on the menu at this south-side restaurant. You'll find chops, steaks and such seafood as rainbow trout and yellowfin tuna served amid a rough-hewn wood decor. 'Nothing fancy, just good food and friendly service.

Keystone Cooker
$$ • 8601 Keystone Crossing • 574-0790

Another popular Keystone at the Crossing lunch spot, the Cooker is great for dinner too. You'll find tasty American specialties such as meatloaf, pot roast and plenty of good sandwiches and fries. But don't fill up on the delicious biscuits and butter your server will bring out (although we can't resist asking for a second basket).

Kopper Kettle
$$$ • 315 W. Main St., Morristown • 763-6767

Henry Ford, Herbert Hoover, Charles Lindbergh and Jane Pauley have all signed the guestbook at this venerable and well-regarded Shelby County restaurant. The historic home is filled with antiques, statuary and art objects from all over the world. But famous and not-so-famous visitors come for the absolutely delicious fried chicken and traditional accompaniments served family style. Don't skip the homemade banana cream pie.

Malibu Grill
$$ • 4503 E. 82nd St. • 845-4334

Voted by readers of *Indianapolis Monthly* magazine as a restaurant worth its sometimes considerable wait for a table, the Malibu Grill excels at offering something for everybody, from pizza and pasta to steak and burgers.

Tasty bread with marinara for dipping is on the table right away. It's casual, trendy and comfortable.

Marble's Southern Cookery
$$ • 2310 Lafayette Rd. • 687-0631

Marble's and mom have good food in common — that is, if you come from the South. This buffet's ribs, chops, catfish and side dishes all have that distinctive taste reminiscent of areas south of the Mason-Dixon Line. A tidy place (though on a past-its-prime thoroughfare), Marble's does a brisk business with an ever-changing menu. Don't miss the bread pudding.

Moe & Johnny's
$$ • 5280 N. College Ave. • 255-5220

Hearty home cooking is on the menu at the South Broad Ripple family establishment. The "big dinners" (turkey, meatloaf and the like) come with three sides and will make you think you're at Grandma's for Sunday supper. Enjoy the retro '40s ambiance; wall murals depict a street scene of days gone by.

Palomino
$$$ • 49 W. Maryland St. • 974-0400

This stylish street-level restaurant near Circle Centre offers excellent fare, a high-energy atmosphere and top-notch service. The rotisserie oven turns out great chicken, but we also love the salmon with pasta. If you're in more of a traditionalist mood, you can always choose pizza or prime rib.

Penn St. Bar and Grill
$$$ • 135 N. Pennsylvania St. • 231-6050

If it's dessert you want, it's dessert you'll get. Renowned for its death-by-chocolate after-meal treats, this downtown lunch-only restaurant also features a fine selection of pasta dishes. The chef keeps the rotating menu lively with an array of health-conscious chicken and beef entrees. But don't be afraid to loosen the belt and indulge in dessert and enjoy the stylish decor.

Plump's Last Shot
$$ • 6416 Cornell Ave. • 257-5867

Bobby Plump is an Indiana basketball legend. He sunk the basket that won the state

Malibu Grill was once voted by readers of a local magazine as an eatery worth its wait for a table.

championship in 1954 for Milan High School, the smallest school ever to win state. His son, Jonathan, runs this new Broad Ripple restaurant that, in addition to loads of basketball memorabilia, offers real Hoosier specialties such as venison and bluegill.

Rick's Cafe Americain
$$$ • 39 W. Jackson Pl. • 634-6666
An extensive menu with lots of appetizers, salads, sandwiches and entrees, such as pasta, chicken, seafood and steaks, plus live jazz and a convenient and comfortable Union Station location make Rick's a fine choice for a casual yet cozy evening.

Rick's Cafe Boatyard
$$$ • 4050 Dandy Tr. • 290-9300
This location on the water at Eagle Creek reservoir offers a nice view (especially from the outdoor deck), live music and a varied menu of fresh fish, steaks, chicken and pasta. It's become quite popular; the wait for a table can be long. If it proves too long, do what we do: Find a seat in the bar, enjoy the music and order from there.

Shaffer's
$$$ • 6125 Hillside Ave. • 253-1404
Shaffer's is the city's only fondue restaurant — that's right, fondue. Though perhaps reminiscent of early '70s dinner parties, Shaffer's take on this retro classic proves excellent — and a lot of fun. We're especially fond of the dessert fondues and the wine list.

Teller's Cage
$$$ • 1 Indiana Sq. • 266-5211
The food's great at the Teller's Cage (we especially enjoy the steaks, veal and lamb), but most people go to this restaurant to enjoy the view as well. The restaurant, on the 35th floor of the NBD bank tower, offers a great view of the city skyline, which is especially nice at night.

Steakhouses

Broad Ripple Steak House
$$$ • 842 Westfield Blvd. • 253-8101
Featuring a Southwestern flair to the cuisine, the Broad Ripple Steak House features hand-cut steaks and a number of excellent pasta and seafood dishes, including an entree called kick-ass swordfish. You can also enjoy outdoor dining at this popular corner establishment. Indoors, you'll find a Southwestern-inspired decor as well.

Bynum's Steakhouse
$$ • 3850 S. Meridian St. • 784-9880
A south-side landmark, Bynum's serves up thick, fresh-cut steaks, prime rib and lobster tail to very loyal customers in a nice-but-not-fancy setting. Situated in a residential area, Bynum's boasts a sort of antique-themed decor: Old signs and tools decorate the walls. Charming glass lamps adorn each table.

George's Place
$$$ • 2727 E. 86th St. • 255-7064
Want an especially thick steak tonight? No problem at George's, where steaks are cut at your table to your exact specifications. Diners can also enjoy a variety of seafood selections and sample the daily special. You'll see lots of suit-and-tie types, especially at lunch; George's proves popular with Keystone at the Crossing power brokers.

Mountain Jack's

$$$ • 5910 E. 82nd St. • 842-5225
3650 W. 86th St. • 872-4500

Both locations of this popular steakhouse serve excellent prime rib, seafood and, of course, top-notch steaks in a casual atmosphere. We love the filet; the vegetable soup is tasty too. Servers build your salad at the table to your specifications.

Ruth's Chris Steak House

$$$$ • 9445 Threel Rd., (96th and Keystone) • 844-1155

Yes, it's a chain, but what a chain it is. This is the place for beef, and the steaks (and everything else, including the lamb) are incredibly tender and well-cooked. Service is professional and attentive, and the English lodge-style decor is handsome and classic. But cheap it's not. Everything is a la carte, and the selections do add up. This is definitely either special occasion or expense account dining. Still, it's worth it. Try out the new Ruth's Chris location downtown.

St. Elmo Steak House

$$$$ • 127 S. Illinois St. • 635-0636

Known for its mammoth, done-just-right steaks, extra spicy shrimp cocktail and impeccable black-tie service, St. Elmo maintains nearly a century of fine dining. Next to the posh Canterbury Hotel, the downtown restaurant plays host to the city's business elite and celebrities passing through. Even Metallica stopped in. You don't have to be a rock star to afford St. Elmo but, like Ruth's Chris, this isn't an everyday kind of place. If someone offers to take you, go.

Asian

Bangkok

$$ • 7269 N. Keystone Ave. • 255-7799

You'll find excellent Thai fare at this unassuming strip mall restaurant. Bangkok wins plenty of local awards, and if you want to sample a variety of the tasty, sometimes spicy, dishes, try the lunch buffet. Don't miss the soup and the Thai toast.

Daruma

$$ • 3508 W. 86th St. • 875-9727

This Japanese restaurant offers delicious and unusual specialties always beautifully presented. Older kids might enjoy the novelty of being seated Japanese style (see our Kidstuff chapter) and being served by the attentive, kimono-clad wait staff. Daruma offers excellent sushi, sukiyaki, tempura and steak.

Forbidden City

$$ • 2605 E. 65th St. • 257-7388
3837 N. High School Rd. • 298-3588
3938 E. 82nd St. • 845-8989
3517 W. 86th St. • 872-2888

If hot and sour soup is your barometer of fine Chinese food, then Forbidden City deserves your attention. The restaurant, with north- and west-side locations, plus a superb north-side buffet and a northwest-side express, also does a fine job with other offerings from an extensive menu that offers Hunan, Szechuan and Mandarin cuisine. We especially like the green pepper beef and cashew chicken. Call ahead for dinner reservations. You can get quick service on carryout. Or stop in at lunchtime and enjoy an entree, soup and egg roll for a very reasonable price.

Kang's Express

$$ • 2989 W. 71st St. • 297-3451

The specialty at this little northwest-side establishment is the excellent Korean fare. Be sure to try the spicy kimchi (fermented vegetables) and the chop chae bab (a sweet stir fry with rice noodles). Prices are low, authenticity and quality are high.

Oriental Health Cuisine

$ • 86th St. and Allisonville Rd. • 578-3066

Delicious and healthfully prepared, the food at this Castleton restaurant makes use of extra-fresh veggies, seafood and pasta. The vegetarian, vegan and macrobiotic dishes earn this establishment an entry in our vegetarian category too.

Sakura

$$ • 7201 N. Keystone Ave. • 259-4171

This north-side sushi bar, quite popular among the local Japanese community, serves excellent seafood beautifully presented. If sushi isn't your favorite, try the tempura; it's served in lovely lacquer boxes. But do give the sushi a try. We love the softshell crab, the futomaki and the mackerel. If time is a concern, keep in mind that a lunch hour can easily stretch into an hour and a half (or even two if you really get into the convivial atmosphere that sharing sushi inspires).

Sansui
$$ • 1329 S. Range Line Rd. • 848-9050

Another good option for sushi, Sansui is large and spacious. A helpful staff will gladly explain the menu offerings and offer guidance for those unsure about what sort of sushi to try. Combination platters are a good option. Sansui also offers tasty tempura and steaks.

Sizzling Wok/Thien Huong
$$ • 7280 N. Michigan Rd. • 298-9001

Though this northwest-side eatery offers Chinese and Vietnamese food. Try the excellent Vietnamese fare such as sauteed beef rolls, Vietnamese pancakes and fish in clay pot. The bare bones interior is nothing fancy, but with the fresh vegetables, sophisticated flavors and cooked-just-right seafood, you won't miss a fancy place setting.

Yen Ching
$$ • 1300 E. 86th St. • 844-1810
8512 E. Washington St. • 899-3270

A local favorite, Yen Ching specializes in Mandarin and Szechuan cuisine. Try the house specials: moo shu pork, sizzling beef and Peking duck. Pricier at dinner, the lunch selections offer good value and an easy-on-the-wallet way to check out some of Yen Ching's specialties.

Bakeries

Those with a sweet tooth — or a taste for toast — will appreciate the baked goods from these local ovens.

Boyden's Southside Bakery
$ • 3953 S. Meridian St. • 784-2992

Offering quick service on decorated cakes, Boyden's opens at 4 AM every day with plenty of doughnuts, danish and coffee cakes for early risers.

Bread of Life Bakery
$ • 2274 W. 86th St. • 872-5251

Delicious bread that makes wonderful toast is the specialty here. We especially like the honey millet variety. Atlas Supermarket also stocks the hearty loaves.

Charlotte's Bakery
$ • 2142 N. Mitthoeffer Rd. • 897-9671

Eastsiders stop in at Charlotte's for fresh doughnuts, pies, cakes and cookies.

Crawford's Bakery and Deli
$ • 1609 N. Capitol Ave. • 924-2494

This is a popular stop for workers on their way downtown and for employees of Methodist Hospital right across the street. Regulars love the doughnuts, Danish and long Johns. And the deli serves up a great quick lunch.

Great Harvest Bread Co.
$ • 1069 Broad Ripple Ave. • 251-2222
1426 W. 86th St. • 872-2222
8923 S. Meridan St. • 885-9999
11856 Allisonville Rd., Fishers • 849-5555

The line is out the door on Saturday morning, but the fresh baked loaves are worth the wait. We're particularly fond of the sprouted wheat and cinnamon walnut. Try a slice; they give free samples.

Krispy Kreme
$ • 5060 W. 38th St. • 299-3587
6706 E. 82nd St. • 578-3081
1080 E. 86th St. • 581-0095

This new chain has wooed plenty of local doughnut lovers since it opened, and we must admit we're converts. Don't miss the warm-from-the-oven glazed doughnuts and the apple cinnamon variety.

Long's Bakery
$ • 2300 W. 16th St. • 632-3741
39 Jackson Pl. (Union Station) • 635-4252
2301 E. Southport Rd. • 783-1442

There's nothing like a Long's doughnut and a hot cup of coffee to get you going on a cold morning.

Roselyn Bakeries
$ • General Office, 2425 E. 30th St.
• 925-8901

These corner bakeries — nearly 40 of them scattered across the city — offer great sweets. We can't get enough of the delicious powdered sugar-covered cookies called Mexican wedding cakes and the seasonally decorated goodies.

Taylor's Bakery
$ • 6216 Allisonville Rd. • 251-9575

Three generations of this family have been serving up sweet treats — and three generations have been enjoying them. Try the coffee cakes and danish.

Cafeterias

Ed & Marge's Cafe
$ • 320 N. Meridian St. • 635-0132

Don't miss the roast beef Manhattan or the beef and noodles at this busy downtown lunch place. And be sure to add on the peach cobbler. But if you linger too long over dessert, Marge might shoo you out. There's always a line of customers, and someone's always looking for a table.

Gray Bros.
$ • 555 S. Indiana Ave., Mooresville • 831-3345

This Mooresville cafeteria is plenty popular among Indianapolis residents who don't mind the drive if the food is good. And at Gray Bros., it is. Nothing fancy, just hearty cafeteria fare served up at reasonable prices.

Jonathan Byrd's
$ • 100 Byrd Way, Greenwood • 881-8888

This giant among cafeterias can serve 400 diners (with banquet facilities for hundreds more). Locals of all sorts flock to this Greenwood establishment for traditional cafeteria fare: a little bit of everything.

Laughner's
$ • General Office, 4004 U.S. Hwy. 31 S.
• 783-2907
20 N. Franklin Rd. • 356-3388
4030 U.S. 31 S. • 787-3745
6880 E. 82nd St. • 845-9011
1616 E. 86th St. • 846-1112

A local family began this statewide cafeteria chain around 1900. And with Hoosiers' fondness for roast beef, baked fish, fried chicken, liver and onions, macaroni and cheese, green beans and fruit pies, the chain will likely be around a lot longer.

MCL
$ • Corporate Office, 2730 E. 62nd St.
• 257-5425
6010 E. 10th St. • 356-1587
2121 E. 62nd St. • 253-1908
116th and Keystone • 844-9217
5520 Castleton Corner Ln. • 845-5717
1251 U.S. 31 N. • 881-7525
3919 Lafayette Rd. • 293-1121
8135 Pendleton Pike • 898-5455
6002 Crawfordsville Rd. • 241-9497
10202 E. Washington St. • 897-6956

An offshoot of the original Laughner clan started up another cafeteria chain, and the two restaurants serve a similar menu. Though cafeteria devotees could probably spot the subtle differences, we think MCL and Laughner's are both very good at what they do.

Cajun

Jazz Cooker
$$ • 925 E. Westfield Blvd. • 253-2883

This popular Broad Ripple restaurant serves up delicious Cajun specialties in an old Victorian-style house, complete with a wrought-iron fence around the garden dining area. Inside you'll find nicely set tables, a strolling saxophonist and great jambalaya, crawfish etouffe and delicious black bean soup.

INSIDERS' TIP

Food court fans should check out downtown's Circle Centre. You're sure to find enough fast food options to please the whole family.

Henry Grattan is a great place to enjoy a just-poured Harp and conversation.

Photo: Jeff Hauersperger

Continental

Glass Chimney
$$$$ • 12901 Old Meridian St. • 844-0921

Long a favorite for special occasions and expense account dinners, the Glass Chimney boasts traditional continental dining in an elegant atmosphere. Discriminating diners will also find an extensive wine list and a selection of vintage ports. For more casual dining, wine and cocktails, try the Deeter's Nasch and Nip next door. (At both you'll find excellent selections from Chef Dieter Puska.)

Eagle's Nest
$$$$ • Hyatt Regency, 1 S. Capitol Ave. • 632-1234

One of the city's most popular choices for a romantic dinner, the Eagle's Nest, atop the Hyatt Regency downtown, offers beautiful views of the city, and the rooftop room actually rotates. If you can stop staring into each other's eyes, try the prime rib, filet mignon or the salmon. If you're keeping an eye on costs, note that extras such as salads and sides are indeed extra.

The Marker
$$$ • Adam's Mark Hotel, 2544 Executive Dr. • 381-6146

Service is wonderful at The Marker; relax and let them take care of everything. Don't go looking for innovative cuisine. Rather, The Marker offers classic choices such as salmon, veal, chicken and beef deliciously prepared. And everything on the dessert tray looks good too. Choose something luscious and enjoy the country lodge ambiance.

Midtown Grill
$$$ • 815 E. Westfield Blvd. • 253-1141

Minimalist decor, attentive service and excellent food characterize the trendy Midtown Grill. The high energy level creates a vibrant atmosphere. Try the wild mushroom ravioli for a delicious vegetarian selection. We can also recommend the tropical grilled chicken salad and the goat cheese in grape leaves.

The Restaurant at the Canterbury Hotel
$$$$ • 123 S. Illinois St. • 634-3000

This vintage building received a facelift during Circle Centre construction. Now as beautiful outside as in, it boasts a distinctive ambiance: plush upholstery, cushy carpeting and well-set tables. This well-regarded restaurant features Continental and American cuisine; it's known for the Dover sole meuniere, rack of lamb and dessert souffles (which must be ordered in advance). Afternoon tea is served Monday through Saturday from 4 PM to 5:30 PM; be sure to make reservations.

Delis

Shapiro's Delicatessen
**$ • no credit cards • 808 S. Meridian St.
• 631-4041
2730 W. 86th St. • 872-7255**

A local landmark since 1905, Shapiro's sets the standard around here for deli fare. And "around here" means the Midwest when it comes to Shapiro's — it's that good. Patrons line up daily for fresh sliced roast beef, chicken soup with matzo balls and thick, creamy cheesecake. Or you can order it all to go. You just can't beat these Kosher specialties. You can stack up the corned beef sandwich against New York's Carnegie Deli any day.

Schlotzsky's Deli
**$ • 9605 E. Washington St. • 899-3737
3958 E. 82nd St. • 849-6636**

These casual delis are, admittedly, a chain (out of Austin, Texas), but they bake their own terrific sourdough bread with which they make tasty deli sandwiches as well as pizzas. We love the smoked turkey sandwich and the chicken and pesto pizza. The soup of the day is a good bet too.

Deli Jack's
$$ • 9413 N. Meridian St. • 843-1609

You'll find great sandwiches at this Carmel eatery, creations such as the classic Italian piled high on bread from the Great Harvest Bread Co. We like the veggie sandwich with its homemade spinach dip. You can also get tasty Chicago-style hot dogs and pizza too.

Drive-ins

Bill's Fabulous '50s
**$, no credit cards • 6310 Rockville Rd.
• 244-1950**

This kitschy establishment features roller skating carhops who balance trays loaded with frosty mugs of root beer, onion rings, Coney dogs and tenderloins. Turn on your headlights for service. While you're waiting, the kids can pop a quarter in the outdoor jukebox that's stocked with such titles as "Sh-Boom, Sh-Boom" and "Monster Mash." Enjoy the retro experience, and check out the classic cars.

Dog 'N Suds
$ • no credit cards • 5914 Crawfordsville Rd. • 241-4746

You'll get surprisingly quick service at this shiny new drive-in around the corner from the Indianapolis Motor Speedway, and you'll find delicious root beer, crispy fries and really tender tenderloins. The city's newest drive-in, located in the parking lot of a busy strip mall, is quite popular, and parking places fill up fast on weekend evenings.

Edward's Drive-In
**$, no credit cards • 2126 Sherman Dr.
• 786-1638**

This longtime southeast-side establishment serves up excellent jumbo tenderloins and tasty onion rings; the Coneys are pretty good too. Curbside service is quick, but you can also eat indoors.

Mug 'N Bun
**$, no credit cards • 5211 W. 10th St.
• 244-5669**

This is certainly a popular spot on weekend evenings. You won't find roller skating carhops, just good food and good service. We love the thick onion rings, rich and creamy root beer, Coneys and tenderloins — all the traditional drive-in fare. There's also a (heated) outdoor seating area.

Ethiopian

Queen of Sheba
Ethiopian Restaurant
$$ • 936 Indiana Ave. • 638-8426

Take along some friends and enjoy sharing food around the messob, a woven lidded table upon which a platter of food is placed. All the dishes are presented atop a thin crepe-like bread called injera. Diners tear off hunks of bread and scoop up bites of such Ethiopian specialties as cega (tender beef in a red pepper sauce), yemisir alecha (yellow split peas) or tekil gomen (cabbage and carrots). The food is unusual and downright delicious.

French

Chanteclair
$$$$ • 2501 S. High School Rd. • 243-1040

This is a great place to celebrate any special occasion; it's especially nice for a romantic anniversary dinner. You'll enjoy the elegant atmosphere and fine French cuisine; we recommend the sauteed shrimp and scallops. A strolling violinist adds to the romantic ambiance. Jackets are required for men.

Chez Jean Restaurant Francais
$$$$ • 9027 S. Ind. 67, Camby • 831-0870

Barbara and Jean Milesi operated this charming restaurant for more than 30 years; their son now runs this French favorite. Longtime patrons wax practically poetic over the bouillabaisse and crepes Suzette. Make reservations for dinner, and also reserve a room at the adjacent inn for a close-to-home romantic getaway.

Renee's
$$ • 839 E. Westfield Blvd. • 251-4142

This cozy country French restaurant consistently wins local awards for best Broad Ripple restaurant, best dessert and best carryout. It's deserving of such kudos. We love the chicken dijonnaise, ragout niçoise, the apple dumpling and banana cream pie. It's also tough to top Renee's in the casually romantic category. The place is small and fills up fast; though you can probably walk in and get a table at lunch on a Tuesday, make reservations for a weekend dinner.

Z'Bistro
$$$ • 160 S. Main St., Zionsville • 873-1888

Another delightful country French restaurant, Z'Bistro is definitely upscale. The food is excellent, as is the wine list, and the wait staff is knowledgeable about both. Relax and enjoy the atmosphere with its fresh flowers, well-set tables and antique bar. Linger over a bottle of wine, then take a stroll through charming Zionsville.

German

Cafe Europa
$$ • 4709 N. Shadeland Ave. • 547-4474

This tiny restaurant boasts excellent fare; you'll find a variety of schnitzels (try the zesty pfefferrahmschnitzel), hearty fried potatoes, sweet red cabbage, homemade spaetzel. Don't pass up the delicious apple strudel for dessert. Enjoy accordion music on weekend evenings.

Gisela's Kaffeekranzchen
$$$ • 112 S. Main St., Zionsville • 873-5523

This Zionsville establishment specializes in bratwurst, knockwurst, pork chops and, of course, the delicious desserts, including Black Forest cherry torte that Gisela's is known for. The charming upstairs restaurant, with its cozy dark wood ambiance, will make you believe you really are in a cozy Black Forest cafe. Regulars recommend the $15.95 Saturday night buffet.

Heidelberg Cafe
$$ • 7625 Pendleton Pike • 547-1230

This east-side eatery also offers a gift shop in addition to such traditional German favorites as schnitzels, wursts and chops. You'll also find excellent breads, cakes and pastries. The food's good, and you'll enjoy browsing among the plentiful German-themed knick knacks.

Haus Anna
$$ • 67 N. Madison Ave. • 887-0439

Named for the owner's mother, this little Greenwood restaurant really is in a house, though from the outside it's rather nondescript. Inside, you'll find lots of tables, walls covered in Bavarian posters, knick knacks and a cuckoo clock marking the time. Try

---

INSIDERS' TIP

Stonycreek Farm in Hamilton County provides a great chance to get away from the fast pace of weekday life. Kids can pet the animals or pick a pumpkin in the fall.

one of the specialties from owner Edelgard Stutler's native Bavaria. We can heartily endorse the sauerbraten and spaetzel, the jaegerschnitzel and most definitely the Black Forest cherry torte.

Rathskeller
$$ • 401 E. Michigan St. • 636-0396

In the Athenaeum's basement (formerly known as Das Deutsch Haus), the Rathskeller feels like a pub in the Black Forest. Dark wood, leaded glass and a fireplace complete with Faustian relief set the tone. The smell of sauerkraut and strudel complete the experience. Ask *der frau* for a tall stein and get ready to enjoy.

Greek and Middle Eastern

Acropolis
$$ • 1625 E. Southport Rd. • 787-8883

A fun place to take the kids (see our Kidstuff chapter), the Acropolis offers belly dancing on weekend evenings. The Greek specialties are excellent; for a real feast, try the sampler plate. We can also recommend the lamb. And if kids don't care for Greek fare, they'll find plenty of alternatives such as breaded shrimp and french fries.

Aesop's Table
$$ • 600 N. Massachusetts Ave. • 631-0055

It's fun to browse through the art galleries on Mass Ave. (see our Arts chapter), then stop in for lunch or dinner at this charming Mediterranean-style cafe. It's a bit subdued compared to other Greek places. No one belly dances or shouts "*Opa!*" over flaming plates of saganaki, but we like it. It's casual, yet a bit sophisticated.

Greek Islands
$$ • 906 S. Meridian St. • 636-0700

The low ceiling here is scorched from where jovial servers ignite dishes of flaming cheese with shouts of "*Opa!*" This place is small, crowded and boisterous, but Greek Islands is the place for authentic Mediterranean fare done well and offered with good will. They serve up a great Greek salad.

Hellas Cafe
$$ • 8501 Westfield Blvd. • 257-6211

The spanikopita at this little Greek place in Nora just may be the best in town. You can also count on the leg of lamb and the souvlaki. Hellas also serves some American favorites, but we never pass up the great Greek specialties.

Mediterrano Cafe
$$ • 5941 E. 86th St. • 595-0399

Be sure to try the babaganooj at this pleasant lace-curtained cafe. It's delicious, as are the lamb curry and baklava. The attentive service makes it all even better at this cafe tucked into a Castleton strip mall.

Parthenon
$$ • 6319 N. Guilford Ave. • 251-3139

The longtime Broad Ripple favorite ranks as a lot of folks' favorite restaurant. You'll see all sorts here: young parents with babies (the little ones watch transfixed as the costumes of the weekend belly dancers shimmer and jingle), artist types and office workers enjoying an outdoor lunch (in nice weather, of course). Though the gyros are especially good, we can make a meal of a maza plate and a Greek salad.

Zorba's
$$$ • 30 N. Main St., Zionsville • 733-0633

We love the appetizer maza plate at this new Zionsville restaurant. It's a simple little place, with little in the way of decor, but the food, including the babaganooj on the maza plate, is excellent. For real variety, follow your appetizer with a combo platter. And take home some baklava to enjoy later.

Indian

India Garden
$$ • 830 Broad Ripple Ave. • 253-6060

This tiny Broad Ripple restaurant specializes in authentic northern Indian cuisine. To sample a variety, try the excellent lunch buffet. Don't miss the puffy bread, baked just minutes before it appears. Tasteful decor with an Indian flair and well-set tables contribute to the comfortable ambiance.

Star of India
$$ • 1043 Broad Ripple Ave. • 465-1100
5929 E. 82nd St. • 578-4400

The 82nd Street location opened in the summer of 1995, an expansion that attests to the restaurant's popularity. The bright red chicken wins rave reviews. Both locations offer delicious authentic Indian fare.

Taj of India
$$$ • 5929 E. 82nd St. • 578-4400

A wide-ranging menu offers diners tons of options at this Castleton restaurant. We love the lamb specialties, but you'll find plenty of vegetarian options as well. The combination specials are a great way to sample and to have leftovers to take home.

Italian

Ambrosia
$$$ • 915 Westfield Blvd. • 255-3096

Hidden among a row of Broad Ripple restaurants, Ambrosia is as its name implies. The place has a studio look, but it retains an intimacy unavailable at many restaurants. And you'll fall for the food. Try the pesto or the seafood fettuccine Alfredo; you won't be sorry.

Amici's
$$ • 601 E. New York St. • 634-0440

Off the beaten path, this old house nonetheless plays host to one of the city's finest Italian restaurants. Open a bottle of red wine, sample the sauces and pretend you're in a place only the locals who speak Italian know. They have a good jukebox too. On the menu you'll find traditional Italian specialties; we've never been disappointed in any pasta dish.

Bacco
$$$ • 1260 W. 85th St. • 582-1362

This is an excellent little Italian place that belies its strip mall location. Photographic prints and artwork line the textured terra-cotta walls. The menu highlights seafood; be sure to try one of the seafood/pasta specialties. We like the spaghetti alla pescatora: spaghetti tossed with shrimp and clams and ringed with mussels.

Benvenuti
$$$$ • 1 N. Pennsylvania St. • 633-4915

This elegant 14th-floor restaurant provides one of the city's best fine dining experiences. Sophisticated without being stuffy, Benvenuti provides stylish, comfortable surroundings, excellent service and wonderful Northern Italian cuisine, with such excellent appetizers as homemade ravioli of lobster and a delicious roasted red bell pepper soup. Jackets are required for men.

Bravo
$$ • 8651 Castle Creek Pkwy. • 577-2211

This spirited restaurant proves loud and boisterous; the high, open ceiling contributes to the noise, but we like the high energy level. Reminiscent of a Roman cafe, Bravo offers terrific pasta dishes (some served in huge bowls). Diners will also find wood-fired pizzas and steaks. Service is friendly and efficient, and the atmosphere is conducive to lingering and enjoying the ambiance.

Iaria's
$$ • 317 S. College Ave. • 638-7706

One of the city's favorite Italian joints, this place is small, casual and fun. You'll see movers and shakers discussing business over their lasagne and parents with kids trying to get Junior to finish his spaghetti and meatballs. After dinner you can wander next door to the Action Bowl (see our Parks and Recreation chapter) for a little duck-pin bowling.

Milano Inn
$$$ • 231 S. College Ave. • 264-3585

Celebrity photographs of famous faces and local heroes line the entryway walls at Milano Inn, and the place is almost always packed. Make a reservation, and come with friends to really enjoy the place. Though not especially fancy, the food is plenty good. Try the La Dolce Vita the sweet life (veal and chicken stuffed with proscuitto and mozzarella) or the fresh tomato pizza. For excellent take-out, stop in at one of the half dozen Milano's Pasta to Go locations around town.

The Old Spaghetti Factory
$$ • 210 S. Meridian St. • 635-6325

We broke our rule about chain restaurants

to include The Old Spaghetti Factory because it's a great place to take the family. You get your money's worth and then some. Meals come with salad, bread (we like to slather on the garlic butter), entree, coffee and spumoni ice cream for dessert. Choices are limited primarily to pasta, after all, spaghetti is in its name, but there's plenty of variety within those parameters. We especially like the spaghetti topped with mizithra cheese and meat sauce; the tortellini and lasagna are good too. And the decor, with its monstrous chandeliers, fringed lamps and trolley car dining, is always a hit with the kids.

Papa Joe's
$$ • 2441 Lafayette Rd. • 925-3593

This place used to be known as Joe's Hole in the Wall, and it remains a little neighborhood joint. Nothing fancy, just good Italian classics in comfortable surroundings. Try the lasagna; we've heard customers send their compliments to the chef after indulging in this popular dish. We also like the sauce, and you can even buy it by the quart to take home.

Tuscany
$$$ • 838 Broad Ripple Ave. • 253-7475

At Tuscany part of the appeal is the streetside Broad Ripple location. The Northern Italian specialties, steaks and seafood prove consistently good, and the atmosphere is tough to beat — especially if you get a table near the sidewalk. Order a nice bottle of wine, and dig in to a plate of pasta.

Vito Provolone's
$$ • 8031 S. Meridian St. • 888-1112

This little south-side place offers a nice variety of standard Italian dishes in a cozy setting. There's not much room to wait for a table, but once you're seated, you'll enjoy the food. Try the mix-and-match "pastabilities," and pair up some fettuccine with Vito's vodka sauce. Or maybe some linguine with pesto.

Java Joints

Though we can't quite claim the same passion for coffee you'll find in San Francisco or Seattle, Indianapolis boasts plenty of places to enjoy a hot cup of joe. Take along

a book or a friend, and soak up some atmosphere.

The Abbey
$ • 771 Massachusetts Ave. • 269-8426
5909 E. 86th St. • 598-9864

You'll find comfy chairs and an eclectic crowd, including college kids and retirees. Try the delicious pastries and desserts to along with the java.

Cafe Espresso at Border's Books and Music
$ • 8785 N. Keystone Ave. • 574-1775

A favorite bookstore expanded, and its Keystone at the Crossing location includes a coffee bar, something regular patrons have been pining for since competitor Barnes and Noble opened. Expect to see all sorts of customers, from families to young professionals, since Borders has a large and loyal following.

Barnes and Noble
$ • 3748 E. 82nd St. • 594-7525

Featuring terrific Starbucks coffee, this massive bookstore draws plenty of professional types, reading and writing group members and a cadre of coffee shop regulars.

Cafe Patachou
$ • 4911 N. Pennsylvania St. • 925-2823

This neighborhood cafe, which in addition to coffee also serves up excellent omelets and cinnamon toast as well as a terrific turkey sandwich, attracts moms with kids (there's a toy-stocked play corner), couples sharing *The New York Times* and *Chicago Tribune* and a variety of neighborhood regulars.

Cath Inc.
$ • 126 N. Delaware St. • 685-0600
222 E. Market St. • 634-0600
705 E. 54th St. • 255-1075

With its three locations (two downtown and one in the Meridian-Kessler neighborhood) Cath serves a wide range of customers. Office workers stop in for a "Good Morning" muffin and a cup of mocha java before heading to work. The Meridian-Kessler location attracts an assortment of regulars from this diverse neighborhood.

Coffee Zon
$ • 137 E. Ohio St. • 684-0432

This downtown shop moved a few doors down Ohio Street a few years ago. It still offers a pastry case and hot java and a handy spot to stop in for a cup before work.

Cornerstone Coffee and Espresso Bar
$ • 651 E. 54th St. • 726-1360

This newish shop, furnished in American garage-sale chic, has become popular, like Cath, its nearby neighbor, with young people from the Broad Ripple area as well as dog-walkers and baby stroller-pushers from Meridian-Kessler. (We've seen dogs waiting patiently outside the door, though there are outside tables.)

Finale Dessert Cafe
$ • 3953 E. 82nd St.
• 841-3953

The focus here is on desserts, but you'll also find excellent java to enjoy along with a serving of the supreme chocolate mud cake.

Fine Grind
$ • 111 Monument Circle • 635-2223
8323 N. Michigan Rd. • 876-9892

These shops sell fresh roasted coffee and accessories in addition to offering walk-up counter service.

40 West Coffee Cafe
$ • 40 W. Jackson Pl. • 686-1414

This street-level coffee shop in the building that houses the Omni Severin offers wonderful salads, sandwiches, desserts and coffees.

Mexican

Acapulco Joe's
$$ • 635 N. Illinois St. • 637-5160

Joe, before he died, would burst into the restaurant and sing "God Bless America" at least twice an hour. Now Kate Smith does it via record, but little else has changed. "Aca Joe's" remains a hit with the downtown office crowd for the simple reason that the tacos and tostadas (and everything else) taste good and are priced right. Make sure you munch on the fresh chips and squirt-bottle salsa.

El Sol de Tala
$$ • 2444 E. Washington St. • 635-8252
1353 W. 86th St. • 255-4300

You'll miss El Sol if you're not careful, but this near east-side eatery is worth finding. The authentic Mexican food earns universal raves among those who find it (though the neighborhood doesn't). Still, many of the city's most prominent citizens know where it is, and they also know not to miss the guacamole and the chile rellenos. And now a north-side location, situated amid the many 86th Street strip mall restaurants, carries on the tradition.

FYI

Unless otherwise noted, the area code for all phone numbers in this guide is 317.

La Jolla
$$ • 921 Broad Ripple Ave.
• 253-5252

One of the best things about this popular Broad Ripple restaurant is the porch. It's great to grab a table outside, sip a Margarita and watch the goings on in this eclectic neighborhood and nightlife district. Oh, and the food's good too. La Jolla offers a healthful take on Mexican fare with a number of vegetarian options as well as traditional tacos and tostadas.

Zorro's
$$$ • 1300 E. 86th St. • 571-1001

Don't come looking for refried beans or a giant chimichanga. Zorro's specializes in Pacific Mexican cuisine, with an emphasis on seafood preparations almost tropical in origin. The fish and shrimp in banana leaves is excellent; so is the classic chicken mole. A stylish decor and reasonable prices also make this new restaurant appealing.

Pizza

Arni's
$$ • 3443 W. 86th St. • 875-7034

A great family choice (see our Kidstuff chapter), Arni's has won "best decor" awards from *Indianapolis Monthly's* People's Choice poll for six years running. The bar is full of life-size cutouts of celebrities; the dining rooms sports bicycles on the ceiling. And the pizza and salads are great.

Bazbeaux
$$ • 334 Massachusetts Ave. • 636-7662
832 E. Westfield Blvd. • 255-5711

The city's original gourmet pizza joint, Bazbeaux remains one of the most interesting, due primarily to its locations. The tiny house in Broad Ripple sees crowds hanging around the sidewalk waiting for tables; admire the wall paintings at the trendy Mass Ave. address. Whichever location you try, don't miss the quattro formaggio (four cheese) pizza.

Puccini's Smiling Teeth
$$ • 1508 W. 86th St. • 875-9223
3944 E. 82nd St. • 842-4028

Two locations offer easy access to this north-side favorite where you'll find a variety of gourmet pizzas as well as several pasta dishes. We like the barbecue chicken and smoked gouda pizza; traditionalists opt for the "ultimate warrior" with pepperoni, sausage, onions and much more. And the "veg head" is a tasty vegetarian alternative.

Some Guys
$$ • 6235 Allisonville Rd. • 257-1364

The gourmet pizza here proves great; we especially like the barbecue chicken variety. And the logo, a face on a pizza slice is cool, too.

Union Jack Pub
$$ • 924 Broad Ripple Ave. • 257-4343
6225 W. 25th St. • 243-3300

The incredibly thick Chicago-style pizza at Union Jack is sure to fill you up; in fact, you'll probably have to ask for a box for the leftovers. These popular pizza joints boast somewhat different crowds: The west-side location tends to be rowdier, the Broad Ripple crowd more given to conversation.

Pubs

(Check out our pub listing in the Nightlife chapter for more entertainment-oriented information about Pubs.)

Aristocrat
$$ • 5212 N. College Ave. • 283-7388

Though the Aristocrat does indeed feel like a pub, with dark wood and a cozy bar, it offers family dining and a very popular Sunday brunch. In nice weather, ask for a table outside; the sidewalk landscaping makes this a very pleasant option.

Corner Wine Bar
$$ • 6331 N. Guilford Ave. • 255-5159

Not really a pub, the Wine Bar is just what its name implies: a great place to sit outside in popular Broad Ripple, sip a Cabernet, nibble on fruit and cheese and watch the world go by.

Elbow Room
$$ • 605 N. Pennsylvania St. • 635-3354

The quintessential pub, this popular downtown spot does a brisk business; it's tough to get a table at lunch. After work you'll see tables full of friends and coworkers hashing over the day's events. The burgers are great here; an order of nachos is huge. You'll find plenty of sandwiches and some steaks on the menu.

Henry Grattan
$$ • 745 Broad Ripple Ave. • 257-6030

This Irish bar is a great place to enjoy a just-poured Harp and some conversation. The food, mostly traditional pub fare, is pretty good, the service friendly and the atmosphere inviting. It's has a traditional pub-style ambiance with lots of dark wood and plenty of old photographs lining the walls.

Legal Beagle
$$ • 20 N. Delaware St. • 266-0088

As its name implies, this place is a lawyer hangout. And why not? It's across from the City-County Building. But don't let that scare you away. Regular folks will find the standard bar fare done well and the legal-themed decor pleasant. If you listen carefully, you might hear the inside dope about the latest big trial.

Loughmiller's
$$ • 301 W. Washington St. • 638-7380

First, don't mispronounce the name. It's a hard consonant: Lock-miller's. Second, don't miss the club sandwich. And third, the salads are splendid. Loughmiller's is a lunchtime favorite among state employees, politicos and conventioneers (it's across the street from the Statehouse and behind the Westin Hotel), and it has a fine beer selection.

Melody Inn
$$ • 3626 N. Illinois St. • 923-4707

"The Mel," as it's affectionately known, has a storied past and a cameo in Dan Wakefield's book, *Going All The Way.* Popular among all types of folks, from college kids and softball teams to the after-work crowd and neighborhood regulars, the Mel offers the standard bar fare served in plastic baskets that won't disappoint. Plus, the beer is cold, and the shots are affordable.

Pawn Shop
$$ • 5906 N. College Ave. • 251-1111

This classic Broad Ripple pub remains extremely popular and features a varied menu. The chili is always good, the fries are plentiful and you'll find some surprises, such as the vegetarian water buffalo sandwich. Often crowded, this comfortable neighborhood hangout is a great place to get together with friends.

Brew Pubs

Broad Ripple Brew Pub
$$ • 842 E. 65th St. • 253-BREW

In addition to terrific beers (we especially enjoy the redbird ale), this microbrewery offers great fish and chips, daily specials and a number of excellent vegetarian dishes. Note that kids are welcome (in the front dining room, which is separate from the bar).

Oaken Barrel Brewing Co.
$$ • 50 Airport Pkwy. • Greenwood • 887-2287

Another entry into the microbrewery business (also see the Broad Ripple Brew Pub entry), this south-side place has much more of a family atmosphere than the Brew Pub. But the food's good, and the beers are great. Try the raspberry wheat variety.

RockBottom Restaurant and Brewery
$$ • 2 N. Meridian St. • 681-8180

Situated downtown near Circle Centre, this new establishment focuses more on food than brews with its pork chops, smoked salmon, pastas and salads. Check out its line of house brews too.

Alcatraz Brewing Co.
$$$ • 49 W. Maryland St. • 488-1230

This Circle Centre brew pub/restaurant enjoys a good reputation with downtown lunchers who like the sandwiches and pizzas. We're particularly fond of the ribs and the garlic-y fries and coleslaw. And there's the beer of course; the dark brew is especially good. Try one, and check out the prison-themed decor.

Circle V Brewing Co.
$$ • 8310 Craig St. • 59-59-ALE

You'll find a variety of traditional pub fare at this family-friendly Castleton restaurant. The spacious dining room, with its spiffy blue and silver industrial-style decor, is open and comfortable; call-ahead priority seating is available, and you might need it on busy weekends. Prices are reasonable, and the beer, with Hoosier-themed names, is good too.

Regional

Fletcher's of Atlanta
$$$$ • 185 W. Main St., Atlanta • 292-2777

This small eclectic eatery run by local chef Fletcher Boyd boasts excellent service and a creative menu. Its location in the tiny northern Hamilton County town of Atlanta might be a drawback to some, but it really is worth the 45-minute drive (take U.S. 31 north to County Line Road then east to Atlanta). You'll enjoy a casual, hip ambiance; there's artwork on the walls (and more in an upstairs gallery), beautifully set tables and a crowd dressed in everything from jeans to evening wear. You'll also find a seasonally changing menu and top-notch service. We can heartily recommend Hog Heaven, a marinated pork chop and pork loin dish. Salads prove excellent as well. Fletcher's is expensive, but worth it.

Panache
$$$ • 60 S. Elm St., Zionsville • 873-1388

This tiny Boone County town boasts plenty

of excellent restaurants, and Panache, which specializes in seasonal modern American food, is certainly among them. The small, casual restaurant features an interesting menu that changes periodically, but if you see a lamb dish, try it. Attentive service makes the dining experience even more enjoyable.

Peter's Restaurant and Bar
$$$$ • 8505 Keystone Crossing, 465-1155

Chef Peter George is very well-regarded around Indianapolis, and plenty of patrons would call his cigar-friendly restaurant the best in the city. Making use of seasonally available herbs and produce, he creates excellent regional American dishes — lamb, game and fresh fish. You'll find Lake Superior whitefish, Indiana duckling and roast venison. Salads are great too; we like the hearts of romaine with black walnuts, apples and bleu cheese. His restaurant is upscale, yet casual, with a beautiful open kitchen and inviting bar.

Snax
$$ • 2413 E. 65th St. • 257-6291

Diners will find a delicious variety on the tapas-style menu. Order a number of dishes and enjoy grazing (and sampling each other's selections). The seasonally changing menu might include red bean chili with smoked onions, a fall vegetable strudel or mixed greens with smoked salmon. Most selections are in the $4-to-$8 range.

Something Different
$$$ • 2411 E. 65th St. • 257-7973

A new decor featuring shades of green, gold and maroon has given a new look to this well-regarded upscale eatery. Chef Anthony Hanslits revises the menu monthly ensuring innovation and variety with such dishes as leek flan with smoked pheasant, game bird strudel, grilled walleye or perhaps chickpea-stuffed red pepper. Whatever the season, you're sure to find excellent fare.

Russian

Moscow Nights
$$ • 3532 W. 86th St. • 875-0777

Though the modern, minimalist decor doesn't look particularly Russian, the food certainly is. An interesting menu includes caviar-stuffed eggs, Russian-style perogy and delicious borscht. The owners, who hail from the former Soviet Union, serve up authentic dishes that are as delicious as they are unusual.

Russia House
$$ • 1475 W. 86th St. • 876-7990

You'll feel like a Cold War-era spy sitting in this tiny cafe, with its lace curtains and fabric-draped walls. The borscht is excellent here, as are the Siberian pelmeni (small meat-filled dumplings). If you're lucky, you'll get to hear a sultry chanteuse sing Russian ballads on weekend evenings. It'll help you keep up the James Bond masquerade.

Seafood

Fisherman's Dock
$$ • 3451 W. 86th St. • 876-FISH
3838 E. 82nd St. • 578-FISH

Fresh fish is flown in daily for lunch and dinner at this restaurant, which also features hand-cut steaks, poultry, pasta and even a kids' menu. Two locations offer plenty of convenience for northsiders who enjoy the fresh seafood and casual ambiance of these popular eateries.

Hot Tuna
$$$ • 40 W. Jackson Pl. • 687-5190

Though we can't help thinking of the early '70s rock band when we think of this place, the name refers to the food, not the music. A relaxed hotel dining room on the first floor of the downtown Omni Severin, Hot Tuna is casual, yet it offers professional, attentive service. Enjoy the complimentary appetizer your server will bring out, but be sure to try the lightly breaded fried calamari; it's some of the best in town, extra tender and done just right. The pan-browned walleye is great too.

Keystone Grill
$$$ • 8650 Keystone Crossing • 848-5202

Popular for lunch among Keystone at the Crossing office workers, the Keystone Grill remains a good choice for dinner as well, especially if you have a yen for fresh seafood.

Though the menu changes, look for such specialties as rainbow trout, grilled Norwegian salmon or farm-raised catfish. You'll find a number of steak and poultry dishes as well; one of our favorites is the linguine with mussels and clam sauce.

Key West Shrimp House
$$$ • 6714 E. 82nd St. • 635-5353

This longtime local landmark moved north from the near south side, and you can now enjoy its traditional seafood specialties. The restaurant kept the traditional nautical theme as much as was possible. Regulars enjoy the variety of shrimp dishes, fresh seafood, lobster and oysters (though you'll also find steaks, chicken and pasta).

Kona Jack's Fish Market and Sushi Bar
$$$ • 9413 N. Meridian St. • 843-2600

Kona Jack's advertises the city's freshest fish and seafood, and the north-side establishment has won over plenty of locals who appreciate the wide selection and the staff's willingness to slice an order to fit the requirements of your favorite recipe. The sushi bar proves popular as well, the atmosphere upscale but inviting.

New Orleans House
$$$ • 8845 Township Line Rd. • 872-9670

Come to this seafood buffet ready to indulge, and be sure you have plenty of time set aside to really enjoy it (the menu suggests a two-hour dinner, and we agree). Eat your fill of steamed shrimp, oysters on the halfshell, smoked salmon, clams and crab legs. And don't miss the frog legs that servers bring around for diners to try. Enjoy the bountiful buffet as well as the relaxed country club sort of atmosphere.

Soups, Salads and Sandwiches

Bay Window
$ • 202 W. Main St. • 882-1330

This homey, cozy little spot in Old Towne Greenwood is a great place to stop after browsing through the old downtown area (see our Shopping chapter). You'll find a tasty selection of sandwiches and soups; we like "Mary's Favorite" a turkey and cranberry sauce combo on dark rye paired with a cup of the homemade cream of broccoli soup. Try the ooey-gooey butter cake or the pumpkin crunch pie for dessert.

Benvenuti The Bakery
$ • 1 N. Pennsylvania St. • 686-9615

Though Benvenuti, the "parent" restaurant to this bakery, is quite posh, this offshoot offers the same excellent quality in a casual lunch and carry-out location. Everything in the display case looks great; be sure to sample the salads and some focaccia. And if you really want to indulge, try the tiramisu and one of the tiny chocolate cream puffs for good measure.

Between Bread
$, no credit cards • 136 N. Delaware St. • 638-4174

If gazpacho is on the menu, order it. If not, then any of the soups will please. But, as the name implies, sandwiches star here, and patrons line up daily at this restaurant in an alley near the City-County Building. Be patient, the line moves quickly, and it's worth the short wait.

Brother Juniper's
$, no credit cards • 339 Massachusetts Ave. • 636-3115
150 E. 16th St. • 924-9529

A religious order runs the place (hence the name), and the whole-Earth food tastes divine. Fresh soups and sandwich combinations fuel many a downtown worker, and the pies are wonderful. It's a miracle, though, that fights don't break out over tables at the always busy Mass Ave. location. Herron art school students run in for a sandwich at the 16th Street address.

City Market
$ • 222 E. Market St. • 634-9266

At this historic downtown marketplace, lunchtime diners find a wide variety to sample. Libby's Deli offers great sandwiches and deli sides, Pameer serves up delicious Afghani fare, the Rice Bowl has terrific egg rolls, and you'll find plenty more food stands throughout the market. For dessert, stop by Cath for cookies, muffins or coffee, or pick up some fresh fruit at a market stand (also see our Shopping chapter). Inside dining is at a premium, but on sunny days the outdoor tables, benches and ledges offer great spots to enjoy lunch and people-watch. Many stands do not accept credit cards.

Illinois Street Food Emporium
$ • 5500 N. Illinois St. • 253-9513

In the heart of the Butler-Tarkington neighborhood you'll find a great little shopping district, the Shoppes at 56th Street (see our Shopping chapter). And within that is the Illinois Street Food Emporium, which offers great deli fare and excellent pastries and desserts. We can heartily recommend the avocado-and-turkey croissant; you'll also find plenty of heart-healthy options. The side salads are great too; try the wild rice variety. Grab a table inside, eat outdoors or enjoy a walk through the neighborhood.

Petite Grill
$ • 443 N. Pennsylvania St. • 631-3500

This long, narrow space in a downtown office building is indeed petite, but the Petite Grill can satisfy any appetite. From its big-as-the-plate tenderloin to the crunchy onion rings, the food is good, so be ready to eat. For lesser appetites there is lighter fare; early risers will find breakfast too.

Vegetarian

Essential Edibles
$ • 429 E. Vermont St. • 266-8797

Very popular among the downtown lunch crowd, Essential Edibles is known for its creative approach to vegetarian cuisine. You find such specialties as grilled eggplant sandwiches, mushroom paté and a range of pasta and grain salads. And if you see a flier advertising an upcoming cooking class, sign up.

Essential Edibles Too
$ • 115 E. 49th St. • 931-1080

This carry-out cafe brings the best stuff from the downtown location to the popular Meridian-Kessler neighborhood. Be sure to try the focaccia, the herb breads and the vegan cookies. They'll make a believer out of you.

Oriental Health Cuisine
$ • 86th St. and Allisonville Rd. • 578-3066

Though also listed in our Asian food category, we include Oriental Health Cuisine here for its vegetarian, vegan and macrobiotic dishes. Pasta is made daily, and you'll find extra-fresh vegetables served in creative preparations.

FYI

Unless otherwise noted, the area code for all phone numbers in this guide is 317.

While there's something going on in Broad Ripple seven nights a week, the busiest nights are Thursday, Friday and Saturday. That's when it's clear that Broad Ripple is an ancient Sumarian term for party.

Nightlife

Your work is done, and now you're ready to have some fun. Where do you go? What can you do? Well, it just so happens that those questions are the core of this chapter.

What follows is a look at some of what Indianapolis has to offer in the way of live music, dance clubs, pubs and movie theaters.

To help you navigate through the choices, we've primarily arranged this chapter geographically. For example, if you're downtown and want to check out the nightlife there, flip to our "Downtown" section and read through our "Jazz and Blues," "Rock/Pop," "Dance Clubs," "Pubs and Comedy" categories. You can do the same for Broad Ripple and the Northwest, Northeast, South, East and West sides of town. If, however, you're looking for a particular concert venue or want to take in a movie, turn to our separate "Concert Venues" and "Movie Theaters" sections at the end of the chapter.

Go now. A good time awaits.

Where to Start

In addition to this chapter, which provides specifics in terms of names, addresses and telephone numbers, the following publications provide schedules of events and activities on a weekly basis.

Weekend, 633-9079, a weekly arts and entertainment insert appears in the Friday editions of *The Indianapolis Star* and *The Indianapolis News*. It includes movie listings, live music schedules for both concert venues and clubs and information about performing arts events, stage productions, museum exhibitions, lectures and so forth.

NUVO, 254-2400, a free weekly newspaper, which is published each Thursday, covers news, public issues and arts and entertainment. In the case of the latter, *NUVO* pro-

vides a comprehensive schedule of events as well as a detailed list of area clubs and the performers appearing at them.

Downtown

When it comes to nightlife, downtown offers something for everyone. From cozy hotel lounges to smoky blues clubs, hot dance spots to chummy little pubs, you're bound to find someplace you like. And since the downtown district is relatively compact, you can walk from one place to another until you do.

Jazz and Blues

Chatterbox Tavern
435 Massachusetts Ave. • 636-0584

For classic jazz in a classic jazz setting, this tiny, smoky, hole-in-the-wall bar in the Mass Avenue arts district is it. Some of the city's best musicians show up to play at the Chatterbox after midnight, once their early evening gigs are over.

Rick's Cafe Americain
39 W. Jackson Pl. • 634-6666

On the second level of Union Station, this restaurant/bar features jazz that's as tasty as its entrees.

Slippery Noodle Inn
372 S. Meridian St. • 631-6974

This place just south of Union Station is Indiana's oldest (c. 1850) continually operating tavern. With blues performers on stages upstairs and down, it's also the best place in town to hear local, regional and national blues. And if all that great music makes you hungry, the Noodle's full-service kitchen is open well past midnight.

Photo: Meredith Goldberg

A midnight crowd waits in the rain to enter the Land Shark on Broad Ripple Avenue in June.

Rock/Pop

America Live!
39 W. Maryland St., Ste. H-7 Circle Centre • 630-5483

Occupying nearly 50,000 square feet on the fourth floor of the downtown mall, America Live! is an entertainment complex containing three nightclubs — Gator's, Flashbaxx and World Mardi Gras — as well as a beer pub and two restaurants. Based on a beach theme, Gator's is a high-energy dance club featuring state-of-the-art audio, video and lighting. Done up in 1970s-style decor, Flashbaxx is a dance club that features '70s and '80s music. For live music, World Mardi Gras combines a New Orleans atmosphere with local, regional and national performers. The music here includes jazz, rhythm 'n' blues and rock.

But if all you want is someplace to have a beer and shoot some pool, try Brewski's. With more than 80 varieties of beer on hand, along with an array of pool tables and electronic games, it's designed for fun.

There are also two full-service on-site restaurants, The Big Easy Cafe and Sports City Cafe, for those times when having too much fun makes you hungry.

The Cozy
115 E. Wabash St. • 638-2100

A combination restaurant and nightclub, this place is tucked away in an alley-like street between Pennsylvania and Delaware streets, making it a bit hard to find. But it's worth the search. The Cozy has a large dance floor, pool tables and TVs throughout broadcasting sports. There's live music — blues, rock and funk — on the weekends and a mixture of recorded music the rest of the week.

Culture Club
235 S. Meridian St. • 756-9606

With three floors of live and recorded reggae, house and Top 40 music, this club attracts a multicultural crowd that comes to dance the night away.

Hooters
39 W. Jackson Pl., Union Station • 267-9637
If you're looking for a place in the sun but can't afford it, this bar/restaurant with its Florida beach theme might suffice. There are rock 'n' roll oldies on the jukebox, so kick back, relax and let the good times roll.

Ike & Jonesy's
17 W. Jackson Pl. • 632-4553
Offering a mix of live and recorded music — '60s rock, R&B and Top 40 stuff — this c. 1950s-style diner is a favorite after-work watering hole for downtown workers looking to unwind. It's an uninhibited kind of place, and it's loud. But you can have yourself a good time here without much effort. (A word of advice: Don't wear your favorite clothes here unless you're prepared to overlook the spills that happen in crowded bars.)

Rathskeller Restaurant
401 E. Michigan St. • 636-0396
On Friday and Saturday nights, this German restaurant inside the Athenaeum adds live music to its menu. If your taste runs to rock and R&B, drop by for some schnitzel and tunes.

Dance Clubs

In addition to the dancing at the previously mentioned live music clubs, the following clubs offer dancing to recorded music.

Faces Night Club
2145 N. Talbott St. • 923-9886
While you'll see members of other races and ethnic groups in the crowd, this club 2 miles north of downtown is predominantly an African-American nightspot, and an elegant one at that. This is a no-jeans-and-T-shirts kind of place. Faces' patrons dress to go out. From very nice casual clothes to beautifully tailored suits and dresses, the people who go to Faces jump sharp. The music here ranges from rhythm

'n' blues to jazz, sometimes live, sometimes not. In either case, there's room to dance.

Jackson Street Bar
234 S. Meridian St. • 266-8444
In a New Orleans-style setting, the music, which is primarily dance pop from the '80s and '90s, motivates until the wee hours — or until your feet weep for relief.

Pubs

For food-related information, please see our "Pubs" category in the Restaurants chapter.

The Elbow Room
605 N. Pennsylvania St. • 635-3354
A downtown landmark for decades, The Elbow Room is as much restaurant as pub, but that doesn't diminish its value as a place to relax for an evening over a good imported beer. The music emanating from speakers throughout the place ranges from '70s radio hits to contemporary stuff.

Filibusters
Westin Hotel, 50 S. Capitol Ave. • 262-8100
Sit and sip in the pub where the pols do — this hotel pub is across the street from the State Capitol and the state office complex, so it attracts its fair share of state and local government officials and plenty of weary conventioneers from the nearby Convention Center.

Louisiana Street Bar
123 W. Louisiana St. • 631-2221
This street-level bar in the Crowne Plaza hotel offers a respite after a hard day. Its kitchen serves a variety of food until midnight, so you can have a late dinner as well as a nightcap.

Comedy

Indianapolis Comedy Connection
247 S. Meridian St. • 631-3536
A local downtown comedy classic, the Comedy Connection hosts a variety of the nation's best touring comedy talent. Past acts

have included such rising starts as Tim Allen, Rosie O'Donnell and Ellen DeGeneres.

Broad Ripple

This is entertainment central. In just a few square blocks, this north-side village contains more nightlife options than any other section of town. While there's something going on in Broad Ripple seven nights a week, the busiest nights are Thursday, Friday and Saturday. That's when it's clear that Broad Ripple is an ancient Sumarian term for party.

Jazz

Jazz Cooker
925 E. Westfield Blvd. • 253-2883

If you can't get down to New Orleans for the real thing, this place is a good alternative — order up some red beans and rice, then kick back for some Big Easy jazz.

The Jazz Kitchen
5377 N. College Ave. • 253-4900

This is the city's hottest jazz club, a place where the best local, regional and national musicians come to cook. You can see everyone from local favorites, such as Affinity and Steve Allee, to performers of international stature such as Maynard Ferguson.

Midtown Bar & Grill
815 E. Westfield Blvd. • 253-1141

In the heart of Broad Ripple, this place offers cool jazz in an intimate environment. This is a tablecloths-and-candles kind of place where a throaty sax or some smoothly fingered ivories remind you how sensuous jazz can be.

Pop/Rock

The Vogue
6259 N. College Ave. • 259-7029

Let's start with the king. This former movie theater is the state's top spot on the rock club circuit — the place to see (and hear) the best in local and regional bands and national acts the caliber of Taj Mahal, Buddy Guy and Johnny Cash.

The Vogue is a great place to see performers at their best — or in some cases, their worst, but that's not the club's fault. It's hard to beat a table by the balcony railing: You can see everything going on on-stage without having to crane to see around anyone. The only problem is ordering; when the band's cranked up, communicating with your waitress can be a challenge. Just wave your bottle around and point at it, then hold up the appropriate number of fingers.

On Sunday nights, The Vogue hosts "Boing," an alternative dance party popular with the local gay community.

C.T. Peppers
6283 N. College Ave. • 257-6277

Live music that defies categorization, including rock, jazz, blues and reggae, along with pool, darts and electronic games make this Vogue neighbor a local favorite. And Peppers' kitchen cooks up great chow.

The Patio
6308 Guilford Ave. • 253-0799

A smaller version of The Vogue, this cramped club is the kind of place your mother would frown upon — the floor's too sticky, the air's too smoky and the music's too loud. In other words, it's perfect. At The Patio, you're apt to hear anything from punk to funk — and apt to see anyone from Polo-shirted frat boys to totally tatooed bikers.

J.C. Bistro
834 Broad Ripple Ave. • 255-8755

On the main drag through the village, this club is a contemporary version of the fern bars of the 1970s. Though festooned with mirrors and hanging plants, it manages to book some of the best acts in the area. The music here ranges from radio covers to alternative tunes, reggae to acoustic.

Dance Clubs

Eden
6235 N. Guilford Ave. • 475-1588

For "a different point of view from the top of Broad Ripple," this club inside a former VFW hall is home to cutting edge dance music. The patrons here run the gamut from smartly dressed to multiply pierced. Rave on, Garth.

Landsharks
810 Broad Ripple Ave. • 254-8157

A mix of live and recorded music, along with a beach party atmosphere, makes this a place "where good fins get together." If you can't make it down to the islands, this is an inexpensive alternative, unless you're looking for some sun. But then, who goes to a nightclub for that?

Pubs and Bars

For food-related information, please see our "Pubs" category in the Restaurants chapter.

Average Joe's
816 Broad Ripple Ave.
• 253-5844
Mineshaft Saloon
812 Broad Ripple Ave.
• 253-5844
Rock Lobster
820 Broad Ripple Ave.
• 253-5844

These three clubs, which bill themselves as "Broad Ripple's Party Trifecta," offer recorded music, pool tables, air hockey, video games and sports TV. Take advantage of domestic and imported beer specials throughout the week and spicy chicken wings for sustenance.

Broad Ripple Brew Pub
840 E. 65th St. • 253-2739

In a manner of speaking, this is the testing facility for the on-site microbrewery. Freshly brewed beers in several varieties, including seasonal brews, are available in a relaxed pub setting.

The Corner Wine Bar
6331 Guilford Ave. • 255-5159

For those times when you'd like to sit and sip a glass of wine while talking with a friend, this place at the corner of Guilford Avenue and Westfield Boulevard is perfect. Domestic and imported wines and beers are available.

Henry Grattan
745 Broad Ripple Ave. • 257-6030

No this isn't some guy's house — it's an Irish pub, complete with brass rails and dark wood. It's the kind of place that beckons on a rainy afternoon.

Melody Inn
3826 N. Illinois St. • 923-4707

Not actually in Broad Ripple, but a couple miles southwest, the Melody Inn is still as cool as any BR nightspot. Perched on the eastern edge of the Butler-Tarkington neighborhood, the Melody is a throwback to 1960s college-bar chic complete with wraparound booths and a long oak bar. It's got a jukebox jammed with everything from Sinatra to Oasis, and on weekend nights you can hear local jazz and folk performers live. The clientele is a lively mix of folk from the surrounding neighborhoods and college kids.

The Pawn Shop Pub
5906 N. College Ave.
• 251-1111

Sometimes you find a place that feels like home the minute you walk in the door — a "Cheers" sort of place. This is one of those places, complete with a horseshoe bar, brass footrests, dim lighting, and friendly bartenders. There's no music, live or recorded because The Pawn Shop is where you go when you want to while away a few hours shooting the breeze.

The Red Key Tavern
5170 N. College Ave. • 283-4601

This is the classic neighborhood bar: Formica-topped tables and vinyl chairs, a jukebox in the corner and a bar lined with regulars. It's a great place to spend an evening alone or with a friend.

Union Jack Pub
924 Broad Ripple Ave. • 243-3300

This place is reminiscent of those oak-and-brass bars you find in college towns everywhere. The collegial atmosphere is ideal for quaffing a few brews along with some of the great pizza this place is famous for (yeah, yeah, the British aren't exactly known for their pizza, but it's just the name of the place, not it's culinary identity). See the "Pizza" category in our Restaurants chapter.

Comedy

Broad Ripple Comedy Club
6281 N. College Ave. • 255-4211

This club upstairs from C.T. Peppers features a variety of regional and national comedians, including such favorites as Michigan's own Heywood Banks and song parodists Pinkard and Bowden. On the third and fourth Mondays of each month, BRCC hosts Comedy Showcase, which features local and regional acts.

Northwest

Rock/Pop

Shooters II
5522 Georgetown Rd. • 388-0022

Tucked away in a strip mall, this live music club features a wide variety of bands from classic rock and Top 40 to the blues in a blue jeans, casual atmosphere.

Dance Clubs

Memories
7820 North Michigan Rd. • 879-0759

This is a place where the past and the present combine to create the time of your life. Enjoy DJ dancing every Thursday, Friday and Saturday, plus a game room and big-screen sports. This is home of the Notre Dame Club of Indianapolis, so be prepared to cheer on the Fighting Irish during football season.

Pubs and Bars

For food-related information, see the "Pubs" category in our Restaurants chapter.

Benchwarmers Sports Food and Spirits
3850 DePauw Blvd. • 871-5655

A congenial sports bar inside the Holiday Inn North, Benchwarmers has TVs throughout for those crucial sporting events. It also has billiards, shuffleboard and NTN (a sports and trivia game). On Saturday nights, enjoy a DJ and dancing.

Northeast

Rock/Pop

Cocktail Cove
82nd St. and Allisonville Rd. • 576-9800

Live music and televised sports — need we say more? This is a place where folks go to see and be seen — the kind of place where tanning contests and martinis are *de rigueur*. When you're looking for a port to ride out a storm, anchor yourself here.

Whirligig's
8787 Keystone Crossing • 846-2700

This high-energy club inside the Radisson Hotel features both local bands and DJs. On weekends, this place really hops, and the dance floor's packed. Dress up a little, and lighten up a lot.

Pubs and Bars

Legends Sports Bar & Grill
8250 Center Run Rd. • 576-9238

With a DJ pumping out dance tunes every night, it's easy to see why Legends is, well,

---

INSIDERS' TIP

Every Thursday evening in August, Ameritech teams up with the Indianapolis Zoo to present "Animals and All That Jazz," a combination of live jazz, good food and all the Zoo's attractions. It's a favorite of families looking for something different to do.

legendary for fun. If you're rhythmically challenged, you can spend your time shooting pool, eating (the food here is also, uh, legendary), or just leaning back in your chair working on your smile.

Comedy

Crackers Comedy Club
Fashion Mall, Keystone at the Crossing • 846-2500

Featuring such hilarious comedians as Brad Garrett, Crackers is longtime staple of the local nightlife scene. And its upscale setting makes it easy to sell to affluent northsiders.

South

Jazz

The Jazz Cellar
522 E. Raymond St. • 788-4521

This club, which is on the lower level of the Fireside South Restaurant, features a variety of local and regional jazz artists. As the name implies, this underground club is a cozy, intimate place, just right for a tête-à-tête over an after-dinner brandy.

Jazz in Action
1105 Prospect St. • 686-6006

Ensconced on the fourth floor of the Fountain Square Theatre, this club offers great music and a good view of the historic area around it. Here you'll hear everything from covers of jazz classics to new compositions and improvisations.

Rock/Pop

Celebration Lounge
520 E. Thompson Rd. • 787-8341

Inside the Holiday Inn South, this club features live music on the weekends, including classic rock, country, funk and '50s goldies. During the week, there's a DJ. And there's a jukebox, along with a buffet, in the back of a fin-tailed Cadillac.

The Fountain Room
1103 S. Shelby St. • 686-6010

This place in the Fountain Square area offers patrons a chance to time travel back to the 1950s for a weekend sock hop. Dance to live and recorded music.

Lady Luck Billiards
911 N. State Rd. 135, Greenwood • 885-1962

In the downstairs portion of this two-level club you can catch a potpourri of area bands and musical styles including rock, reggae, funk, etc. Upstairs, you can shoot some pool. And all over the place, you can keep an eye on televised sports.

Comedy

One-Liners Comedy Club
50 Airport Pkwy., Greenwood • 889-LAFF

Owned in part by local comedian Dave "The King" Wilson, this south-side club is a great spot to catch local and regional acts.

East

Rock/Pop

Zanies Too
5914 E. 10th St. • 357-6022

This club defines intimate. It's small enough that when a band's on stage, you can count the change in the bass player's pocket. The music here is primarily rock and blues, both acoustic and electric.

Dance Clubs

Ritz Nightclub
3525 N. Shadeland Ave. • 549-2222

Inside the Quality Inn East, you'll find this club, home of DJ'd dance tunes, six nights a week. The crowd tends to be young and on-the-prowl, the clothes tend to be trendy and the music tends to be loud '90s dance tunes. Nobody sits (for long) at the Ritz.

Comedy

Ritz Nightclub
3525 N. Shadeland Ave. • 549-2222

Every Monday evening at this club inside the Quality Inn East is "Comedy Nite," with comedian Ty Wilson hosting the open-mic festivities.

West

Jazz

Rick's Cafe Boatyard
4050 Dandy Tr. • 290-9300

Anchored on the shore of Eagle Creek Reservoir, this restaurant offers up some choice live jazz. Very classy ambiance and a great view of Eagle Creek Reservoir, this is a place where you can learn firsthand what's hot and what's cool and how jazz contains the best of both.

Country

In Cahoots
111 N. Lynhurst Dr. • 487-9065

Inside a building the size of an airplane hangar, this club near the airport is home of the Texas two-step and host to some of country's best up-and-comers. Join in free dance lessons. And if all that dancing makes you hungry, this is the only nightclub in the country with a Taco Bell inside it.

Western Star Dance Hall
6447 W. Washington St. • 486-8100

Part of a dining-dancing establishment, the hall has a 1,500-square-foot, hardwood dance and a high-quality sound and light system.

Indianapolis Jazz Greats

When you're sitting in one of the local jazz clubs, soaking up the ambiance and the music, consider this: Indianapolis has long been an important contributor to American jazz. In fact, from the 1920s through the mid-1960s, the city was one of the centers of jazz in this country, on a par with other jazz hotspots such as Chicago and St. Louis.

Close-up

And the city's roster of significant jazz artists, past and present, includes names known to any jazz buff. Among them are:

David Baker: Chair of the Indiana University School of Music's jazz department, Baker, a trombonist, has played with the likes of Stan Kenton and Quincy Jones. As a composer and arranger, he's both highly regarded and in constant demand.

Erroll Grandy: Known as the "godfather of Indianapolis jazz" for his affect on the local jazz scene of the 1940s, '50s and '60s, Grandy was both a gifted pianist and an inspiration to several generations of jazz musicians. At various times, he backed such well-known figures as Dinah Washington, Billie Holliday and Count Basie.

Slide Hampton: An innovative trombone player and acclaimed jazz composer, Hampton played with and arranged music for some of the best-known names in jazz: vibes

Photo: The Indianapolis Star and The Indianapolis News

Jazz trombonist J.J. Johnson is an Indianapolis native.

player (and distant cousin) Lionel Hampton, Maynard Ferguson and Art Blakey, among others. Today, he's one of the international jazz world's most respected figures.

Freddie Hubbard: A major player in the development of jazz in the second half of the 20th century, trumpet player Freddie Hubbard, both solo and in tandem with others, influenced the sound and stretched the boundaries of modern music.

J.J. Johnson: Another innovative trombonist, Johnson more than any other player affected the evolution of the instrument in contemporary music. From the way he played to what he played, Johnson explored the potential of his instrument in a manner that redefined what a trombonist can do.

Wes Montgomery: One of the 20th century's most influential jazz guitarists, Montgomery won accolades from musicians, critics and fans for his inventive playing. Guitarists today continue to sing his praises and study his techniques, while fans continue to listen to such Montgomery recordings as the 1965 Grammy Award winner "Goin' Out of My Head" and 1967's bestselling jazz LP *A Day in the Life*.

Photo: The Indianapolis Star and The Indianapolis News

Wes Montgomery was one of this century's most influential jazz guitarists.

Today, Wes (who died in 1968) is memorialized both in a namesake park at 34th Street and Hawthorne Lane and in the annual Wes Montgomery Jazz Festival held in Washington Park each August.

Monk Montgomery: Wes's older brother Monk was the first jazz musician to record with an electric bass, which he did in 1953. A member of Lionel Hampton's band in the early 1950s, Monk also played with Wes and their younger brother, Buddy, in the Wes Montgomery Trio, as well as with a variety of other musicians.

Buddy Montgomery: Younger brother of Wes and Monk, Buddy played piano with Miles Davis as well as with his brothers in the Wes Montgomery Trio. Today, he remains a widely respected composer and player, occasionally returning to Indianapolis from his home in Oakland, California, for concerts.

Eat what you like in the Western Star Dinner House, then work it off in the dance hall.

Rock/Pop

Quincy's
2544 Executive Dr. • 381-6137

Hear some of the best live sounds around in this club in the Adam's Mark Hotel. Performers range from Top 40 and classic rock cover bands to the local Afro-Caribbean mambo maniacs, Dog Talk.

And when there isn't a band on stage, the DJ's working hard to keep the beat.

Comedy

ComedySportz Arena
3121 W. 30th St. • 926-3368

This is improvisational comedy up close and personal. Teams of "actletes" create scenes based on audience suggestions while a ref regulates the humor (as in keeping it clean yet funny).

Quincy's Comedy Cabaret
2544 Executive Dr. • 381-6137

Every Tuesday evening, this nightclub in the Adam's Mark Hotel hosts a comedy night.

Concert Venues

Hilbert Circle Theatre
45 Monument Cir. • 262-1110

Home of the Indianapolis Symphony Orchestra, this former movie theater is now a gorgeous concert hall. When not in use by the ISO, it is occasionally used for other classical or jazz performances. (Also see entry in The Arts chapter.)

Clowes Memorial Hall
4600 Sunset Ave. • 940-9696

This performance hall on the campus of Butler University is Indianapolis's version of the Kennedy Center for the Performing Arts. In the acoustically marvelous Clowes auditorium, you can see Broadway shows, operas, jazz ensembles, rock groups, dance performances, readings and lectures by well-known writers. (Also see entry in The Arts chapter.)

Deer Creek Music Center
12880 E. 146th St. • 776-3337

One of the premier amphitheaters in the Midwest, Deer Creek is set amid 220 acres of beautiful countryside about 15 miles north of Indianapolis. During its season (May through October), it hosts an array of performers. The 1996 roster included such diverse acts as the Allman Brothers, Sting, Neil Young, Phish and Lyle Lovett. At Deer Creek, you can hear the stars beneath the stars. (Also see entry in The Arts chapter.)

Indiana Roof Ballroom
140 W. Washington St. • 236-1870

On the fourth floor of the Indiana Repertory Theatre building downtown, the Spanish-style ballroom was built in the 1920s. Since being renovated in the early 1980s, the Roof has become a popular site for Big Band dances as well as dinners, receptions and occasional concerts by such performers as Harry Connick Jr. (Also see entry in The Arts chapter.)

Murat Theatre
502 N. New Jersey St. • 635-2433

In this wonderful old theater inside the Murat Shrine Temple, you can catch an array of acts. Performance artist Laurie Anderson, singers Tony Bennett and Sarah McLachlan and jazz saxophonist Branford Marsalis have performed at the Murat.

Recently renovated, it is one of downtown's truly wonderful music venues.

Madame Walker Urban Life Center & Theatre
617 Indiana Ave. • 236-2088

Built to commemorate Madame C. J. Walker, creator of the Walker System of hair care products and America's first black female millionaire, this beautifully restored building houses both a ballroom and a theater. The center offers events year-round, including Jazz on the Avenue, performances by local, regional and national musicians every Friday evening; and the Walker Repertory Showcase, a series of stage productions by and about the black experience. (Also see entry in The Arts chapter.)

Movie Theaters

Out-of-the-Ordinary Theaters

Hollywood Bar & Filmworks
247 S. Meridian St. • 231-9255

If your idea of heaven is having someone serve you food and drinks while you watch a movie, then the door to this downtown establishment may just be the Pearly Gates. The Filmworks features new and classic films in a

---

INSIDERS' TIP

The first Friday of every month, the Indianapolis Museum of Art hosts "First Friday," a combination of live jazz, wine and hors d'oeurves and admission to the museum's galleries. It's a popular event with singles hoping to meet someone interesting amid all the music and art.

high-tech cinema setting complete with at-your-seat food and beverage service. One of the city's best-kept secrets, the Filmworks is fast gaining popularity among people who appreciate first-rate movies, atmosphere and service.

Irving Theater
5507 E. Washington St. • 357-3792
This small two-screen theater on the eastside shows both second-run Hollywood releases and independent films. It also has great popcorn.

General Cinema Castleton Square
North Parking Lot • 849-3471
The three screens in this small complex show a combination of offbeat Hollywood and independent films. It's long been among local film buffs' favorite cineplexes.

United Artists Theatres
**Circle Centre, fourth floor,
49 W. Maryland St. • 237-6356**
While this nine-screen cinema complex is a lot like other first-run multiple-screen complexes in the area, it includes some elements that set it apart, namely motion simulators in a virtual-reality theater. While you can go watch a movie in the same old static setting you're used to, you can also go participate in a virtual-reality scenario that will literally move you (and your seat).

First-Run Theaters

General Cinema Corporation
Clearwater Crossing (12 screens), 82nd Street and Dean Road, 595-6234

Eastgate Mall (six screens), Shadeland Avenue and Washington Street, 377-1117

Glendale Center (three screens), 5988 N. Rural Avenue 253-6491

Greenwood Park Mall (seven screens), 1251 U.S. 31, Greenwood, 888-7224

Lafayette Square (five screens), 3919 Lafayette Road, 293-6200

Regal Cinemas
Shiloh Crossing (12 screens), 10400 Rockville Road, 273-8958

Village Park Plaza (12 screens), Highway 31 North, Westfield, 843-1666

Sony Theaters
Sony Cherry Tree (10 screens), 9529 E. Washington Street, 357-3792

Sony College Park (10 screens), W. 86th Street and Michigan Road, 872-4345

Sony Greenwood (10 screens), U.S. 31 and Fry Road, 881-3905

Sony Lafayette Square (eight screens), Lafayette Road and Georgetown Road, 299-0852

United Artists
In addition to the Circle Centre cineplex, UA also has theaters at: Eagle Highlands (10 screens), 4015 Shore Drive, 298-2574.

Second-Run Theaters (a.k.a. "cheap seats")

Greenbriar Cinema (two screens), W. 86th Street and Ditch Road, 253-3015

Speedway Cinema (two screens), 5694 Crawfordsville Road, 487-2890

Woodland Cinema, N. Keystone Avenue and 116th Street, 846-2425

Cinemark Theatres, Greenwood Corners (eight screens), U.S. 31 and Stop 11 Road, 882-0202

Washington Market (eight screens), 10455 E. Washington Street, 898-1990

Drive-Ins

ABC Drive-In Theatre, junction of State Roads 37 and 32, 767-5565

Clermont Deluxe Outdoor Theatres I & II, 10310 E. U.S. Highway 136, 291-1560

Tibbs Drive-in, 480 S. Tibbs Street, 343-6666

You'll discover tiny shopping districts tucked into neighborhoods, vibrant collections of specialty stores and enough strip centers and shopping malls to keep you busy year round — especially during the holidays.

Shopping

Local residents once complained they had to travel to Chicago to find decent shopping. If that ever was true, it's certainly no longer the case. Indianapolis has seen an exciting growth of shopping possibilities in the past five or so years. A Fashion Mall expansion brought Jacobson's, and later Parisian, to the city, and now, with the opening of Circle Centre, residents and visitors are able to enjoy the well-known customer service of Nordstrom and the variety of The Limited stores, as well as an additional Parisian location, not to mention the 100 or so specialty shops that fill Circle Centre.

Excellent shopping can be found all across the city. You'll discover tiny shopping districts tucked into neighborhoods, vibrant collections of specialty stores and enough strip centers and shopping malls to keep you busy year round — especially during the holidays.

Except for malls and a few special categories, shopping is grouped in this chapter by location. Indianapolis is a very drivable city; you can get from one side of town to the other in less than 30 minutes. So hit the bank machine, grab the credit cards and head out to explore the city with a shopping bag in hand.

Just don't forget where you parked the car.

Shopping Districts

Downtown

With the opening of Circle Centre, in September 1995 (see our Close-up in this chapter), downtown is experiencing a renewed emphasis on shopping. But in addition to the new mall, the area around Monument Circle offers lots of terrific specialty shops such as **Bash Seeds**, 103 N. Delaware Street, a downtown mainstay since 1902, which stocks an extensive selection of seeds as well as garden accessories in an old-fashioned interior. The **Rocky Mountain Chocolate Factory**, 28 Monument Circle, sells sinful specialties, such as fudge, truffles and marvelous caramel apples. For an indulgence of a different sort, check out the custom designs at **Reis-Nichol's Jewelers**, 47 S. Pennsylvania Street; **Goodman Jewelers**, 30 Washington Street, a full-service jeweler, has been a downtown mainstay for years and hung in there throughout all the construction of recent years. **Redwood & Ross** men's clothiers, 11 S. Meridian Street, also saw its share of nearby construction as Circle Centre went up.

Even with some construction projects continuing, just about everything downtown remains easy to reach. A short walk on Pennsylvania Street will take you to **Architectural Center Bookstore**, at 47 S. Penn, which stocks an interesting selection of interior and graphic design titles as well as books on restoration and home repair. Writing, or writing instruments, to be exact — remains the focus at the **Hoosier Pen Company**, 155 W. Washington Street, where you'll find a wide selection of both fountain and ballpoint pens.

And even though it's not right downtown, **Odyssey Map Store**, 902 N. Delaware Street, is worth a quick drive (or a long walk). The shop stocks thousands of maps and globes and travel guides, a must for anyone dreaming about a getaway.

City Market
222 E. Market St. • 634-9266

A market at this site was planned by the city as early as 1821, and the original building, completed in 1886, still boasts food stalls and produce stands, though the emphasis these days is on eating rather than shopping. Lunchtime is the best time of day to visit; the market is crowded with downtown workers who want to grab a corned beef sandwich at **Libby's Delicatessen**, Chinese food from the **Rice Bowl** or Afghani fare from **Pameer** (see our Restaurants chapter). Still, the market is a great place to pick up imported olive oil at **Aesop's Kitchen and Cupboard** or health food from **The Good Stuff**. Whatever you find, stop for a while and enjoy a cup of coffee and a pastry at **Cath Inc.** or take it outside on the plaza, where tables and benches provide a place to people watch.

Massachusetts Avenue
From New York St. to College Ave.

The downtown section of this diagonal street has become something of an art district, with a variety of small galleries representing plenty of talented, innovative artists (see The Arts chapter for more information).

In addition to art, the street offers a number of restaurants and interesting shops (see our Restaurants chapter). The shops include: **Stout's Shoes**, a traditional full-service shoe store with an old-fashioned but still-operational system of baskets and pulleys to retrieve selections from the stock area. The **Mass. Ave. Knit Shop** offers all the raw materials necessary for a terrific afghan. **Priscilla's** floral shop offers artful arrangements in beautiful containers. Farther down the street, near the corner of College Avenue, **Chatham's on the Avenue** offers a browsable mix of fine cards and gifts (the store takes its name from the neighborhood: Chatham Arch). Don't miss the delicious desserts at **The Abbey** coffeehouse next door. Or come back to the area around midnight and hear some great jazz at the **Chatterbox**.

Fountain Square
South of downtown, 1000 block of Virginia Ave. and Prospect St.

Drive into this historic shopping district, and you'll feel like you've entered a small town. It even boasts a **Fountain of Mystery** bookstore, **Fountain Square Antique Mall** and several small restaurants.

Around Town

Old Towne Greenwood
Downtown along Main St.

Though the community of Greenwood has become known for its massive Greenwood Park Mall, you'll find a small but charming area in the old business district downtown. **Making Thyme** offers herbs and related gift items. **Kooler's Boutique** is a traditional dress shop, and **Bauman Interiors** offers beautiful home furnishings and accessories. You'll also spot the **Bay Window**, a small lunch place with excellent soups and sandwiches. Don't miss the well-regarded **Kids Ink** children's bookstore around the corner on Madison Avenue.

The Shoppes at 56th and Illinois
5600 block of Illinois St.

This small shopping district in the Butler Tarkington neighborhood offers considerable convenience with a handy supermarket and liquor store, plus a variety of specialty shops. The locally owned **Tarkington Tweed** offers fine clothing for women and men including an impressive array of ties. You'll also find fashions at the **Oxford Shop**. The nearby **G. Thrapp Jewelers** manufactures beautiful designs in-house. Other shops include **Charles Mayer & Co.** gifts, **Reardon Tennis**, **Kids Ink** bookstore, **Kincaid & Sons** meat market, **Banura** for Middle Eastern food and the **Illinois Street Food Emporium** for sandwiches, salads and bakery items.

Pennsylvania and 49th Street Shops
Corner of Pennsylvania and 49th

Another small neighborhood shopping area, this little enclave is situated in the midst of the Meridian Kessler neighborhood. Here you'll find **Cafe Patachou**, a popular European-style coffee shop, **D&Z Gifts**, and **Essential Edibles Too**, a vegetarian carry-out cafe. Antiques lovers enjoy **Hope's Shop**, and just across the street is **Collections Antiques Etc.** with an eclectic array of fine antiques and furnishings. Neighborhood residents also patronize **Hamaker Pharmacy** and **Friendly Foods**.

Broad Ripple
Broad Ripple Ave. between College Ave. and Westfield Blvd.

You could easily spend a whole day — and evening — in this arty, eclectic neighborhood exploring its many shops, galleries and restaurants (see our Restaurants and Nightlife chapters too). The area is compact enough to explore on foot, though parking, available along the streets and in one lot, is at a premium. Finding a spot on a warm weekend night, when the neighborhood is full of people milling about the sidewalk cafes and walking from one nightspot to another, can be a real challenge. You'll have less trouble during the day, though the neighborhood is still a busy place.

Shops abound. Many are in older Victorian cottages, and the best way to find them is simply to wander the side streets. You'll discover unusual fragrances at **Moorman's Perfumes**, offbeat fashion designs at **Dinwiddie's**, useful art and home accessories at **The Bungalow**, cards and gifts at **Chelsea's**, and furniture from the 1920s through the '50s, as well as glass, pottery and accessories at **Blue Sun Gallery**. **Turandot** stocks unusual and artistic gifts and home accessories. **Artzy Phartzy** offers an array of clothes, art and offbeat gift items. **Artifacts** specializes in original art and gift items, and **Marigold** stocks unique women's apparel. **Protocol** also offers distinctive fashions, but check out its just-as-distinctive interior.

Many more shopping possibilities exist in and around Broad Ripple, including a number of resale boutiques and bookstores.

South Broad Ripple
College Ave. between 46th and 54th sts.

The SoBro area, situated along the Col-

lege Avenue corridor, features a number of interesting shops, most of which are clustered around intersections. In addition to several antiques shops, a branch of **Habig's Garden Shops** and **Modern Times** bookstore, the neighborhood boasts one of the city's best gourmet grocery stores, **Atlas Supermarket**, where Indianapolis native David Letterman worked as a bag boy. You'll find African-American books and gifts at **X-Pressions**, children's "gently worn" clothes at **Casey's Closet**, distinctive timepieces at **Clockworks**, used furniture and antiques at **Bluemingdeals** and **Barn Village Antiques** and delicious desserts at the **Broad Ripple Pie Company**, **Cath** and **Cornerstone** coffee and espresso bar.

Nora
86th St. between Meridian St. and Westfield Blvd.

Though Nora remains a residential area as well as a shopping district, it is also home to a considerable variety of specialty shops. In addition to grocery and discount store shopping, you'll find gift items at **Perry Luggage & Gifts**, **The Accent Shop** and **Killybegs** and original jewelry designs at **Aronstam**. Look for fashionable kidswear at **The Blue Bear** and **New Generation Kids**. Those with a green thumb will want to check out **Habig's Garden Shop** and its **Garden Cottage** expansion right across the street.

Keystone at the Crossing
Keystone at 86th St.

This popular north-side shopping district has grown in the last few years with a Fashion Mall expansion (see entry below under "Malls") and the development of specialty shops anchored by **Borders Books and Music**, a huge book/music/video/software emporium complete with its own coffee bar, **Cafe Espresso**.

Clearwater Shoppes and Clearwater Crossing
82nd St. and Dean Rd.

This area too has burgeoned in the last few years and now boasts quite a sizeable

FYI

Unless otherwise noted, the area code for all phone numbers in this guide is 317.

and varied selection of stores and restaurants. You'll find kids' clothes at **Chocolate Soup**, fine wines and spirits at **The Wine Gallery**, a **Barnes and Noble** bookstore complete with an espresso bar, **Leland's** fireplace accessories, **Expressions Custom Furniture**, **Houseworks** home decor and accessories and many more upscale retailers.

Castleton
82nd St. and Allisonville Rd.

By the early 1990s, what was once a small village had become the county's most intensively developed shopping district. Indeed, Castleton boasts nearly 20 shopping centers within just 2 square miles. You can find just about anything you want, including party supplies, sporting goods, computers, kidswear and just about everything in between. Though the many strip centers boast a multitude of small shops, some of the major area stores are **Graham's Crackers**, 5981 E. 86th Street, which stocks a huge inventory of collectibles and gifts, and the expansive **Kittle's Home Furnishings**, 8600 Allisonville Road, which boasts an **Ethan Allen** gallery and its in-house design studio. And in the midst of it all is Castleton Square Mall.

West 86th Street
Between Meridian St. and N. Michigan Rd.

Work your way west along this stretch of a very busy street where you'll find several popular strip malls, such as **North Willow Commons**, and such stores as **Courtyard Cottage**, which specializes in intimate apparel; **Mary V**, offering fine women's wear in larger sizes; **Arnold's Men's Store** for updated traditional clothing; **Collections 94** with its out-of-the-ordinary fashions; **Little Women and Company** for girls' special occasion dresses and even the tea parties to wear them to. And **Wells Flower & Gift House**, across from St. Vincent Hospital, offers browsers a great selection of gift items. The area also boasts plenty of specialty dining spots (see our Restaurants chapter for more info).

Zionsville
Northwest of Indianapolis off N. Michigan Rd.

This charming village, with its bricked Main Street, distinctive boutiques, restaurants and specialty shops, provides a good day's worth of shopping. Like Broad Ripple, which was itself once a separate village, Zionsville is compact enough to explore on foot. Here you'll find a number of antiques shops (see our "Antiques" section in this chapter), as well as **Potpourri**, **Stacy LaBolts**, **Lilly's Boutique Gallery** and the **Children's Clothier** for fine apparel; and the **Tin Soldier**, the **Gift Horse** and the **General Store** for unusual gift items and home accessories. Other specialty stores include **Avalon Jewelers**, the **Village Clock** shop, **Ironwood** book shop, **My Mother's Doll Shop** and the **Rug Gallery**. Refer to our Restaurants chapter for the scoop on Zionsville's many excellent eateries.

Malls

The Greater Indianapolis area boasts malls on all sides of town; all are easily worth a morning or afternoon of browsing. You'll find major department stores, specialty shops, theaters and plenty of dining options, from sit-down restaurants to grab-a-sandwich food courts.

Circle Centre
49 W. Maryland St. • 681-8000

Downtown became a shopping destination once again with the opening of Circle Centre in September 1995 (see the Closeup in this chapter). Integrated with the historic buildings of downtown are **Nordstrom** and **Parisian** department stores and loads of interesting shops, such as **FAO Schwartz** for toys, the **Warner Bros.** store for Looney Tunes-inspired gifts and clothes and **Godiva Chocolatier** for delicious treats. You'll also find a United Artists theater, nightclubs and terrific restaurants, including the popular **California Cafe** and **Palomino** (see our Restaurants chapter for more on Circle Centre dining).

Castleton Square
82nd St. and Allisonville Rd. • 849-9993

Near one of the city's busiest intersections, Castleton Square Mall remains a very popular shopping destination. Anchored by a new **L.S. Ayres**, as well as **Lazarus**, **JCPenney**, **Sears** and **Montgomery Ward**, the mall also offers a dozen shops unique to the city. Serious browsers can relax with a cup of coffee from **Barnie's** or enjoy an above-it-all view at **Lazarus' Top of the Mall** restaurant, where window-side tables overlook the mall below. Or take in a movie; Castleton's cinema is known for its highbrow and offbeat flicks. The area around the mall along 82nd Street abounds with strip centers; nearby you'll find everything from natural foods to doughnuts, from computer gear to sporting goods.

Eastgate Consumer Mall
7150 E. Washington St. • 352-0951

This east-side bargain-hunter's dream offers plenty of off-price possibilities, though few of the traditional mall extras such as fountains and fancy food courts. Here you'll find **Burlington Coat Factory**, which in addition to coats stocks good quality menswear, dresses, kids' clothes and even baby furniture.

The Fashion Mall
Keystone Ave. and 86th St.

Anyone looking for the unusual, the designer name and the out of the ordinary has to hit the Fashion Mall. Anchored by **Jacobson's**, which offers a Chanel boutique, and Parisian, the mall's two upscale department stores are linked by loads of small and not-so-small shops specializing in designer labels, distinctive accessories and other pricey items. You'll find such national names as **Banana Republic**, **Eddie Bauer**, **Abercrombie & Fitch**, **Crabtree & Evelyn** and **The Sharper Image**. Local retailers such as **The Mole Hole** feature fine gift items, while **M.G. Tates** stocks great kitchen gadgets and home accessories. **Kits & Kaboodle** features unique, collectible and educational toys. The mall offers food court dining as well as the always-popular **Dalt's** and **TGI Friday's**, both excellent lunch spots (though you may have to wait for a table). The adjacent Radisson Plaza Hotel also offers fine dining at **Waterson's** and a more casual atmosphere at the **Keystone Cafe**. Keystone at the Crossing (where Keystone crosses 86th Street), as

the area is called, boasts several other fine restaurants and a new shopping area.

Keystone Square
116th St. and Keystone Ave. • 848-6889

North on Keystone Avenue, where Indianapolis merges into Carmel, you'll find this compact mall that includes women's fashions at **Plotner's Style Shop**, retro sports-related items at **Johnny's Sports Nostalgia** and good-condition used sporting goods at **Play It Again Sports**. The mall also includes a Target discount store.

Glendale Center
6101 N. Keystone Ave. • 251-9281

One of the city's oldest enclosed malls, Glendale is anchored by **L.S. Ayres** and **Lazarus** and is home to 100 specialty shops. Stores include **This End Up** furniture, **Lechter's** housewares, **African Art and More** and **Watercolor Indiana**. There are also plenty of specialty clothiers. The mall houses longtime favorite **Swensen's** ice cream and sandwiches. You can also catch a first-run flick or a bargain movie, and the unique shops and nightlife of Broad Ripple are nearby.

Greenwood Park Mall
1251 U.S. Hwy. 31 N., Greenwood
• 881-6758

This south-side mega-mall has it all: movies, plenty of specialty shops, restaurants and such major department stores as **L.S. Ayres**, **Lazarus**, **JCPenney**, **Sears** and **Montgomery Ward**. Billed as the state's largest mall (though Fort Wayne's Glenbrook Square also claims the title), this is where TV stations go to shoot videotape of the holiday shopping crush. The massive parking lots really do fill up; just try to find a space the weekend after Thanksgiving. But for an all-day mall extravaganza, you can't beat it. And the whole mall area offers one strip center after another providing even more possibilities.

Lafayette Square
38th St. and Lafayette Rd. • 291-6390

West-side shopping focuses on Lafayette Square, where nearly 100 stores, including **L.S. Ayres**, **Sears**, **Lazarus**, **JCPenney** and **Mont-**

gomery Ward, offer buyers a wide variety of shopping options. In addition to the standard mall theater and specialty shops, you'll even find G.C. Murphy's, a traditional dime store complete with a lunch counter and deliciously sticky caramel corn. The immediate area, along both Lafayette Road and W. 38th Street, provides plenty of strip center shopping; you'll find shops specializing in fabric, menswear, ceramic tile, garden supplies and more.

Washington Square
10202 E. Washington St. • 899-4567

Especially popular among eastsiders and those who live in nearby Hancock and Shelby counties, Washington Square provides shoppers with 120 stores, including the major anchors of L.S. Ayres, Lazarus, Sears, Montgomery Ward and JCPenney. You'll find housewares, gift shops, specialty clothiers, shoe stores, movies and plenty of fast food options. E. Washington Street offers an abundance of shopping; you could spend a day working your way east, stopping at huge furniture stores, small dress shops, discount dens and other emporia.

Antiques

Read on, and you'll soon see that Greater Indianapolis has plenty to offer any antiques buff.

There's also the renowned 35-mile stretch of U.S. 40 extending east from Knightstown to Richmond that might just be heaven on earth. Known as Antique Alley, this highway stretch provides access to some 700 antique dealers. If you're in the mood for a drive, you won't want to miss it.

Indianapolis

Antique Barn Village/ Barn Village Antiques
5209 N. College Ave. • 283-5011

In the area where Broad Ripple meets Meridian Kessler (called "SoBro" for South Broad Ripple), this shop buys and sells a little bit of everything, including furniture, clocks, dolls, signs, music boxes, antique toys, art deco radios, pottery, patio furniture, paintings, rugs and statuary. It's a browser's paradise that's open seven days a week.

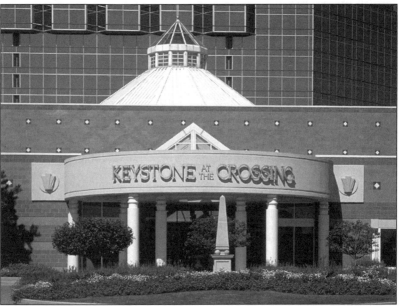

Photo: Jeff Hauersperger

One of the nicest places to shop on the city's north side is Keystone at the Crossing.

The Antique Centre
3422 N. Shadeland Ave. • 545-3879

With 75 showcases of collectibles and 10,000 square feet of furniture and accessories, it's easy to see why this place bills itself as "the place to start your treasure hunt." You'll also find American Indian artifacts and antiquarian books. It's open Tuesday through Sunday.

Antiques N More
3440 N. Shadeland Ave. • 542-8526

From sterling flatware to oak and mahogany armoires, tables and more, this place sells it — and buys it, including entire estates. It's open seven days a week.

Blue Sun Gallery
922 E. Westfield Blvd. • 255-8441

This Broad Ripple area shop carries furniture from the 1920s to the 1950s as well as glassware and pottery. It's open Tuesday through Saturday and is closed Sunday and Monday.

Collections Antiques, Etc.
113 E. 49th St. • 283-5251

With a focus on 19th-century European furnishings and accessories, Collections is an upscale shop in the heart of the Meridian Kessler neighborhood. It's open Monday through Saturday and is closed on Sunday.

Colonial Antiques
5000 W. 96th St. • 873-2727

Specializing in architectural antiques (fireplace mantles, doors, windows, pillars, etc.) this northwest-side shop also buys and sells a variety of other items. It's open Friday and Saturday, noon to 5 PM and Monday through Thursday by chance or appointment.

Earl's Auction Company
5199 Lafayette Rd. • 291-5843

You'll find antique furniture, firearms, tools and a live auction every Tuesday. It's open for inspection of goods Monday through Saturday; the auction is Tuesday at 4 PM.

Finds Antiques
1764 E. 86th St. • 571-1950

This shop in the Northview Mall caters to an upscale crowd. Here you'll find period furniture, porcelains, lamps, Oriental rugs and decorative accessories. If you've got something to sell or something you're curious about, Finds offers professional appraisals. It's open Tuesday through Saturday and is closed Sunday and Monday.

Fountain Square Antique Mall
1056 Virginia Ave. • 636-1056

With more than 70 dealers, this is the largest two-story antiques mall in the city. Looking for an old oak hutch? An antique watch? A tin milk box? Look here. It's open seven days a week.

Hope's Shop
116 E. 49th St. • 283-3004

Specializing in glass, china, kitchenware and dolls, this small Meridian Kessler shop also offers expert appraisals. It's open Tuesday through Saturday; it's closed Sunday and Monday.

In Praise of the Porch
1764 E. 86th St. • 571-1950, 675-9485

Across the street from North Central High School, this shop deals in antique wicker furniture and accessories. It's open Tuesday through Saturday and is closed Sunday and Monday.

Indianapolis Downtown Antique Mall
1066 Virginia Ave. • 635-5336

In the historic Fountain Square district (c. 1870, the oldest continually functioning commercial district in Indiana), this mall consists of 40 shops on two floors. Here you'll find everything from Depression glassware and American art pottery to furniture, quilts and Hummel figurines. It's open seven days a week.

Quality Antiques
1105 Shelby St. • 686-6018

This store in the Fountain Square Theatre Building specializes in lamps, furniture and barware from the '50s. You'll also find deco-era items and primitives, as well as other collectibles and rare oddities. It's open seven days a week. If shopping makes you hungry, right next door you'll find the **Fountain Diner**, an authentic 1959 diner.

Recollections
5202 N. College Ave. • 283-3800

From antique toys and musical instruments to hand tools and costume jewelry, this shop's got it. It's open Monday through Saturday and is closed Sunday.

Red Rose Vintage Clothing
834 E. 64th St. • 257-5016

There's used clothing and there's vintage clothing — this Broad Ripple shop buys and sells the latter. This is where to go if you're in need of a genuine flapper dress or 1940s suit. It's open Monday through Saturday and is closed Sunday.

Shadeland Antique Mall
3444 N. Shadeland Ave. • 542-7283

The oldest and largest antiques mall in the city, this east-side facility contains 99 dealers who buy and sell a range of antique items, including furniture, musical instruments, radios, toys, books, sheet music, lamps, china, glassware, rugs, jewelry, etc. It's open seven days a week.

Solomon-Jones
2850 N. Meridian St. • 926-5555

Offering antiques, traditional interior design assistance and appraisal service, Solomon-Jones focuses on an upscale clientele. It's open Monday through Saturday and is closed Sunday.

Trash to Treasures
5505 N. Keystone Ave. • 253-2235

Operated by longtime Indianapolis antiques dealer Virginia Lucas, this shop is a stockpile of both stuff and knowledge. Whether you're looking for a table, a lamp or someone who knows antiques, this place is worth a trip. It's open Thursday through Saturday.

Downtown Goes Uptown with Circle Centre

Wow! That's the reaction many people have the first time they see Circle Centre. And who can blame them? This 800,000-square-foot, four-level shopping and entertainment complex in the heart of downtown Indianapolis, which opened for business on September 8, 1995, is no run-of-the-mill mall.

In addition to including the only Nordstrom department store in Indiana, Circle Centre includes an array of other upscale retailers — the city's second **Parisian** department store (the other is at the Fashion Mall on the north side), an **FAO Schwartz** toy store, **The Museum Company**, **Doubleday Book Shops**, **The Body Shop**, **Guess Home Collection** and **Kitchen Express**. It also includes a variety of restaurants and nightclubs as well as a United Artists cineplex with nine theaters and a virtual reality arcade.

In all, there are nearly 100 Circle Centre tenants, making it the retail/entertainment complex that city planners long envisioned as an essential component of downtown revitalization. Its construction capped a two-decade-long effort to once again make downtown Indianapolis an inviting place for residents and visitors.

With other components already in place (sports and performing arts venues, hotels, a convention center, a zoo, museums and housing), what was needed to round out downtown redevelopment was a project that would revitalize the once-bustling shopping district.

As in other cities around the country, most of Indianapolis's major retailers had abandoned the downtown area for suburban shopping malls. The stores that remained (a handful of clothing and shoe stores, some jewelers, a few newsstands and book shops) survived due to patronage by downtown office workers.

But on evenings and weekends, no one shopped downtown.

Yet as the convention business boomed, and as sports venues sprouted, people began coming downtown on Saturday and Sunday afternoons. And civic leaders took a look at what was missing: a place for all these people with time on their hands and money in their pockets to go either before or after their events. Why not send them shopping?

That was the genesis for one of the largest construction projects in Indiana's history. Circle Centre was conceived and constructed to lure shoppers — including out-of-town conventioneers and area residents — to the downtown district.

With a $310 million price tag, the project was developed by a joint public-private partnership between the City of Indianapolis and Circle Centre Development Company, which is itself a partnership between real estate development and management company Simon Property Group Inc. and 19 corporate investors. According to the International Council of Shopping Centers, a corporate collaboration of this magnitude was unprecedented in retail development.

Designed by the New York firm Ehrenkrantz & Eckstut Architects, Circle Centre's architecture combines the facades from eight older buildings with new construction to achieve a graceful, elegant appearance that's both comfortable and contemporary. Inside, arched skylights running the length of the mall allow natural light in, and storefronts run the gamut from elegantly understated (**Coach**, **Ann Taylor**) to unexpectedly funky (**Junkyard**, a unisex clothing store). The overall effect is urban and urbane — at once cosmopolitan, metropolitan and fun.

The Stores

The largest of the mall's tenants, and one of its two anchor stores, is **Nordstrom**, which is housed in a 28,000-square-foot facility. Famous for customer service (there's an in-store concierge), the Seattle-based department store carries very high quality merchandise, including more than 150,000 pairs of shoes (including hard-to-find sizes) in five shoe departments as well as 35 specialty departments offering designer clothing and accessories for men, women and children. Elegant is the operative word at Nordstrom.

Parisian, a Georgia-based department store chain, is the second anchor. It covers 145,000 square feet and specializes in fine-quality clothing, shoes and accessories for men, women and children. One innovative touch for restless kids is an in-store jungle gym, while for harried adults the store offers personal shopping services. Like Nordstrom, Parisian prides itself on customer service.

In addition to the anchors, Circle Centre contains stores that cater to a wide variety of needs and desires. At **Abercrombie & Fitch Co.** you'll find rug-

Photo: Frank Espich

Here's a wide-angle shot of the main concourse at Circle Centre taken from the north end of the fourth level looking south.

ged, contemporary sportswear for men and women, while at **Banana Republic** the clothes for both sexes are classic and comfortable. For women, there's **Everything But Water** that sells swimwear; in a somewhat drier mode, there's **Bebe**, which offers a private collection of business and casual clothes.

Men can drop by **Structure**, which sells European-design sportswear, or **Britches Great Outdoors**, home of both casual and business clothes. For kids, the mall offers **Baby Guess?** and **Guess? Kids** as well as **Gap Kids**.

If you've got a hankering for chocolate, there's **Godiva Chocolatier**, where you'll find more than 70 types of freshly made candies. Or if you prefer smelling sweet things to eating them, try **The Body Shop** or **Garden Botanika**, both of which deal in natural hair and body products.

If it's art you're after, take a peek inside **Niang African Art and More**. Also, stop by **Papyrus** for handmade greeting cards, imported gift wrap and collector-quality fountain pens.

If you're an avid reader (you're reading this, right?), the **Doubleday Books Shops** offer more than 17,000 fiction, travel, cooking, lifestyle and children's books, while at **Sam Goody** you'll find more than 35,000 CDs and cassettes as well as videotapes, laserdisks and computer software.

In other words, there's something for everyone at Circle Centre.

Parking

Realizing that the success of Circle Centre would in part depend on overcoming Central Indiana residents' reluctance to venture downtown where parking could sometimes be a problem, mall developers included underground parking garages in its design. Well-lit and well-marked with icons to help you find your car again once you've finished shopping, Circle Centre's garages contain 2,700 spaces. For maximum safety, the garages are patrolled regularly by a private security company. The cost for up to three hours of parking is $1.

Hours

Circle Centre is open Monday to Saturday, 10 AM to 9 PM, and Sunday, noon to 6 PM. Individual tenants, notably restaurants, nightclubs and movie theaters, are open on different schedules.

Boone County

Brown's Antique Shop
315 N. Fifth St., Zionsville • 873-2284

Established in 1945, Brown's consists of three buildings filled with furniture. It's open seven days a week.

The Sow's Ear
76 S. Main St., Zionsville • 873-2785

Specializing in Hummel figurines, Lalique glassware, music boxes, slot machines and art glass, this shop is open Monday through Saturday.

Hamilton County

Acorn Farm Antiques
15466 Oak Rd., Carmel • 846-2383

This shop in a 10-room Colonial house is home to a variety of quality items, including furniture, brass, silver, copper, glass, china and paintings. It's open Tuesday through Saturday.

Antique Emporium
1055 S. Range Line Rd. • 844-8351

Here you'll find fine quality furniture from country casual to formal as well as handmade

Oriental rugs and accessories. It's open Tuesday through Saturday.

Antiques Galore & More
110 E. Main St., Westfield • 867-1228
When you're looking for Victorian furniture, art glass, art pottery and Indiana art, stop by this place that specializes in the unique and unusual. It's open Wednesday through Saturday and by appointment.

The Antique Mall of Carmel
622 S. Range Line Rd., Carmel • 848-1280
This mall features 30 booths of quality antiques and collectibles. It's open seven days a week.

Antiques & Stuff
18386 Moontown Rd., Noblesville • 896-3416
Whether you're in the mood for an old steamer trunk, a ceramic water jug or a rolltop desk, this shop is worth a stop. Even though it's a bit off the beaten path, it's worth the trek to find out what owner Judy Williams has on hand. It's open evenings and weekends.

R. Beauchamp Antiques
16405 Westfield Blvd., Westfield • 896-3717
With more than 16,000 square feet of American and European antique furnishings, Oriental rugs and accessories, this shop claims to have one of the largest selections of goods in the Midwest. It's open Tuesday through Saturday.

Bound to Be Found Antiques
74 N. Ninth St., Noblesville • 776-1993
With stock that runs the gamut from old toys and advertising ephemera to military items and primitives, this place on the east-side of Noblesville's square is bound to be found by serious antiquers.

The Collector's Door
44 S. Eighth St., Noblesville • 773-4777
A man's antiques shop, this place stocks tools and nautical instruments as well as sports- and travel-related antiques. It's open Monday through Friday.

Lazy Acres Antiques
77 Metsker Ln., Noblesville • 773-7387
Inside a c. 1872 barn and carriage house, this shop specializes in American, primitive and folk art. It's open seven days a week.

Noblesville Antique Mall
20 N. Ninth St., Noblesville • 773-5095
Within the walls of this restored 1880s building are three floors of furniture, glassware, art, jewelry and antiquarian books. It's open seven days a week.

Strawtown Pottery & Antiques
12738 Strawtown Ave., Noblesville • 984-5080
Offering a selection of quality antique furniture, handmade pottery and Native American artifacts, this shop is open Tuesday through Saturday.

Union Street Antiques/The Jonathon Westfield Company
120 N. Union St., Westfield • 896-3566
From Windsor chairs and tin lighting to folk art and handmade furniture, you're apt to find it here. It's open Monday through Saturday.

Hendricks County

Gilley's Antique Mall
1209 W. Main St., Plainfield • 839-8779
This mall, which consists of two buildings and more than 250 booths, is open seven days a week. During the summer, Gilley's also hosts weekend flea markets.

Specialty Stores
Book Nooks
At Insiders' Guides we have a penchant for bookstores, and in a city like Indianapolis, with a wide variety of top-notch offerings, we couldn't help sharing our favorites with you. For information about the city's vibrant literary life, please see our Literary Life chapter.

City Market is a favorite place for workers and shoppers to meet for lunch.

General Interest Bookstores

B. Dalton Bookseller

Castleton Square • 849-6240
Glendale Square • 257-1373
Washington Square • 899-4150
Greenwood Park Mall • 888-4436

One of the original chains, B. Dalton has downsized many of its stores in recent years. Still, the local outlets regularly stock some 25,000 titles, including a good selection of computer books. There are also in-store newsstands that carry a selection of mainstream magazines and newspapers. B. Dalton stores are open seven days a week.

Barnes & Noble Bookstore

3748 E. 82nd St. • 594-7525

This store in the Clearwater Crossing complex contains thousands (it claims more than 100,000) of new and backlist books as well as a large remainder section. The magazine racks are jammed with a huge assortment of popular and offbeat publications. Buy a couple and plop down at a table in the in-store coffee shop, order a cappuccino and relax.

Barnes & Noble also hosts a number of book discussion groups (see entry in the "Reading Groups" section of The Literary Life chapter), book signings and other writer-related events. Call or drop by for more information.

Barnes & Noble is open seven days a week.

Bookland

137 W. Market St. • 639-9864

This small store just east of the State Capitol building carries one of the largest stocks of newspapers and magazines in Indiana along with an array of paperback books. It's open seven days a week, 6 AM to 7 PM.

Borders Book Shop

5612 Castleton Corner Ln. • 849-8660

For several years, this has been the place serious readers go. With more than 125,000 titles in stock and a well-informed and well-read staff, it's the store all the others in town have to compete with. It's a reader-friendly place, with chairs, benches and couches scattered throughout the store to encourage book browsing and conversation.

It, too, has an extensive selection of magazines and newspapers, including a special section just for literary publications. Border's hosts a variety of public events, including book signings, readings and reading groups (see entry in the "Reading Groups" section of The Literary Life chapter).

Borders is open seven days a week.

Borders Books and Music
8675 River Crossing Blvd. • 574-1776

This is the new kid in town, having opened for business in September 1995. In nearly 33,000 square feet of space, it contains not only 100,000-plus books, but also more than 50,000 music selections, more than 8,000 videotapes and some 2,000 CD-ROMs and floppy disks. It also contains an in-store espresso bar, Cafe Espresso, which serves a Borders blend of coffee (strong enough to keep you awake so you can read one more chapter!). Like it's older, well-established predecessor (see previous entry), this Borders hosts readings, book signings and other literary activities. It's open seven days a week.

Chapters Bookshop
8660 Purdue Rd. • 872-2665

While not as large as Barnes & Noble or Borders, this locally owned northwest-side store has a reputation as a place where a staff that knows about books takes good care of customers who care about books. What it lacks in size, Chapters tries to make up for in service and attractions. Though small, it manages to snare its share of writers on book tours, hosting several book signings every year. Chapters is open seven days a week.

Coopersmith's
The Fashion Mall, Keystone Crossing • 574-9718

An upscale bookstore in an upscale mall setting, Coopersmith's is a comfortable place to browse the latest releases and bestsellers. It is open seven days a week.

Doubleday Book Shops
Circle Centre, 39 W. Maryland St. • 632-4910

With 17,000 titles lining the shelves in a home-library type of setting, this store in Circle Centre caters to an upscale crowd. There are special sections devoted to fiction, cooking, travel, lifestyles, art and children's books. Armchairs encourage you to relax and peruse books, while free gift wrapping makes giving a book as a present an easy decision. It's open seven days a week.

Indiana News Co. Inc.
14 W. Maryland St. • 636-7680

In a funky old building across the street from Circle Centre, Indiana News carries a huge selection of out-of-town and foreign newspapers and magazines, sports publications, racing forms and paperbacks. It's open seven days a week from 6 AM to 6 PM.

Waldenbooks
Castleton Square • 849-2175
Washington Square • 898-5537
Greenwood Park Mall • 882-0270
1430 S. Range Line Rd., Carmel • 575-0062

A longtime rival of B. Dalton, Waldenbooks has also undergone some downsizing in the past few years. Still, the local outlets remain viable sources for recently published fiction and nonfiction titles as well as for mainstream magazines and newspapers. Hours vary according to location.

Specialty Bookstores

Architectural Center Bookstore
47 S. Pennsylvania St. • 634-3871

For books on architecture, interior and graphic design, restoration and repair, landscaping and related subjects, this small shop is a gold mine. It's open Monday through Friday, 11 AM to 4 PM.

Downtown Comics
111 N. Pennsylvania St. • 237-0397
5767 E. 86th St. • 845-9991

Both locations carry new and collector comics, graphic novels, role playing games and trading cards. Hours vary by location.

Dreams & Swords Bookstore
6503 Ferguson St. • 253-9966

This "feminist family bookstore" in Broad Ripple is a good source of books on women's social, political and sexual issues.

Kids Ink Children's Bookstore
5619 N. Illinois St. • 255-2598

A real success story, local-style, Kids Ink is one of the Midwest's most respected children's book retailers due to the efforts of owner and founder Shirley Mullin. It's also a real find for aspiring authors of children's or young adults' books. In addition to selling such books, Kids Ink also hosts book signings and helps coordinate Butler University's annual children's literature conference (see the "Literary Events" section of The Literary Life chapter).

Pasitu Enterprise
309 W. 42nd St. • 927-9297

This small shop specializes in Islamic and African-American literature.

X-Pression
5912 N. College Ave. • 257-5448

This shop specializes in ethnic books and gifts. It's also a great place to meet African-American writers on book tours.

Religious Bookstores

Abba Christian Bookstore
3330 N. Emerson Ave. • 546-4406

This small store specializes in African-American art and history, theology and used/rare books.

Agape Bookstore
2131 Mitthoeffer Rd. • 894-1110

This east-side shop carries Christian books, music, cards, and gifts.

Berean Christian Store
8811 Hardegan St. • 888-0682

This County Line Mall store stocks Christian books, Bibles, music, videos and Sunday School supplies.

Family Bookstore
10202 E. Washington St. • 897-9908

In Washington Square between JCPenney

Photo: Randy Baughn

A gorgeous interior greets shoppers to the Fashion Mall.

and L.S. Ayres, this shop stocks a variety of Christian books, music, gifts, Bibles and church supplies.

Herald Discount Christian Bookstore
7850 E. 96th St. • 842-8942
For 10 percent to 50 percent off religious books, Bibles, music and cards, this is the place to shop.

John 3-16 Christian Store
1056 Broad Ripple Ave. • 253-9114
Here you'll find Bibles, books, music, cards and gifts.

Krieg Brothers Catholic Supply House
119 S. Meridian St. • 638-3416
A downtown institution for years, Krieg Brothers specializes in religious books as well as in a variety of Catholic supplies.

Light & Life Bookstore
5062 Pike Plaza Rd. • 293-9922
From books and Bibles to robes and church supplies, this northwest-side store carries a wide assortment of religious items.

Romar Christian Book Store
7767 U.S. 31 S. • 882-3006
5458 E. 82nd St. • 842-5115
Both Romar sites stock books, music, cards, Bibles and church supplies.

Unity Bookstore
907 N. Delaware St. • 635-4066
This downtown shop is a good source of metaphysical, New Age and self-help books and tapes.

Used and Rare Books

All-About Books
5136 N. Keystone Ave. • 475-1869
This shop buys and sells rare, used and collectible books.

Blue River Books
6219 Guilford Ave. • 254-3031
A wonderful Broad Ripple place, Blue River

specializes in Indiana history, modern first editions, military history, Americana and biography. In addition to books, the shop also deals in historical prints and ephemera.

The Book Rack
8013 E. Washington St. • 897-2173
6144 W. 25th St. • 297-8968
3780 S. East St. • 783-2473
County Line Mall, Greenwood • 881-3010
These shops buy, sell and trade used paperbacks.

Book Shop — Barely Used Books
616 Station Dr., Carmel • 843-1855
This store in the Target Mall deals in both hardcover and paperback as well as used records.

Book World, Inc.
5620 Crawfordsville Rd.
• 241-4000
7775 E. Washington St. • 359-0099
Both Book World locations buy, sell and trade used paperbacks and comic books.

Broad Ripple Bookshop
6407 Ferguson St. • 259-1980
When you visit Broad Ripple Bookshop, you'll enter an old house stacked high with wonderful texts — a book lover's paradise. This shop deals in old, rare and out-of-print books in such subject areas as Indiana, Civil War, Americana and art. You'll also find children's books and modern first editions.

Fountain of Mystery Books
1119 Prospect St. • 635-2583
This is a good source for mysteries, true crime and science fiction.

Half-Price Books
8316 Castleton Corner Dr. • 577-0410
1551 W. 86th St. • 824-9002
844 N. U.S. 31, Greenwood • 889-1076
Local outlets of this national used book chain, these three stores buy and sell books, magazines, CDs, LPs and audio and video tapes.

Old Library Book Shop
6219 Guilford Ave. • 254-3031
Actually housed in the former site of the

Broad Ripple Library (it's now a few blocks east in Broad Ripple Park), this shop is actually a used book cooperative of some 20 dealers. Here you'll find art books, children's books, American literature and general interest books. It's open Monday through Saturday, 11 AM to 6 PM.

Gourmet Groceries

Looking for hoisin sauce, tahini, Stilton or an exotic spice for your favorite recipe? You're sure to find them at one of these specialty food stores. (But don't forget the major chains. You'll find a good selection of specialty items at **Cub**, **Marsh** and **Kroger**: All have locations around town.)

A-1 Oriental Supermarket
3709 N. Shadeland Ave. • 546-5252

This specialty grocery, one of the state's largest, stocks foods items from China, Japan, Korea, the Philippines, Thailand and Latin America. It's fun to just browse, and kids enjoy checking out the unusual candies and treats. But if you need any sort of Asian specialty item, this is the place to go.

Atlas Supermarket
5411 N. College Ave. • 255-6800

This full-service grocery, where David Letterman worked as a bagboy, stocks the usual stuff in addition to a wide variety of specialty ingredients and gourmet and imported foods. You'll find shoppers crowding through the narrow aisles and clustered around the popular deli counter.

The Cheese Shop
8702 Keystone Crossing • 846-6885

Check out the Cheese Shop in the Fashion Mall for a variety of fancy imported foods and gourmet take-out in addition to the specialty cheeses.

Corner Gourmet
3832 E. 82nd St. • 598-0621

This Clearwater Crossing shop offers enough goodies for any gift basket. Stock up on coffees, dips, mixes, oils, jams and jellies as well as cool gadgets and tableware.

Gourmet Emporium
1450 W. 86th St. • 879-8995

This shop, situated among the many strip malls along W. 86th Street, features fine wines, imported meats and cheeses and top-notch cookware and accessories.

Kahn's Fine Wines and Spirits
5369 N. Keystone Ave. • 251-9463

This well-regarded shop sells a wide variety of wines, and the knowledgeable staff will be happy to help you find what you're looking for or maybe steer you to something new. The shop now stocks gourmet foods.

Marsh
Locations all over town, Corporate Offices: 9800 Crosspoint Blvd. • 594-2100

You'll find these expansive well-stocked stores all across the city. They boast excellent bakeries and delis. Don't pass them up when you're looking for specialty ingredients.

Meijer
1425 W. Carmel Dr. • 573-8300
72 N. Ind. 135 • 885-3000
5349 Pike Plaza • 387-2400
11351 E. Washington St. • 894-6700

Though not really what we call gourmet, Meijer gains inclusion here due to its unique grocery/department store stock (shoes, clothes, toys, hardware and household goods in addition to grocery and fresh produce) and its 24-hour-a-day schedule.

Nuts Plus
4217 Lafayette Rd. • 299-4628
11554 Westfield Blvd. • 575-8952

Here you'll find an assortment of imported foods and spices from India, Pakistan and the Middle East.

O'Malia's Food Market
General Office: 867 W. Carmel Dr. • 573-8088

These full-line upscale groceries stock

plenty of specialty foods amid very pleasant surroundings of carpeted floors, attractive decor. Check out the baked goods and meat counters. Though primarily on the north side, O'Malia's maintains a store, complete with a cooking school kitchen, in downtown's Lockerbie neighborhood.

Sakura Mart
2450 E. 71st St. • 254-9598

This offshoot of the popular Sakura Japanese Restaurant sells an array of imported Asian ingredients as well as fresh seafood and sushi-to-go.

Jewelers

Hofmeister Personal Jewelers
3809 E. 82nd St. • 577-7070

In this lovely Lake Clearwater building, you'll find a small staff of professionals, including five full-time goldsmiths, dedicated to customer service. Hofmeister, a family business, offers everything from simple engagement rings to lavish custom designs. Manufacturing of the firm's award-winning designs is done in-house. It's also an official Rolex dealer.

Reis-Nichols Jewelers
47 S. Pennsylvania St. • 635-4467

This family-owned business stresses personal service and designs and manufacturers its award-winning designs at its downtown facility. It also handles Masonic, emblematic and award jewelry and employs a certified Rolex watchmaker.

Outdoors and Recreation

Gaylan's
Castleton Corner Shopping Center, Allisonville Rd. and 86th St. • 842-9606

Galyan's sporting goods supermarkets, with several locations in the metropolitan area,

stock just about anything you'd need for just about any sport. The north-side location even includes a wall to simulate rock-climbing and the instruction to learn to do it.

Outdoor Ventures
73 E. Epler Ave. • 784-1255

Stocking new and used military surplus, camping, caving and rapelling gear, this shop also offers training classes and adventure trips.

Play It Again Sports
2110 Broad Ripple Ave. • 257-0036

These shops at several locations in the metropolitan area buy and sell new and used sporting goods. You can often get good deals on secondhand equipment, stuff used a few times before its former owner decided that perhaps rock climbing was a bit too strenuous.

Sitzmark
930 S. Range Line Rd. • 844-8222

Known primarily as a ski outfitter, Sitzmark also carries backpacking, hiking, rock climbing and in-line skating gear.

Don's Guns
96th St. and Keystone Ave. • 574-0800

You'll see Don Davis' cheesy ads on late-night TV hyping his shops that sell an array of firearms as well as hunting and fishing supplies at several locations. The stores also boast indoor shooting ranges.

FlyMasters
8232 Allisonville Rd. • 570-9811

The city's only store specializing in fly fishing offers a course to introduce novices to the sport.

Visitors — and even longtime residents — may be surprised at the variety of sights to see in the Indianapolis area.

Attractions

Attractions in Indianapolis boast a certain historic flair, and visitors and newcomers remark upon the city's many monuments, statues and historical markers. We like to commemorate people and events around here. Scattered throughout downtown you'll find statues immortalizing the likes of President Benjamin Harrison and the young Abe Lincoln, as well as such sculpture as "Jammin' on the Avenue," a free-form collage of musical instruments in the Lockefield Gardens area. And, of course, Miss Indiana herself, the statue named "Victory" that tops the Soldiers and Sailors Monument. You get a great sense of history by walking up to some of these monuments, touching them, reading the inscriptions and getting a feel for what earlier residents thought was important enough to immortalize. Most of our museums also offer a historical perspective, though you can find plenty of modern galleries as well (see our Arts chapter).

Indianapolis features numerous examples of historic architecture; indeed, a stroll through downtown is a veritable walking tour. Use the following descriptions as a guide, and pick up a map from the City Center, 201 S. Capitol Avenue (see its listing below). Those who prefer to tour in style can take a horse-drawn carriage; many drivers can tailor a tour to suit your interests. You'll see these hansom cabs all over downtown on weekends and can almost always find them waiting along downtown streets, especially on the weekends.

While we've tried to highlight our major attractions in this chapter, you'll also find some listed elsewhere in this book. The Children's Museum, for example, certainly ranks as one of the city's top draws, but for a detailed discussion of its many wonders, see our Kidstuff chapter. Ditto for the Indianapolis Zoo and Conner Prairie. And don't forget to check our Sports chapter for a look at some of the venues that earned Indianapolis its "amateur sports capital" label.

Visitors — and even longtime residents — may be surprised at the variety of sights to see in the Indianapolis area. From Rembrandts to railroads, local museums offer something for every interest. Some, such as the Eiteljorg, the Indiana State Museum and the National Art Museum of Sport, lie within walking distance of downtown, but most others, including the Indianapolis Museum of Art and The Children's Museum, require at least a short drive. Our notable monuments, historic sights and architectural attractions however, clustered as they are in the downtown area, can be easily toured on foot, if you have plenty of time and some comfortable shoes. A few exceptions, including Crown Hill Cemetery and historic North Meridian Street, require transportation for more comfortable sightseeing.

What follows is a guide to the museums, monuments and historic sights that make Indianapolis something to see.

General Attractions

Indianapolis City Center
201 S. Capitol Ave. • 237-5200

Any sightseeing should really begin at the Indianapolis City Center.

Need some help getting the lay of the land? Take a look at the 13-by-13-foot model of downtown. Touch a button, and local landmarks light up, allowing you to see just how far Circle Centre is from Monument Circle (not far at all — an easy walk) or from Indiana Avenue (a healthy hike). The place offers plenty of souvenirs as well, including the requisite selection of mugs, T-shirts and tote bags. You could easily fill one of those bags with brochures; the City Center offers more than 300 highlighting local and statewide attractions.

Circle Centre
49 W. Maryland St. • 681-8000

This beautifully designed downtown mall incorporates both historic architecture and modern design. The 800,000-square-foot collection of department stores, specialty shops, restaurants and night clubs — even a movie theater — provides plenty of entertainment options right in the midst of other downtown attractions.

Indianapolis/Marion County Public Library
40 E. St. Clair St. • 269-1700

This impressive building, with its striking lobby and seductive book stacks, ranks as many people's favorite downtown spot. Situated as it is near the American Legion Mall, the library offers a great view of downtown from the front steps. Inside are more than 1.5 million books and plenty of out-of-the-way reading spots in which to enjoy them. The Riley Room on the lower level offers a great children's collection. Plenty of special events, such as lectures, film series, readings and small-scale theater productions, are offered here at the Central Library as well as at the many branches across the city. The library opens 9 AM to 9 PM Monday through Friday, 9 AM to 5 PM Saturday and 1 PM to 5 PM Sunday. The library is closed on major holidays as well as over the Memorial Day weekend, when the 500 Festival Parade that takes place nearby makes it nearly impossible to reach the door.

IMAX 3D Theater
650 W. Washington St. • 233-4629

A part of White River State Park (see our Parks and Recreation chapter), the new IMAX Theater uses film 10 times the size of normal movies. These larger-than-life films seem to reach out and grab viewers, who wear polar-ized glasses to view the special effects. The new theater opened in late 1996 near the Indianapolis Zoo and the Eiteljorg Museum.

Indianapolis Zoo
100 W. Washington St. • 630-2001

You'll find this beautiful downtown zoo within walking distance of the Statehouse and the Eiteljorg Museum. Its centerpiece, an $8.5 million Waters Building, offers piranhas, penguins and even underwater viewing of polar bears at play. The zoo opens daily at 9 AM, and admission is $9 for adults, $6.50 for seniors, $5.50 for kids ages 3 through 12 and free for tots younger than 2. See our Kidstuff chapter for more details.

Canal Walk
Ohio and West sts. • 632-1824

Situated below street level, this stretch of the renovated Central Canal provides a lovely spot for walking or jogging, and on any nice day you'll see loads of downtown workers doing both. The areas designated by the purple Canal Walk signs feature beautiful landscaping, fountains, bridges and plenty of people enjoying them during lunch. The State Office Building cafeteria opens onto the Canal at the Ohio Street Basin; you can eat indoors or tote your lunch out to one of the handy picnic tables. It's a pleasant spot to rest after touring of the Statehouse or the Eiteljorg. Kids like the pedal boats; see our Kidstuff chapter for details. The Vermont Street Plaza includes two fountains, staircases and a wrought iron pedestrian bridge that spans the canal, making it a popular spot for downtown weddings. The Walnut Street Basin offers landscaped paths, a 110-foot steel truss bridge, plus easy ramp access for those with disabilities.

Capitol Commons
Corner of Washington St. and Capitol Ave.

This beautiful park, reminiscent of a formal English garden, boasts a huge fountain

INSIDERS' TIP

When ogling the exterior of our impressive Statehouse, don't be too startled by a sudden burst of loud, raucous laughter when you think no one else is around. The recorded noise is just the state's nonviolent way of shooing away pigeons.

Photo: Randy Baughn

Arts and artifacts of the American West are exhibited in the Eiteljorg Museum.

as its centerpiece and smaller ones at either end. Surrounding the fountain are grassy areas, flower beds, walkways and seating areas; it's a favorite lunch spot for brown baggers. Across Washington Street is the Statehouse; beneath the garden is an underground parking garage.

Henry Street Farmers' Market
Meridian and Henry sts.

This downtown farmer's market opens at 8 AM till noon from early May through October just three blocks south of Circle Centre. Visitors will find fresh fruits and vegetables, herbs, flowers, breads, jams and jellies, as well as the occasional musician or street performer.

Museums

Indianapolis Museum of Art
1200 W. 38th St. • 923-1331

The 152 acres along White River and the Central Canal where the Indianapolis Museum of Art is located may be one of the prettiest spots in the city. The wooded grounds feature trails, gardens, a greenhouse, numerous statues scattered about and the huge Robert Indiana "LOVE" sculpture (the letters L, O, V and E are stacked atop each other). Don't miss a stroll outside before or after visiting the museum itself. Four pavilions house the museum's collections, which include Renaissance works, Old Masters, 19th-century French pieces and outstanding collections of Asian and African art. A recent expansion enlarged the museum's capacity considerably, and it boasts plenty of flexibility for showcasing the many traveling exhibits the IMA hosts.

The building is also home to Civic Theater. The IMA opens 10 AM to 5 PM Tuesday through Saturday (to 8:30 PM on Thursday) and noon to 5 PM Sunday; you can usually join a docent-led tour at 2 PM. Contributions are encouraged. Special exhibits often require admission.

The Children's Museum
3000 N. Meridian St. • 924-5431

You don't need a kid in tow to take in the incredible array of attractions at The Children's Museum; you'll see plenty of adults wandering about on their own or showing their spouses exhibits they remember from their own childhood (the huge stuffed polar bear is a longtime museum favorite, though more high-tech displays abound). The museum opens daily from 10 AM to 5 PM; it stays open till 8 PM on the first Thursday of each month. Admission is $6 for adults, $5 for seniors, $3 for kids ages 2 through 17 and free for kids younger than 2. See our Kidstuff chapter for detailed information on this local landmark.

Conner Prairie
13400 Allisonville Rd., Fishers • 773-0666

Another notable sight highlighted in our Kidstuff chapter, Conner Prairie interests history buffs of all ages. A living history museum showcasing Indiana life in 1836, the village wins kudos for authenticity. In addition to its impressive historical details, Conner Prairie is also noted for its handmade salt glaze pottery and the winter Hearthside Suppers, held in the restored Conner home. See our Festivals and Events chapter for more information on the January through March Hearthside Suppers.

Conner Prairie opens Tuesday through Friday from 9:30 AM to 4:30 PM, on Saturday from 9:30 AM to 5 PM and Sunday from 11:30 AM to 5 PM. Admission is $9 for adults, $8.50 for seniors and $6.50 for kids ages 6 through 12.

Indiana State Museum
202 N. Alabama St. • 232-1637

The former Indianapolis City Hall building is home to the Indiana State Museum, which often hosts traveling exhibits from the Smithsonian. On permanent display are geological and historical exhibits highlighting life in Indiana. Don't miss the huge Foucault pendulum that, due to the Earth's rotation, endlessly knocks down strategically placed wooden pegs. The museum opens Monday through Saturday from 9 AM to 4:45 PM and on Sunday from noon to 4:45 PM. Admission is free. See our Kidstuff chapter for more information.

Eiteljorg Museum of American Indians and Western Art
500 W. Washington St. • 636-9378

Art and artifacts of the American West are exhibited in this beautiful museum. The building's design was inspired by Southwestern adobe architecture, but the native wildflowers and prairie grasses that grace the eastern side of the building are pure Indiana. Inside, the museum showcases works by such artists as Georgia O'Keefe and Frederick Remington as well as works by Taos group artists Joseph Henry Sharp and Victor Higgins. Displays also include excellent examples of Native American textiles, pottery, basketry and beadwork. .

The Eiteljorg is open 10 AM to 5 PM Tuesday through Saturday and noon to 5 PM Sunday. It also opens Mondays in from Memorial Day through Labor Day; it's closed Thanksgiving, Christmas and New Year's Day. Admission is $5 for adults, $4 for seniors, $2 for children ages 5 to 17 and free for children 4 and younger. (See The Arts chapter for more details.)

National Art Museum of Sport
University Place Conference Center, 850 W. Michigan St. • 274-2339

Housing what is thought to be the nation's largest collection of fine art depicting athletics, this collection includes works representing 40 different sports. Included is a series of Winslow Homer wood engravings of mid-19th century leisure sports and a group of works depicting the games of the Inuit people, as well as a few oddities such as a silkscreen print done by Muhammad Ali. The museum can accommodate most visitors during regular business hours (9 AM to 5 PM), but because of its location within the University Place Conference Center, groups should call to schedule a visit. Admission is free.

Indiana Transportation Museum
Forest Park Ind. 19, near downtown Noblesville • 773-6000

Although plenty of adults visit this Noblesville museum on their own, check our Kidstuff chapter for more information on exploring the steam, diesel and electric trains of the past. Hours are 11 AM to 5 PM Wednesday through Sunday; admission is $3 for adults, $2 for kids.

Indianapolis Motor Speedway Hall of Fame Museum
4790 W. 16th St. (Gate 2) • 241-2500

An Indianapolis must-see is the Hall of Fame Museum at the track. Though the rau-

"The Greatest Race Course In The World"®

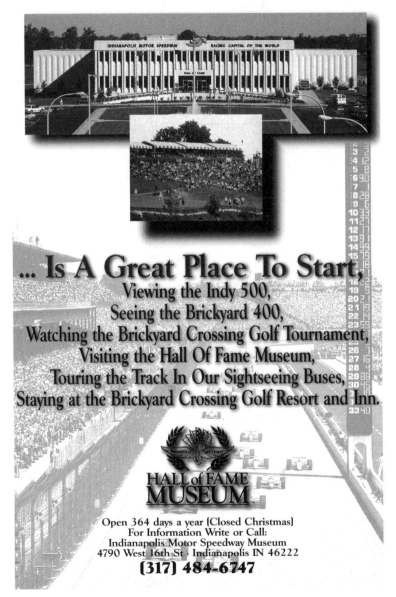

... Is A Great Place To Start,

Viewing the Indy 500,
Seeing the Brickyard 400,
Watching the Brickyard Crossing Golf Tournament,
Visiting the Hall Of Fame Museum,
Touring the Track In Our Sightseeing Buses,
Staying at the Brickyard Crossing Golf Resort and Inn.

HALL of FAME MUSEUM™

Open 364 days a year [Closed Christmas]
For Information Write or Call:
Indianapolis Motor Speedway Museum
4790 West 16th St · Indianapolis IN 46222

(317) 484-6747

cous fans who gather outside the Speedway the night before the race may offer more excitement, anyone who's heard Paul Page announce "a new track record" will want to view the museum's collection of antique race cars and racing memorabilia. Included in the exhibit is Ray Harroun's yellow Marmon "Wasp," winner of the first Indy 500 in 1911. Visitors can also take a $2 guided spin in a tour van around the famous oval, if it's not in use for racing or testing. An adjacent memorial area honors Louis Chevrolet and other racing pioneers, and the Speedway Hotel and Brickyard Restaurant offer convenient dining and accommodations.

The 18-hole Brickyard Crossing, a championship course designed by Pete Dye, features holes 7, 8, 9 and 10 in the track's infield. The museum is open from 9 AM to 5 PM every day except Christmas. Admission is $2 for adults; kids younger than 16 get in free.

Hook's Historic Drug Store and Pharmacy Museum
1202 E. 38th St. • 924-1503

Though now a part of the a national chain, Hook's drugstores were a part of Indianapolis since John Hook opened his first store here in 1900. This little museum, with its reproductions and antique pharmacy memorabilia, opens 11 AM to 5 PM Tuesday through Sunday and earns mention in our Kidstuff chapter for its soda fountain and candy counter. See that chapter for more details, and be sure to sample a traditional chocolate soda.

Indiana Medical History Museum
Old Pathology Building, 3000 W. Washington St.
• 635-7329

This museum, once a part of Central State Hospital, remains the oldest surviving pathology lab in the country and was built to study the causes and effects of mental illness. Listed on the National Register of Historic Places, the museum boasts 15,000 medical artifacts such as 19th-century surgical equipment, patent medicines, a Civil War doctor's kit and 19 rooms, including labs, a library and lecture hall. The museum opens 10 AM to 4 PM

FYI

Unless otherwise noted, the area code for all phone numbers in this guide is 317.

Wednesday through Saturday or by appointment. Admission is $3 for adults; kids 6 and younger get in free.

Wishard Memorial Hospital Nursing Museum
1001 W. 10th St. • 630-6233

This museum, housed in two rooms in the older section of Wishard Hospital, chronicles the advances in nursing since 1883. Take a look at the antique hypodermic needles, much larger and scarier than those used today, and the 1920s-era surgical amphitheater to see how much medical equipment has — lucky for us — changed. Though the museum is open 9:30 AM to 11:30 AM Wednesdays only, call 630-6432 to set up a group tour from 9 AM to 4 PM weekdays. Admission is free.

American Legion Mall and Headquarters Museum
700 N. Pennsylvania St.
• 635-8411

This fourth-floor museum displays the outfit and equipment of a doughboy along with dioramas of World Wars I and II and the Vietnam Conflict. History buffs and veterans will enjoy the military artifacts. It's free and open from 8 AM to 4 PM weekdays, but the grassy, sunken mall is open at all times. The inviting green space is a favorite among the lunchtime crowd and those looking for some shade on a hot, sunny day.

Monuments

Indiana Soldiers and Sailors Monument
Monument Cir., Meridian at Market St.
• 233-3247

"To Indiana's Silent Victors," the monument stands in tribute to more than 210,000 Hoosiers killed in the Civil War and more than 4,000 killed in the War with Mexico. A basement museum features photographs, weapons and uniforms from the War Between the States. Atop the monument's limestone shaft, up 330 steps, is an observatory with a striking view of downtown. The monument's base provides another haven for lunchers who enjoy sitting next to bubbling fountains that drown out city noises. Admission is free, and it's open daily except some holidays.

World War Memorial
431 N. Meridian St. • 232-7615

Built on a hill over an underused and acoustically perfect auditorium, the war memorial's awe-inspiring Shrine Room reminds visitors of attractions in the nation's capital. Multicolored light refracted through stained glass illuminates a huge American flag suspended over an altar commemorating fallen war heroes. Built as the centerpiece of a five-block plaza, the war memorial also features the statue "Pro Patria" on its south steps. Inside, a collection of wartime relics dates back to Indiana's founding, and listings of the state's war dead line the wide staircases. This memorial opens daily from 8 AM to 4:30 PM, except July 4th, Thanksgiving, Christmas and New Year's Day. The

monument was built, as its inscription reads, to "vindicate the principles of peace and justice in the world."

Veterans Memorial Plaza
Between Meridian and Pennsylvania sts., between the old Federal Building and American Legion Headquarters

This five-block park anchored by the War Memorial provides a calming haven when downtown work gets too hectic. University Park, south of the memorial, features a lively fountain full of prancing nymphs and sprites and monuments to Benjamin Harrison, Abraham Lincoln and Schuyler Colfax (Grant's vice president). In Obelisk Square to the monument's north is another fountain, this one with a miniature black-and-gold Washington Monument in the center along with the country's 50 state flags, placed in order of when the states entered the Union. The park's a nice place to stroll, feed the squirrels or do a little people-watching.

USS Indianapolis Memorial Plaza and Monument
700 North St. along the Central Canal

Just past midnight on July 30, 1945, the USS *Indianapolis* was hit and sunk by Japanese torpedoes just after delivering parts of two atomic bombs to the Pacific island of Tinian. Of the 1,197 men who served aboard the ship, 880 lost their lives. This $1 million monument and plaza to honor them includes a limestone and granite representation of the destroyer set next to the downtown canal. The name of each crew member aboard the ship when it sank is listed on the back with a special designation for those who died. Aside from its key role in delivering the nuclear bomb parts, the *Indianapolis* also served as President Franklin Roosevelt's ship of state on several occasions.

Historic Sights

Those who enjoy walking tours can easily spend a day or two exploring downtown Indianapolis. Keep in mind that most of these historic attractions lie within the downtown Mile Square, and none are too terribly far apart.

Madame Walker Urban Life Center
617 Indiana Ave. • 635-6915

This beautiful building, with its Egyptian and African design motifs, was built to house the business of Madame C.J. Walker, America's first African-American female self-made millionaire. The restored structure houses the impressive Walker Theater; an hour-long tour of the building is available; call to schedule one. Combine a tour with a Friday night Jazz on the Avenue show, and really get a feel for the place and neighborhood, which once featured numerous jazz joints that attracted the biggest names in the business.

Most of the historic Indiana Avenue neighborhood has given way to IUPUI, but you can tour the Walker building from 8:30 AM to 7 PM Monday through Saturday; admission is $2 for adults and $1 for seniors older than 65 and kids younger than 19. Be sure to call for reservations.

Indiana Statehouse
Market St. at Capitol Ave. • 232-8880

Before its centennial renovation in 1988, prison inmates occasionally painted the Statehouse's interior walls a drab green, and little attention was given to its historic features. The renovation, which cost five times the original $2 million price tag, renewed the original hand-painted details, beautiful brass chandeliers and marble floors. From the governor's office, which features a desk made of teak decking from the USS *Indiana*, to the Supreme Court chambers with original brass spittoons, the Statehouse now evokes a feeling for the city's long history as a seat of government.

The Indiana General Assembly still meets here beginning in early January each year for either a short or long session. Guided tours are available by appointment between 9 AM and 3 PM weekdays, or stop at the information desk on the rotunda's north side for pamphlets that provide a self-guided Statehouse tour.

Indiana Theatre
134 W. Washington St. • 635-5252

Home to the Indiana Repertory Theatre, the state's only professional resident theater company, the Spanish Baroque Indiana Theatre building was a 1920s movie palace. Now it features three stages and a variety of performances. The elaborate Indiana Roof ballroom on the sixth floor, with its star-studded domed "sky" and decor that recalls a Spanish village, is a wonderful place to enjoy a concert or dance to nostalgic Big Band music. New Year's Eve dinner-and-dancing celebrations are a great way to ring in the New Year. Tours of the IRT

INSIDERS' TIP

For a beautiful view of the Statehouse, go to the south end of the Capitol Commons garden and look north. For an excellent view of Downtown, stand on the steps of the Indianapolis-Marion County Public Library and face south. Don't forget your camera! Both are great photo opportunities.

and "The Roof" are available by appointment. (See The Arts chapter for more information.)

Union Station
39 Jackson Pl. • 267-0700

Built on the site of the nation's first Union station, the current building was erected in 1888. Though in disrepair when renovation began in the early 1980s, the station saw 200 trains a day during the busy years of WWII. Renovated as a festival marketplace with shops and restaurants, the facility struggled to find a niche among other downtown attractions and Circle Centre. As of this writing, Union Station was scheduled to close, and its future remains uncertain.

Hilbert Circle Theatre
45 Monument Cir. • 262-1110

You wouldn't guess it now, but 20 years ago a down-at-the-heels Circle Theatre — the city's first movie palace — was showing Beatles film festivals. Now restored, the impressive building is home to the Indianapolis Symphony Orchestra and provides a wonderful venue for its many musical events. Families especially enjoy taking the kids to the Yuletide Celebration concerts. Tours of the building can be arranged in advance; cost is $1 per person.

Christ Church Cathedral
125 Monument Cir. • 636-4577

This beautiful Gothic church (the subject of Eli Lilly's book *The Little Church on the Circle*) is worth a quick peek or a formal tour, which are usually available after services or by calling ahead to schedule a group visit; the church is often open for touring during downtown festivals. The oldest Episcopal congregation in the city still worships here at the Circle's only remaining church. It's a lovely setting for services or for the church's many music programs. See our Places of Worship chapter for more information.

City Market
222 E. Market St. • 634-9266

Completed in 1886, the historic central building still houses fruit stands, meat markets and a variety of specialty food stalls. Don't miss the Greek imports at Aesop's Kitchen & Cupboard, gourmet coffee and pastries at Cath Inc. and what may be the city's best coney dog at Libby's Deli. Though seating is limited, you can scout out a table on the upper level balcony and listen to mid-day concerts by local musicians. Or take your lunch outdoors and enjoy it on the plaza. Kids find the place entrancingly bohemian (you'll find it listed in our Kidstuff and Restaurants chapters too).

Photo: Randy Baughn

The Indianapolis State Museum is open seven days a week and admission is free.

The market opens 6 AM to 6 PM Monday through Friday and 6 AM to 5 PM Saturday.

James Whitcomb Riley Home and Lockerbie Square
528 Lockerbie St. • 631-5885

Riley lived here for 23 years until his death in 1916 and penned much of his poetry here. The 1872 house is furnished with period pieces. Riley's room includes some of his personal effects: clothes, top hat, a self portrait and his pen, with which he may have composed such famous poems as "Little Orphant Annie" and "When the Frost is on the Punkin." The home opens 10 AM to 3:30 PM Tuesday through Saturday, noon to 3:30 PM Sunday. The museum closes on most holidays, but opens with free admission on the poet's October 7th birthday. Otherwise, admission is $2 for adults and 50¢ for kids ages 7 to 17.

The surrounding Lockerbie Square neighborhood, with its cobblestone streets, tiny gardens and charming homes, is considered one of the best Victorian restorations in the country and is bounded by Michigan, New York, Davidson and East streets. (See our Neighborhoods chapter for more details.)

Athenaeum
401 E. Michigan St. • 636-0390

This 1892 landmark began as a social club and illustrates the city's German heritage; indeed people with a German background still make up the city's largest ethnic group. The Rathskeller's dark wood and Faustian ambiance evoke an Old World feel. Stop in for lunch, and try the brats and sauerkraut (see our Restaurants chapter for details). The Athenaeum now houses the American Cabaret Theatre and a YMCA.

Murat Shrine Temple
510 N. New Jersey St. • 635-2433

Looking like you took a turn at the Athenaeum and ended up in the Sahara, this nearly 90-year-old building on the National Register of Historic Places boasts a definite Middle Eastern motif, especially the Egyptian Room. Hour-long tours guide you through the newly renovated historic structure, which some say houses a resident ghost. Stories of a semitransparent spectre appearing in a box seat,

footsteps crossing the stage, doors slamming shut and lights turning on by themselves have spooked visitors and workers alike.

Some think it is the ghost of Elias J. Jacoby, a former potentate of the shrine. He died in 1935 while getting ready for the shrine's New Year's Eve Party. The lights that some insist they've seen have appeared to rise from Jacoby's favorite box seat. To try to see for yourself, call the shrine and arrange a visit. You can tour the shrine on Monday, Wednesday and Friday from 9 AM to 3 PM. See our Nightlife chapter for details on the Murat as one of our top-notch live music venues.

Scottish Rite Cathedral
650 N. Meridian St. • 262-3100

Kids think this Tudor Gothic structure looks like a castle, and they're right. The impressive Masonic temple building, built in 1929, has been deemed by an international architectural association as one of the most beautiful buildings in the world. The temple's magnificent details, such as the ballroom's black-and-white walnut parquet floor and the rare Russian white oak used in the auditorium enhance the impressive architecture. An hour-long tour is available by checking in with the guide at the North Street door. Stop by 10 AM to 3 PM Monday through Friday; groups should call ahead.

Kemper House
1028 N. Delaware St. • 638-5264

Called "the wedding cake house," this 1873 home was built as a wedding present and really will remind you of a wedding cake, with its many columns and gingerbread trim. Restored by Eli Lilly, the home now houses the offices of Historic Landmarks. Three small rooms are filled with Victorian furnishings and can be rented for meetings and such. Though the home doesn't open for tours, those who really want to view the interior can call to make special arrangements.

Benjamin Harrison Home
1230 N. Delaware St. • 631-1898

Our country's 23rd president lived here from 1875 to 1901, and many of the original Victorian furnishings can be seen during a tour of the home; tours generally start on the hour and half hour. Knowledgeable guides will fill you in on the life of Benjamin Harrison as well. The Fourth of July Ice Cream Social is a popular summertime celebration. The president himself (well, a believable costumed interpreter) attends the annual community event. The home is open 10 AM to 3:30 PM Monday through Saturday and 12:30 PM to 3:30 PM Sunday; it's closed on major holidays and during the first two weeks in January. Admission is $3 for adults, $2.50 for seniors and $1 for students.

Morris-Butler House
1204 N. Park Ave. • 636-5409

This 1866 home was restored by Historic Landmarks and gives modern-day visitors a glimpse into a Victorian Indianapolis home, complete with lace curtains at the windows and an Indiana-made Wooton desk. A tour takes an hour, and the home is open 10 AM to 4 PM Tuesday through Saturday and 1 to 4 PM Sunday; groups should call ahead for an appointment. Admission is $3 for adults, $2

Historic Stores

When Circle Centre, Indianapolis' new downtown mall, opened, it included historic elements unusual in mall design. Ehrenkrantz & Eckstut Architects of New York, specialists in historic renovations, designed the new mall to incorporate eight storefronts from the late 1800s.

Though most of the facades are purely ornamental, three function as either entrances or exits. Enter through the former House of Crane storefront, an Italianate Revival-style facade, and you'll find yourself in one of Nordstrom's espresso bars. This building front was the only one to be restored without being taken down. Most of the others, which include the Chicago School-style J.F. Darmody Building, the impressive black art deco Rost Jewelers on Illinois Street, the Italianate Revival Rothschild Building and the Italian Commercial Revival P.W. Jackson Building on Meridian Street, were disassembled and stored. The cast iron facades of the Wilking and the Levey Brothers buildings, for example, were taken apart and stored on the grounds of Central State Hospital.

The storefronts camouflage the mall in places and create the feel of separate buildings. Carefully reassembled and skillfully incorporated into the mall's design, the historic facades provide a reminder of the area's past as the city's warehouse district.

Photo:The Indianapolis Star and The Indianapolis News

Historic storefronts are part of Circle Centre. The facades were preserved even though the original buildings were destroyed.

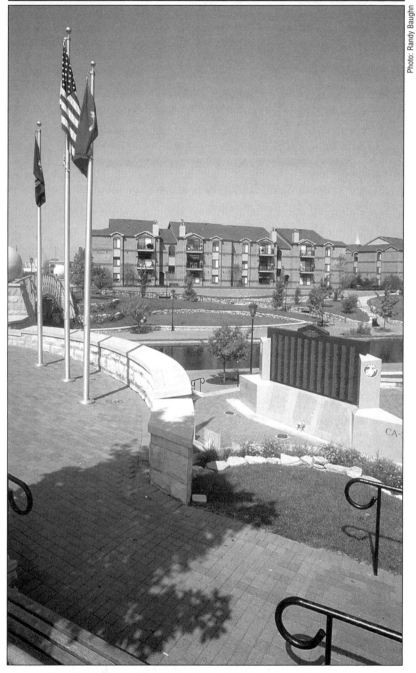

The USS Indianapolis Memorial is located on the canal walk.

for children ages 6 through 16 and free for kids younger than 6. The home is closed on holidays and during January.

Crown Hill Cemetery
700 W. 38th St. • 925-8231

This is the nation's fifth largest cemetery, and its rolling, expansive grounds can provide a morning or afternoon's worth of history. You'll find the graves of bank robber John Dillinger, President Benjamin Harrison and Hoosier poet James Whitcomb Riley. In fact, Riley's memorial is atop Strawberry Hill (also known as "the crown"), the highest natural point in the city, offers a great view of the downtown skyline. You can pick up a tour map at the gatehouse; the grounds are open every day. (See our Literary Life chapter for additional information on Riley.)

Mansions at Marian College
3200 Cold Spring Rd. • 929-0299

On the grounds of this private college northwest of downtown are two notable mansions that provide an inside look at how local movers and shakers once lived. Built for one of the Speedway founders, the James A. Allison Mansion, called Riverdale, boasted a pipe organ and an indoor pool. Much of the first floor has been restored; some of it is furnished with the original custom-made furniture. Also on the grounds is the Wheeler-Stokely Mansion, dubbed Hawkeye, and built for another Speedway founder. Pick up the *Mansions of Marian* booklet, available at the college bookstore, for more details, and book the $2 per person tours in advance.

Historic Meridian Street
38th to 56th sts.

This historically designated stretch of U.S. Highway 31 boasts some of the city's most beautiful homes. Many of these Meridian Street mansions date from the 1920s, and residents take great pride in the historically accurate restorations. Beautiful yards, especially in the spring, make this neighborhood perfect for a stroll. You can also see plenty of sightseers driving slowly past the magnificent houses. Several annual home shows, including Meridian in Bloom, spotlight the area that often hosts the annual Decorators' Show House. (See our Annual Events and Festivals chapter.)

Indianapolis offers enough attractions to provide weekends full of kid-oriented sightseeing, plus plenty of activities to keep youngsters occupied year round.

Kidstuff

One refrain you'll hear over and over in Indianapolis is that it's a great place to raise a family. And indeed it is. It's a backyard-barbecuing, softball-playing, bicycle-riding kind of town. Many of our most popular events boast a definite family flair, and Indianapolis offers enough attractions to provide weekends full of kid-oriented sightseeing, plus plenty of activities to keep youngsters occupied year round.

Not only can we claim the world's largest children's museum and one of the biggest city parks in the nation, but also the area abounds with opportunities for kids to participate in sports, the arts and the community. Even most restaurants — except the poshest, of course — are kid-friendly. Indeed, a trip to an ethnic restaurant, where kids can try to eat with chopsticks or watch wide-eyed as jingling, scarf-draped belly dancers perform, can be great fun for the whole family.

In fact, many of the attractions listed in this chapter could have easily been included elsewhere and just might keep the grownups amused as well. The Children's Museum, for example, is a guaranteed crowd-pleaser, and we know plenty of parents who relish an opportunity to slip on some knee-pads and crawl through indoor playgrounds right behind Junior.

This chapter's suggestions include a variety of possibilities, from kid-pleasing stores and restaurants to unique museums and outdoor activities. Though by no means all-inclusive, our suggestions include well-known, can't-miss attractions as well some out-of-the-ordinary options. At any rate, this list will certainly get you started exploring the city from a kid's point of view.

Of course, it helps if you have at least one youngster tugging you along.

Attractions and Museums

Here are our picks for the city's best sights from a kid's perspective. Don't be surprised if they ask to go to some of these places again and again. Say yes; they're all worth a return trip.

Children's Museum
3000 N. Meridian St. • 924-5437

This is it, the primo point of interest for kids in Indianapolis. The Children's Museum ranks as the largest such facility in the world, and the place is filled with exhibit after exhibit highlighting science, cultures, history, the arts and just plain fun. The best part is that things are designed to be touched, examined, climbed on and crawled through.

Generations of kids have stared in awe at the enormous stuffed polar bear; youngsters often ask their parents if they remember seeing it when they were kids (this writer certainly does). The same goes for the Egyptian mummy, the working carousel, the hard-to-believe-it's-not-real limestone cave. Well, you get the idea.

The place really must be seen to be believed. A recently renovated entrance features the world's largest water clock, and kids are fascinated with the bubbling timepiece. Of course, they also dig the Indy race car, the log cabin, the planetarium and the computers. And the CineDome theater, which opened in the summer of 1996, shows movies specially made for the large-format. The theater's five-minute signature movie explores Indianapolis from a kid's perspective and includes footage of parades, the State Fair and shots from a hot air balloon. Look around during the movie; you'll see kids and adults alike swaying slightly in their seats as the film takes them "flying."

Around here, parents start bringing the kids to the Children's Museum even before they can walk, and there's stuff even for the tiniest ones to do. Playscape, a gallery for the preschool crowd, includes water and sand play, art supplies, animal costumes to dress up in and plenty of things to climb through, around, under and over. There's also an extra-soft area for babies to explore.

In other galleries, school-age kids will love exploring the very convincing replica of an Indiana limestone cave, slipping into a real submarine and wondering about Wenuhotep, the 2,500-year-old Egyptian mummy. Teenagers can work on academic and community projects in CFX, the Eli Lilly Center for Exploration. Teens also like the late-night laser light shows, set to the music of such groups as Pink Floyd and Led Zepplin, in the planetarium.

During October, the Children's Museum also operates a haunted house. One of the city's best (and least gory), it also offers lights-on tours for little ones with friendly characters handing out treats.

The museum is open 10 AM to 5 PM seven days a week; it's closed on Christmas and Thanksgiving. Though subject to change, at the time of this writing admission fees are $3 for youths ages 2 to 17; $6 for adults 18 to 59; and $5 for seniors. The museum is open late, and admission is free the first Thursday evening of each month from 5 to 8 PM. Annual family passes can be purchased for $40. Theater, SpaceQuest Planetarium (and its laser light shows), computer center, carousel and haunted house tickets must be purchased separately. Parking is free.

Indianapolis Zoo
1200 W. Washington St. • 630-2001

Designed as a zoo without cages, the Indianapolis Zoo provides a wide-open look at wildlife from the jungles, plains, deserts and oceans. Home to more than 3,000 creatures, the zoo features a world-class Waters Complex with penguins, polar bears and daily dolphin shows. The Deserts Biome provides an arid environment for birds, lizards and tortoises to fly, slither and creep across your path. And, of course, lions, tigers and bears — even eagles — can be spotted outdoors. For a little more interaction, kids (and grownups too) can ride camels and elephants; a train takes visitors around the park in a more conventional manner.

It's a beautiful facility, with well-designed and well-maintained walkways throughout. It's especially festive when decked out with thousands of lights for Christmas at the Zoo, but note that lines can be long for this popular holiday outing.

The zoo opens daily at 9 AM year round; closing times vary seasonally from 4 to 5 PM. Don't let a little chilly weather deter you from a visit; the animals are often more active when it's cooler than in the heat of an Indiana summer. Admission is currently $9 for adults, $5.50 for kids 3 to 11 and $6.50 for seniors; parking costs an additional $3.

Eiteljorg Museum of American Indians and Western Art
500 W. Washington St. • 636-9378

The Eiteljorg offers one of the finest collections of Native American and Western art in the nation (see our Arts and Attractions chapters), and kids will enjoy the artist-in-residence series that features Native American artists demonstrating their work. Take a look at the 38-foot totem pole near the entrance of the museum. This pole, inspired by one that stood for years in the Golden Hill neighborhood, was created by a fifth-generation Alaskan carver. Raised in April 1996, the pole will stand outdoors for two years; it will then become a permanent indoor exhibit.

The museum, which is within walking distance of downtown, is open 10 AM to 5 PM Tuesday through Saturday and from noon to 5 PM Sunday; it's also open Mondays from Memorial Day through Labor Day. It's closed on Thanksgiving, Christmas and New Year's Day. Admission is $5 for adults, $2 for kids 5 to 17 and for full-time students, and $4 for seniors. Parking is free.

Conner Prairie
13400 Allisonville Rd., Fishers • 776-6004

Ranked by *Midwest Living* as among the best Midwest historical sites and by *Vacations* magazine as one of the 10 best U.S. family vacations, Conner Prairie is indeed one of the area's most interesting attractions. The living history village frozen in time offers visitors the chance to experience life in 1836 and watch as costumed interpreters go about their business. Visit the schoolhouse, the blacksmith shop or watch village residents celebrate a typical 1836 wedding (in June). Visitors can also tour the original Conner home, built by settler and statesman William Conner, which has been restored and furnished; it now looks as it might have when it was built in 1823. Kids used to overflowing toy boxes and bookshelves will be surprised at the nursery, where they can look around a 19th-century kid's room.

In addition to touring the historic areas, visitors can also experience hands-on activities such as candle-dipping and soap-making in the Pioneer Adventure Area. The modern Museum Center houses exhibits, a gift shop, bakery and Governor Noble's Eating Place, a fully modern and casual dining room.

Be sure to check out some of the many special events at Conner Prairie throughout the year. Some of the most popular include the summertime Symphony on the Prairie series; the Apple Store produce market, open in September and October; the Headless Horseman at Conner Prairie during October; and Conner Prairie by Candlelight and the Festival of Gingerbread in December.

The historic areas are open April through November. Hours in those months are 9:30 AM to 4:30 PM Tuesday through Friday, 9:30 AM to 5 PM Saturday, and 11:30 AM to 4 PM Sunday. The village celebrates Independence Day each year with A Glorious Fourth in Prairietown and is open on Memorial Day and Labor Day; Conner Prairie is closed on Easter and Thanksgiving. During the winter, it opens only for special events. Admission is $9 for adults, $8.50 for seniors and $6.50 for kids 6 to 12; tours of the William Conner home cost an additional $1.50. Conner Prairie is 6 miles north of Indianapolis near the community of Fishers.

Indianapolis Motor Speedway Hall of Fame Museum
4790 W. 16th St. • 484-6747

Racing fans of all ages will get a kick out of visiting the Indianapolis Motor Speedway

(see our Attractions and Auto Racing chapters), where they can gaze at speedsters of the past and imagine themselves behind the wheel of the Marmon "Wasp," winner of the first 500-Mile Race in 1911. Kids enjoy the 15-minute bus tour around the track itself (an extra $2 per person). If a youngster's heart is set on a spin around the oval, take note: Track tours aren't available when racing teams are out there testing or during inclement weather — both of which happen often during spring in Indiana.

The museum is open from 9 AM to 5 PM every day except Christmas. Admission is $2 for adults 16 and older.

Indiana State Museum
202 N. Alabama St. • 232-1637

Highlighting the state's natural and cultural history, the Indiana State Museum (see our Attractions and Arts chapters), offers kids a glimpse into Indiana's Ice Age past as well as daily life in historic Indianapolis. Kids (OK, grownups too) stand around watching the 85-foot Foucault pendulum that, due to the Earth's rotation, continuously knocks over little wooden pegs placed on the floor. Freetown Village, a living history exhibit at the Indiana State Museum, was created in 1982 to teach African-American history. Costumed interpreters present a view of daily African-American life in Indianapolis in 1870. (See the "Seasonal Specialties" section later in this chapter for information on the winter holidays' Toy Soldiers Playground.)

The Indiana State Museum is open 9 AM to 4:45 PM Monday through Saturday; noon to 4:45 PM Sunday. Admission is free.

Hook's Historic Drug Store and Pharmacy Museum
1202 E. 38th St. • 924-1503

The main attraction here for kids is the soda fountain and candy counter that came from an Indiana ice cream shop. They can enjoy an old-fashioned ice-cream soda while Mom and Dad browse through the outstanding collection of pharmacy and drug store relics (see our Attractions chapter).

FYI

Unless otherwise noted, the area code for all phone numbers in this guide is 317.

The drug store is at the Indiana State Fairgrounds and opens from 11 AM to 5 PM Tuesday through Sunday (though the store may close up by 4:30 PM if business is slow).

Indiana Transportation Museum
Forest Park, on Ind. 19, near downtown Noblesville • 773-6000

Even in these days of cyberspace, kids remain fascinated by railroads, and at the Indiana Transportation Museum in nearby Noblesville, they can examine steam, diesel and electric trains and even take a ride on the former Nickel Plate Railroad (rides are offered on weekends only and require an additional fare).

The museum is open 10 AM to 5 PM Tuesday through Sunday from Memorial Day through Labor Day; it opens on weekends in May and from Labor Day through Halloween. Admission is $4 for adults and $2 for seniors and kids 4 to 12.

Indiana State Police Youth Education and Historical Center
8500 E. 21st St. • 899-8293

Offering one of the nation's finest collections of police-related paraphernalia, the Historical Center features vehicles, firearms, photos, displays and souvenirs. State police officers often conduct tours; call for details.

The center is open 8 to 11 AM and 1 to 4 PM Monday through Friday; it's also open 9 AM to 4 PM every third Saturday from April through October. Admission is free, though donations are accepted.

Geokids
Indianapolis International Airport • 487-7243

This interactive exhibit, developed in conjunction with the Children's Museum, aims to teach school-age kids about geography, weather and travel with such appealing displays as a 6-foot rotating globe and a 3-D floor map of the United States.

Stuff to do Downtown

Even if they're stuck downtown, surrounded by conventioneers, with no hope of ever getting more than walking distance away from the hotel, kids (and their parents) can still find plenty to do. Here are a few of our favorite outings.

Indiana Soldiers and Sailors Monument
Monument Cir. • 233-3247

Challenge the kids to climb the 330 steps to the enclosed balcony for a great view of downtown; you can take the elevator and beat them there. In warm weather, locals enjoy lunch on the Monument steps. The kids won't be able to resist a trip inside the Rocky Mountain Chocolate Factory, 28 Monument Circle, which boasts a delicious assortment of chocolates and caramel apples.

City Market
222 E. Market St. • 634-9266

This historic market, with ethnic food shops, gourmet coffees and some of the city's best deli fare, can seem like the most bohemian place in the world to a kid. Local musicians often perform during the weekday lunch rush when the market is most exciting (see our Restaurants and Shopping chapters). Get in line, get some food and find a table along the upstairs balcony or take some sandwiches outside and enjoy lunch on the open-air plaza. Many City Market stands are open 6 AM to 6 PM Monday through Friday and 6 AM to 5 PM Saturday.

Indiana World Skating Academy
201 S. Capitol Ave. • 237-5555

A competition site for the 1987 Pan Am Games, these two indoor ice-skating rinks across from Union Station offer year-round public skating (call for a schedule) as well as lessons, private parties and hockey, figure skating and speed skating camps and clinics.

Canal Walk
West and Ohio Sts. • 632-1824

This urban oasis sits below street level and offers a handy place to rest if you've been touring the Statehouse or the Eiteljorg. Kids, however, aren't big on cooling their heels, so load the family onto a pedal boat and cruise along the canal. The boats, which seat up to five passengers, are available from 10 AM to 6 PM on weekends from mid-April through mid-

Photo: Guy Reynolds

These cubs relax at the Indianapolis Zoo.

May and mid-September through October. During the summer, you can pedal along from 4 to 9 PM Monday through Friday and 10 AM to 11 PM Saturday and Sunday. Boats cost $6 per half-hour or $10 per hour (plus a 5 percent sales tax).

American Legion Mall
700 N. Pennsylvania St.

Though kids might not dig poking among a bunch of war mementos in the Legion museum, they might appreciate the chance to throw a Frisbee or toss a football around the expansive grassy areas of the American Legion Mall. We even see kite flyers here on blustery March afternoons. The mall area is great for picnic lunches; kids love stopping at one of the hot dog vendors who park their carts in the area.

Indianapolis-Marion County Library
40 E. St. Clair St. • 269-1700

Just across St. Clair Street from the American Legion Mall is our impressive public library. Take the kids to the ground-level Riley Room, a relaxing spot (complete with rocking chair) to read a book with the little ones.

Stores and Restaurants

Though you can find great shopping and dining possibilities all over town, here we offer some bona-fide, kid-tested suggestions.

Shops

Toys R Us
8250 Castleton Corner • 841-9334
4575 W. 38th St. • 297-0338
9251 E. Washington St. • 897-0320
1650 E. County Line Rd. • 882-5838

Yes, it's a chain, but this mega-store is a kid's paradise, with aisle upon aisle of toys, games and electronics. Here you can find everything from traditional Barbies and GI Joes to the latest in Sega and Nintendo. Selection remains excellent even at Christmastime, when stores stay open into the wee hours to accommodate sneaky parents playing Santa.

Kits & Kaboodle
8701 Keystone Crossing • 574-3333

This shop exudes personality and offers a gold mine of unusual gift ideas for your favorite kid. Here you'll find shelves stocked with a wide variety of cool stuff, including science-related toys, traditional teddy bears, collectible dolls, stamp pads and stickers galore. Looking for paper dolls, Brio or those doctor office bead mazes? This is the place. It's also a great source for unusual little stocking stuffers. We went looking for those little figures we remembered from childhood, clowns and animals that bend back and forth when you push up on the base . . . and found them.

Kids Ink Children's Bookstores
5619 N. Illinois St. • 255-2598
13632 N. Meridian St. • 844-6516
199 Madison Ave. • 882-1090

One of the Midwest's leading kid's-only book retailers, Kids Ink stocks more than 15,000 children's books, plus hundreds of toys and cassettes. The knowledgeable staff will help you find whatever you're looking for, from Pat the Bunny to The Babysitters' Club. The stores also schedule story hours and special events.

The Great Train Store
39 Jackson Pl. • 634-6688

This Union Station shop is the place for model train enthusiasts as well as for fans of Thomas the Tank Engine, star of PBS's *Shining Time Station*. Railroad-themed books and accessories make this a favorite of parents, and little ones like to watch as real electric trains (situated up high and out of reach) run through the place.

Comic Carnival and S-F Emporium
Information Hotline • 257-1450

With locations all over town, this popular comic book shop caters to X-Men fans of all ages. It stocks a wide variety of titles, both new and traditional, including a top-notch science fiction selection.

Pacers Home Court Gift Shop
300 E. Market St. • 263-2164

Pro-sports fans can stock up here, and after three straight seasons with the Pacers in the NBA playoffs, Pacer paraphernalia have become hot items. You can find a good variety of T-shirts, sweatshirts and other game

gear in this downtown shop at street level beneath Market Square Arena.

Cookie Cutters
3906 E. 82nd St. • 842-7753

This one we've included for Mom and Dad — or anyone who's tried to trim a preschooler's bangs. If you can't get the little ones to sit still for a haircut (and who can?), try this place. The kids-only shop caters to little tikes with video monitors instead of mirrors in front of the chairs; they can watch *Barney* instead of worrying about scissors too close to their ears. But the "chairs" themselves may be the biggest attraction. Kids can sit in a Jeep, race car, fire truck or VW Bug while speedy stylists quickly clip. Prices seemed reasonable (about $12 at the time of this writing), but note that appointments are necessary.

Restaurants

Chuck E Cheese's
5501 E. 82nd St. • 849-7324
8804 U.S. 31 S. • 887-0646
4910 W. 38th St. • 299-2544
8109 E. Washington St. • 897-2751

Kids love this place more for the games than for the pizza, and it's almost always full of token-toting tots clamoring for just one more game of Skee-Ball or Whack-a-Mole. Some parents get a headache just pondering such an excursion, but birthday parties at Chuck E Cheese's remain extremely popular. And while it ain't gourmet, the pizza really isn't bad at all.

Arni's
3443 W. 86h St. • 875-7034

The pizza is really good at Arni's, and the restaurant offers a wide variety of sandwiches, salads and specialty items as well. But it's still a kid kind of place, and youngsters love the decor, which features bicycles on the ceiling and scooters on the walls. It's loud, comfortable and casual, and no one cares if a little one drops pizza on the floor.

Bill's Fabulous '50s
6310 Rockville Rd. • 244-1950

This west-side drive-in features roller-skating carhops balancing trays full of icy root beer mugs and baskets of giant tenderloins and onion rings. You turn on your lights for service, and while you wait, the kids can pop a few quarters in the outdoor juke box; they can select from such vintage titles as "Purple People Eater" and "Monster Mash." A few Hula-Hoops are usually lying around in case Mom or Dad feel like demonstrating how it's done. Bill's is a silly, kitschy kind of place, but it's a summertime hangout for classic car buffs who like to park their '57 Chevys and kibbitz with other motorheads.

The Old Spaghetti Factory
210 S. Meridian St. • 635-6325

A downtown family favorite, the Spaghetti Factory offers good food, ample portions and low prices in an offbeat building full of fringed Victorian lamps and monstrous chandeliers. Kids enjoy eating in the trolley car situated in the middle of the restaurant. Be warned that the wait for a table can be quite long; although the restaurant doesn't take reservations, you can call ahead to put your name on the list.

Acropolis
1625 E. Southport Rd. • 787-8883

This family-oriented south-side restaurant boasts authentic Greek fare as well as more standard menu items; just about anyone can find something they like if gyros, moussaka and other Greek specialties don't appeal. But everyone is sure to enjoy the belly dancing offered on weekend evenings. The whole place will be clapping along.

Daruma
3508 W. 86h St. • 875-9727

Though not recommended for the youngest of kids, Daruma nonetheless offers older ones a unique dining experience that includes sitting on the floor in traditional Japanese style. Beautifully prepared and deliciously different, the food, brought to the table by kimono-clad servers, is sure to intrigue young diners.

Wok 'n' Roll
1041 Broad Ripple Ave. • 257-3663

This isn't China, the menu says, and while you won't discover authentic Oriental fare at this tiny Broad Ripple eatery, you will find such fun and tasty specialties as Cashew-Cashew Geshundeit Chicken and A Hunka Hunka Burnin' Love. The award-winnning interior is decorated with woks and Chinese checkerboards; the order counter looks like a giant take-out box.

Back to Nature

When the kids tire of tagging along while Mom and Dad browse through yet another museum or antique shop, take them outdoors and turn 'em loose for a while. Here are a few places to soak up some sunshine.

Eagle Creek Park
7840 W. 56th St. • 327-7110

This huge northwest-side park is one of the perks of living in Indianapolis (see our Parks and Recreation chapter). It's big, beautiful and loaded with stuff for kids to do. Situated along Eagle Creek Reservoir, the park includes a sandy beach, a marina where you can rent a Sunfish or windsurfer, lots of hiking trails, smooth paved roads for biking or jogging, a newly remodeled nature center, playgrounds and picnic areas. As part of the parks department, it also offers classes, camps and programs for all ages. An admission fee ($2 per vehicle on weekdays and $3 per vehicle on weekends) is charged.

Marott Park
7200 block of N. College Ave.

This park and nature preserve, located surprisingly enough between the busy shopping districts of Broad Ripple and Nora, offers a small open area for picnicking or Frisbee-playing, but its main draw are the wooded trails leading down to White River, where kids can skip stones, wade and watch for wildlife (see our Parks and Recreation chapter).

Garfield Park & Conservatory
2450 Shelby St. • 327-7184

Garfield Park's formal sunken gardens are being restored, and the renovated conservatory, a warm, tropical oasis especially appealing in the winter, reopened in late 1996. Kids love the jungle atmosphere, and a 15-foot waterfall completes the rain forest illusion (see the Parks and Recreation chapter). The conservatory is open 10 AM to 5 PM Tuesday through Saturday and noon to 5 PM Sunday; admission is free.

Central Canal
Westfield Blvd. in Broad Ripple

The Central Canal is home to a large year-round community of ducks and geese who waddle up on shore at the first sign of a human with a loaf of bread. Though several Broad Ripple businesses sell little bags of high-priced bread crumbs, stop in at the Kroger store, 6220 Guilford Avenue, in the middle of Broad Ripple and pick up a couple loaves of white bread for less than a buck. The birds will eat it up. In fact, some of the geese are bold enough to

Photo: Randy Baughn

Holiday Park features three separate play areas and great trails that lead down to White River.

take a slice right out of your hand. But remember that a big hissing goose can scare the littlest kids and intimidate older ones as well; just shoo the flock away or empty out the bread bag if the birds get too demanding.

Holcomb Gardens
4600 Sunset Ave. • 940-9351

Located on the Butler University campus, this beautiful area is great for biking and strolling near the pond and along the Central Canal. The Holcomb Observatory and Planetarium, 940-9333, are cool too. The facility offers public shows at 7 PM and 8:15 PM on Friday and Saturday.

Playgrounds and Water Parks

When the kids are bouncing off the walls and need to burn off some excess energy, it's time for a trip to a playground or water park. And the choice isn't necessarily determined by the season. Indianapolis kids can play and swim all year round. In addition to commercial facilities, the parks department offers plenty of options. While you can find great city parks and aquatic centers all over town, here are some favorites.

Holliday Park
6349 Spring Mill Rd. • 327-7180

Probably the best playground in the city, Holliday Park (see our Parks and Recreation chapter) features three separate play areas designed for different ages. A fenced area for the littlest ones includes a low, wooden climbing and sliding structure, but kids seem more interested in the bigger ones that include tubes, ladders and terrific slides. A climbing feature that kids refer to as "that spiderweb thing" provides plenty of places to perch and survey the action. And though you won't find teeter-totters or merry-go-rounds, the park does boast swings, including popular tire swings with room for several kids at a time. A group called Friends of Holliday Park has put a lot of effort into refurbishing the play area and the trails that lead down to White River. As at Marott Park, kids love to wade along the shallow riverbanks. As they splash around looking for minnows and snail shells, you'll find it hard to remember you're in the middle of the city.

Indy Island Aquatic Center
8575 E. Raymond St. • 862-6867

Though nearly a dozen city parks boast swimming pools, the parks department now offers six aquatic centers with water slides, sand play areas and lap pools (see our Parks and Recreation chapter). However, Indy Island, at the new Warren Middle School at the corner of Post Road and Raymond Street, is the state's only indoor water park. It wins rave reviews — especially in the middle of winter — for its 150-foot water slide, a water playground, geysers and a meandering lazy river. Indy Island hours are noon to 5 PM and 6:30 PM to 9:30 PM Monday through Friday, noon to 5 PM and 6 to 8 PM Saturday and Sunday. Admission is $4.50 for adults and $3.50 for children ages 3 to 17.

Discovery Zone
5926 Crawfordsville Rd. • 244-4386
1238 U.S. Highway 31 N. • 889-7529
3720 E. 82nd St. • 577-1565
9493 E. Washington St. • 899-4386

"DZ," as it's called, always seems frenzied, but kids love the maze of tubes, tunnels, ball bins and bungee rooms. Kick off your shoes, rent some knee pads and take off after the kids as they climb, crawl and slide through these top-notch indoor playgrounds. Though adults may prefer to sink into the ball pit and stay there, kids love climbing across ropes and discovering new places to hide. They also enjoy the roller slide, which can prove a bit much for grown-up posteriors.

Local Discovery Zones are open 10 AM to 8 PM Monday through Thursday, 10 AM to 10 PM Friday, 9 AM to 10 PM Saturday and 11 AM to 7 PM Sunday. Admission is about $6 for kids 3 to 12 and around $4 for tots 1 and 2. Accompanying adults (and babies younger than 1) are admitted free. Call about group rates and popular birthday packages.

The Little Gym
1300 E. 86th St. • 581-0429

Kids as young as 4 months (and as old as 12) can take classes here. Music and movement are the focus for the tiniest ones, while older kids can sign up for gymnastics, sports skills, karate and other programs. Birthday parties and Mom's day out sessions are also available. Call for class schedules and details.

Gymboree
126th St. and Gray Rd. • 57-GYMBO

Babies, toddlers and preschoolers (newborns through age 5) can climb, crawl, play and explore with Mom or Dad during the play programs at this popular Carmel facility. Call for info on introductory classes.

Thunder Island Water & Recreation Park
19830 U.S. Hwy. 31 N., Westfield
• 896-5172

Kids can cool off with bumper boats, a water slide and children's pools as well as enjoy miniature golf and go-carts. Thunder Island also features an adult pool and a driving range. The park opens 10 AM to 7 PM daily for golf and go-carts starting April 1. Kids can make a splash from 11 AM to 7 PM daily from Memorial Day weekend and through the end of August (plus Labor Day weekend). Admission is $10.75 for adults; $9.50 for ages 4 to 12.

The Sporting Life

In a state like Indiana, where many kids pick up a basketball before they learn to walk, you'd expect sports to be popular. And you'd be right. But kids around here do more than just practice their free throws. You'll find youngsters on the baseball diamond, the tennis court, the soccer field and even on the water learning to sail. And, yes, you'll find kids as young as 3 hustling up and down a court with a pint-size round ball learning basketball basics even before they head off to preschool.

But for many kids, school teams provide their primary opportunity to participate in sports. Local public schools and most private schools offer a variety of sports activities. Churches also sponsor teams and leagues,

and some programs have grown quite large. **Tabernacle Presbyterian Church**, 926-9426, the **Jewish Community Center**, 251-9467, and the **First Baptist Church of Indianapolis**, 844-3559, work with thousands of kids (they needn't belong to the church to participate). In Hamilton County, the **Carmel Dads Club**, 846-1663, organizes leagues in several sports.

Here are a few more of our favorite ways to build team spirit.

Boys and girls ages 8 through 18 can sign up to play baseball on one of the city's more than 16 **Little League** teams; more than 400 sluggers participate each season, which lasts from early May through mid-August. Call 897-6127 for sign-up information. **Indy Parks and Recreation**, 327-0000, also sponsors baseball and softball leagues.

Older boys — ages 15 through 18 — can participate in **American Legion** baseball leagues. Call 654-8135 for information. And the **Indiana Amateur Baseball Association**, 923-3484, sponsors leagues that allow high school- and college-age young men to hone their skills in hopes of winning a college scholarship.

The **Amateur Softball Association**, an Olympic-affiliated group, organizes leagues across the city for both kids and adults. Call 783-9644 with kid-related questions.

Though the first experience many youngsters have with organized basketball is in elementary school, Indy Parks and Recreation runs leagues and clinics, some for kids as young as 3 or 4. And local **YMCAs** offer plenty of opportunities to shoot hoops as well as to play soccer, racquetball and volleyball, swim and do gymnastics and aerobics — you name it. Call the Y's general office at 266-9622.

Those who prefer swinging a racquet to dribbling a ball can participate in **Washington Township Schools' Community Tennis Program**, which boasts an excellent reputation. Taught by professional instructors and top high school and college players, these summer clinics offer all levels of instruction —

even a basic skills class for preschoolers. The popular program is held at the North Central High School Community Tennis Center, 1801 E. 86th Street, 259-5377.

When it comes to sports camps, local parents know to call **Butler University**, 283-9375, where kids can participate in a wide range of day and overnight sport camps. Youngsters can spend part of their summer vacation honing their skills in baseball, football, soccer, volleyball and gymnastics.

For kids who'd rather be sailing, **Eagle Creek Park** offers a sailing day camp through Indy Parks and Recreation. And for those who prefer a horse of a different color, Indy Parks offers a **Galloping Guys and Gals** camp. Call the parks department at 327-0000 for details. The **Indy School of Gymnastics**, 872-5948, has produced dozens of state and regional gymnastic champs — even a bronze medalist at the World Gymnastics Championships. It offers recreational classes for preschoolers and older kids as well as competitive team programs.

Kids who've gotta dance can check out **Barb & Company Dance** studio, 872-6486. Home to the Indianapolis Junior Dance Company, this facility offers classes for kids as young as 3 at all levels of interest in ballet, jazz, tap and ballroom dancing, plus acting, movement, fencing, tumbling and lots more. The **Performing Arts Center of Carmel**, 844-9131, also offers a variety of dance and gymnastic instruction as well as musical theater courses and voice lessons.

For those who'd rather watch, the Indianapolis Indians sponsor a **Knot Hole Club** for kids 14 and younger. For an annual price of about $8, kids get free general admission (when accompanied by an adult), plus a newsletter and a T-shirt. Kids especially enjoy games when the Famous Chicken or the Philly Phanatic perform. The Indians now play in beautiful Victory Field right downtown. Kids enjoy taking a blanket along and watching the game from the grassy hills just over the outfield fence.

The Indiana Pacers, who play at Market Square Arena, 300 E. Market Street, also sponsor a kids' program, and the group now sports a new name: **Boomer's Buddies** (Boomer is the Pacers mascot). For about $10 per child,

kids ages 6 though 14 receive a number of ticket discounts, coupons good at concession stands and at the Home Court Gift Shop and usually a Pacers T-shirt or hat. Call 263-2100 for information.

Seasonal Specialties

Indianapolis kids often judge the passage of time by the changing festivities. Though you'll find some of these (and many more) in our Events and Festivals chapter, here's a quick year-round guide to kids' favorite seasonal events (organized from a kid's perspective, starting when school begins).

August

WENS Skyconcert Downtown on the banks of
White River • 266-9700

Everyone knows that a kid's year really begins when summer ends and school starts, usually just before or just after Labor Day. Marking the end of summer is the WENS Skyconcert on Labor Day weekend. Families find a place to park on the west side of downtown, tune their radios to 97.1 and settle back for a super fireworks display synchronized to music.

October

October, a favorite month among the preschool and elementary-school crowd, brings plenty of Halloween-related festivities.

Hayrides

Kids and their families can enjoy hayrides at Conner Prairie, where the Headless Horseman makes a visit. The fun, rather than frightening, performance is a hit with younger kids. Call **Conner Prairie** at 776-6000. **Eagle Creek Park**, 327-7110, also offers autumn hayrides through a spooky (if you use your imagination) setting, though you'll find no one galloping around without a head. Hamilton County's **Stonycreek Farm**, 773-3344, offers hayrides as well. Call ahead to make reservations.

Pumpkin Patches

Stonycreek also boasts a pumpkin patch where kids can select just the right gourd to carve. **Waterman's Farm Market** at 7010 E. Raymond Street, also offers pumpkin picking. Call 356-6995 to see when the potential jack-o'-lanterns are ready. For a pleasant autumn drive in addition to a pumpkin, head west to Danville's **Beasley's Orchards and Gardens**, 2304 E. Main Street, 745-4876; or east to Greenfield's Tuttle Orchard, 5717 N. County Road 300 W., 326-2278. If you decide to brave the crowds of Brown County during autumn, you'll find a good selection of already-picked pumpkins (as well as apples and cider, Indian corn and decorative gourds) in **Bean Blossom**, a wide spot in the road on Ind. Highway 135 before you get to Nashville.

November

Celebration of Lights
Monument Cir. • 237-2222

Once Halloween is over, kids can begin looking forward to winter holidays. The Celebration of Lights, held on Monument Circle the Friday night after Thanksgiving, includes the lighting of the 284-foot-tall Soldiers' and Sailors' Monument, turning it into the world's largest "Christmas tree."

Christmas Tree Farms

Choosing their own evergreen at a tree farm can be fun for kids, and by Thanksgiving weekend, many tree farms around the county are ready to hand you a saw and let you cut down your own. A favorite is **Watt's Christmas and Train Shop**, 9180 Hunt Club Road (in the Zionsville area), 873-2365. **Stonycreek Farm**, 773-3344, where field trips full of kids pick pumpkins in the fall also features Christmas trees. And just west of Indianapolis on U.S. Highway 36 in Avon (about 5 mils west of I-465), **Cartlidge Christmas Trees** offers thousands of Scotch and white pine trees.

Toy Soldiers Playground
At the Indiana State Museum, 202 N. Alabama St. • 232-1637

Also opening the weekend after Thanksgiving is the Toy Soldiers Playground. The

Santaland Express train, which many adults remember from the former downtown L.S. Ayres, chugs through the museum's display of mechanical figures and Christmas scenes.

Christmas at the Zoo
1200 W. Washington St. • 630-2001

Also running throughout December is Christmas at the Zoo, a celebration that turns the Indianapolis Zoo into a twinkling wonderland of light displays.

Hanukkah

Children also enjoy the many activities surrounding Hanukkah, the Jewish festival of lights, held at local synagogues (see our Places of Worship chapter).

Kwanzaa
Crispus Attucks Middle School, 1140 Martin Luther King Jr. St. • 226-4611

Indianapolis Public Schools' Kwanzaa Celebration includes a candle-lighting ceremony as well as singing, storytelling, dancing and drumming. Call for details on the time and date of this late-December event.

February

Kidsfest
100 S. Capitol Ave. • 637-4574

This late-February event fills the RCA Dome with kid- and family-oriented displays. Hands-on activities in arts, sports, education and recreation offer plenty of excitement.

March

High school basketball fans become increasingly frenzied throughout March as Hoosier Hysteria takes hold of just about everyone — especially high school students. The late-March Indiana High School Athletic Association boys basketball championships determine the state's best team and signal an end to winter in Indiana, although bad weather and basketball often go hand-in-hand around here. We generally expect snow during the sectional, regional, semistate and state finals; it's more of a surprise when the white stuff doesn't fall. (Easter egg hunts, held at parks around the city, serve as a more reliable harbinger of spring.)

Easter Egg Hunts

Indy Parks and Recreation, 327-0000, sponsors great Easter festivities in March or April, depending on when Easter falls. Check out the **Broad Ripple Eggstravaganza** and **Eagle Creek Park's Easter Egg Hunt** (kids are separated into age groups). The parks department also offers parties, egg decorating, breakfast with the Easter bunny and even an after-dark "moonlight madness" hunt. You'll also find good hunts at Garfield Park, Watkins Park and Municipal Gardens; all are part of Indy Parks.

St. Patrick's Day Parade
Downtown

Even though it's quite possible that March 17 will prove snowy and blustery, kids welcome the downtown St. Patrick's Day parade as a bona-fide sign of spring in Indianapolis. They enjoy the kilt-clad pipe and drum bands, floats and clowns. And the candy, of course,

that the little ones seated along the curb always scramble for.

May

Big Wheel 500
500 Major Taylor Velodrome, 3649 Cold Spring Rd. • 327-0000

At this popular pre-500 event, kids ages 2 to 5 race Big Wheels at the Velodrome while the whole family enjoys games, food and entertainment. Don't forget the camera; it's a great photo opportunity. And don't drag Junior's own Big Wheel along; a ride for the race is provided. Pre-registration for the mid-May event is $3; the race-day price is $5 per child. Call to pre-register.

Summer

Though school isn't quite out yet (most continue into the first week of June), the Memorial Day weekend — and of course the 500 Festival Parade and the race — mark the first real weekend of summer. Although it's just

Photo: Guy Reynolds

Make friends at the Indianapolis Zoo with A.J., the Aldabra tortoise.

about as likely to be cool and rainy as hot and sunny, this is also when the outdoor pools in local parks open — another landmark in the year of a kid.

In June, U-pick farms, often the same that offer pumpkins in October (see earlier entry), feature ultra-fresh strawberries and, a bit later, blackberries and raspberries. But you'd better hurry; by July, the berries are just about gone. But that's OK. Fourth of July celebrations mark the apex of a kid's summer, and there are plenty of opportunities to celebrate.

Conner Prairie hosts its Glorious Fourth (see our Festivals and Events chapter for such summer spectacles) and downtown's Fourth Fest brings thousands of families to the sidewalks and parking lots around town to watch the fireworks that start about 9 PM.

Though they may not be as ingrained as 500 activities, Brickyard 400 events in early August, including Circlefest and the race itself, are sure to become signposts that, even though temperatures may reach the 90s, a kid's summer is winding down. By the time the Indiana State Fair rolls around in mid-August, school is just around the corner.

Out-of-Town Options

Though Indianapolis boasts plenty to do, sometimes a special trip is in order. And while our Daytrips and Weekend Getaways chapter offers plenty of possibilities, here are a few that will especially please the kids.

Billie Creek Village
U.S. 36, Rockville • 569-3430

West of Indianapolis in Parke County (known for its autumn covered-bridge festival), Billie Creek Village features a re-created turn-of-the-century village with 30 historic buildings, a tree-lined creek, covered bridges and one of the Midwest's largest consignment craft shops. Plenty of special historical events, such as the state's largest Civil War re-enactment, are held here, in addition to craft fairs, ice cream socials and music festivals. Some of the kids' favorites include the Maple Fair, when you can watch maple syrup being made, and Halloween "fright rides." They also like the General Store, with its 20-foot candy counter, homemade fudge and the old-fashioned Coke

machine that vends those little kid-size glass bottles.

The whole county just crawls with cars during the October covered-bridge festival; traffic can be heavy, and kids can get impatient. It may be advisable to schedule a visit to avoid the mid-October festival; the bridges can be seen year round, and Billie Creek Village itself proves more enjoyable for kids when it's less crowded.

Located 1 mile east of Rockville, Billie Creek Village opens from Memorial Day through Halloween and for special events; it offers limited operation the rest of the year. Admission is free during the week; on weekends it's $3.50 for visitors age 4 and older. You can also purchase a $20 annual pass.

Carthage, Knightstown & Shirley Railroad
112 W. Carey St., Knightstown • 345-5561

The CK&S Railroad offers hour-long rides on tracks that were once part of the Big Four Railroad (Cleveland, Cincinnati, Chicago and St. Louis Railroad). Passengers board the vintage coach car at the former site of a New York Central freight and passenger station in Knightstown, about 30 miles east of Indianapolis off I-70. The coach, caboose and open platform car travel south to Carthage, crossing the old National Road (U.S. Highway 40) and passing under the old "Pennsy" railroad bridge. The engine is "run around" for the return trip. Both depots offer refreshments, railroad-related memorabilia and equipment displays to examine. (As a special bonus for parents, Knightstown is loaded with antiques shops.)

Trains depart Knightstown on weekends May through October at 11 AM Friday; and 11 AM, 1 and 3 PM Saturday and Sunday. Round-trip fares are $6 for ages 12 to adult, $4 for kids 3 to 11.

Holiday World/Splashin' Safari
Hwy. 162 • (800) GO-SANTA

For years known as Santa Claus Land, Holiday World is one of the country's oldest amusement parks. More elaborate than Old Indiana, Holiday World boasts the largest wooden roller coaster in Indiana and Kentucky, bumper boats, a white-water rapid-style ride and all the traditional amusement park favorites. And, of course, Santa himself, who reads to kids in the Storytime Theater.

It also offers its own water park, called Splashin' Safari, which includes a wave pool (with free use of inner tubes), a 350-foot water chute, a 300-foot water tunnel, plus (and this is what distinguishes Splashin' Safari from other water parks) two areas — Butterfly Bay and Crocodile Isle — for the littlest kids.

Though Holiday World offers a fun, kid-oriented weekend getaway, it's not especially convenient to Indianapolis. It's way down in southern Indiana, 7 miles south of I-64. But the kids will think it's worth the drive.

New in 1996, the Watubee, a six-story-tall white water raft slide, gained a mention in a *Parents* magazine "Top Theme Park Thrills" article.

Holiday World opens weekends in May, September and October and every day during June, July and August; Splashin' Safari opens weekends in May and September and every day during June, July and August. General admission is $17.95; $11.95 for seniors and kids under 48 inches tall.

Indiana State Parks
Department of Natural Resources
• 232-4125

Indiana boasts a wonderful network of state parks (see our Parks and Recreation chapter), and any of them can provide a day or weekend of fun for families. Recreation guides that detail operating hours and amenities of each state park, reservoir, forest, fish and wildlife area and historic site are available free from the DNR. Here are some highlights.

Brown County State Park is probably the most popular among Indianapolis residents. On Ind. Highway 46 near artsy-craftsy Nashville, Brown County State Park is sometimes crowded, and its housekeeping cabins are often booked two years in advance. But except

for the busiest holiday weekends, you can almost always find a camp site (there are more than 400 available). For those who prefer a little less nature, the park offers a very comfortable inn, the Abe Martin Lodge. There's also a pool, great scenery and plenty of wildlife (but please don't feed the deer).

McCormick's Creek State Park, Indiana's first state park, is just as beautiful as Brown County and somewhat less crowded. Situated 14 miles northwest of Bloomington on Ind. 46, the park provides rugged terrain, caves and scenic waterfalls — perfect for hiking. Again, cabins are often booked way in advance, but more than 300 campsites are available. And the Canyon Inn offers cozy accommodations (and — just in case you can't get the campfire going — a great breakfast buffet).

Turkey Run State Park offers a great chance to take the kids canoeing. Sugar Creek runs right through it and boasts great views of sandstone ravines and shady forests. Rent a canoe at one of several liveries near the park; they'll drop you off and pick you up later. Southwest of Crawfordsville on Ind. 47, Turkey Run provides plenty of activities within the park as well, including horse and bicycle rentals, and Turkey Run Inn has an indoor pool.

FYI

For Teens

Though it's a great place to be a kid, Indianapolis doesn't especially cater to teenagers, and unless they're involved in sports, many claim to have a tough time finding something to do. They like to hang out in offbeat Broad Ripple, but they have no real place to go there; restaurants prove pricey, and the many nightspots are strictly for the 21-and-older set. Coffee shops such as the Village Idiot, where you don't need an ID, just a taste for java, have become favorites of

INSIDERS' TIP
Sign the kids up for the Indianapolis Indians' Knot Hole Club. For one low price, they get in to all home games and receive an Indians T-shirt too.

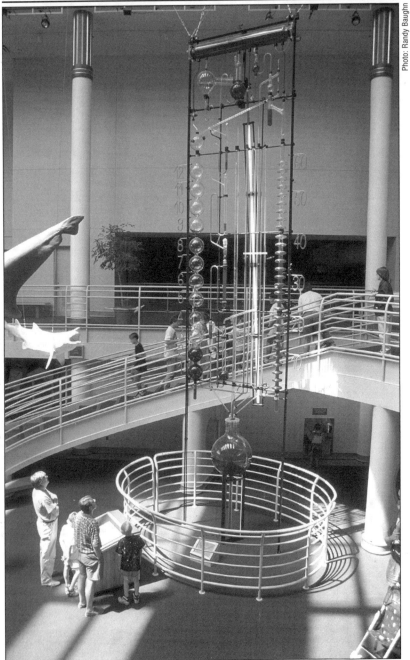

The Children's Museum features the world's largest water clock.

older teens and the much ballyhooed Generation X crowd.

Parents may have to do some digging, but activities do exist for those kids too old for playgrounds but too young for college. Best bets include teen classes at the Indianapolis Art Center and those sponsored by Indy Parks and Recreation as well as programs offered by local YMCAs. (Refer to "The Sporting Life" earlier in this chapter for more ideas.)

Indianapolis Art Center
820 E. 67th St. • 255-2464

The art center offers kids and teens lots of creative options. Past classes have included puppetry, collage, ceramics and printmaking, all taught in the center's studios. The center also sponsors a fine arts summer day camp. Costs for week-long classes and camp do prove pricey; most cost more than $100 for art center members. Family memberships are available for $40. The center also offers a terrific array of adult classes (see our Arts chapter).

Indy Parks and Recreation
1426 W. 29th St. • 327-0000

New classes begin every few months with each new season (see our Parks and Recreation chapter), and the Fun Guides list the many options sponsored by Indy Parks. The guides are available free from the parks department; call to add your name to the mailing list. Teens (and younger kids too) enjoy the sports clinics, horseback riding, dance classes, cooking courses, photography and art instruction.

YMCAs
General Office, 615 N. Alabama St.
• 266-9622

With more than a half-dozen locations around town, the Y offers convenience coupled with a great variety of fitness, culture and arts-related courses. Membership is required for full access to all the facilities, but limited memberships are available (for summertime swimming, for example).

Around here, fairs and festivals highlight our history and ethnic heritage as well as our love for sports.

Festivals and Events

To get to know an area, you just have to attend its festivals. Sample the food, watch the people and get a feel for what makes a region special. Indianapolis is no exception. Around here, fairs and festivals highlight our history and ethnic heritage as well as our love for sports. Pick any month and you'll find plenty going on around the city. Art fests begin in May and continue throughout the summer, and food fests — where the focus is on eating — begin with Holy Rosary's Italian street fair in early June and continue 'til September's Greek Festival. Food vendors abound at Midsummer Fest and Circlefest, and, speaking of food, plenty of locals eat their way through the State Fair in August, filling up on such specialties as hot buttered corn on the cob, Hoosier rib-eye sandwiches and warm, sugary elephant ears.

Fall yields apples, and plenty of nearby orchards and small towns celebrate with fresh-pressed cider and just-picked Winesaps and Granny Smiths. The holiday season, which seems to begin just after the haunted houses close their creaky doors, brings plenty of activity as well. Flipping through our local calendar, you'll also find an abundance of sports-related events, from the Indiana High School Athletic Association's basketball finals to the Circle City Classic (also see our Sports chapter). In May, of course, the action at the track is the main topic of conversation, and you'd better pull together at least one black-and-white outfit to have ready for the many 500-related parties and events.

But to really find out what's going on in Indianapolis, get involved with some of the organizations that put on these annual shows. Regardless of the fair or festival, you'll meet a bunch of dedicated volunteers who'll help introduce you to what happens behind the scenes, where the action really is.

Although we've noted whether an event charges an admission fee, be sure to call ahead for specific rates; fees may have changed since this writing.

January

Hearthside Suppers
13400 Allisonville Rd., Fishers, Conner Prairie • 776-6000

Guests to the historic William Conner home at Conner Prairie, a living history village north of the city, help prepare authentic 19th-century dinners and learn to eat with a knife (forks weren't in use yet, and everything at Conner Prairie is authentic). After the dinners, which despite the low-tech cooking methods really are delicious, guests play old-fashioned parlor games and tour the restored home. Reserve early for these popular dinners that run through March. Admission is $40 to $45 per person.

Greater Indianapolis Garage Sale
Indiana Convention Center, 100 S. Capitol Ave. • 262-3452

This popular annual event is a must for bargain hunters across the city. Scour the more than 700 booths for all sorts of treasures. Who knows what you'll find! Admission is $3.

Indianapolis Home Show
Indiana State Fairgrounds, 1202 E. 38th St. • 298-7111

Anyone building, remodeling or just

dreaming about it will want to check out this venerable home show that includes as a centerpiece a home built indoors. You'll find lots of booths, vendors and tons of home improvement options. Crowds are largest on weekends when lines to tour the home can be quite long. Watch for discount admission coupons at local businesses. Admission is $7.

February

Kid's Fest
RCA Dome, 100 S. Capitol Ave. • 262-3452
The dome is home to a working carousel during this kidstuff extravaganza. Hands-on sports and arts activities offer plenty for kids and parents to do, and 100 exhibitors showcase children's products and services. Admission is $4 to $6; kids younger than 2 are admitted free.

The Annual Carquest World of Wheels
Indiana Convention Center, 100 S. Capitol Ave. • 262-3452
Car collectors, shade-tree mechanics and motor heads of all ages descend upon the Convention Center to scope out the custom cars, trucks and specialty vehicles that make this show an annual favorite. Admission is $6.

Indianapolis Boat, Sport and Travel Show
Indiana State Fairgrounds, 1202 E. 38th St. • 632-2666
The city's oldest sport show draws outdoor enthusiasts inside to check out the latest in hunting, fishing, camping and boating equipment. Take a stroll through the displays, poke your head into a lavish RV and make plans for your summer vacation. Admission is $7.

IHSAA Girls' Basketball Finals
Market Square Arena, 300 E. 38th St. • 846-6601
Hoosier Hysteria starts early when players from across the state square off in this annual contest to determine the best in girls' basketball. Admission is $12.

The Writers' Center Anniversary Celebration
Rathskellar at the Athenaeum, 401 E. Michigan St. • 929-0625
This event spotlights local award-winning writers who read their works to an appreciative audience. Donations are accepted.

March

NCAA Division 1 Men's and Women's Indoor Track and Field Championships
RCA Dome, 100 S. Capitol Ave. • 262-3452
Spectators will find plenty to watch during this two-day exhibition of athletic prowess as the top collegiate competitors from across the country vie for All-America honors. Admission is $12 to $17.

Flower and Patio Show
Indiana State Fairgrounds, 1202 E. 38th St. • 255-4151
Just when you think spring will never arrive, this terrific annual event offers show-goers a chance to stop and smell the daffodils. Visitors can wander through numerous garden displays designed by area landscape professionals, pick up pointers from local gardening guru and Marion County Extension Agent extraordinaire Dick Crum, purchase English ivy or an African violet or join a local garden club. Admission is $7.

St. Patrick's Day Parade
Downtown • 237-3855
Put on something green and head downtown for this festive hour-long parade. Office workers on their lunch breaks vie with kids clutching green balloons for the best curbside spots to watch one of the city's favorite parades. Catch green bagels tossed to the crowd by O'Malia Supermarket employees, or scramble with the kids for candy. Or you can just enjoy the spectacle and the Gordon Pipers as they fire up their bagpipes. Admission is free.

IHSAA Boy's Basketball Finals
RCA Dome, 100 S. Capitol Ave. • 846-6601
The state's top-four teams compete in this

Come to the Indiana State Fair...

An Entire Summer Jam-Packed Into Just 12 Days.

Thrilling rides,

Fresh Buttered Corn,

America's Music &

Blue Ribbon Fun!

...A Well-Preserved Tradition

annual example of Hoosier Hysteria at its most rampant. Sold out for more than 60 years, the event draws more than 40,000 spectators, and downtown crawls with wild-eyed basketball fans. Admission is $12.

April

Decorators' Show House
Location to be announced, St. Margaret's Guild, P.O. Box 40793, Indianapolis 46240

The volunteers of St. Margaret's Hospital Guild organize this late-April through mid-May showcase for local interior designers to benefit Wishard Hospital. As the show house nears completion, motorists will notice the many signs along Meridian Street marking former show homes. Decorators often transform a Meridian Street mansion (sometimes two), though both the Stokely and Allison mansions at Marian College have served as show houses as well. Admission is $12.

500 Festival of the Arts Exhibit
Children's Museum, 3000 N. Meridian St.
• 636-4556

More than 4,000 Marion County students from grades K through 12 submit artwork for this juried competition, and all entries are displayed during May at the Children's Museum. It's fun to peruse the paintings and drawings as you go from level to level at the museum. Museum admission is $3 to $6.

May

Indianapolis Life 500 Festival Mini-Marathon
Monument Cir. • 636-4556

If you want to watch rather than participate in this early May event, dubbed the country's largest half-marathon, tag along with someone who works in a downtown highrise, preferably one with lots of windows. The more than 14,000 registered participants in the mini, which now attracts top runners from across the country, start at Monument Circle, and it's great fun to watch the masses move down the streets. While race-car drivers hope for warm, dry days in May, those participating in the mini long for overcast skies or even a light drizzle.

If you want to enter the race, you can receive an entry form by sending a self-addressed stamped envelope requesting an entry to 201 S. Capitol Street, Indianapolis, 46225. No entries are accepted after April 1. There is a $20 to $25 entry fee for participants

Children's Folk Dance Festival
Indiana Convention Center 100 S. Capitol Ave. • 924-7060

This traditional rite of spring, sponsored by Indy Parks and Recreation, is in its 26th year. The high-spirited early May festival involves 1,000 kids from 25 schools and offers plenty of music, dancing and demonstrations. Admission is $3.

Qualifications
Indianapolis Motor Speedway, 4790 W. 16th St. • 481-8500

Those who decline to join the 400,000 or more spectators who attend the race each year can still experience some racing excitement by attending the qualifications, which draws a smaller crowd — just a quarter-million fans on the first day. The two weekends leading up to the race determine the starting positions for the 33-car field, and everyone who's in a race pool monitors the action to find out where their driver will start. Admission is $10.

Broad Ripple Art Fair
Indianapolis Art Center grounds, 820 E. 67th St. • 255-2464

If, for some unfathomable reason, you're not either attending or listening to qualifications, check out the season's first art fair, usually the weekend before the race. The weather is notoriously unpredictable this time of year, however, and though last year's fest saw warm temperatures and clear skies, it's just as likely to be rainy in May, much to the chagrin of both artists and race car drivers. But with a little sunshine, this venerable art festival offers a great opportunity to browse

the booths, sample gourmet food and enjoy live music. The Art Center is just north of Broad Ripple off College Avenue, but fair-goers can often find a better parking spot at Broad Ripple Park and catch a shuttle bus to the Art Center. Admission is $6.

500 Festival Kids' Day
Monument Cir. • 636-4556

At this free event, kids race Big Wheels, make arts and crafts, play games and participate in educational activities such as Eli Lilly's "Chemisty is a Blast." Kids' Day attracts approximately 30,000 people. More than 12,000 prizes ranging from jump ropes to bicycles are given away during this early May event.

Indianapolis 500 Carburetion Day
Indianapolis Motor Speedway, 4790 W. 16th St. • 481-8500

OK, so today's high-tech race cars don't have carburetors anymore. This last practice day, the Thursday before the race, still boasts its traditional name. Popular among those who don't mind calling in "sick" and showing up at work the next day with a sunburn, Carburetion Day includes semifinals and finals of the Miller Genuine Draft Pit Stop Contest between four racing teams. Admission is $5.

Hulman Hundred
Indiana State Fairgrounds, 1202 E. 38th St. • 927-7500

Ever-popular A.J. Foyt presents this dirt car race on the State Fairgrounds' oval the Friday night before the 500. The 100-mile competition, which attracts more than 30 cars, is part of the USAC Silver Crown series. Admission is $10.

Delco Electronics 500 Festival Parade
Downtown • 636-4556

More than 150,000 spectators attend this annual day-before-the-race extravaganza, which features floats, bands and, of course, the 33 race car drivers. Grandstands are set up along the route for ticketholders, who are issued props and costumes to interact with the parade units, turning the event into the nation's only participatory parade. Though grandstands full of ticketholders fill some of the best viewing areas, plenty of spectators tote along lawn chairs and pick their own perfectly free spot to watch the festivities. Admission is $12.50.

500 Ball
Indiana Convention • 636-4556

Kicking off the greatest weekend in motor sports, the 500 Ball has become one of the city's most celebrated black-tie events with spectacular decorations, unique food presentations and plenty of music and dancing. Tickets cost $150.

Indianapolis 500-Mile Race
Indianapolis Motor Speedway, 4790 W. 16th St. • 481-8500

Called the world's largest one-day sporting event, the greatest spectacle in racing attracts nearly a half-million people to the track in late May. The infield area, which once hosted race-day denizens who arrived early and spent the day drinking and ogling the opposite sex, has earned the moniker "the snakepit." Efforts to tone down some of the more, shall we say, exuberant fans resulted in a reduction of some of the shenanigans. Those heading to their seats in the grandstands should be sure to bring along the *de rigeur* fried chicken box lunch and plenty to drink. But keep in mind: It's a long way to the restrooms. General admission is $20.

June

Balkan Festival
Sts. Constantine and Elena Romanian Orthodox Church, 3237 W. 16th St. • 638-4162

Forget the fighting in the Balkans for a while and soak up that area's culture as those of Serbian, Romanian and Macedonian descent share their music, food and dance at this two-day festival in early June. Admission is $2.

Italian Festival
Holy Rosary Church, 520 Stevens St. • 636-4478

You just can't beat the combination of a warm early June evening, a cup of cappuccino and a plate of pasta — unless maybe you add some cannoli. Festival-goers, some 30,000

each year, can also enjoy music, a traditional religious procession and church tours.

Woodruff Place Flea Market
Woodruff Pl., between 10th and Michigan sts. • 685-0571

This neighborhood, developed in the late 1800s by James Woodruff, features fountains, statuary, grassy esplanades and grand old mansions. Take this early-June opportunity to wander through the neighborhood looking for bargains. You'll find everything from rummage sale knick knacks to antique furniture at this free neighborhood market.

Talbott Street Art Fair
Talbott between 16th and 19th sts. • 257-4687

One of the city's oldest festivals, it was established in 1955 by Herron art students as a way to sell their work at the end of the semester. Now, usually the second weekend after the 500, more than 200 artists working in a variety of media sell their wares in the historic Herron-Morton neighborhood, an area known for its artistic ambiance. You'll find plenty of top-notch artwork — no junk — at this popular fest, one of the last free art fairs around. (See our close-up in this chapter.)

Gus Macker 3-on-3 Basketball Tournament
IUPUI campus, 425 University Blvd. • 687-6064

Approximately 8,000 Hoosier hoopsters participate in this annual roundball roundup that matches competitors according to skill level. Anyone who's ever played driveway basketball will love to play, and it's fun to watch as well. Temporary courts are set up all over IUPUI parking lots for the mid-June double-elimination competition, the second largest on the Gus Macker tour. Entries cost $88 per team.

Meridian-Kessler Home and Garden Tour
Various homes in the Meridian-Kessler neighborhood
38th St. to Kessler Blvd. and Meridian St. to Winthrop Ave. • 283-1021

Get a glimpse inside one of the city's oldest and most prestigious neighborhoods as eight homes and gardens open for tours. The neighborhood is beautiful in the spring, and this tour, which also includes Friday night dinner and dancing, highlights some of the area's best. Walk from house to house to really get a feel for this expansive neighborhood. Admission is $6.

Strawberry Festival
Christ Church Cathedral, 55 Monument Cir. • 636-4577

Nearly 20,000 people stand in line on Monument Circle to buy these sweet treats during this popular day-long berry bonanza in mid-June. Enjoy the sweet taste of an Indiana summer as the Cathedral Women of Christ Church Cathedral dish up homemade shortcake, ice cream, strawberries and whipped cream to raise money for charities. Downtown workers often designate one person to make a strawberry run for the whole office, and the sweet servings are worth the wait.

FYI

Unless otherwise noted, the area code for all phone numbers in this guide is 317.

Deer Creek Fair
Deer Creek Music Center • 12880 E. 146th St., Noblesville • 776-3337

The whole family can enjoy this celebration of music, sports and art. You'll find a full midway, arts and crafts demonstrations and sport competitions at this mid-June festival. Admission is $3 to $6.

Midsummer Fest
Monument Cir. • 637-4574

Celebrate the summer solstice on the Circle with continuous entertainment, lots of music and food, food, food. More than 30 local restaurants and caterers set up booths, and festival-goers can find everything from bratwurst to eggrolls. Admission is $4.

July

A Glorious Fourth
Conner Prairie, 13400 Allisonville Rd., Fishers • 776-6000

Celebrate the Fourth at this living history museum where it's always 1836. Even though Independence Day wasn't yet a national holiday in 1836 (the year represented in Conner Prairie's living history village), visitors to Prairietown can still enjoy a day of patriotic celebration, complete with watermelon, homemade ice cream, a reading of the Declaration of Independence and a noon militia muster. Admission is $6.50 to $9.

Fourth Fest
Pan Am Plaza, 201 S. Capitol Ave. • 633-6363

Music, food and fireworks, all the makings of a perfect Fourth of July, characterize this day-long downtown festival. The fireworks begin after dark, so there's plenty of time to find the perfect place to ooh and ahh. Those who work downtown often set up lawn chairs atop their parking garages, while others scout out spots around the American Legion Mall and the World War Memorial. What you want is a clear view of the NBD bank tower, from which the fireworks are launched. We like to find a piece of grass and spread a blanket somewhere on the IUPUI campus. The near-downtown university offers vast parking lots and is far enough away from the action to muffle the loudest booms (a plus for those with skittish kids) and to reduce the post-fireworks traffic jams.

Indiana Black Expo Summer Celebration
Indiana Convention Center, 100 S. Capitol Ave. • 925-2792

The diverse offerings of this well-known late-July event attracts visitors from across the country. The nation's largest and longest-run-

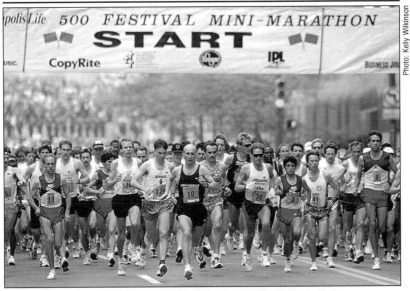

Runners begin the annual Indianapolis 500 Festival Mini-Marathon.

ning celebration of African-American culture and heritage, this festival includes an ecumenical service, music festival, boxing tournament, health fair, youth summit and an art competition and exhibition. Though much of the festivities take place at the Convention Center, other sites across the city also host Expo events. General admission is $6.

County Fairs

For a real taste of small-town Americana, visit any of Central Indiana's county fairs. Most have a week-long run in July, and you likely could spend the whole month tromping through county fairgrounds with an elephant ear in hand admiring livestock and canned goods, playing carnival games and riding the Tilt-A-Whirl. The Shelby County fair also offers harness racing, and though gambling on the trotters is not allowed at the fair (head to Hoosier Park in Anderson for that), top-notch driver Brian Barnes is the one to watch. The Marion County Fairgrounds are at 7300 E. Troy Avenue, 353-2444. Each county around Marion also hosts a fair; see our Area Overview chapter for county information and chamber of commerce numbers. There are admission fees to some fairs.

Hoosier State Games Finals
Various locations • 237-5030

The Hoosier State Games, one of the largest amateur multisport festivals in the country, offers athletes of all ages and skill levels the chance to compete in this statewide competition. The games spotlight 19 sports from bowling to water polo and include traditional Olympic-style opening and closing ceremonies. The goal of the Games is to promote health and fitness for all Indiana residents and to provide an Olympic-type experience for participants. You must be an Indiana resident for at least 30 days prior to your first competition to enter. You must also be an amateur. There is a $6 entry fee.

Kroger Circlefest
Monument Cir. • 237-2222

More than 30,000 visitors flock to the Circle in late July for this family-oriented festival, which offers plenty of food and music for Mom and Dad, plus a children's entertainment area. Now a part of the Brickyard 400 Festival, Circlefest kicks off the NASCAR celebration. Admission is $4.

August

Brickyard 400

Indianapolis Motor Speedway, 4790 W. 16th St. • 481-8500

Local race fans wholeheartedly welcomed this new Speedway event in early August 1994, when the first race resulted in a purse of $3.2 million, the richest in NASCAR history. Those who want to find out what stock car racing is all about before the big event can check out qualifications ($10 admission), when the cars will be on the oval for two days of practice prior to the race. See our Auto Racing chapter for more information. General admission is $20.

Brickyard Crossing Championship

Brickyard Crossing Golf Resort and Inn, 4400 W. 16th St. • 484-6709

This Senior PGA Tour tournament is played on the course that winds in and around the Indianapolis Motor Speedway. Admission is $8. (See our Sports chapter for more information.)

RCA Championships

Indianapolis Tennis Center, 755 University Blvd. • 632-8000

Big names in men's professional tennis hit town in mid-August for this nine-day event. (See our Sports chapter for more information.) Admission ranges from $8 to $50.

Indiana State Fair

Indiana State Fairgrounds, 102 E. 38th St. • 927-7500

August in Indiana means the State Fair, and that means corn on the cob, Hoosier rib-eye sandwiches, pork chops, lamb kabobs, elephant ears and lemon shake-ups. And all that food means more than one trip — it's at least two trips' worth of stuff to see. Of course, there are the animals, which according to sur-veys are the No. 1 attraction. Be sure to check out the world's largest male hog, a huge creature, and the tiny piglets born each year during the fair's 12-day mid-August run. Watch 4-H'ers spend hours fluffing fleece and combing manes to ready their animals for competition; these dedicated kids often camp out in the animal barns to be near their charges.

In addition to the animals, kids can't resist the midway; there are plenty of kiddie rides for the little ones as well as scarier contraptions for daredevils. Free stages offer plenty of entertainment, the Pepsi Coliseum usually hosts a wide variety of livestock shows and such performers as Randy Travis, Clint Black, Garth Brooks and Dolly Parton have filled the Grandstand. So have another elephant ear and enjoy! Admission is $3.

African American Arts Festival

30th St. and Fall Creek Pkwy. • 924-5908

At this free fest along the banks of Fall Creek, you'll find music, dance, storytelling and arts and crafts from Africa and across the United States. Plenty of food vendors offer refreshments at this mid-August family festival.

Traders Point Hunt Club Charity Horse Show and County Fair

Wild Air Farm, 7750 E. Hunt Club Rd., Zionsville • 873-5552

This highly regarded mid-August horse show features hunters, jumpers, a children's horse show and a country marketplace. Admission is $3 to $5.

Amish Country Market

Hamilton County Fairgrounds 2003 E. Pleasant St. • 545-1970

Come early to beat the crowds of shoppers at this popular late-August market. Buyers and browsers snap up Amish baked goods, craft items and one-of-a-kind gifts at the county fairgrounds in Noblesville; proceeds benefit the Julian Center women's shelter. Several

INSIDERS' TIP

Indiana Black Expo's Summer Celebration in July is the largest event of its kind in the nation and draws visitors from across the country for its annual array of festivities focused on African-American culture.

buildings house the goodies, but be prepared for crowds everywhere. If you're taking the kids, note that the market gets so packed with browsers that baby strollers must be parked outside the buildings. But don't get so wrapped up in shopping that you miss the food. Admission is $4 to $6.

Indiana Avenue Jazz Festival
Madame Walker Urban Life Center
617 Indiana Ave. • **236-2099**

Local and national jazz artists perform on the Avenue, a street with a rich music history, during this week-long event that includes an all-day festival with street food, art booths and clothing vendors. Try to catch a performance in the Walker Theater, a beautiful building that features African/Egyptian architecture.

September

WENS Skyconcert
Banks of White River, west side of downtown • **266-9700**

The "lite rock" radio station, WENS, broadcasts music synchronized to a spectacular fireworks display Labor Day weekend. Head over to the west side of downtown, find a patch of grass along the river (or, as mentioned before, on the IUPUI campus), turn up the car radio and enjoy the show.

NHRA U.S. Nationals
Indianapolis Raceway Park,
9901 Crawfordsville Rd. • **291-4090**

Approximately 150,000 fans crowd into Raceway Park each Labor Day weekend for this popular end-of-summer drag, the richest in the Winston Drag Racing Series. These high-powered monsters reach speeds of 300-plus mph and travel a quarter-mile in four seconds. Admittedly exciting, all that horsepower can also be deafening, so take along some ear plugs. Admission ranges from $5 to $53.

Oktoberfest
German Park, 8600 S. Meridian St.
• **888-6940**

We know it's not October yet, but forget the calendar and join in this traditional fall fa-vorite complete with beer, brats and oompah bands. Stretching over two weekends in early September, it's part of the state's largest celebration of German culture. Admission is $4.

Greek Festival
Holy Trinity Greek Orthodox Church, 4011 N. Pennsylvania St. • **283-3816**

One of the city's most popular food fests, visitors to the church grounds in the Meridian-Kessler neighborhood enjoy homemade gyros, shish kabobs and baklava at this early-September event. Sample baked goods and watch as parish children in traditional garb demonstrate Greek folk dances. Admission is $3.

Penrod Arts Fair
Indianapolis Museum of Art,
1200 W. 38th St. • **923-1331**

Attracting nearly 20,000 people, this juried fine arts fair in early September spotlights the work of more than 200 artists, dancers, actors and other performers. The 30-year-old festival is held on the beautiful 152-acre IMA grounds. Admission is $15.

Fiesta
American Legion Mall, Downtown
• **636-6551**

This free day-long mid-September party celebrates traditional Hispanic culture of North and South America with music, dancing, craft booths and plenty of food vendors.

Hoosier Storytelling Festival
Indianapolis Art Center, 820 E. 67th St.
• **255-7628**

Bring the kids to this late-September festival and enjoy imaginative yarns from a variety of storytellers plus workshops on telling your own tales. Some sessions are geared toward school-age kids; some toward the younger set. Call for details on times. Cost is $8 per session. Kids younger than 6 can enjoy for free.

Western Festival
Eiteljorg Museum, 500 W. Washington St.
• **636-WEST**

You'll find plenty for the whole family at this celebration of Western life, including a chili cook-off, concerts, mountain men demonstrations, cowboy storytellers and trick ropers as well as exhibits at the museum. Admission is $5; kids 12 and younger get in free.

October

Coca-Cola Circle City Classic
RCA Dome, 100 S. Capitol Ave. • 237-5222

This contest spotlights two historically black colleges and has grown to include more than 20 related events, including a princess pageant, golf tournament and parade. One of the highlights of the early-October game is the halftime show when the McDonald's Battle of the Bands provides plenty of high-stepping, hand-clapping entertainment. Admission ranges from $10 to $25.

The Headless Horseman at Conner Prairie
Conner Prairie, 13400 Allisonville Rd., Fishers • 776-6000

This amusing — not scary — evening includes a hayride through Conner Prairie's apple orchard where visitors may catch a glimpse of the headless horseman, watch costumed interpreters perform the *Legend of Sleepy Hollow* and enjoy an animated version as well. Admission is $4.

Pack Up the Car. Let's Go to a Festival!

Though we have plenty of terrific festivals in Indianapolis, it's fun to experience some in other parts of the state. Here's a handful of Indiana festivals worth the drive.

Close-up

Maple Fairs

The last weekend of February and the first weekend of March finds Parke County dripping with maple syrup. At Billie Creek Village, a mile east of Rockville on U.S. 36, visitors can view a primitive maple camp and sample maple candy and maple cream (and enjoy wagon rides, crafts and more good food as well). Call 569-3430 for details.

Photo: Auburn Cord Duesenberg Museum

Check out classic cars such as this 1929 Duesenberg during A-C-D Days, a Labor Day weekend fest celebrating Auburn's automotive heritage.

Parke County also hosts maple sugaring demonstrations at sites throughout the county (no admission charge). Call 569-5226 for information.

Wildflower Forays

Usually held the last weekend in April, this celebration of spring shows off acres of flowers at the T.C. Steele State Historic Site, off Ind. 46 near Nashville. Visitors can tour the gardens and enjoy plenty of musical entertainment with no admission charge. Call (812) 988-2785 for information.

You can usually count on plenty of blooms during the last weekend in April and the first weekend in May in Madison, and the Madison in Bloom Festival celebrates the spring color. Visitors can tour private gardens not generally open to the public in Madison's historic district. There is an admission charge of $9. Madison is in south central Indiana, east of I-65, on the Ohio River. Call (812) 265-2335 for details.

Weekend Warriors

Mid-May in Blackford County, northeast of Indianapolis off I-69, sees hundreds of costumed participants arrive for the annual Civil War Re-enactment. Watch battles and a wedding; enjoy afternoon tea, and witness a re-enactment of the 1862 draft riot. There is an admission charge of $5. Call 348-2938 for more information.

The Memorial Day weekend draws plenty of history buffs to Vincennes, on U.S. 41 in southwestern Indiana, for its well-known Spirit of Vincennes Rendezvous. The event features 1700-to-1840-era artists and craftspeople at work and includes early American foods, kids' games and battle re-enactments. There is an admission charge of $3.50; $1 for kids. Call (812) 882-7079 for information.

Pickin' and Grinnin'

Visitors to Petersburg, a small community in southern Indiana, will get an earful the first weekend in June when the town hosts the Indiana State Pickin' and Fiddlin' Contest. Musicians will compete in guitar, mandolin, banjo, harmonica and fiddle, and visitors can sing along to the old-time bluegrass music. There is an admission charge of $5. Call (812) 354-8155 for details.

For another bluegrass get-together, head to Bean Blossom, south of Indianapolis on Ind. 135, to the mid-June Annual Bluegrass Festival. The longest-running bluegrass event in the country marked its 30th year in 1996. Admission fees range from $13 to $18; three-day passes are available as well. Call (615) 868-3333 for more information.

Something Fishy

Here are three choices for those eager to sample a real Hoosier tradition: the annual community fish fry. In late June, anyone hungry for wall-eye and codfish sandwiches, generally served up with coleslaw and fruit pie, can head to Fairland, a tiny burg in Shelby County; call 835-7744; Palmyra, a tiny burg in Harison County; call (812) 364-6122; or Jonesville, a tiny burg in Bartholomew County; call (812)-522-7728. At all three you'll find live music, entertainment and craft booths with no admission charge.

A Week in Fort Wayne

After the Fourth of July celebrations are over, Fort Wayne gears up for its huge Three Rivers Festival, a week-long extravaganza with a parade, lots of art, children's events and fireworks. Most events are free. Call (219) 745-5556 for details.

But if you miss Three Rivers, catch Fort Wayne's late-July Indiana Highland Games. This celebration of Scottish heritage, with pipe and drum bands, Highland dancing and clan tents is held at Zollner Stadium at Concordia Lutheran High School. Be sure to arrive early to see all the events, including the athletics competition. There is admission fee of $7. Call (219) 436-0705 for information.

Historic Heritage

Enjoy great food and admire the work of 350 artists and crafters at the mid-August Amish Acres Arts and Crafts Festival in Napanee in northeastern Indiana. You'll also find two entertainment stages and plenty of great food (see our Daytrips and Weekend Getaways chapter for more on Amish country and call 219-773-4188 for more information).

For another angle of history, attend the Annual Traditional Pow-wow at the Boone County 4-H Fairgrounds in Lebanon, northwest of Indianapolis off I-65, scheduled for the third weekend of August. You'll enjoy Native American dancing, singing, food and arts and crafts. Call 482-3315 for details. There is a $4 admission fee; $2 for kids.

For a look at Indiana's automotive heritage, head to Auburn, off I-69 in DeKalb County during Labor Day Weekend. Tour the art-deco Auburn Cord Duesenberg Museum; Saturday afternoon brings scores of antique cars for Parade of Classics. Check out how much such antiques go for at the classic car auction. After the parade, you can get a close-up look at the cars while they're parked downtown. Call (219) 925-3600 for information.

Even More History

Early October brings visitors to Greenfield, east of Indianapolis in Hancock County, to celebrate Hoosier poet James Whitcomb Riley during James Whitcomb Riley Days. Visitors enjoy arts and crafts, a fine arts show and, of course, a poetry contest. There's no admission charge. Call 462-4188 for more information.

Enjoy a re-created gathering of French and Indians at Fort Ouiatenon Historic Park near Lafayette in west central Indiana during the Feast of the Hunters Moon. Peruse authentic crafts, enjoy military demonstrations and indulge in tasty cooked-outdoors food. There is a $7 admission charge; $3 for kids. Call 742-8411 for details.

Annual Haunted House
Children's Museum, 3000 N. Meridian St.
• 924-5431

The museum guild sponsors this October tradition that opens mid-month and boasts a different creepy theme each year. Last year's was dubbed the International House of Haunts, with spooky displays including the Amazon "Brain" Forest. Much less gruesome than many local haunted houses, the Children's Museum's exhibition even offers lights-on tours for the littlest kids. Admission is $3.50.

Halloween Zoobilee
Indianapolis Zoo, 1200 W. Washington St.
• 630-2001

Kids dressed as goblins, ghouls or even Power Rangers can participate in a costume contest, go trick-or-treating at different spots throughout the zoo, roast marshmallows and

enjoy crafts and magic shows. Admission is $5.50 to $9.

Pumpkin Harvest Festival
Stoneycreek Farm, 11366 Ind. 38 E., Noblesville • 776-9427

Throughout October, visitors to this Noblesville-area farm can hitch a ride on a haywagon to the pumpkin patch, see farm animals, explore a haunted barn and even have lunch at the Country Market. Admission is $2 on weekends.

Victorian Day Celebration
Crown Hill Cemetery, 700 W. 38th St.
• 925-8231

Forget the idea of spooky cemeteries. Crown Hill is a beautiful spot to enjoy a day of Victorian-era events such as Civil War re-enactments, live entertainment and a Victorian gown exhibit. Food is available, and visitors can even take a carriage or stagecoach ride. Admission is $7 for adults and $2 for kids.

November

Christmas Gift and Hobby Show
Indiana State Fairgrounds, 1202 E. 38th St. • 927-7500

Get in the Christmas mood early at one of the season's biggest bazaars. For more than 40 years, this annual extravaganza, billed as the world's largest, has been providing crafts, gift ideas and holiday food to its faithful visitors, many of whom come back year after year. Admission is $6.

Toy Soldiers Playground
Indiana State Museum, 202 N. Alabama St. • 232-1637

Gather up the kids and take along a camera. This exhibit, which traditionally opens the weekend after Thanksgiving, features the old L.S. Ayres Santaland Express train that many locals remember from their own childhoods. Enjoy carolling choirs in the rotunda while little ones give Santa their wish lists.

FYI

Unless otherwise noted, the area code for all phone numbers in this guide is 317.

Winterland Holiday Drive-Thru Light Show
Indiana State Fairgrounds, 1202 E. 38th St. • 927-7500

Load up the car and head to the fairgrounds to view more than 5 million lights in displays that stretch for 2.5 miles. The Midwest's largest holiday display is illuminated from mid-November through early January.

Celebration of Lights
Monument Cir. • 237-2222

For more than 30 years, Indianapolis residents have been braving the cold on the Friday night after Thanksgiving to watch the lighting of "the world's largest Christmas tree." Strung with lights, the monument does indeed resemble a tree, and the whole family will cheer as a local child flips the switch that lights up the 284-foot-tall monument.

December

Christmas in the Village
Main St., Zionsville • 873-3836

Stroll the streets of this charming Boone County town during the holidays and enjoy specialty shops, unique restaurants and plenty of festive holiday decorations.

Kroger Christmas at the Zoo
1200 W. Washington St., Indianapolis Zoo • 630-2001

All through December the zoo sparkles with more than 150,000 twinkling lights and animated displays. Lines can be long (and the weather chilly) for this popular holiday event where kids can ride a camel, see real reindeer and enjoy a special holiday dolphin show. Zoo admission is $5.50 to $9.

Conner Prairie by Candlelight
Conner Prairie, 1300 Allisonville Rd., Fishers • 776-6000

Walk through Prairietown during December and talk with costumed interpreters who explain Christmas celebrations c. 1836. Christmas wasn't the extravaganza it is today, and kids will likely be surprised at the simplicity of the holiday observation. Admission is $7.50 to $9.50.

Holiday Candlelight Tour
Various locations • 639-4534

Enjoy a Historic Landmarks walking tour that takes visitors to the Morris-Butler, Kemper and President Benjamin Harrison homes, all decorated for a Victorian holiday. Admission is $8.

INSIDERS' TIP

Zionsville's Christmas in the Village, with its quaint brick streets, unique shops and thousands of twinkling lights, is guaranteed to put just about anyone in the Christmas spirit.

Garfield Park Conservatory Poinsettia Show
Garfield Park and Conservatory, 2450 S. Shelby St. • 327-7184

This traditional holiday poinsettia show has continued for nearly 60 years, and though the conservatory closed for months for renovation, it reopened in early 1997. The flowers are spectacular during the show, and later in the month you can get a good price on the poinsettias during the annual sale.

Indianapolis Auto Show
100 S. Capitol Ave., Convention Center and RCA Dome • 262-3410

Traditionally held the weekend after Christmas, the Auto Show provides a place to go to escape a houseful of visiting relatives when not much else is going on. Lust after the latest in automotive technology and plan next year's Christmas wish list. Admission is $5.

Street Art

What began as a way for Herron art school students to sell their work at the end of the semester has evolved over the years into a popular weekend street fair that stretches along three blocks of one of the city's unique historic areas. Talbott Street Art Fair, usually held in early June, stretches for several blocks, beginning at the Herron School of Art building at 16th and Talbott streets.

When it began in the late '50s, patios were turned into display areas, and artists hung their canvases on carriage house walls. Now, more than 250 craftspersons from 21 states exhibit their wares in this well-regarded juried show. When you walk along Talbott Street during the rest of the year, you can see little painted lines on the streets marking booth space; you'll see many familiar faces if you attend the fair regularly.

Photo: The Indianapolis Star and The Indianapolis News

Paintings, drawings and sculptures are just a sample of the variety available at the annual Talbott Street Art Fair in early June.

Be prepared for crowds. Go with the flow and wander through the displays. You find ceramicists, painters, metalworkers, sculptors, wood carvers and just about every other artistic specialty imaginable — and some you couldn't even imagine. It's all good though; you'll find no hokey junk.

Talbott Street Art Fair turned 40 in 1995, and the venerable art fest, the oldest of its kind in the state, remains one of the best. Traditionally held the second weekend after the Indy 500, the weather is often hot, but participating artists prefer high temperatures to the spring-in-Indiana thunderstorms that keep browsers and buyers away. There is no admission charge.

Since the city's founding, literature has played a significant role in the cultural life of Indianapolis.

Literary Life

Is there literary life in Indianapolis? Yes, most definitely. There are a number of literary groups and events for writers and readers alike. There is a superb public library system as well as a wonderful state library and some fine university libraries. And there are plenty of very good bookstores. You'll find a lot of writers living in and around Indianapolis: poets and novelists, children's authors and journalists, historians and playwrights, screenwriters and biographers, authors of romances, mysteries and science fiction.

Yes, there is literary life in Indianapolis, and there always has been. In fact, the city was once (and many maintain, may yet be again) the literary center of the Midwest.

A Brief History

Since the city's founding, literature has played a significant role in the cultural life of Indianapolis. When Indiana's first state treasurer, Samuel Merrill, left the old capital of Corydon for Indianapolis in 1824, he brought with him the contents of the state library as well as those of his own personal book collection. To Merrill, life without literature was unthinkable.

So unthinkable that in 1850, he bought one of the city's two existing bookstores and increased its inventory. He also established the Merrill Publishing Company, which initially focused on producing law books but eventually expanded into trade books. By the early 20th century, the firm, which through a series of mergers became Bobbs-Merrill, was one of the leading trade publishers in the United States. On its roster were such bestselling Indiana authors as James Whitcomb Riley, Meredith Nicholson, George Ade and Booth Tarkington, who collectively were known in publishing circles as "The Big Four."

In fact, those four writers, along with other Bobbs-Merrill authors such as Maurice Thompson (*Alice of Old Vincennes*) and Charles Major (*When Knighthood Was in Flower*), were important contributors to an era known as Indiana's Golden Age. Comprised roughly of a period from 1880 to 1920, the Golden Age was a time when Indiana and Indianapolis gained and sustained national attention for their contributions to American culture, politics and commerce. (While Bobbs-Merrill is no longer in operation, Indianapolis is currently home to a number of other publishing firms.)

The literature produced by Indianapolis writers in the Golden Age ranged from scholarly nonfiction to mystery and romance. Attorney and politician Albert Beveridge's four-volume biography, *The Life of John Marshall*, published in 1916, garnered widespread acclaim. Meredith Nicholson's *The House of a Thousand Candles* mixed mystery with romance to become a national bestseller.

The Golden Age ended with World War I, and Indianapolis lost its position as the literary center of the Midwest to Chicago. But the city continued to contribute to American literature. In fact, two of the most significant figures in the development of contemporary writing were Indianapolis natives and members of the famous Lost Generation in post-WWI Paris.

Margaret Anderson, an Indianapolis native and founder of the *Little Review*, a literary magazine based at various times in Chicago, New York and Paris, was an early supporter and publisher of such rising literary stars as Ernest Hemingway and James Joyce. And her friend Janet Flanner, who often wrote under the pen name of Genet, was a regular contributor to *The New Yorker* and author of a number of widely respected books including *An American in Paris* and *Paris Journals*.

Another Indianapolis-bred writer who gained national stature in the wake of a war — this time World War II — was novelist Kurt Vonnegut Jr. The son of a prominent Indianapolis architect, Vonnegut witnessed the horrors of war firsthand, including the firebombing of Dresden, Germany, an event that colored his outlook on war and on America. In the 1960s and '70s, Vonnegut's biting satire and black humor, evident in such books as his anti-war masterpiece, *Slaughterhouse Five*, made him one of the country's most popular writers.

The roster of significant 20th-century writers from Indianapolis also includes novelist and nonfiction writer Dan Wakefield, poets Etheridge Knight and Mari Evans, fiction writer and essayist Susan Neville and historian Alan T. Nolan.

Reading

For avid readers, Central Indiana is a gold mine of book discussion groups, some independent, others hosted by branch libraries or by bookstores, that meet regularly throughout the area. And there are a number of reading and lecture series sponsored by the Indianapolis-Marion Public Library, the Writers' Center, the Butler University Writers' Studio and the Indiana Humanities Council.

And finally, Indianapolis can claim dozens of bookstores ranging from large general interest stores such as Borders, Barnes & Noble, and B. Dalton to small, specialized shops dealing in children's books, mysteries, religious books, feminist books or comic books.

Whether you yearn to write a book or just like to keep your nose buried in one, Indianapolis has something for you. Read on.

Bookstores

You can learn a lot about the vitality of a community's literary life by the number and variety of bookstores it contains, and by this measure Indianapolis is in good shape. At last count, there were some 60 bookstores, including those with more than one location, in the Greater Indianapolis area. (For a detailed listing, see our Close-up in the Shopping chapter.)

Reading Groups

Like the literary salons and clubs of the past, reading groups (aka book discussion groups) bring book lovers together to talk about books and authors. In Indianapolis, there are dozens of these groups, many of which are privately run. But there are also many more that are open to the public, namely those operated by area libraries and bookstores.

If you like to talk about what you read the following groups welcome newcomers. (Meeting days and times are subject to change, so check with individual locations for confirmation.)

Library Groups

Several reading groups meet at Indianapolis-Marion County Public Library branches. Each of the following groups is general in interest — that is, they read a range of books, fiction and nonfiction, rather than focusing on specialized types of books. Some people attend more than one group, others prefer to find a group they're comfortable with and leave it at that. The choice is yours.

The Broad Ripple Book Discussion Group
Broad Ripple Library 1550, Broad Ripple Ave. • 269-1791

This groups meets the second Tuesday of each month from 10:15 to 11:15 AM.

The Brown Library Book Review Group Brown Library
5427 E. Washington St. • 269-1864

This groups meets six times a year, usually in the spring and fall, on the second Thursday of the month from 1:30 to 2:30 PM.

The Nora Book Discussion Group
Nora Library, 8625 Guilford Ave. • 269-1830

This group meets the first Tuesday of each month from 10:15 to 11:15 AM.

The Southport Library Book Discussion Group
Southport Library, 2630 E. Stop 11 Rd. • 269-1873

This group meets on the fourth Monday of each month from 7 to 8 PM.

Bookstore Groups

Bookstores have a vested interest in hosting reading groups because they attract regular groups of avid readers to their sites and promote reading. Both of these are pluses for booksellers. But the real point is getting books into the hands of people who want to read and talk about them.

What sets bookstore groups apart from the library groups is that they tend to be focused on specific topics or interests. Two of the city's largest bookstores also host some of its liveliest specialized reading groups.

Borders Book Shop
5612 Castleton Corner • 849-8660

Long a popular haunt for true book lovers, Borders has a really knowledgeable staff (as in, people who read books as well as sell them) and a browser-friendly environment. Because of its popularity, it was a natural place for reading groups to congregate, and they do.

The Classics Club meets on the second Wednesday of each month at 7:30 PM.

The Mystery Club meets on the third Wednesday of each month at 7:30 PM.

The Military History Club meets on the first Thursday of each month at 7:30 PM.

The Contemporary Fiction Club meets on the fourth Wednesday of each month at 7:30 PM.

The Lavender Book Club, which deals with gay and lesbian topics, meets on the third Thursday of each month at 7:30 PM.

Barnes & Noble Bookstore
3748 E. 82nd St. • 594-7525

A relative newcomer to the local literary scene (this store opened in 1994), Barnes & Noble has attracted a loyal following, in part for its friendly atmosphere and in-store coffee shop, which invites customers to relax and read over a cup o' joe. Like Borders, B&N hosts a variety of reading groups.

The African American Discussion Group meets on the first Thursday of each month at 7:30 PM.

The Indy Fiction Lovers meet on the first Tuesday of each month at 7:30 PM.

The Coffee and Book Chat groups meets on the second Monday of each month at 10 AM.

The Women's Issues group meets on the third Thursday of each month at 7:30 PM.

The Singles Who Love Books group meets on the third Thursday of each month at 7:30 PM.

The Literature and Medicine group meets on the fourth Thursday of each month at 7:30 PM.

The History Reading Group meets on the fourth Wednesday of each month at 7:30 PM.

The Blue Blazer International Reading Group, which reads and discusses titles from the Great Books program, meets quarterly. Call Barnes & Noble for the date, time and topic.

FYI

Unless otherwise noted, the area code for all phone numbers in this guide is 317.

Literary Organizations, Facilities and Programs

Indiana Arts Commission (IAC)
402 W. Washington St. • 232-1268

This statewide arts agency promotes and sponsors several programs of interest to writers, including biannual fellowship grants to help writers underwrite the costs of writing projects and the artists-in-education program, which provides matching grants to schools for writing residencies. The IAC also helps underwrite reading and storytelling series as well as literary events and publications.

Indiana Humanities Council (IHC)
1500 N. Delaware St. • 638-1500

In addition to helping fund reading and lecture series, this statewide organization, an affiliate of the National Endowment for the Humanities, is the sponsoring agency for the biannual WORDSTRUCK literary festival (see the "Literary Events" section of this chapter).

Butler University Writers' Studio
4600 Sunset Ln., Jordan Hall 304
• 940-9861

Founded by award-winning fiction writer and essayist Susan Neville, a member of Butler's English department, the Writer's Studio provides students direct access to the experience, skills and advice of area poets, novelists, journalists and playwrights through its fellowship program. The studio also sponsors the annual Visiting Writer Series that presents lectures and readings (most of which are open to the public) by nationally known writers such as Grace Paley and hometown hero Kurt Vonnegut Jr. (see our Literary Stars Close-up in this chapter), along with such Indiana favorites as Michael Martone and Scott Russell Sanders.

Indianapolis-Marion County Public Library
40 E. St. Clair St. • 269-1700

Standing on land donated by local literary legend James Whitcomb Riley (see our Literary Stars Close-up in this chapter), the Indianapolis-Marion County Public Library's downtown facility, which is known officially as the Central Library, is one of the city's architectural and literary treasures. Inside this lovely old building (Greek Doric style, c. 1916), you'll find some 1.7 million books, magazines, newspapers, audio tapes, CDs, films, videotapes, artwork and other items.

There were two or three early and unsuccessful attempts at creating libraries in Indianapolis before an impassioned sermon by Rev. Hanford A. Edson of the Second Presbyterian Church on the Thanksgiving Day 1868, on the need for a free, public library led 113 citizens to form the Indianapolis Library Association. After four years of fund-raising and policy-making, the Indianapolis Public Library opened in one room of a school at the intersection of Pennsylvania and Michigan streets. Its collection consisted of 12,790 books.

From that early effort, the library began to grow, including expanding its service area in 1968 to all Marion County (except Beech Grove and Speedway, which maintain their own community libraries). Today, in addition to the Central Library, the Indianapolis-Marion County Public Library system contains 21 branch libraries and an extension services division that provides library programs to neighborhood community centers.

Among the library's many programs are several of interest to writers and readers, including readings and workshops presented by local and national writers. Every March, the library hosts the Marian McFadden Memorial Lecture, which, on alternate years, features a renowned author of adult or children's books, such as Saul Bellow, Chris Van Allsburg, Madeline L'Engle and Tom Wolfe.

Several of the branch libraries also host book discussion groups (see entries under the "Reading Clubs" section of this chapter) for readers who like to talk about books as well as read them. And for those whose love of literature outpaces their finances, six times a year the library holds used book sales at the Extension Services building at 2450 N. Meridian Street.

For information on the schedule of specific events and activities, pick up a copy of the library's bimonthly newsletter, *Reading in Indianapolis*, which is available at the Central Library and all branches. The Central Library is open Monday through Friday, 9 AM to 9 PM; Saturday, 9 AM to 6 PM; and Sunday 1 to 5 PM. Branch library hours vary by site.

The Writers' Center Inc.
3200 Cold Spring Rd. • 929-0625

From its headquarters in St. Francis Hall on the campus of Marian College, the Writers' Center, which is Indiana's only comprehensive community-based literary organization, offers workshops, special-interest writing groups, educational programs and readings by regionally and nationally prominent poets, fiction and nonfiction writers. Among its programs are the annual Naptown Invitational Reading Series and the Visiting Writers Series. The Center also plays an active role in the planning and development of the biannual WORDSTRUCK literary festival (see related Close-up in this chapter). Additionally, it hosts open readings at The Slippery Noodle Inn, a downtown blues club.

The Writers' Center publishes *Literally*, a quarterly newsletter, which provides up-to-date information about literary events in the area and information about upcoming writing con-

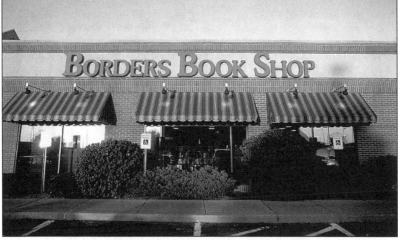

Many reading groups congregate at Borders Book Shop at Castleton Corner.

tests and publications that are seeking submissions. The Writers' Center Press offers Indiana writers opportunities to publish in its semiannual magazine, *The Flying Island*, as well as in occasional chapbooks and through various competitions.

The organization's Marian College office houses a resource library of literary publications, writers' aids, reference books and an informal meeting space for Center members.

Membership to the Writers' Center is $30 per year for individuals in Marion and adjoining counties, $20 for non-local, students and seniors.

Whether you're interested in poetry, scriptwriting, fiction or nonfiction, chances are the Writers' Center offers a workshop, discussion group or publication that will meet your needs. Call for a schedule of classes and events.

Indiana State Library
140 N. Senate Ave. • 232-3675

Established in 1825, this state-run institution is the central repository of all documents and publications pertaining to Indiana's government as well as a regional repository for U.S. government documents. Additionally, it's a treasure trove of materials, including books, maps, letters, pamphlets, brochures, newspapers, magazines, manuscripts and photographs, from the state's territorial days to the present. The on-site genealogy division is a popular resource for writers, scholars, historians and families. The library's staff is both knowledgeable and helpful in seeing that writers and readers make best use of the available resources.

In addition to housing the library collections, the State Library building, which is just west of the State Capitol, is also home to the Indiana Center for the Book (see following entry) and the Indiana Historical Society. The State Library is open Monday through Friday, 8 AM to 4:30 PM; the genealogy department is open Saturday from Labor Day to Memorial Day, 8 AM to 4 PM.

Indiana Center for the Book
140 Senate Ave. • 232-3569

Established in 1989 to stimulate public interest in books, reading, publishing and literacy throughout the state, the Indiana Center for the Book periodically sponsors programs, discussion groups, lectures and exhibitions. Affiliated with the Library of Congress's national Center for the Book, the Indiana Center works with writers, educators and librarians to develop projects aimed at encouraging appreciation for books from both an aesthetic and educational perspective.

University Library at IUPUI
755 W. Michigan St. • 274-0472

One of the first libraries in the United States designed for the electronic information age, this new facility (c. 1993) on the campus of Indiana University-Purdue University of Indianapolis (IUPUI) contains a fiber optics network that allows voice, video, data and graphics to be transmitted to multimedia stations throughout the library. There are also 100 on-site workstations that provide patrons with free access to the World Wide Web and the Internet.

Of course, the library also contains more traditional resources too — a half-million books, an extensive microfilm and microfiche collection and a periodicals department that subscribes to 3,000 magazines and newspapers from around the world, including an array of popular and obscure literary publications.

The library, which is open to the general public and IUPUI students and staff, is open Monday through Thursday, 8 AM to 11 PM; Friday, 8 AM to 9 PM; Saturday, 8 AM to 7 PM; and Sunday, 10 AM to 11 PM.

Literary Events

WORDSTRUCK
Indiana Humanities Council, 1500 N. Delaware St. • 638-1500

Produced biennially by the Indiana Humanities Council in cooperation with more than two dozen area cultural organizations, WORDSTRUCK is a free, citywide event that celebrates the power and pleasure of books and reading through public programs such as lectures, readings and workshops by regionally and nationally known writers. In the past, the four-day event has attracted such notables as Kurt Vonnegut Jr. and Dan Wakefield, both products of Indianapolis. (See our Literary Stars Close-up in this chapter.)

Butler University Midwinter Children's Literature Conference
4600 Sunset Ave. • 940-9861

Since 1991, this annual conference has been held on the campus of Butler University each February. Conference participants attend presentations and workshops given by internationally known, award-winning children's book authors and illustrators, children's book editors and agents, university professors, book critics, teachers, and librarians. Past speakers have included Avi, Kathryn Lasky, Jerry Pinkney and conference organizer (and acclaimed local author) Valiska Gregory.

In addition to conference activities, there are a variety of other community activities, such as readings, lectures and book signings, that are open to the public, free of charge.

Visiting Writers Series
Butler University Writer's Studio, 4600 Sunset Ave., Jordan Hall 304 • 940-9861

In keeping with its ongoing commitment to the city's literary life, Butler University hosts this series that brings poets, novelists and nonfiction writers to town for readings and lectures throughout the fall and winter. The events are held on the university campus, either in Robertson Hall or Clowes Memorial Hall, and most are open to the public. In the past, such notable writers as Grace Paley, Robert Bly and P.J. O'Rourke have taken part in the series. Contact the Butler Writer's Studio to be put on the series mailing list, or watch the events calendars in *The Indianapolis Star* and *The Indianapolis News*.

Literary Landmarks

Meredith Nicholson Residence
1500 N. Delaware St. • 638-1500

Formerly home to early 20th-century nov-

INSIDERS' TIP

The near-east side neighborhood of Woodruff Place, between Michigan and 10th streets near the Indiana Women's Prison was likely the setting of Booth Tarkington's *The Magnificent Ambersons*. Many of the area's homes have been restored and are indeed magnificent.

The Ruth Lilly Poetry Prize

It's no secret that poets don't get rich, at least not from writing poetry. But a select few do once in a while win prizes that enrich both their reputations and, to some degree, their bank accounts. The Ruth Lilly Poetry Prize is one such prize.

In fact, it's one of the most desirable prizes in the literary world, in so far as its cash value is concerned. Established in 1986 by wealthy arts patron and poetry fan Ruth Lilly, a member of the Eli Lilly and Company founder's family, the annual prize includes a $75,000

Photo: The Indianapolis Star and The Indianapolis News

David R. Wagoner grew up in Whiting during the 1930s.

honorarium that makes it one of the richest literary awards in the world.

Chosen by a three-member panel — the editor of the Chicago-based *Poetry* magazine and two poets of the editor's choice — the Ruth Lilly Poetry Prize recipient is judged on the merits of his or her body of work. The official citation reads that the prize is given "to an American poet whose accomplishments warrant extraordinary recognition."

Since its inception, the list of Lilly prize winners reads like a Who's Who of American poetry: Hayden Carruth, Adrienne Rich, Donald Hall, David Wagoner, Philip Levine, Mona Van Duyn, Anthony Hecht, John Ashbery and Charles Wright. (Of that list, only Wagoner has connections to Indiana, having been born in the northwestern town of Whiting.)

Apart from its generous honorarium, the Ruth Lilly Poetry Prize is important for another reason. In an era when poets and poetry are increasingly devalued, the prize bestows a sense of value to an ancient and honorable literary art form.

---

elist and nonfiction writer, Meredith Nicholson, this lovely brick structure now houses the offices of the Indiana Humanities Council. As such, it's not open for public tours, but you might want to call and ask if there's a time you could come by and look around.

James Whitcomb Riley House
528 Lockerbie St. • 631-5885

Without a doubt one of the city's best-known landmarks, literary or otherwise, this two-story brick Victorian was Riley's home for the last 23 years of his life. And it looks as if he just stepped out for a minute (there's a pen on his desk and a hat on his bed) rather than for eternity (he died in 1916).

This house, with its faded, worn rugs and furniture, is a mecca of sorts for Riley fans who come from around the world to pay homage to a poet who parlayed a penchant for rustic dialect and simple rhythms into bestsellerdom. Among his best-known works are such schoolroom mainstays as "'Little Orphant Annie" and "When the Frost Is on the Punkin'."

The Riley House, which is listed on the National Register of Historic Places, is open Tuesday through Saturday 10 AM to 4 PM and Sunday noon to 4 PM. It's closed on major holidays. Admission is $2 for adults, $1.50 for seniors, 50¢ for children 7 to 17 and free for those 6 and younger.

James Whitcomb Riley Grave
Crown Hill Cemetery
700 W. 38th St. • 925-8231

Atop the Strawberry Hill, at the highest natural point in Indianapolis, Riley's grave is one of the city's memorable memorials. It's a great place for a picnic, especially on a clear sunny day when you can gaze out on the city as it spreads out in all directions from Crown Hill.

Note the small headstone next to Riley's Greek temple that reads, "The Poet's Favorite Niece." That's her only identification — and her only legacy.

To find Riley's memorial, enter the cemetery at the 34th Street gate and follow the signs.

Booth Tarkington House
4270 N. Meridian St.

Formerly the home of Pulitzer Prize-winning novelist and playwright Booth Tarkington, this magnificent Tudor-style mansion is still a private residence and therefore not open for tours. But it's worth driving by just to catch a glimpse of the elegance in which one of the city's literary lions once lived.

INSIDERS' TIP

The achievements of Indiana's pioneer poet laureate, Sarah T. Bolton, are remembered with a bronze plaque in the rotunda of the Statehouse.

Literary Stars

Throughout its history, Indianapolis has had its share of literary stars. Some lived here during their youth and left to make their reputations elsewhere; others called Indianapolis home in the midst of their fame. Among the best known of the city's luminaries, past and present, are:

Sara T. Bolton (1814-1893)

Indiana's unofficial poet laureate, Bolton came to Indianapolis in 1831, having married local newspaper publisher Nathaniel Bolton. Here she raised two children, worked on political and social causes and wrote poems. Probably her best-known work was the nationally distributed "Paddle Your Own Canoe," which contained the lines:

Nothing great is lightly won
Nothing won is lost
But if you succeed you must
Paddle your own canoe.

Close-up

Janet Flanner, aka Genet (1892-1978)

The daughter of a prominent Indianapolis family, Flanner got her early training in writing as an arts reporter and reviewer for *The Indianapolis Star*. When she was 26, she married and moved to New York, rarely returning. Moving once again when she was 30, this time to Paris, she finally found her voice as a writer when she began doing a column for *The New Yorker* in 1925; using the pen name Genet, she wrote a semimonthly "Letter from Paris," as well as other pieces for the magazine for 50 years. She also wrote a number of books, including *An American in Paris* (1940) and *Paris Journals*, 1944-1965 (winner of a National Book Award in 1966).

Etheridge Knight (1931-1991)

From his beginnings as a poet while imprisoned in the Indiana State Prison, Knight went on to become one of the country's best-known and most-respected African-American poets. Winner of a number of writing awards, Knight was also in demand as a reader and workshop leader at universities and prisons. Among his best-known collections of poems are *Poems from Prison* (1968), *Belly Song and Other Poems* (1973), and *Born of Woman* (1980). In 1986, his book, *The Essential Etheridge Knight* won the Before Columbus American Book Award.

Meredith Nicholson (1866-1947)

The author of 29 books and scores of essays and stories, Nicholson began his writing career on the staff of *The Indianapolis News*. From there he went on to success as a businessman, but dissatisfied, he continued to write. The success of his history of Indiana, *The Hoosiers*, in 1900 led Nicholson to turn to writing full-time. Among his best-known works are the novels *House of a Thousand Candles* and *A Hoosier Chronicle* and a volume of biographical sketches entitled *Old Familiar Faces*.

Nicholson gave up writing in the 1930s, becoming at the behest of President Franklin Delano Roosevelt a diplomat, serving at posts in Paraguay, Venezuela and Nicaragua.

Booth Tarkington (1869-1946)

Son of a local circuit court judge, Tarkington turned a boyhood penchant for mischief and theatrics into a lucrative career as a fiction writer and playwright. A

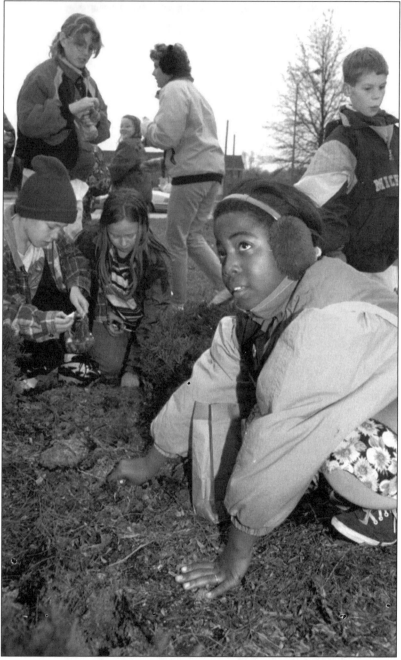

Photo: The Indianapolis Star and The Indianapolis News

Educational and fun opportunities abound for kids in Indianapolis.

graduate of Princeton University where he was a star in the drama department and editor of three publications, Tarkington nearly derailed his career through his drinking. Despite his love of alcohol, he managed to capture national attention in 1899 with the publication of his novel, *The Gentleman from Indiana*.

Other books and plays followed, but meanwhile, his first marriage floundered. Finally, in 1912, he went on the wagon — his career blossomed even further as he turned out such well-received books as *Penrod*, a collection of stories about a eponymous young hero, and *The Magnificent Ambersons* (1919) and *Alice Adams* (1921), both Pulitzer Prize-winning novels. Tarkington is widely regarded as one of Indianapolis' leading early 20th-century literary lights, along with Riley and Nicholson.

Photo: The Indianapolis Star and The Indianapolis News

Kurt Vonnegut Jr. is one of America's leading satirists.

Kurt Vonnegut Jr. (1922-   )

Born into a prominent family (Kurt Vonnegut Sr. was a well-known architect), Vonnegut left Indianapolis to serve in World War II. After the war, he joined General Electric's public relations department where he remained for several years while writing stories and novels on the side. Widespread popularity of such Vonnegut books as *God Bless You Mr. Rosewater*, *Player Piano* and *Slaughterhouse Five* in the 1960s and 1970s allowed him to write full-time. Since then, he has continued to be one of America's leading satirists and social critics.

Dan Wakefield (1932-   )

The author of such novels as *Going All the Way* and *Starting Over* and nonfiction books such as *New York in the Fifties*, Wakefield left Indianapolis for New York in 1952. There he made a name for himself as a journalist, contributing to such publications as *Atlantic Monthly* and *Esquire*. Wakefield returns frequently to his hometown for readings and speeches.

Clearly, the arts are more than window-dressing in Indianapolis: They're a vital part of the city's economic infrastructure and a vital part of people's lives.

The Arts

First, let's acknowledge the obvious: When it comes to the arts, Indianapolis is no New York. But it is the hub of artistic activity in Indiana. The arts are well-represented here, at least insofar as the mainstream is concerned.

If you're looking for avant garde, cutting-edge stuff, you'll have to look hard. Experimentation happens here but not to the extent that you'll find in more cosmopolitan cities. Chalk that up to Midwestern conservatism, both in attitude and in funding. Corporate and foundation coffers tend to open more freely if the artist or organization requesting help is producing safe, noncontroversial art. Still, safe as most of it is, the art being produced here on many fronts is high quality — a reflection of the caliber of the artists and the arts organizations in the community. Sometimes on extremely tight budgets, creators and presenters alike not only find ways to make ends meet but also to produce credible, commendable works of art.

The arts have a significant impact on the local economy. According to a study commissioned by the Arts Council of Indianapolis and conducted by Indiana University's Center for Urban Policy and the Environment, the total annual impact of the arts on the city's economy is $46 million. What's more, there are some 4,000 people employed by 200 local arts organizations — and they account for a payroll of $35 million. Clearly, the arts are more than window-dressing in Indianapolis: They're a vital part of the city's economic infrastructure and a vital part of people's lives. Arts organizations report a collective attendance total of nearly 5 million people annually. The arts are alive and well in Indianapolis.

But don't take our word for it. Go see and hear for yourself.

Support Organizations

Indiana Arts Commission (IAC)
402 W. Washington St. • 232-1268

This state agency is responsible for promoting the arts and providing financial assistance to arts organizations and artists throughout Indiana. Using funds from the National Endowment for the Arts and those allocated to it by the state legislature, the IAC operates a number of programs ranging from artists fellowships to a popular and widely admired arts education program that puts painters, poets, potters, percussionists and a potpourri of other artists into classrooms statewide.

Indiana Humanities Council (IHC)
1500 N. Delaware St. • 638-1500

Using funds from the National Endowment for the Humanities and from contributions made by corporations, foundations and individuals, the IHC funds the development of programs and projects (lectures, discussion groups, film series and readings) aimed at exploring the cultural and academic life of Indiana. One such program is the popular biannual WORDSTRUCK a weeklong celebration of Indiana's literary life. (For more on this, see our Literary Life chapter.)

The Arts Council of Indianapolis
47 S. Pennsylvania St., No. 701 • 631-3301

This private, nonprofit organization is charged with providing financial, planning, programming and management assistance to arts organizations, artists and the local community. It also operates the city's newest arts facility — the Artsgarden, Circle Centre's arts information center inside the glass-enclosed arch that spans West Washington Street (see the close-up in this chapter).

Indiana Advocates for the Arts/ Indiana Citizens for the Arts
401 E. Michigan St. • 638-3984

These jointly run organizations are non-profit, volunteer-driven arts advocacy groups that lobby the state legislature on behalf of the arts, work within communities around the state to promote and raise awareness of the arts, and stress the value of arts education for children and adults alike.

Indiana Black Expo Inc.
3145 N. Meridian St. • 925-2702

In addition to staging the largest annual African-American exposition in the country, Indiana Black Expo also provides information about and support for the efforts of local African-American artists, writers, musicians and performers.

Indiana Film Society
820 E. 67th St. • 255-2464

Based at the Indianapolis Art Center, this organization presents films and film series with the intention of educating the public about the artistic aspects of film-making. (Of course, if in the process of getting educated, you also have a lot of fun, no one's going to mind.)

Very Special Arts of Indiana Inc.
1605 E. 86th St. • 253-5504

Dedicated to making the arts accessible to very special audiences (children and adults with physical and/or mental disabilities) this organization funds hands-on arts programs and projects. It also conducts workshops to train artists and teachers how to create arts activities for people with special needs.

Young Audiences of Indiana Inc.
3050 N. Meridian St. • 925-4043

Affiliated with Young Audiences, a national arts education organization, this nonprofit operation provides schools, community centers, parks, libraries and museums statewide with arts programs for school children. The roster of Young Audiences of Indiana usually contains some 60 visual artists, storytellers, danc-

ers, actors, musicians and writers from throughout the state.

Penrod Society
P.O. Box 40817, Indianapolis 46240 • 252-9895

Named for Penrod Schofield, the hero of local author Booth Tarkington's Penrod stories, this organization promotes and supports various arts events and activities in Indianapolis. One of its most visible activities is its annual fund-raiser, the Penrod Arts Fair (see separate entry in the "Arts Events" portion of this chapter). Beneficiaries of the society's largesse include the Indianapolis Museum of Art, the Indianapolis Symphony Orchestra, the Indiana Repertory Theatre and Dance Kaleidoscope.

Arts Indiana Inc.
47 S. Pennsylvania St., Ste. 701 • 686-2250

This is the corporate entity responsible for publishing *Arts Indiana*, the only statewide publication devoted exclusively to reporting on the arts and cultural life in Indiana. Published monthly from September through June, Arts Indiana explores the human, social and political aspects of the arts — literary, performing and visual. Lively writing and uncluttered design make reading this magazine a pleasure — its statewide focus makes reading it a must if you want to feel at all informed about what's going on not only in Indianapolis but throughout Indiana.

"Making art accessible" is a facet of many an arts organization's mission statement — Arts Indiana does exactly that.

Performing Arts Facilities

Circle Theatre
45 Monument Cir. • offices, 262-1110 • box office, 639-4300

Home of the Indianapolis Symphony Orchestra, the Circle Theatre is the second-oldest building on Monument Circle. Originally built in 1916, it was the city's first facility devoted exclusively to showing movies. But by the time it closed in 1981, the Circle Theatre had degenerated to the kind of place that attracted customers who wore overcoats year-round.

The theater didn't sit vacant long before supporters of the Indianapolis Symphony Orchestra arranged to buy it and renovate it as the orchestra's permanent home. The renovation process, with such painstaking tasks as recasting plaster moldings, involved scores of local construction and craftspeople.

In 1984, the ISO (Indianapolis Symphony Orchestra) staged its first concert in the theater's gorgeous (and acoustically wonderful) auditorium. In the years since, the Circle Theatre has reclaimed its role as one of the city's premier venues. On evenings when the orchestra is performing, the sidewalk in front of the Circle Theatre is thick with a lively mix of concert-goers, from formally clad socialites to blue-jeaned music students.

FYI

Unless otherwise noted, the area code for all phone numbers in this guide is 317.

Clowes Memorial Hall
4600 Sunset Ave. • 940-9696

Prior to its move to the Circle Theatre, the ISO called Clowes Memorial Hall, on the campus of Butler University, home for 20 years. Often referred to simply as Clowes, this facility was built in the early 1960s with donations from the family of the late George Henry Alexander Clowes, a wealthy business professional and local arts supporter.

While no longer the home stage for the ISO, the acoustically superb Clowes auditorium continues to feature an array of performing arts, including the road versions of Broadway shows, chamber music and choral groups, ballets, and operas, as well as pop, rock and jazz artists.

Murat Temple
502 N. New Jersey St. • 635-2433

The local headquarters for the Shriners, the Murat Temple is renowned for its theater. Built in 1910, it's the oldest surviving downtown stage; the Egyptian-influenced architecture provides an exotic counterpoint to the eclectic mix of performers who appear at the Murat — from Tony Bennett to Laurie Anderson, Broadway touring companies to comedy acts, the theater hosts a variety of acts year round.

Recently refurbished, the Murat now contains 2,681 seats, making it the largest theater in Indianapolis. And despite some of the alterations made during the refurbishing process (such as the removal of all balcony-level box seats), it's still one of the most elegant live-performance venues around.

Madame Walker Urban Life Center
617 Indiana Ave. • 236-2099

Another downtown theater that's a great discovery is the one inside the Madame Walker Urban Life Center. The Walker Building was originally built in 1927 to commemorate the late Madame C.J. Walker whose Indianapolis-based cosmetics manufacturing firm had made her America's first black female millionaire. Over the years, neglect took its toll on the structure, but in 1979 efforts began to save it. After an extensive $5 million renovation, the building became the Madame Walker Urban Life Center, opening for business in 1984. Four years later, the 950-seat, fourth-floor Walker Theatre opened.

The Walker Theatre, once the site of performances by such renowned black artists as Louie Armstrong and Lena Horne, now hosts Jazz on the Avenue concerts every Friday night. It's also the site for the annual Indiana Avenue Jazz Festival, a four-day celebration of jazz that features well-known musicians. Additionally, other local and national jazz events and gospel, rhythm 'n' blues and urban-music performers appear at the Walker.

In addition to music, the Walker hosts stage plays and films. It's home to the Walker Repertory Showcase, which provides opportunities for local African-American theater companies to present productions in conjunction with the Walker Theatre. It also houses a youth arts program for young actors, writers, dancers, musicians and visual artists.

Ruth Lilly Theater
3000 N. Meridian St. • 921-4000

This 350-seat facility, named for local arts and education patron Ruth Lilly, is on the first level of The Children's Museum of Indianapolis. It offers a variety of family fare ranging from children's music favorite Raffi to local and national children's theater productions. (For more information on the museum and its many programs and attractions, see our Kidstuff chapter.)

The Warren Performing Arts Center
Warren Central High School,
9500 E. 16th St.
• 898-9722

This is one of the city's most technologically advanced arts facilities. Constructed in 1983 at a cost of $10.5 million, it's comprised of a 1,000-seat grand auditorium, a 150-seat studio theater, a dance studio and several rehearsal halls. While used on a daily basis by the school's drama and music classes and groups, the center is the site of school-related concerts, theater/dance productions and community and off-Broadway shows.

Christel DeHaan Fine Arts Center
University of Indianapolis,
1400 E. Hanna Ave.
• 788-3212

The city's newest arts venue, the DeHaan Fine Arts Center is named for local arts patron and businesswoman Christel DeHaan. The center includes the two-tiered Ruth Lilly Performance Hall, an art gallery, art studios, sound-isolated practice rooms for instrumental and vocal musicians and an 80-seat lecture hall.

Considered the equal of any concert hall in the country, the center's performance hall utilizes 28-inch-thick walls, a sound-reflecting chandelier and acoustic drapes that can be adjusted for specific types of performances from symphonic orchestras to electronic music. During its first year of operation, the center presented a variety of performing arts productions ranging from student and faculty recitals to modern dance, from folk singer/storyteller Jean Redpath to poet Carolyn Forche.

Deer Creek Music Center
12880 E. 146th St. • 776-3337

Since it opened in 1989, this facility has earned a reputation among performers and fans alike as one of America's best amphitheaters. On 220 lovely, rolling acres in Hamilton County, Deer Creek contains 6,200 pavilion seats, 81 corporate boxes and room for another 14,000 people on the surrounding lawn. During any given May-to-September season, you can catch pop, rock, heavy metal, jazz and country performers on the Deer Creek stage. It also hosts the weeklong, family-oriented Deer Creek Festival every June (see our Annual Events chapter for more information).

Indiana Roof Ballroom
140 W. Washington St. • office, 236-1870
• events line, 236-1877

On the top floor of the Indiana Repertory Theatre (see separate entry under the "Theater Companies" portion of this chapter) is the Indiana Roof Ballroom. Under its 40-foot-high domed ceiling, which is dappled with stars and clouds, audiences attend performances by the likes of jazz guitarist Earl Klugh or glide across the floor to the music of Guy Lombardo's Royal Canadians (yes, Guy's gone, but his band plays on). In addition to buying tickets to Roof events, you can also buy packages that include dinner and a room at the adjacent Embassy Suites hotel. Call the Indiana Roof's office for details.

Market Square Arena
300 E. Market St. • box office information, 639-2112

While clearly not designed for the nuances of a piano sonata or the subtleties of classical ballet, Market Square Arena (or MSA, as it's known locally) does serve as a venue for rock, pop and country performances as well as for assorted productions by such road companies as Disney, Jim Henson's Muppets and, yes, the ubiquitous Mighty Morphin Power Rangers.

Theater Companies

Indiana Repertory Theatre
140 W. Washington St. • offices, 635-5277
• box office, 635-5252

If you spend any time wandering around the stretch of W. Washington Street between N. Illinois and N. Capitol, you'll spot the Indiana Repertory Theatre. Looking every bit the gorgeous c. 1927 movie palace that it is, the IRT building houses a professional theater operation that presents both classic and contemporary stage productions. During its October-to-May season, this is the place where works by Shakespeare and Moliere rub shoulders with those by Neil Simon and August Wilson.

The IRT is actually three theaters in one: a 600-seat main stage, a 250-seat upper stage and a 150-seat cabaret. In the heart of downtown's hotel, retail and convention district, the IRT attracts more than 100,000 theater-goers every year, while its educational outreach program provides another 40,000 school children opportunities to experience live theater.

The IRT offers a variety of series: the Mainstage Series; a Senior Discount Series; the Culture Collection, which is a miniseries featuring African-American playwrights and actors; an American Sign Language/Audio described series for patrons who are hearing- or sight-impaired; a Student Series; an Opening Night Series; and an Upperstage Family Series. There are also Saturday Brunch, Sunday Tea Talk and Tuesday Pub Night series. Ticket prices for these options vary, and series packages are available. To learn more, contact the IRT box office.

The Phoenix Theatre
749 N. Park Ave. • offices, 635-2381 • box office, 635-7529

As the city's premier site for contemporary theater productions, the Phoenix offers issue-oriented dramas and comedies that are apt to make you think about what you've seen. In addition to staging productions, the Phoenix also hosts workshops and classes for aspiring playwrights and actors. It also sponsors the Festival of Emerging American Theatre, an annual playwriting competition that attracts entries from around the world.

Season subscriptions are available, as are single-admission tickets. For a season schedule and ticket prices, contact the Phoenix box office.

Beef & Boards Dinner Theatre
9301 N. Michigan Rd., 872-9664 • group reservations 876-0503

Since 1973, Beef & Boards has been home to Broadway-style plays and musicals. As the only year-round Equity theater in town, it recruits professional performers both locally and nationally. In addition to productions of such stage gems as *West Side Story* and *Brigadoon*, B&B also hosts concerts from the likes of B.B. King and the Wright Brothers.

Ticket prices vary; season discount memberships are available, as are group rates for parties of 20 or more. A table for two will cost you $5 extra.

American Cabaret Theatre
401 E. Michigan St. • 631-0334

If you too think that "Life is a cabaret," then the American Cabaret Theatre, inside the turn-of-the-century Athenaeum Turners building, is for you. Founded in New York in 1975, ACT moved to Indianapolis in 1990. Since then, it has gained a reputation for presenting high-energy, professionally staged musical productions. Call for a schedule and ticket information, then get ready for a good time.

Indianapolis Civic Theatre
1200 W. 38th St. • offices, 924-6770 • box office, 923-4597

Founded in 1914, the Indianapolis Civic Theatre is the oldest continuously operating community (nonprofessional) theater in the United States. Inside a facility on the lower level of the Indianapolis Museum of Art, the Civic's small, paid staff works with a cadre of volunteer actors and technicians to produce musicals, dramas and comedies for its 700-seat mainstage theater and experimental productions in a separate 90-seat theater known as Studio C.

The Civic Theatre also sponsors the Junior Civic, one of the city's longest-running youth theater programs. It offers classes to kids in 1st through 9th grades. There are various ticket options and prices. To learn more, contact the Civic's box office.

Asante Children's Theatre
P.O. Box 22344, Indianapolis, Ind. 46222 • 638-6694

Speaking of kids, the Asante Children's Theatre is one of the city's new bright lights. Founded in 1991 by veteran actress Deborah Asante, the group is based at the Christamore House, a community center on the near-east side. Created as a means of educating children about both theater and African culture, Asante Children's Theatre holds annual citywide auditions to fill the 30 slots it has open for children between the ages of 8 and 18. During its September-to-June season, the troupe stages three productions at the Madame Walker Urban Life Center, 617 Indiana Avenue. For information, call Asante Children's Theatre.

Theatre on the Square
627 Massachusetts Ave. • 637-8085

This small but well-respected theater dedicates its seven-production season to contemporary and lesser-known plays and musicals, presented in intimate settings. Housed in a renovated building on the northeast edge of the Mile Square, Theatre on the Square consists of a 150-seat main stage and an 80-seat cabaret.

A schedule and ticket information are just a phone call away.

Edyvean Repertory Theatre at CTS
1000 W. 42nd St. • offices, 927-8052 • box office, 923-1516

In its theater on the campus of the Christian Theological Seminary (CTS), the Edyvean features both classical and contemporary stage plays and musicals during its six-show season. In 1992, it introduced Indiana's first audio description service for visually impaired audience members. The 425-seat theater also contains FM sound-enhancement equipment for the hearing impaired.

Making theater accessible to adults with disabilities has long been important at the Edyvean. Since 1982, the theater has been home to the Jumping Mouse Players (see following entry). For information on the Edyvean's season, contact the box office.

The Jumping Mouse Players
1000 W. 42nd St. • 927-8054, TDD (800) 743-3333

This touring company, which is based at the Edyvean Theatre, is made up of performers with learning and/or developmental disabilities. This nonprofessional troupe is open to anyone 16 or older who is physically, mentally or developmentally challenged. The group creates its

Photo: Randy Baughn

Walker Theater has hosted its share of jazz music, bringing Friday nights alive on Indiana Avenue.

own material, utilizing acting, dance, mime, song and improvisation to entertain and educate its audiences. The Jumping Mouse Players perform in schools and churches, at colleges and for civic groups and clubs statewide.

Indianapolis Children's Theatre
5630 E. Washington St. • 322-1711
This professional, non-equity theater puts on an annual series of productions for families and children and offers classes in theater-related subjects.

NAPI REP/New Artists Productions
3909 N. Meridian St. • offices, 923-4581
• box office, 547-6338
NAPI REP is a professional, nonunion theater company established specifically to assist African-American playwrights, actors, directors, craftspeople and technicians in their efforts to learn about and work in live theater. The company's season runs September to June, during which time it presents five productions on the IRT's upperstage and cabaret.

In 1993, NAPI REP was one of 20 theater companies in the United States selected to perform at the National Black Theatre Festival; that same year, the company also performed at the International May Time Festival in Ireland. NAPI REP is an offshoot of the African-American production company New Art-

ists Productions. To learn about forthcoming productions, call the NAPI office.

Footlite Musicals
1847 N. Alabama St. • 926-6630
Since 1956, Footlite Musicals has been dedicated to presenting musical theater to Central Indiana audiences. On its home stage in the Hedback Theatre, this all-volunteer community theater group produces four shows a year. In 1991, Footlite was designated the No. 1 community theater in America when its production of Stephen Sondheim's *Into the Woods* won the American Community Theatre Association's national competition. Experience Judge Footlite's quality for yourself; call for a schedule and ticket information.

Soul People Repertory Theatre
1951 Suffolk Ln. • 876-0853
Dedicated to theater works by and about African-Americans, this organization stages many pieces by new playwrights.

Buck Creek Players Inc.
7820 Acton Rd. • 862-7022
This all-volunteer theater produces a variety of comedies, dramas and musicals throughout the year, relying on the talents of experienced amateurs to mount and perform the productions.

Epilogue Players Inc.
7824 Copperfield Dr. • 926-3139

This theater company consists of performers older than 50. It puts on a variety of comedic and dramatic productions on stages throughout the area.

Music

Indianapolis Symphony Orchestra
The Circle Theatre, 45 Monument Cir.
• box office, 639-4300 • offices, 262-1100

The Indianapolis Symphony Orchestra (a.k.a. ISO) is one of the few professional symphony orchestras in America that operates on a full 52-week schedule, performing nearly 200 concerts a year. It's also one of the few orchestras that owns and maintains its own concert hall, the aforementioned Circle Theatre. The orchestra also performs in parks and other public sites throughout Indiana and at Conner Prairie (see the Attractions and Kidstuff chapters) during the annual *Symphony on the Prairie* summer series.

Since 1987, the ISO's conductor has been internationally acclaimed maestro Raymond Leppard. Under his direction, the orchestra has attained international acclaim of its own, performing to critical accolades throughout the United States and Europe and releasing several well-received recordings. (In 1994, the ISO began a series of one-hour syndicated radio programs; called *Indianapolis On The Air*, the 13-week series is heard on more than 175 radio stations nationwide.)

The ISO presents several programs throughout the year. In addition to its 21-week *Classical Series* and its seven-week *Symphony on the Prairie Series*, there is a *Pops Series* conducted by Erich Kunzel; a *Studio Series* that combines Maestro Leppard's analysis with performances of classical masterworks; a *Family Series*; the always popular Yuletide Celebration performance; and the *Sound of the City and Indiana* series that take the ISO out to parks and community centers throughout Indianapolis and the state.

Ticket prices vary, and subscription packages are available. Discounts are available for seniors, students and children.

The Heartland Film Festival

Tired of gratuitous sex and violence? Yearning for movies that aim higher than daredevil chases and explosions? Looking for films that aspire to enrich or enhance viewers' lives rather than merely titillate or thrill? Then you're ready for the Heartland Film Festival.

Close-up

Since its debut in 1992, the Heartland Film Festival has become a well-respected addition to the national film community. Created as a vehicle for honoring life-affirming films — that is, films that illuminate and celebrate the best in human nature — the four-day long October festival has attracted such movie world luminaries as directors Robert Wise and Sydney Pollack, film critics Jeffrey Lyons and Michael Medved, and producers Don Hahn (*The Lion King*) and Branko Lustig (*Schindler's List*) to Indianapolis for workshops and screenings.

Founded by Jeffrey Sparks, who now serves as its artistic director, the Heartland makes good use of the talents and connections of Indiana natives who've gone on to success in Hollywood. Writer/producer Matt Williams (*Roseanne* and *Home Improvement*), director David Anspaugh and screenwriter Angelo Pizzo (*Hoosiers* and *Rudy*) have contributed time and energy to the festival.

As it has gained exposure, the Heartland has also gained access to the works of both independent and mainstream filmmakers. At the 1994 festival, for example, Walt Disney Studios' film *Squanto: A Warrior's Tale*, premiered, as did Miramax Family Films', *Gordy*. At the same time, the festival featured such independently produced documentaries as *Satya: A Prayer for the Enemy* about Tibetan nuns' nonviolent response to the Chinese occupation of Tibet, and *Moving the Mountain*, which is about one of the Tienneman Square protest leaders. (*Moving the Mountain*, produced by rock star Sting's wife, Trudi Styler, went on to win the festival's top prize, the Crystal Heart, which is literally that, along with a check for $25,000.)

The festival's films are shown at a variety of sites ranging from the Madame Walker Urban Life Center and the Circle Theatre to the Hollywood Bar & Film Works and Union Station. Ticket prices vary, and festival packages are available. For information, contact the Heartland Film Festival, 613 N. East Street, 464-9405.

Photo: Rob Goebel

The Crystal Heart Award is a cherished prize provided during the event each October.

Indianapolis Symphonic Choir
4600 Sunset Ave. • 940-6461

Founded in 1937 by Fabien Sevitzky, music director of the ISO, and Elmer Steffen, music director of the local Roman Catholic archdiocese, the Indianapolis Symphonic Choir has become one of the city's musical treasures. Comprised of some 120 trained singers, the choir not only performs with the ISO but also stages concerts on its own, including the popular holiday presentation, Festival of Carols. In addition to appearances throughout Indiana and nearby states, the choir has performed at Carnegie Hall in New York City and the Kennedy Center in Washington, D.C. Call for a schedule and ticket information.

Indianapolis Opera
250 E. 38th St. • offices, 283-3531 • box office, 940-6444

If it's arias you crave, the Indianapolis Opera is happy to oblige. Since its founding nearly 20 years ago, this renowned company has garnered praise for its high musical and production standards. Under the guidance of general director Nando Schellen, former artistic director of Amsterdam's Sweelinck Conservatory and associate director of the Netherlands Opera, Indianapolis Opera stages four productions each season at Clowes Memorial Hall, three with the Indianapolis Symphony Orches-

tra and one with the Indianapolis Chamber Orchestra. To ensure the quality of the productions, singers are selected through national auditions.

And to ensure audience understanding, the company hosts pre-performance discussions of an opera's plot and characters as well as of opera history in general. Ticket prices vary, and subscription packages are available through the Clowes box office.

Indiana Opera Theatre Inc.
7515 E. 30th St. • 253-1001

While formally known as the MacAllister Awards and Festival Opera Theatre, this organization is still widely known by the name under which it operated for well more than a decade — Indiana Opera Theatre. Regardless of its name, it has earned a reputation for imaginative stagings of operatic works. Its production of Gilbert and Sullivan's *Trial by Jury*, for instance, was performed in a local courtroom.

This organization is also the sponsor of the well-respected MacAllister Awards, which, through a series of nationwide auditions, recognizes the skills of young (younger than 36) opera singers. The annual competition, which is named for local business professional and arts patron P.E. MacAllister, includes divisions for professional singers, college singers (younger than 25) and youth (ages 13 to 18).

For schedules and ticket information, contact the opera's office.

Indianapolis Children's Choir
Butler University, 4600 Sunset Ave.
• 940-9640

From the moment of its first meeting in 1986, the Indianapolis Children's Choir has been an unqualified success. Founded by Henry Leck, former assistant director of the Indianapolis Symphonic Choir, the Children's Choir has become a well-respected part of not only Indianapolis' musical community but the world's as well.

With 700 members between 9 and 14, the ICC is actually a collection of 10 choirs, organized according to youngsters' levels of musical comprehension and ability. In addition to performing locally, the ICC has sent touring contingents to Europe, Australia and New Zealand; it has also done a number of recordings, including one with the Canadian Brass. The choir has performed at places as diverse as Carnegie Hall and the former Nazi concentration camp at Dachau.

To get a sense of how popular the ICC is in this town, count the number of cars and minivans you see bearing the Indianapolis Children's Choir sticker in a window or on a bumper. You'll be surprised how quickly they add up.

Contact the ICC office for schedules and ticket information.

Cathedral Arts Inc.
47 S. Pennsylvania St., No. 401 • 637-4574

Cathedral Arts acts as an umbrella organization for a number of musical programs and events, including two chamber ensembles, Suzuki & Friends and the Ronen Chamber Ensemble, and the acclaimed International Violin Competition.

Founded in 1980 by Indianapolis Symphony orchestra concertmaster Hidetaro Suzuki, the eponymous Suzuki & Friends has attracted a loyal and enthusiastic following. The ensemble usually performs five concerts each year in the Ruth Lilly Theater at the Children's Museum of Indianapolis. They also occasionally perform at other sites, including the Circle Theatre and the Christel DeHaan Fine Arts Center on the campus of the University of Indianapolis.

The Ronen Chamber Ensemble, which was also founded by ISO members (principle clarinetist David Bellman and cellist Ingrid Bellman), performs wind instrument selections. Ronen concerts are held in the Wood Room of the Circle Theatre.

One Cathedral Arts program that attracts significant attention internationally is the quadrennial International Violin Competition. The

Photo: Randy Baughn

The Murat Temple is renowned for its theater.

brainchild of the late violin master and Indiana University Music School professor Josef Gingold, the IVC brings 50 of the world's finest young violinists to Indianapolis every four years for two weeks of intense competition. The results are cash prizes as well as performance and recording contracts that are the richest in the history of violin competitions.

While the IVC is popular locally, it's even more popular outside the state. In 1982, a PBS documentary on the competition won a number of prestigious television awards; four years later, the BBC broadcast a seven-part series of excerpts from the 1986 contest. American Public Radio and the Voice of America both broadcast the violinists' stage performances.

The next International Violin Competition will be held in Indianapolis in 1998.

To get schedules and ticket information for any of these Cathedral Arts programs, contact the organization.

Indianapolis Chamber Orchestra Inc.
4600 Sunset Ave. • 940-9607

Founded in 1984, this nonprofit 32-member orchestra is modeled after London's renowned chamber orchestra, the Academy of St. Martin-in-the-Fields. Under the baton of conductor Kirk Trevor, the orchestra performs an annual six-concert series at Clowes Hall, which also serves as its headquarters. Contact the Clowes box office for ticket information.

Indianapolis Arts Chorale
P.O. Box 17446, Indianapolis, Ind. 46217 • 787-1874

If you're a choral music fan, lend an ear to the Indianapolis Arts Chorale. Consisting of 40 singers (doctors, teachers, ministers, executives and homemakers), the chorale performs a variety of vocal music ranging from the compositions of Haydn and Brahms to excerpts from Gilbert and Sullivan in settings that include high school auditoriums, churches, the Indianapolis Museum of Art and the Indiana Statehouse.

A subscription to the Chorale's six-concert, October-to-May program is available by contacting the Chorale directly — or you can buy single-event tickets before each performance.

Cathedral Concerts-Choral Masterworks
55 Monument Cir., Ste. 600 • 635-4577

This group presents an annual concert series of choral works featuring performances by the Cathedral Choir of Men and Boys, the Cathedral Girls' Choir, the Indianapolis Festival Singers and the Indianapolis Festival Orchestra.

Indianapolis Handbell Ensemble
379 Bolin Ct., Carmel • 575-1001

A professional handbell ensemble, the IHE performs at both public and private events throughout Central Indiana.

Philharmonic Orchestra of Indianapolis
P.O. Box 503, Indianapolis 46206 • 283-5234

An all-volunteer group comprised of professional and amateur musicians, this orchestra performs classical and pops concerts at venues throughout the city.

Carmel Symphony Orchestra
P.O. Box 761, Carmel, Ind. 46032 • 844-9717

Largely a volunteer organization (only 15 of the orchestra's 63 musicians are paid), the Carmel Symphony Orchestra still manages to produce a full season, including family concerts, orchestral concerts, chamber music concerts and educational concerts. Events take place at various sites, including churches, high school auditoriums and area parks.

This is a community orchestra that, due to Central Indiana's large contingent of well-trained musicians (many of whom are graduates of Indiana University's prestigious school of music), doesn't sound like a community orchestra. These folks got chops! For a schedule and ticket information, contact the orchestra's office at the telephone number listed above.

Drums of West Africa
4037 Graceland Ave. • 283-7681

Guided by founder Prince Julius Adeniyi, Drums of West Africa utilizes a variety of authentic African percussion instruments to showcase the rhythmic traditions of West African cultures. In appearances before audiences from elementary school children to adults, in settings from school gymnasiums to concert halls, Drums of West Africa offers living proof that music is at once personal and universal. Watch for newspaper announcements of a performance, then go: Just be prepared to be wowed both by the music and by Adeniyi's infectious joy.

The Festival Music Society
6741 N. Central Ave. • 251-5190

Since its founding in 1961, this nonprofit organization has been staging annual performances of early classical music, that is, music from the Medieval, Renaissance, Baroque and Classic periods. The organization's program, which is held each July, includes both concerts and lectures, bringing in such noteworthy performing groups as the Cologne Chamber Orchestra, the Paris Consort and Hesperus (the ensemble-in-residence at the Smithsonian Institution's National Museum of American History).

Contact the society for a schedule and ticket information.

American Pianists Association
4600 Sunset Ave. • 940-9945

The American Pianists Association, which has its headquarters at Clowes Hall on the Butler University campus, hosts two significant biennial musical events in the city: the National Piano Fellowship Auditions and the American Jazz Piano Competition. The Ninth Biennial National Piano Fellowship Auditions will be held in 1997, while the Third Biennial Jazz Piano Competition is in April 1996. In addition, the winners of the National Piano Fellowship Auditions appear annually at PianoFest, a series of piano performances held at the Circle Theatre's Wood Room and at the Indianapolis Museum of Art.

Fine Arts Society of Indianapolis
1400 E. Hanna Ave. • 788-3291

Since 1968, this organization has been a leader in the production of classical music radio in Indianapolis. A public charitable trust, the society broadcasts more than 100 hours of classical music programming each week on WICR (88.7 FM), a noncommercial radio station operated by the University of Indianapolis. In 1986, the society received a George Foster Peabody Award for excellence in broadcasting.

In addition to its radio programs, the society also sponsors a variety of fine and performing arts events and annually honors a civic leader for contributions to the cultural life of the community with its Diploma of Honor.

Dance

Dance Kaleidoscope Inc.
4600 Sunset Ave. • office, 940-6555 • box office, 940-4597

Dance Kaleidoscope (or DK as it's known in dance circles) is Indiana's only professional, modern dance company. Under the direction of world-renowned dancer and choreographer David Hochoy, the eight-member troupe stages a full professional season, performing at the Indianapolis Civic Theatre, on the lower level of the Indianapolis Museum of Art, 1200 W. 38th Street.

DK's repertoire consists of pieces choreographed by such leading modern dance pioneers as Martha Graham and by such contemporary artists as Fred Mathews. In addition to its concerts, DK also conducts workshops and demonstrations in schools throughout Indiana. The company also offers the Jaffee-Hall Emerging Indiana Artist Award, which gives Indiana dancers a chance to be part of a professional dance company for a season. For a DK season schedule and the lowdown on tickets, contact the Indianapolis Civic Theatre's box office.

Ballet Internationale/Indianapolis Ballet Theatre Inc.
502 N. Capitol Ave., Ste. B • office, 637-8979 • box office, 921-6444

If ballet is your pleasure, Ballet Internationale/Indianapolis Ballet Theatre is your ticket. Around since 1959, BI/IBT has gradually transformed itself from a struggling local ballet troupe into a high-quality touring company and major regional ballet company.

Stylistically patterned after the Ballet Russe de Monte Carlo, IBT mixes classic ballets with contemporary and original works. That means that, in addition to traditional ballets, you can see works by such 20th-century choreographers as Jose Limon and George Balanchine. You'll also enjoy the Christmas classic, *The Nutcracker*.

In addition to performing locally at Clowes Memorial Hall and the Warren Performing Arts Center, the BI/IBT tours extensively. To date, it has danced for more than 65,000 people in 24 states and in Canada. And the BI/IBT Academy, housed in the company's downtown facilities, offers students professional training.

For a performance schedule and ticket information, contact BI/IBT's offices.

Indianapolis Dance Company
P.O. Box 30345, Indianapolis 46230 • 846-2441

The Indianapolis Dance Company (IDC) combines a variety of dance styles — modern, ballet, jazz, ethnic and avant-garde — in eclectic performances intended to challenge traditional notions of what dance is (or should be). Under the guidance of founder and artistic director Gregory Hancock, the IDC uses dance to entertain and address social, political, religious, cultural and historical issues. The company's productions are staged at Caleb Mills Auditorium, inside Shortridge Junior High School, 3401 N. Meridian Street. The IDC's programs also include a company specifically for high school and college dancers (called IDC ALSO), the annual staging of a modern version of *The Nutcracker* entitled *The Nutcracker?* and a month-long summer dance academy for young dancers.

Butler Ballet Jordan College of Fine Arts
4600 Sunset Ave. • 940-9346

Housed in a contemporary building tucked away on the northeastern corner of Butler University's campus, the Butler Ballet is a troupe of college-age dancers that performs publicly a few times each season. Additionally, the company's facilities serve as a training ground for a variety of young dancers

from throughout the community. There are dance classes available for different age and skill levels.

IUPUI Moving Company
901 W. New York St. • 274-0611

The performing company for dancers attending Indiana University-Purdue University at Indianapolis (IUPUI), this organization stages performances and lecture-demonstrations in ballet, jazz and ethnic styles of dance.

Susurrus
6001 Broadway • 257-6437

A group of artists dedicated to presenting multidisciplinary performances in galleries, theaters and other venues, Susurrus also offers classes in dance, theater and art.

Visual Arts

Museums

Indianapolis Museum of Art
1200 W. 38th St. • 923-1331

Founded in 1883, the Indianapolis Museum of Art (a.k.a. IMA) is one of the oldest art museums in the country. Set amid the beautifully landscaped riverside splendor of the former estate of Josiah K. Lilly Jr. (grandson of pharmaceutical company founder Eli Lilly), the IMA is home to superb collections of J.M.W. Turner watercolors and drawings, old master paintings and contemporary art, and unparalleled collections of Chinese and African art.

The 152-acre site also exemplifies landscape design and botanical gardening at its best. The on-site greenhouse facilities sell flowers, herbs and plants and host year-round gardening and landscaping lectures and workshops.

In addition to the museum's natural appeal to art students and art lovers, the beauty

INSIDERS' TIP

The Indiana State Fairgrounds hosts an incredible variety of events each year. For a monthly schedule, call 927-7500.

of the surrounding grounds attracts picnickers and nature lovers.

During the summer, the IMA hosts musical performances and movies in its outdoor terraced amphitheater. Every September it also hosts the Penrod Festival (see the "Arts Events" portion of this chapter), the city's best-attended outdoor art fair. Throughout the year, the museum is the site of the popular first-Friday program, which offers after-work jazz and wine on the first Friday of each month. This program is particularly popular with singles who see it as opportunity to mingle and meet amid artistic environs.

There is also a wonderful museum shop on the parking-garage level. There you'll find everything from prints and art books to handpainted clothing and fine art jewelry. And if browsing makes you hungry, check out the cafe on the first floor or the Garden on the Green restaurant, which is just down a winding drive north of the museum.

The IMA is open Tuesday, Wednesday, Friday and Saturday from 10 AM to 5 PM, Thursday from 10 AM to 8:30 PM and Sunday from noon to 5 PM. It's closed on Mondays, Thanksgiving, Christmas and New Year's Day. Admission is free; however, there is a charge for admission to special exhibitions within the museum (except on Thursdays when admission to all exhibitions is free). Members are admitted free to all exhibitions. Membership information is available by calling the main switchboard number listed previously.

Eiteljorg Museum of American Indians and Western Art
500 W. Washington St. • 636-9378

It isn't what you expect to find, but on the western fringe of the downtown district, a pale pink building rises like a mesa amid the bustle of Washington and West streets. With a design as contemporary as the gleaming office towers a few blocks east yet as ancient as adobe pueblos, the Eiteljorg Museum of American Indians and Western Art is a Southwestern gem in a Midwestern setting.

The museum is named for its chief benefactor Harrison Eiteljorg, a local industrialist and philanthropist, whose multimillion-dollar collection of Native American and Western artworks and artifacts form the core of its bounty.

In addition to Eiteljorg's collection, the museum exhibits traveling shows that focus on Indian and/or Western subjects; it also hosts a variety of community-oriented events ranging from lecture and film series to workshops, tours and an annual chili cook-off. Its artist-in-residence series features Native American artists demonstrating various arts and crafts.

If museum shops excite you, don't miss the Eiteljorg's. It's filled with Western and Southwestern treasures ranging from gorgeous turquoise and hammered silver jewelry to handwoven blankets and one-of-a-kind baskets.

The Eiteljorg is open Tuesday through Saturday from 10 AM to 5 PM and Sunday from noon to 5 PM. It's closed on Monday except for June, July and August when it's also open Monday. It's closed on Thanksgiving, Christmas and New Year's Day. Admission is $5 for adults, $4 for seniors, $2 for full-time students and children 5 through 17 and free for children 4 and younger.

Indiana State Museum
202 N. Alabama St. • 232-1637

The Indiana State Museum (ISM), housed in the former city hall building, contains wonderful examples of Indiana-related artworks, including an unrivaled collection of paintings and drawings by well-known turn-of-the-century Indiana artist T.C. Steele. (The museum also owns and cares for Steele's former Brown County residence, known as the House of the Singing Winds.)

In addition to Steele, the ISM contains artwork from other notable Indiana artists — J. Otis Adams, William Forsyth, Frank V. Dudley and Adolph Shulz. In keeping with its commitment to collecting and showing Indiana art, the museum also presents exhibitions by various contemporary artists and photographers.

The ISM is open Monday through Saturday from 9 AM to 4:45 PM and Sunday from noon to 4:45 PM. It's closed on Thanksgiving, Christmas and New Year's Day. Admission is free.

University of Indianapolis Galleries
1400 E. Hanna Ave. • 788-3253

Inside the Christel DeHaan Fine Arts Center, these galleries feature works from the

The Christel DeHaan Fine Arts Center includes the two-tiered Ruth Lilly Performance Hall, an art gallery, art studios, sound-isolated practice rooms for instrumental and vocal musicians and an 80-seat lecture hall.

university's permanent collection and an annual series showcasing works from local, national and international artists.

Crispus Attucks Museum
1140 Martin Luther King, Jr. St. • 226-4613

Housed in what was once an all-black high school with a rich cultural and athletic heritage, this museum focuses its exhibits on the achievements and history of African Americans locally and nationally. Call ahead to check the museum's schedule— the building it's in is now a fully operational middle school.

Galleries

Downtown

Dean Johnson Gallery
646 Massachusetts Ave.• 634-8020

This upscale gallery features the work of local, regional and national commercial, graphic and fine artists. Many of the people who exhibit here work for ad agencies, marketing and design companies, architectural firms— in short, they have day jobs that both nurture and limit their creativity. So they go home and make the paintings, drawings,

prints, photographs and other works that show up in this gallery. It's a real find.

Herron Gallery
1701 N. Pennsylvania St. • 920-2420

Herron Gallery, which is part of Indiana University's Herron School of Art, focuses on contemporary art produced within the past decade. The home of student and faculty shows and local, regional, national and international exhibitions, this gallery features artwork that varies from representational to abstract. Herron specializes in exhibitions of contemporary works that you won't likely see anywhere else in the city.

Ruschman Art Gallery
948 N. Alabama St. • 634-3114

Owner Mark Ruschman focuses on exhibiting and selling the work of regionally and nationally known artists such as local painter James Wille Faust and sculptor James Tyler. Exhibitions change monthly.

The Photography Gallery
546 S. Meridian St., Ste. 506 • 634-2444

This gallery on the fifth floor of the Faris Building specializes in the work of contemporary photographers from throughout the Midwest. Here you'll find everything from traditional prints to images that have been altered or manipulated through various processes. Everything here isn't a Kodak moment, but there's always something interesting to see.

Chatham Gallery
702 Massachusetts Ave. • 636-8223

Home of contemporary photos, sculptures and paintings, this gallery offers a lively mix of the familiar and the challenging, and it does it all in a comfortable setting in the refurbished Catham Arch area.

4 Star Gallery
653 Massachusetts Ave. • 488-0729

This is the city's newest gallery, having opened in early 1996. It features contemporary art from artists emerging on the local, regional and national scenes.

Hot House Gallery
546 S. Meridian St., Ste. 511 • 686-0895

Here you'll find the work of the local artists, many of whom have studios in this old industrial warehouse known as the Faris Building. The art here ranges from landscapes to abstracts, from photorealism to surrealism. There are also periodic open houses in the building. Call for information.

The Stutz Business Center
1036 N. Capitol St. • 488-7374

Once the home of the Stutz Automobile Company, this beautiful old brick structure has been refurbished as an office/warehouse/light manufacturing center, with a number of the rental units being appropriated by artists for use as studios. While there's an annual open house, individual artists also allow visitors to drop by.

Van Riper Gallery and Specialty Framing
1036 N. Capitol St., Ste. 220 • 488-8848, 684-9471

In this gallery, housed in the Stutz Business Center, you'll find abstract oils, limited-edition prints, serigraphs and antique furniture. This is also where you can have your prized artwork mounted in museum-quality frames. Be forewarned: This place is open by appointment (or by chance) only.

Galleria de Ros
212 W. 10th St., Ste. A-315 • 632-4017

Also in the Stutz Business Center, this gallery exhibits (and sells) work by local, national and international fine and decorative artists.

Niang African Art & More
49 W. Maryland St. • 638-5629

You'll find this gallery inside Circle Centre. It specializes in African art, jewelry, clothing and artifacts.

A Movable Feast
431 Massachusetts Ave. • 926-2980

You can feast your eyes on A Moveable Feast, an ever-changing bounty of conceptual and expressionistic art by founders Klaas Weert and Rae Witvoen. There's no telling who or what you'll find (photographs, paintings, collages and installations). Call ahead for schedules, artists and other vital details.

Utrillo's Gallery
2630 E. 10th St. • 684-9883

In a small brick building on the near-east side, Utrillo's challenges conventional ideas about what is or is not art by exhibiting fine art side-by-side with objects d'art and thrift (some would say junk) art. Owner Greg Brown also hosts a local cable access program called ARTV, which features homemade art videos and performances by poets and musicians.

The 703 Gallery for the Arts
703 E. 30th St., Ste. 15 • 925-1500

This gallery specializes in originals and prints by African American artists.

Broad Ripple

Indianapolis Art Center
820 E. 67th St. • 255-2464

As the largest fine-arts facility in this part of town, the Indianapolis Art Center anchors the Broad Ripple art scene. The center showcases the work of local and regional artists and artisans and offers more than 90 different art classes for all ages and skill levels. Classes are available in watercolor and oil painting, drawing, photography, jewelry-making and ceramics.

Photo: The Indianapolis Star and The Indianapolis News

St. John Catholic Church, the first Roman Catholic parish in the city, is a familiar part of Indianapolis' historic architecture.

Organized in 1934 as the Art League, the Center has grown to its present status as one of the area's most respected community arts resources. In fact, the demand for more classroom and gallery space fueled a fund-raising effort that resulted in the construction of a new $7.2 million facility. Designed by internationally known architect and Indianapolis native, Michael Graves (who graduated from nearby Broad Ripple High School), the new structure opened in June 1996.

The Art Center also hosts a number of community events throughout the year, most notably the annual Broad Ripple Arts fair, a weekend-long affair during which some 200 artists display and sell their artwork (see listing under the "Arts Events" portion of this chapter), and the annual Children of Color Festival, a one-day arts celebration of diversity for children (and their parents).

The center also has a riverside stage where local and regional jazz, blues and rock musicians perform. Additionally, it periodically hosts storytellers, film series and theater performances.

Admission to the Center's exhibitions is free. All classes require payment of tuition fees, and for other events the Center usually charges admission fees. Call for a schedule of events and exhibitions and information about classes and gallery hours.

Fox Studios Inc.
5901 N. College Ave. • 253-0135

This combination design studio and showroom at the corner of N. College Avenue and Kessler Boulevard creates custom stained, beveled and etched glass lamps, windows, sculptures, awards and decorations.

Hoosier Salon Gallery
6434 N. College Ave. • 253-5340

A showcase for the work of Indiana artists since 1925, this gallery features a solo exhibition by a different artist each month. It also presents an annual juried show at the Indiana State Museum.

Byron and Sons Gallery
6434 N. College Ave. • 257-6741

Housed in the same building as the Hoosier Salon, this gallery also specializes in Indiana artists, specifically those working from 1880 to 1940.

911 Gallery
http://www.911Gallery.org/911/.

One of the first exclusively digital galleries in the country and on the Web, 911 Gallery combines fine art with state-of-the-art technology. While 911's physical gallery in Broad Ripple ceased operation in late 1995 when its owners moved out of state, you can still drop by its cyberspace gallery where you'll find cutting-edge art from electronic media artists.

Artifacts Gallery
6327 N. Guilford Ave. • 255-1178

Artifacts offers an array of contemporary artwork — paintings, prints, drawings, jewelry, ceramics, glass and sculpture — along with such services as design, custom framing and installation.

Eckert Fine Art
726 E. 65th St. • 255-4561

When it comes to 19th- and 20th-century American and European art, Eckert Fine Art is the gallery you'll hear mentioned time and again. This is where you can buy paintings by Hoosier Group members T.C. Steele and Otto Stark and the work of more contemporary artists.

Der Glass Werks Stained Glass
6055 N. College Ave. • 257-7603

Since 1921, Der Glass Werks artisans have been designing and manufacturing beveled, etched and stained-glass windows, panels and other objects that meld artistry with utility.

G. C. Lucas Gallery
6219 N. Guildford Ave. • 254-6460

With an emphasis on contemporary realism, G.C. Lucas Gallery displays the work of current artists alongside select pieces from modern American artists from earlier this century.

Sigman Gallery
930 Broad Ripple Ave. • 253-9953

This gallery offers contemporary art by local and regional artists, including originals, limited-edition prints and posters.

Yael's Atelier
6528 N. Ferguson St. • 255-5528

Here you'll find a working artist's studio, which includes one of the largest privately owned metal-forging furnaces in the country. There are also several presses that Yael Kahanov uses to create her large copper enamel sculptures and prints, many of which can be found in corporate and private art collections throughout the world.

Broad Ripple Gallery and Framing
720 E. 65th St. • 475-9845

For contemporary glass, clay and fiber works done by artists from around the country, look to Broad Ripple Gallery and Framing. This gallery also carries graphics, prints and antique etchings and engravings.

Protocol Gallery
6317 Guilford Ave. • 254-1778

If you'd rather wear art than contemplate it, Protocol fits the bill. Here you'll find innovative, artist-designed clothing and accessories.

Center for Creative Arts
6263 N. Carrollton Ave. • 255-9633

CCA is a nonprofit, artist-run gallery where you'll find paintings, prints, pottery, woodwork and jewelry done by the 45 artists who own and operate CCA. It's art in action.

The Bungalow
924 Westfield Blvd. • 253-5028

The Bungalow exhibits contemporary handicrafts by Indiana and nationally known artisans. The work here ranges from stone, steel and wood sculpture to handcrafted furniture, basketry and pottery.

Folk Arts Imports
6503 N. Carrollton Ave. • 257-7602

This is where you'll find folk art with a global outlook — handicrafts, jewelry, musical instruments and clothing from Asia, Africa, Mexico and South America. Take a peek upstairs and see the large African tribal pieces.

The Potter's House
6503 N. Carrollton Ave. • 253-4178

This is the home of clay wares (mugs, bowls, vases and planters) handmade by potter Karen Van De Waile.

Winthrop Art Gallery
6224 Winthrop Ave. • 255-1127

Here at the oldest art gallery in Indianapolis, owners John and Andie DeCosta specialize in 19th- and 20th-century American paintings. They also offer art and frame restoration services and art appraisal.

North Side

Editions Limited Gallery of Fine Art
4040 E. 82nd St. • 842-1414

The emphasis at Editions Limited is on contemporary art, from abstracts to realism, in a variety of media, done by local, national and international artists.

Details
8663 River Crossing Blvd. • 259-9400

At this shop in North Willow Commons, you'll find ordinary items such as jewelry, pottery, glasswork and greeting cards that are extraordinarily well done.

Renditions Fine Art Gallery
8702 Keystone Crossing • 848-5205

For wildlife art, including originals and limited-edition prints, that lives up to its designation as art, trek to Renditions in the Fashion Mall. From local to international, this place features artists whose work combines artistry with appreciation for wildlife.

The Art Source
8111 Center Run Dr. • 849-3139

This art consulting and resource center is a good place to get advice on everything from locating and buying fine art to displaying it. There's an on-site library of more than 50,000 art works that are available to the public, an experienced staff that's trained to help individuals and businesses collect art and a gallery that exhibits work from a variety of regional and national artists.

Farber Gallery
2922 E. 52nd St. • 253-7400

In this gallery, you'll find 19th- and 20th-century American and European artwork, primarily paintings and bronze pieces.

Noel Studio Inc.
5618 W. 73rd St. • 297-1117

This place is a combination gallery and distribution center for the works of nationally known (and locally based) painter Nancy Noel. You can get framed or unframed prints here, original oils, pastels and sketches. When the artist is on the premises, she signs her prints for collectors.

Arts Events

Penrod Art Fair Indianapolis Museum of Art
1200 W. 38th St. • 923-1331

This is the granddaddy of local art fairs in Indianapolis. Started in 1966 as a means of raising money for the Indianapolis Museum of Art, the Penrod Art Fair has become an end-of-summer institution. Held the first Saturday after Labor Day on the grounds of the Indianapolis Art Museum, it includes some 280 arts, crafts and food booths and performances by area musicians. The fair attracts thousands of people, many of whom come just to people-watch and wander the museum's beautifully landscaped grounds. This is the place to be and be seen for artists, arts administrators, arts patrons and just plain old art appreciators.

Admission is $10 in advance (from the IMA or Marsh Supermarkets) or $15 at the gate. Children 14 and younger are admitted free when accompanied by an adult.

The Broad Ripple Art Fair Indianapolis Art Center
820 E. 67th St. • 255-2464

From its inception in 1970 during the hippie heydays of sand candles and tie-dyed T-shirts, the Broad Ripple Art Fair has evolved into one of the Midwest's best-known art fairs. Held on Memorial Day weekend, this two-day event on the grounds of the Indianapolis Art Center includes some 200 artists displaying (and selling) paintings, sculptures, ceramics,

drawings, prints, photographs and clothing. There are also food and drink vendors and live music from a variety of local bands.

While the crowds aren't as thick as those at Penrod, this fair attracts thousands of visitors, including everyone from gallery owners and serious collectors to babies in strollers (moms and dads in tow, of course) and dogs sporting bandanas. It's a good time for all. Admission is $5 advance, $7 at the gate and $1 for children younger than 12.

Talbott Street Art Fair
Talbott St. between 16th and 19th sts.

Though somewhat smaller than the Broad Ripple fair, this early June event (usually held the second weekend of the month) also attracts large numbers of art patrons and browsers during its weekend-long run. Held on a blocked-off portion of Talbot Street adjacent to the Herron School of Art and Gallery, the fair consists of scores of artists displaying their works and wares. Crowds are often elbow-to-elbow throughout the fair, so be prepared for some jostling as you try to maneuver over to a display you want to see. But it's a friendly environment, so you'll make it — just remember to use your manners. Admission is free.

Hannah Arts Day
Hannah House, 3801 Madison Ave. • 787-8486

Held on the first Saturday in June, this event on the city's south side is the most recent (c. 1994) entry in the art fair lineup. As such, it's not yet as large as the preceding three fairs, but it's gaining momentum. Like the other events, it features artists' displays, food and entertainment. Hannah Arts Day takes place on the grounds of the Hannah House, a historic landmark, which is in itself a work of art. Admission is $5 for adults, $4 for seniors and free for children younger than 12.

Indian Market
Eiteljorg Museum of American Indians and Western Art, 500 W. Washington St. • 636-WEST

With more than 90 booths displaying the

FYI

Unless otherwise noted, the area code for all phone numbers in this guide is 317.

jewelry, pottery, basketry, weavings and carvings of 80 Native American artists, the Indian market is in an art fair category of its own. Add in Native American drums and dances, food and children's activities and you've got a great day out. This, too, is a June event, usually the third weekend of the month. Admission is $5 for adults; children younger than 12 are admitted free. Call the Eiteljorg for details.

The Indianapolis Artsgarden

Arching like a crystalline bridge across the downtown intersection of Washington and Illinois streets, the Artsgarden is the newest addition to the Indianapolis arts scene. This $12 million, 12,500-square-foot glass and steel structure, which is owned and operated by the Arts Council of Indianapolis, was designed to serve both as a venue for showcasing area performing and visual artists and organizations and as a clearinghouse for information about local arts events.

At its apex, the Artsgarden curves 95 feet above street level, making it one of the downtown's architectural focal points, along with, of course, Circle Centre, the city's new downtown shopping and entertainment complex. The Artsgarden links Circle Centre with the National City Bank/Hyatt Regency Hotel and office complex and the Claypool Court/Embassy Suites Hotel shopping and entertainment complex. Literally and symbolically, the Artsgarden serves as a bridge between the arts and commerce.

At least, that's the hope — the facility, which opened in September 1995, is still in the early stages of trying to fulfill its mission as a presenter of performances and exhibitions and as a purveyor of information about area arts events. (Given its accessibility, the Artsgarden is a one-stop-shopping center for schedules, tickets, calendars, maps and directories related to local arts organizations and events.)

While clearly one of the city's most visible and visually arresting arts facilities, the Artsgarden has attracted its share of criticism. Several area performing arts groups have lamented the fact that they weren't consulted during the structure's design stage;

Photo: The Indianapolis Star and The Indianapolis News

The Artsgarden is the newest addition to the arts scene in Indianapolis. The Artsgarden is a 12,500-square-foot glass-and-steel structure that spans Washington and Illinois streets.

as a result, they predict that poor acoustics will prevent it from being a viable site for musical or theatrical activities. Likewise, visual arts organizations have expressed concern about the effects of harsh light and heat upon works of art. (In their defense, the architects have pointed out that the structure's 26,000 square feet of glass is tempered to reduce noise and tinted to reduce light and heat.)

Despite criticisms, proponents insist that the Artsgarden, which includes a portable stage, theatrical lighting and acoustics, dressing rooms and exhibition cases, will ultimately enhance visibility and public awareness of arts organizations and events and artists. And, in a manner of speaking, it already has.

Since the initial unveiling of the design and the ground-breaking ceremonies (presided over by Jane Alexander, chair of the National Endowment for the Arts) in 1994, throughout the 10-month-long construction process, and right on up to the September 1995 opening, the Artsgarden generated plenty of publicity and attracted plenty of public attention — always with the reminder that its purpose is to showcase the arts.

For information about the Artsgarden, contact the Arts Council of Indianapolis, 631-3301.

The Sound of the City

The internationally-acclaimed 87-member Indianapolis Symphony Orchestra invites you to experience the real joy of musical excellence. One of America's few 52-week orchestras, there are always concerts, some 200 every year, for all audiences.

The Pops Series – Erich Kunzel conducts and the Orchestra swings for these evenings of outstanding entertainment.
Hilbert Circle Theatre, September through June.

Ameritech's "Yuletide Celebration"
The sights, sounds and smiles of the season come to life through music, singing, giant puppets and dancing.
Hilbert Circle Theatre, December.

Marsh "Symphony on the Prairie" Series
Food, families, fun, familiar favorites, even Fourth fireworks, all under the fantastic sky at Conner Prairie.
North on Allisonville Road, June through August.

The Classical Series – Highly celebrated maestro Raymond Leppard conducts the Orchestra for these concerts, right in the heart of downtown.
Hilbert Circle Theatre on Monument Circle, September through June.

Enjoy other ISO performances in the Sound of the City, Young People's Discovery, Family and Indiana series in the Hilbert Circle Theatre, other locations around Indianapolis and throughout the State of Indiana. The Indianapolis Symphony Orchestra can be heard on Koss Classics compact discs and on national and regional radio broadcasts.

For complete concert information, call the ISO box office.
In the Indianapolis are **639-4300**; or call toll free **1-800-366-8457**.

INDIANAPOLIS SYMPHONY ORCHESTRA

Raymond Leppard, Music Director

People here love sports.
And they've got plenty
to love.

Sports

Indianapolis takes its sports seriously. A quick look around at the quantity and quality of local sports facilities and events will provide evidence enough. And just try to get tickets to the Indianapolis 500 or the state high school basketball finals.

People here love sports. And they've got plenty to love. Cheer on first-tier professionals (the NBA's Indiana Pacers, the NFL's Indianapolis Colts), farm teams, the International Hockey League's Indianapolis Ice and the American Association baseball's Indianapolis Indians. Attend world-class events in track and field, swimming, diving and gymnastics; local high school competitions; international rowing and cycling; and the Hoosier State Games.

But this isn't your ordinary sports-loving place. In Indianapolis, sports aren't just entertainment — they're an integral part of local economic development efforts. So much so that they were a driving force behind the city's dramatic revitalization in the 1980s.

In Indianapolis, sports are not only good for business, they are good business. It was that realization that led city officials to make sports, specifically amateur sports, a linchpin in the local economy.

Amateur Sports Capital

The 1980s were a decade of rejuvenation for U.S. cities, as civic leaders throughout the nation joined forces with businesses and citizens groups to revitalize sluggish economies and revamp stagnant communities. Critical to each city's efforts was a marketing plan aimed at enhancing its image, making it attractive to public- and private-sector investors and to potential conventioneers and tourists. Of the dozens of cities engaged in image-enhancement efforts, none was more successful than Indianapolis.

Wielding a savvy marketing strategy, community leaders transformed Indianapolis from a faltering industrial center into a city that *Newsweek* dubbed "the Cinderella of the Rustbelt." However, the closest thing to a glass slipper in that transformation was an athletic shoe, an appropriate symbol for a city that used sports to turn itself into one of the most hospitable places in the country for athletes of all ages and abilities.

Today, few places in the United States can rival Indianapolis for the number of amateur sports organizations and world-class training and competition facilities, or for the quantity and quality of sporting events. Presently 20 national and international sports organizations have their headquarters in Indianapolis. Since 1974, the city has built or renovated more than $168 million worth of sports facilities. The availability of those facilities has resulted in Indianapolis hosting more than 330 amateur sporting events, including the 1987 Pan American Games, the 1991 NCAA Final Four and the 1997 NCAA Final Four. Between 1977 and 1991, the direct economic impact of amateur sports in the city was $1.05 billion.

Through deliberate and skillful planning, Indianapolis has become the self-proclaimed "Amateur Sports Capital of the World."

In the Beginning

The roots of the city's sports focus can be traced to the implementation of Unigov, the merger of the city of Indianapolis with surrounding Marion County to form a unified government structure. Agreed to by the Indiana Legislature in 1969, Unigov actually went into effect on January 1, 1970. Immediately the city's population nearly doubled, its geographic size quadrupled, and its tax base multiplied many times over.

That same year, the Amateur Athletic Union (AAU) moved its national headquarters to Indianapolis. At the time, the AAU was the umbrella organization for 13 amateur sports organizations. It helped with the administration of each sport's program, the marketing of its membership services and the regulation of its competitions.

Having the AAU in Indianapolis gave the city a leg up when Congress passed the Amateur Athletics Act of 1978, which directed the formation of independent governing bodies for all sports in which the United States has Olympic athletes. Suddenly the amateur sports groups operating inside AAU headquarters were free to set up separate operations wherever they liked.

Several of the fledgling national governing bodies headed for what they saw as greener pastures: Colorado Springs, home of the U.S. Olympic Committee. However, recruiters with offers of relocation funds and free office space eventually wooed several back to Indiana. Today, in addition to the AAU, Indianapolis is the home of USA Track and Field, USA Gymnastics, U.S. Diving, the U.S. Rowing Association, U.S. Synchronized Swimming, U.S. Water Polo and the U.S. Canoe/Kayak Team.

The reason city officials wanted amateur sports organizations to establish their headquarters in Indianapolis was simple: What better way to ensure that the city would be considered a primary candidate to host national and international events? But before they could sell the city as a viable place to hold events, civic leaders knew they needed high-quality facilities capable of meeting the exacting standards of athletes, coaches and trainers. In other words, expensive facilities.

Enter the Lilly Endowment. Founded in 1937 by the family of pharmaceutical corporation founder Eli Lilly, the endowment's mission in part is to provide financial help to projects aimed at improving the quality of life in Indianapolis.

Fortuitously, Congress had passed a tax act in 1969 that required foundations to give away a minimum percentage of their assets annually. Just as city officials began casting about for ways to fund the building of new sports facilities, the Lilly Endowment was looking for new areas in need of funds. As any athlete will tell you, timing is crucial to success in sports.

With financial support from the Endowment as well as from corporate and municipal coffers, Indianapolis started building athletic facilities and bidding to host national and international events. Today the city can boast having some of the finest facilities in the country and of attracting some of the finest sporting events in the world.

Since 1982, Indianapolis has hosted an array of events, including the 1982 National Sports Festival (now the U.S. Olympic Festival). Indianapolis was the first city in which the festival, traditionally plagued by red ink, made a profit.

FYI

Unless otherwise noted, the area code for all phone numbers in this guide is 317.

That success led to the city being selected as the site for the 1987 Pan American Games. With only two-and-a-half years to prepare for this international event, which is second only to the Olympic Games in terms of prestige and visibility, local planners rallied the resources needed to run it successfully. The bulk of the work that went into organizing and running the Pan American Games was done by some 37,000 volunteers. The Pan Am Games brought 4,453 athletes from 38 countries to Indianapolis and led to $9 million worth of ticket sales.

Since then, Indianapolis has been the site for Olympic trials in track and field, swimming and diving; the NCAA Final Four (1991 and 1997); the 1994 World Rowing Championships; the Grand Prix of Cycling (twice); and the 1991 World Gymnastics Championships, just to name a few. Sports is a growing enterprise.

And like any enterprise, this one owes its success in large part to the quality of its physical facilities.

Sports Facilities

While many cities can boast of having top-notch athletic facilities, few can match Indianapolis in terms of quantity, quality or accessibility. With few exceptions, the city's major

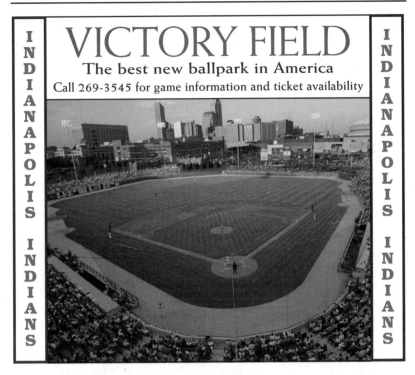

sports facilities are open for use by the public whenever they're not booked for events.

The philosophy behind this policy was simple: Since public money in one form or another helped pay for the construction of many of these facilities, the public has a right to use what it paid for beyond just attending events. (For more information, see our Fitness and Recreation chapter.)

RCA Dome
100 S. Capitol Ave., office 262-3410, box office 262-3389

Like a huge marshmallow, the RCA Dome dominates the southern edge of the Mile Square. One of two domed stadiums in the country attached to a convention center, this 60,500-seat facility is not only the home of the NFL's Indianapolis Colts, it also serves as a site for a variety of amateur sporting events.

In 1984, the Dome hosted the world's largest indoor basketball game when 67,596 people showed up for the U.S. Olympic Team vs. the NBA All-Stars game. In 1991 and 1997

it was the site of the NCAA Final Four, an event it will host again in the year 2000. Every October, it hosts the Circle City Classic, a football game featuring two of the nation's finest black college teams. And since 1979, the NCAA has held its Division I Men's and Women's Indoor Track Championships at the Dome. Call for an events calendar and information on behind-the-scenes Dome tours.

Pan American Plaza
201 S. Capitol Ave., office 237-5794, ice skating information 237-5555

Home to many of the city's amateur sports organizations' headquarters, as well as to the Indiana/World Skating Academy and Research Center. There are two on-site, indoor ice skating rinks: an Olympic-size, 100-by-200-foot rink that's used for training purposes by amateur and professional skaters as well as for classes and public skating; and a smaller, 85-by-200-foot, 1,000-seat rink that's used for competitions. The Research Center tests skaters' physical strengths and weaknesses in comparison to their levels of fitness. The quality of the rinks and the presence of the Research Center has made Indianapolis one of the country's foremost training sites for young figure skaters and hockey players.

The 12-story Pan Am Plaza office tower houses the Indiana Sports Corporation (see our Close-up in this chapter), as well as the national governing bodies (NGBs) for six Olympic sports: rowing, diving, gymnastics, synchronized swimming, canoeing/kayaking and water polo. Other sports organizations calling Pan Am Plaza home include the International Baseball Association, the National Association of Governors' Councils on Physical Fitness and Sports, the Midwestern Collegiate Conference, the Indiana Wrestling Association and Indiana Swimming Inc.

Market Square Arena
300 E. Market St., box office 639-2112, TicketMaster charge line 239-5151

This 16,530-seat facility is the home of the NBA's Indiana Pacers and the IHL's Indianapolis Ice. Built between 1971 and 1974 at a cost of $23.5 million, it has also hosted such noteworthy amateur events as the 1980 NCAA Final Four, the 1982 National Figure Skating Championships and the 1986 Gymnastics Championships of the USA.

Indianapolis Tennis Center
755 University Blvd. • 278-2100

This facility is on the campus of Indiana University-Purdue University at Indianapolis (IUPUI). It features a 10,000-seat stadium court, 18 other outdoor courts and a six-court indoor facility. The permanent site of the RCA Championships (see the "Annual Sporting Events" portion of this chapter), which brings a number of top-seeded men's professional players to town every summer, the Tennis Center is a United States Tennis Association training site. It's also used for a variety of high school and college tennis events.

When not in use for amateur or professional tournaments, the courts are available to Tennis Center members and nonmembers alike. (See our Parks and Recreation chapter.)

Indiana University Natatorium
901 W. New York St. • 274-3518

This is the swimming and diving facility that Olympic gold medalist Greg Louganis once called "the best in the Western Hemisphere." There are three pools in the Natatorium: a main Olympic-size pool, an 18-foot-deep diving pool with five platforms and three springboards and a practice pool with a bottom that can be raised or lowered to accommodate children and people with disabilities.

Photo: Meredith Goldberg

Ivanisevic Goran keeps focused on the ball during the RCA Championships.

The Natatorium has hosted an array of national and international events, including the 1985 Synchronized Swimming World Cup Championships, the 1989 VI FINA World Cup Diving competition, the 1992 World Masters Swimming Championships, seven Olympic trials and 12 NCAA championships.

While the Natatorium is in frequent use by high school, college, national and international athletes, it's also available to the general public. (See our Parks and Recreation chapter.)

Indiana University Track and Field Stadium
901 W. New York St. • 274-6780

After seeing this facility, a writer for *Track and Field News* magazine raved: "If there is a better facility in the U.S. . . . we are unaware of it." Capable of seating nearly 20,000, the stadium features a nine-lane, 400-meter rubber track that is considered one of the world's fastest. The site of the 1988 U.S. Olympic trials, this facility also hosts the annual NIKE Track Classic. When not in use for competitions, the stadium is open to the public. (See our Parks and Recreation chapter.)

Major Taylor Velodrome
3649 Cold Spring Rd. • 327-8356

This facility consists of a 333.3-meter banked track that consistently earns accolades from competitive cyclists. The site of the 1988 and 1989 Grand Prix of Cycling competitions, the velodrome is named for Marshall W. "Major" Taylor, a turn-of-the-century African-American cycling champion from Indianapolis.

Next to the velodrome is the Lake Sullivan BMX Track, which is used for a variety of bicycle motor-cross events.

(For information on public riding at the velodrome or the BMX track, see our Parks and Recreation chapter.)

Hinkle Fieldhouse
Butler University, 4600 Sunset Ave.
• 940-9375

If it were a person, Butler University's Hinkle Fieldhouse would be called a living legend. As it is, it's named for Butler's legendary coach (basketball, football and baseball) and athletic director Tony Hinkle (see our Close-up in this chapter).

When the fieldhouse (then known as Butler Fieldhouse) opened in 1928, it was the largest basketball arena in the United States, a distinction it retained for 20 years. While it has since been eclipsed in size, it hasn't yet been surpassed in atmosphere — if you're looking for a place that radiates history and charm, this is it. Long the home of the Butler Bulldogs, it has also hosted hundreds of high school contests, including numerous state championship games. Prior to the opening of Market Square Arena in 1974, Hinkle Fieldhouse (it was renamed in 1965) was the site of the annual state high school championship game — one of Hoosier Hysteria's ultimate moments.

More recently, this 10,800-seat arena played host to the volleyball events during the 1987 Pan American Games and to the 1994 Midwestern Collegiate Conference Men's and Women's Basketball Championships. Some of the exciting game scenes in the movie *Hoosiers* were shot inside Hinkle Fieldhouse.

Pepsi Coliseum
Indiana State Fairgrounds, 1202 E. 38th St.
• 927-7500

The former home of the Indianapolis Ice, the Coliseum is a 7,839-seat arena that's used for amateur hockey leagues, rodeos, and other sporting events. It's also open to the public for year-round ice skating. (See our Parks and Recreation chapter.)

William Kuntz Soccer Stadium
1502 W. 16th St. • 327-7194

Built for the 1987 Pan American Games, the Kuntz Stadium consists of a 4,500-seat competition field and a 2,000-seat practice field. Operated by Indy Parks and Recreation, this facility now houses youth soccer leagues and hosts a variety of amateur soccer competitions.

Eagle Creek Park
7840 W. 56th St. • 327-7110

The largest municipally owned park in the nation, Eagle Creek is also the home of the Eagle Creek Regatta Course, the only rowing course in the country sanctioned for international competition by the International Federation of Rowing Associations. Site of the U.S.

Photo: Paul Sancya

Jim Harbaugh celebrates a Colts victory.

Rowing National Championships since 1986, the Eagle Creek course also hosted the 1994 World Rowing Championships, the first time this event had ever been held in the United States.

Also at Eagle Creek is a world-class archery range with two competition fields. Originally built for the 1987 Pan American Games, the range is now used primarily for archery classes.

The rowing course and the archery range are open for public use. (See our Parks and Recreation chapter.)

Little League Baseball Central Region Headquarters
9802 Little League Dr. • 897-6127

This is a summer camp and training facility serving 1,000 leagues throughout 13 Midwestern states. On its 30-acre site are five playing fields, a swimming pool, tennis and basketball courts and seating for 2,000.

Hoosier Horse Park
Johnson County Park, N. Camp Atterbury, off 31st St., Edinburgh • (812) 526-5929

Designed for use during the 1987 Pan American Games, the horse park is situated in the 611-acre Johnson County Park, south of Indianapolis. It includes a 14.5-mile cross-country course, three all-weather dressage arenas, a stadium jump arena, a rodeo arena, a flat saddle arena and 192 box stalls. Due to the quality of the facility, Hoosier Horse Park is the site of a variety of amateur equestrian competitions that are free to spectators.

Woodfill Range
Johnson County Park, Edinburgh • (812) 526-6809

A competitive shooting facility, Woodfill Range was also built for the 1987 Pan American Games. Now it's primarily used by soldiers from nearby Camp Atterbury, though it still hosts amateur marksmanship competitions.

Professional Sports

Though Indianapolis bills itself as the Amateur Sports Capital of the World, it hasn't ignored professional sports. To the contrary: The city is home to what might arguably be called one of the most famous professional sporting events in the world — the Indianapolis 500 (see our Auto Racing chapter). It's also home to the Indiana Pacers, who in recent years have become one of the NBA's most exciting teams, and the Indianapolis Indians, long one of professional baseball's best minor league teams. Add to the mix the NFL's Indianapolis

Colts and the IHL's Indianapolis Ice, and it's clear that professional sports are vital factors in the city's overall sports marketing strategy — plus there's the fact that they're a lot of fun.

Indiana Pacers
Market Square Arena, 300 E. Market St. • office 639-2112, MSA Box Office 239-5151

A fixture in Indianapolis since 1967 when the team was one of the earliest American Basketball Association (ABA) franchises, the Pacers and their fans have weathered the fortunes and misfortunes that accompany a long-term relationship. It hasn't always been easy.

In 1967, the late *Indianapolis Star* sports editor Bob Collins and five other investors pooled $6,000 to buy a franchise in the ABA, which was then in the proposal stage. When the upstart basketball organization finally began operating, the Indiana team quickly established its dominance. Relying on the talents of such native sons as Rick Mount, Bill Keller and George McGinnis, as well as such noteworthy acquisitions as Mel Daniels and Roger Brown, the Pacers and coach Bobby "Slick" Leonard showed America what basketball Indiana-style could be. Drawing crowds as large as 8,000 people at a time when the ABA game average was 5,000, the Pacers won three ABA titles, in 1970, 1972 and 1973, and three most valuable player awards: Mel Daniels in 1969 and 1971, and George McGinnis in 1975. They were among the ABA's elite.

And Indianapolis officials showed their appreciation by building Market Square Arena to house the Pacers, who'd been playing their home contests in the Coliseum at the Indiana State Fairgrounds. But in 1976, the ABA went belly-up, and the Pacers became one of only four ABA teams to ante up the required $3.2 million to gain admission to the National Basketball Association.

Resulting financial problems almost destroyed the Pacers. Top players, including McGinnis, left when Indiana couldn't meet their salary demands. In 1977, the team held an unprecedented telethon to meet operating expenses. While the community rallied to help the Pacers, fan support slipped. By the 1982-83 season, attendance at home games was less than 5,000. Making matters worse was the fact that the Pacers consistently finished each season with more losses than wins.

In 1983, local real estate developers Melvin and Herbert Simon bought the Pacers from California businessperson Sam Nassi, who'd owned the franchise since 1979. While the team continued to struggle to find the right combination of players and coaching staff, the Simons' hands-off management style allowed team president and general manager Donnie Walsh and his assistants to run the Pacers. Gradually things improved: By 1987, the Pacers were actually in the NBA playoffs.

In 1994, under the guidance of coach Larry Brown and fueled by the hot-handed three-point shooting of Reggie Miller, the Pacers nearly defeated the tough New York Knicks in the Eastern Conference finals. As it was, they pushed the best-of-seven series to the limit with a fired-up Miller trading courtside jibes with filmmaker/Knicks fan Spike Lee during an unbelievable 25-point rampage in the fourth quarter of Game Five at Madison Square Garden. Though the Knicks finally won that series in Game Seven, the Pacers had served notice that they were once again a force to be reckoned with. Pacer fans became fanatics.

Posters and banners emblazoned with "Pacer Pride" bedecked windows, cars, and lampposts throughout the city. The Pacer gift shop couldn't keep shirts and jerseys in stock. Residents planned their lives around game schedules.

In 1995, the Pacers squared off against the Knicks in the second round of the playoffs. Led by the shooting, rebounding and defensive play of Rik Smits, Dale Davis and Antonio Davis, Indiana prevailed this time. After beating the Knicks, the Pacers dropped a grueling seven-game series to the Orlando Magic in the Eastern Conference Championship.

Unfortunately, 1996 wasn't quite as exciting. Plagued by a series of player injuries that weakened their offense and resulted in uneven performances, the Pacers still managed a 52-30 season. Included in their victories were two over the Chicago Bulls, the team the press often touted as almost invincible. But unlike the previous two years, the Pacers never caught fire in post-season play: They lost their opening round playoff series to the Atlanta Hawks 3-2.

Odd as it seems, despite their popularity, the Pacers aren't a money-making enterprise these days. Or more specifically, they're not a profit-making enterprise. Escalating player salaries, as well as lower-than-the-NBA-average ticket sales broadcast and arena advertising receipts, keep the team in the red. But that hasn't prevented other cities from approaching the Simons about buying the team. In 1993, Toronto investors reportedly offered to buy the Pacers for $100 million. The offer was rejected. Operating deficit or not, Indianapolis without the Pacers is unthinkable.

If you want to see what all the hoopla is about, go sit in Market Square and watch the team in action. Individual ticket prices for Pacers games range from $9 to $32. Group rates are available. For a season schedule and ticket information, contact the Market Square Arena box office.

Indianapolis Colts
7001 W. 56th St. • office 297-2658, tickets 297-7000

It was a dark and stormy night. Sounds like the beginning of a bad story, doesn't it? In a way, it is. It's the beginning of the story of how Indianapolis came to have an NFL franchise. And how Baltimore came to lose one.

When the rancor between owner Bob Irsay and longtime team franchise site Baltimore reached the boiling point in 1984, Irsay, blaming poor playing facilities and declining game attendance, responded to the siren call of Indianapolis. City officials had played on his desire to leave Baltimore by pointing to a newly built domed stadium and guaranteeing him $7 million in annual ticket sales for seven years. They'd also promised a site for a permanent Colts training facility.

That's how a line of Mayflower Transit trucks (at the time, Mayflower had its national headquarters in Indianapolis) happened to appear outside the Colts' Baltimore facility one rainy night in March 1984. Loaded with all of the Colts' gear, the trucks headed west toward Indianapolis. In sports lore, that event has come to be known as the midnight ride of the Colts.

Once the trucks arrived, Irsay and Indianapolis mayor William Hudnut held a press conference, announcing the team's new name, the Indianapolis Colts, and its new home field, the recently opened Hoosier (now RCA) Dome. Indianapolis had officially become an NFL franchise site.

Baltimore wasn't happy. Much howling and hand-wringing ensued, along with many cries of "good riddance." The city of Baltimore filed a lawsuit against the city of Indianapolis, alleging that it had stolen the franchise and could not designate the team as the Colts, a name the suit claimed for Baltimore. That argument was rejected by the court, and the Colts retained their name.

Locally, enthusiasm and optimism were high. The first season, 143,000 Colts fans applied for season tickets. But fans don't win NFL games — teams do. And as a team, the Colts weren't winners. In fact, by 1986, they were floundering; they lost the first 13 games of the season.

In 1987, Irsay decided his team needed a marquee player to turn the team's fortunes around. So in a trade with the Los Angeles Rams, the Colts acquired the services of Eric Dickerson, then the best running back in the NFL. With a talented offensive line protecting Dickerson and running back Albert Bentley backing him up, the Colts seemed poised for greatness.

Under the guidance of coach Ron Meyer, they won the AFC Eastern Division title and went to the NFL playoffs for the first time in 10 years. Though they lost in the first game against the Cleveland Browns, the Colts revived the flagging interest of their Indianapolis fans.

But in the ensuing years, the team's fortunes have wavered. A number of missteps — poor draft choices and trade decisions, player injuries and coaching changes — have resulted in mediocre season records and team morale. Dickerson, who was injured in 1988, finally left the team in 1991 after earning a reputation as a prima donna for his frequent complaints about his teammates, his treatment and his salary.

Another disappointment came when Irsay signed quarterback Jeff George, who had been a local grid star at Warren Central High School. Undeniably talented, George made a lot of noise about his abilities in the press but didn't do much to help the team out of its slump. He,

too, spent as much time complaining as playing before being traded to Atlanta in 1993.

In 1991, the Colts' win-loss record was a dismal 1-15, the worst in the league. With new coach Ted Marchibroda at the helm in 1992, the Colts tied the NFL's record for the best one-season turnaround by compiling a 9-7 season.

The Colts dropped 4-12 in 1993 but rebounded with two straight season-ending victories to go 8-8 in 1994. Running back Marshall Faulk was named the NFL's 1994 Rookie of the Year.

Then came 1995 — the year the Colts proved just how good (and how tenacious) they were. Inspired by the on-field leadership and heroics of quarterback Jim Harbaugh, who led the NFL in passing at season's end, the Colts racked up a record of 11-8; many of the losses were near-misses, with five of them being by four points or less. But the nearest miss of all came during the AFC championship game against the Pittsburgh Steelers. When receiver Aaron Bailey lost his grip on Harbaugh's last-second Hail Mary pass in the end zone. A win would have sent the Colts to the Super Bowl. Still, the Colts received a hero's welcome when they returned to Indianapolis from Pittsburgh. Their long-suffering fans were only too happy to cheer for a team as talented and gutsy as the Colts had proven themselves to be. The only blemish on the 1995 season came a few days later when the Colts director of football operations Bill Tobin fired coach Ted Marchibroda, replacing him with offensive coordinator Lindy Infante. It was a reminder once again that the Colts are a business— and that no one is indispensable.

That's something Infante himself must have been thinking about at the end of the 1996 season. Though they got off to a promising start, going 4-0 before their first loss, the Colts hobbled to a mediocre 9-7 record, plagued by a string of injuries that led to 18 starters spending some part of the season on the sidelines. Among the injured were such key players as Faulk and Harbaugh, though each made it back on the field before season's end.

Still, gutsy as ever, the Colts managed to make the first round of the AFC playoffs, though ironically they were pitted against the Steelers again — in Pittsburgh again. This time the game was less heart-stopping: The Steelers came out on top 42-14, sending the Colts home to regroup for 1997.

In January 1997, the team's longtime owner Bob Irsay died after spending more than a year battling back from a devastating stroke he suffered in November 1995. Among the most colorful figures in the NFL, Irsay was one of the last of the hard-drinking, tough-talking, self-made millionaires in the increasingly corporate-oriented world of professional sports. He was buried in Crown Hill Cemetery.

Long before his death, Irsay had made sure everything was in order for a smooth pas-

Victory Field

On the evening of July 11, 1996, Indianapolis's newest sports venue —Victory Field, 501 W. Maryland Street — made its debut before a sellout crowd of more than 15,000 people. The home field of the city's American Association baseball team, the Indianapolis Indians, Victory Field is an $18 million state-of-the-art baseball facility.

Built in 1995-96, the new stadium replaced a much beloved city landmark, Bush Stadium, which had been the Indians' home field since 1931. While Victory Field lacks the history and the ambiance of its predecessor (Bush Stadium hosted international baseball competition during the 1987 Pan American Games, and it was also used for the baseball scenes in the movies *Eight Men Out* and *Roommates*), it contains amenities that Bush couldn't offer.

Air-conditioned luxury boxes, for instance, and a computerized scoreboard that provides up-to-the-minute scores of Major League Baseball games as well as the score of the game going on in the stadium.

All the seats in Victory are angled toward home plate, so even the fans sitting farthest from the plate can see what's going on without having to twist and turn too much. And there are lawn seats available for some 2,000 people just beyond the outfield wall, a perfect place for a family picnic while waiting to snag a home-run ball.

But in all the hoopla surrounding the opening of Victory Field, Bush Stadium, which was also once called Victory Field, wasn't ignored. At press time for this book, it appeared that the old stadium was going to be converted into (what else?) an auto racing facility.

Photo: Kelly Wilkinson

Victory field became the new home of the Indianapolis Indians in July 1996.

sage of the team to his son Jim, the Colt's longtime general manager. In the short run, the Colts will operate as always. In the long run, no one knows what's going to happen.

In late 1996, Jim Irsay began to discuss publicly the Colts' need for more revenue, something that some observers saw as a precursor to a proposal that the Colts become owners (rather than tenants) of the RCA Dome or as an early warning signal that the team might once again pull up stakes and head for greener pastures, perhaps Cleveland which lost its beloved Browns in 1995.

Jim Irsay said that would never happen — something his father had said to Baltimore fans before moving the teams to Indianapolis. Like father, like son? At the time this book went to press, Colts fans were waiting for the answer to that question.

Fans have been loyal from the start. While home games aren't always sellouts as they were in the first few seasons, it's not unusual for 50,000 or more people to show up for a game. For diehard NFL fans, the thrill of sitting in such a wonderful venue as the Dome has long overridden the sometimes disappointing results. Individually the Colts players are local favorites, appearing in TV and radio commercials, taking part in charitable events and generally making themselves available to the community. That goes a long way toward maintaining good will even during a losing season. Who wouldn't want to support such nice guys?

Individual tickets for Colts games run $15, $23, $25 and $29. Season tickets are $230, $250 and $290. Tickets are available at all TicketMaster locations, including the RCA Dome box office, or by mail-order from the Colts. Call the Colts' ticket line for more information.

Indianapolis Indians
Victory Field, 501 W. Maryland St.
• **ticket office 269-3545**

If you were going to handpick hometown heroes, you couldn't do much better than the Indians. The American Association farm team for the Cincinnati Reds, the Indians have been a part of life in Indianapolis since 1887.

Known as the Indians from the beginning, the club has been affiliated with a number of

Major League teams during the course of its history. Since its first working agreement with the Cincinnati Reds (1939-41), the Indians have been a farm team for the Boston Braves (1946-47), the Pittsburgh Pirates (1948-51), the Cleveland Indians (1952-56), the Chicago White Sox (1957-59, 1962-67), the Philadelphia Phillies (1960) and the Cincinnati Reds (1961, 1968-83). When the Reds refused to allow the use of designated hitters in the minor league, Indianapolis general manager Max Schumacher switched the Indians' affiliation to the Montreal Expos (1984-92). But for the 1993 season, the Indians returned to the Reds' fold where they remain.

During the past few decades, the Indians have readied a number of major leaguers for their careers, including such future stars as Roger Maris, Rocky Colavito and Harmon Killebrew. They've also created their own stars, the most notable being Razor Shines, who personified baseball for Indians fans for a decade before retiring in 1994.

Shines was a multiple-threat player — at first base or third, in the outfield or as a catcher and as a designated hitter who was great in clutch situations. He was also a great motivator of his teammates and of himself. Shines worked hard in the off-season to stay in condition and to improve his game. "He was quite simply the working man's hero," wrote David B. Reddick and Kim M. Rogers of Shines in their 1988 book *The Magic of Indians Baseball: 1887-1987.*

As a team, the Indians have shone in their own right. From 1986 to 1989, the club won four consecutive American Association championships and two Triple-A Alliance World Series.

However, over the course of a century, everything hasn't always been rosy in the Indians' camp. Following the close of the 1956 season, for example, a severe financial deficit nearly killed the team. But city residents revived it by contributing $205,000 in operating capital. When the cash-strapped American Association was forced out of business in 1962, the Indians joined the International League for one season then the Pacific Coast League for five more. Finally, in 1969 the American Association re-formed, with the Indians once again in its fold.

From 1931 until July 1996, the team's home field was Bush Stadium, a wonderful old-time stadium complete with ivy on the walls and a scoreboard on which the numbers were hung by hand. But on July 11, 1996, the lights at the West 16th Street stadium went dark; that was opening night for Victory Field, a new downtown stadium. Constructed at a cost of $18 million, Victory Field was the city's bid to retain the Indians: The team had been complaining for several years about the state of Bush Stadium, which was in need of some major league repairs. (For more on Victory Field, see the Close-up in this chapter.)

Tickets to Indianapolis Indians home games for field-level and upper-view box seats are $8 for adults, $7 for children. For upper and lower reserved seats, tickets cost $7 for adults, $6. For upper and lower grandstand seats, bleachers and lawn seating, tickets are $5 for adults and $4 for children. For a game schedule and ticket information, call the Indians' ticket office.

Indianapolis Ice
222 E. Ohio St. • office 266-1234, Market Square Arena Box Office 239-5151

The top minor league affiliate for the National Hockey League's Chicago Blackhawks, the Ice play their home games at Market Square Arena, 300 E. Market Street. They are the latest in a line of professional hockey teams that have called Indianapolis home since 1939.

The first was the Capitols, a team affiliated with the National Hockey League's Detroit Red Wings. Playing in the newly constructed Indiana State Fair Coliseum, the Capitols won three divisional titles between 1940 and 1946 as well as two league championships (1942 and 1950). When the Red Wings and the State Fair Board couldn't reach a long-term lease agreement for the Coliseum in 1952, the Capitols disbanded.

Over the course of the next 35 years, four more minor league hockey teams called Indianapolis home: the Indianapolis Chiefs (1955-62), a reincarnation of the Indianapolis Capitols (1963), the Indianapolis Racers (1974-78), and the Indianapolis Checkers (1979-87). NHL superstar Wayne Gretzky began his professional career in Indianapolis, playing for the Racers for eight games dur-

ing the 1978 season before moving on to the Edmonton Oilers.

The Ice, an International Hockey League team, debuted in 1988. For the first year of its existence, the Ice had no NHL affiliation. It wasn't until the 1989-90 season that the team became the official farm team for the Blackhawks. That proved to be good timing for Chicago because in that same season the Ice won 53 matches and the IHL's Turner Cup. Since then, the team has continued to be a strong presence on and off the ice and to attract new fans through smart marketing.

Feisty and talented, the young Ice players scrap to keep hockey in the headlines all through the October-to-April season. You don't have to know icing from frosting to enjoy the Ice.

Tickets for Ice home games, which are played at Market Square Arena are $13, $11 and $8; season tickets range from $175 to $285 for half-season to $300 to $475 for whole-season packages.

Tickets are available through all TicketMaster locations, including the MSA box office; season tickets can be purchased by mail from the Ice. Call the team office for information.

Indiana Twisters
Market Square Arena, 330 E. Market St. • office 231-2870, TicketMaster 239-5151

The newest member of the city's professional sports community, the Twisters, a franchise member of the Continental Indoor Soccer League, kicked off its inaugural season in June 1996. In a city where youth soccer leagues abound, the creation of a professional soccer team was long overdue. However, sports fans here have been reared on hoops and fast cars, so it may take awhile before the idea of going to a soccer match really catches on.

Initial crowds for Twisters matches have been supportive, but sparse, with numbers rarely topping 5,000. Still, there is interest, especially among young people who play and enjoy soccer— and among the city's small, but growing immigrant community, many of whose members come from countries where soccer is the major sport.

Tickets for Twisters matches range from $9 to $15, and are available at the Market

Square Arena box office or through TicketMaster.

Indianapolis Motor Speedway
4790 W. 16th St. • office 481-8500, tickets 484-6700

Without a doubt, the Motor Speedway is the city's most enduring professional sports symbol. A local landmark since 1916, it's the site of the annual Indianapolis 500, which is billed as the world's largest one-day specta-tor event, and the newly inaugurated Brick-yard 400, a NASCAR-sanctioned stock car race. (For more information, see our Auto Rac-ing chapter.)

Indianapolis Raceway Park
9901 Crawfordsville Rd. • 291-4090

If you like drag racing, oval track racing or road racing, IRP is heaven. This facility is home to such big-time events as the annual NHRA U.S. Nationals, the Kroger NASCAR

The Indiana Sports Corporation

While no single individual or entity was entirely responsible for turning Indianapolis into a sports capital, the Indiana Sports Corporation certainly played a key role. Established in 1979, the ISC is a not-for-profit, privately funded organization directed at attracting national and international sporting events to Indianapolis and Indiana.

 Close-up

In the beginning, the only ISC employee was Sandy Knapp, the former vice president of promotions and marketing for the Indiana Pacers. In 1980, with the help of a volunteer management team assembled from the business community, Knapp went before U.S. Olympic Committee officials to bid on behalf of Indianapolis for the 1982 National Sports Festival. At the time, most of the sports facilities being touted in the proposal package were merely architectural renderings — the real structures had yet to be built. "We used a lot of smoke and mirrors," Knapp later said of the proposal, which was successful. Indianapolis got the festival. All it needed then were the facilities.

In the end, it got them — and in time. More than 3,000 athletes from around the country came to Indianapolis in the summer of 1982, and many were so impressed by the quality of the facilities and with the city's hospitality that they mentioned their impres-sions in press interviews. Indianapolis gained valuable national attention, the Sports Festi-val earned its first-ever profit, and the ISC proved it could do a lot with a little.

Since then, the ISC has continued its role as advocate for and promoter of India-napolis and Indiana as sports-friendly sites. The organization has coordinated such events as the 1987 Pan American Games, and, under the auspices of its for-profit subsidiary Sports Marketing of Indiana, the 1991 PGA Championship and the GTE (now RCA) Tennis Championships.

One particularly noteworthy event that the ISC organizes annually is the Hoosier

Athletes carry flames to light the torch at the Hoosier State Games, sponsored by the Indiana Sports Corporation.

Photo: The Indianapolis Star and The Indianapolis News

State Games (see our Parks and Recreation chapter). Attracting more than 21,000 athletes of all ages and skill levels to Indianapolis each summer, the Games is one of the largest such events in the country.

Through fund-raisers such as the annual Youthlinks Celebrity Golf Tournament, the ISC is also able to fund sports programs for young people throughout Indiana.

ISC offices are in Pan Am Plaza, 201 S. Capitol Avenue. For more information, call 237-5000.

200 Grand National Stock Car Race and the Miller Genuine Draft Night Before the 500 midget car race. Ah, the smell of rubber, the roar of engines! (For more details, see our Auto Racing chapter.)

Hoosier Park
4500 Dan Patch Cir., Anderson
• 642-RACE

While not actually an Indianapolis sports attraction, Hoosier Park is near enough (about 35 miles north on I-69) to take in, especially if you're a horse racing fan. Indiana's first pari-mutuel track, Hoosier Park features both thoroughbred and harness racing.

Annual Sporting Events

Brickyard Crossing Championship
Brickyard Crossing Golf Resort & Inn, 4400 W. 16th St. • 484-6572

This Senior PGA Tour tournament is played on a course that spreads out around the Indianapolis Motor Speedway. Originally built in 1929, the course was completely redesigned by renowned golf course architect (and former Indianapolis resident) Pete Dye in 1993. The following year, the tournament debuted. It was so successful with players and fans alike that the 1995 event attracted such renowned duffers as Gary Player and Arnold Palmer.

Ticket prices range from $20 for a one-day pass to $100 for a week-long badge that includes access to the course and clubhouse. Group ticket packages range from $600 to $2,100.

Coca-Cola Circle City Classic
Indiana Black Expo, 3145 N. Meridian St. • 925-2702

Established in 1984 as an event for alumni of black colleges, as well as a means of encouraging African-American children to attend college, the Circle City Classic has expanded into one of the country's largest African-American events. For a week each October, thousands of black college alumni (as well as black celebrities and athletes) gather in Indianapolis for a variety of activities, the culmination being the Classic itself, a football game between two of the country's historically black college teams. The sellout game (the proceeds help fund scholarships for black colleges) is played in the RCA Dome.

Tickets to the game are $10, $15 and $25 and are available at all TicketMaster locations, including the RCA Dome box office, or by mail-order from the RCA Dome Ticket Office, 200 S. Capitol Avenue, Suite 150, Indianapolis, Indiana 46225.

The RCA Championships
Indianapolis Tennis Center, 755 University Blvd. • 632-8000, (800) 622-LOVE

Every August some of the biggest names on the men's professional tennis circuit (Jim Courier, Pete Sampras, Todd Martin) come to the city for this nine-day event. Consistently ranked as the "tournament of the year" by the players, the RCA Championships is big-time tennis at its best.

Indianapolis has a long and storied history of support for and involvement with tennis. From 1922 to 1968, it was the site of the Western Open, the oldest amateur tennis tournament in the country. From 1922 until 1965, Indianapolis hosted it every other year; in 1966, it became the tournament's permanent home. However, in 1969, the United States Tennis Association (USTA) moved the U.S. Clay Court Championships to Indianapolis; the Western Open then moved to Cincinnati. As the last tournament before the prestigious U.S. Open, the Clay Courts became an important stop for many of the world's top players eager to fine tune their games for the Open. So popular were the Clay Courts locally that city officials decided to build the Indianapolis Sports Center (now the Indianapolis Tennis Center) in 1978.

Ironically, that same year the U.S. Open switched from clay to hard courts, and players began to shun the Indianapolis tournament and play tournaments on hard courts. By 1986, tournament officials were having a hard time getting top-seeded men's players to commit to the Clay Courts. In 1987, local tournament organizers decided to pave the Sports Center's courts, and the USTA moved the Clay Courts to South Carolina.

In 1988, a $13 million construction project began, turning the Sports Center into the Tennis Center. In addition to paving the existing clay courts, a new tennis stadium replaced the old one, and an indoor tennis complex was added. Impressed with the results, the USTA made the Indianapolis Tennis Center a regional training center and announced the creation of a new sanctioned hard court tournament, the one now known as the RCA Championships.

FYI

Unless otherwise noted, the area code for all phone numbers in this guide is 317.

Other tennis highlights throughout the years have included the Indiana Loves, a member of the short-lived World Tennis Team league (1975-78). The Loves played matches at the Indiana Convention Center and Market Square Arena. And from 1982-92, the Indianapolis Racquet Club hosted a Virginia Slims Ginny circuit tournament (1982-87) and a Kraft series tournament (1988-92), both sanctioned by the Women's Tennis Association.

Individual session tickets for the RCA Championships range from $8 to $50, depending on seat locations and sessions. Season tickets range from $150 to $400. Tickets are available at the Indianapolis Tennis Center box office or by mail.

Youthlinks Indiana Celebrity Golf Tournament
Indiana Sports Corporation, 201 S. Capitol Ave., Ste. 1200 • 237-5000

A joint presentation of the Indiana Sports Corporation and Indiana Black Expo, the Youthlinks Celebrity Golf Tournament is held in late June each year. The event attracts present and former professional and Olympic athletes, coaches, broadcasters, politicians and sports executives from throughout the country to Indianapolis for a day of golf dedicated to raising money to help fund youth sports programs and scholarships.

Past Youthlinks participants have included Olympic speed skater Bonnie Blair, former Indianapolis 500 champion Tom Sneva, CBS sports announcer Billy Packer, screenwriter Angelo Pizzo (*Hoosiers* and *Rudy*), former Indiana University head football coach Bill Mallory and Indiana's senior U.S. Senator Richard Lugar.

Since its inception in 1988, Youthlinks has raised more than $2.5 million for such programs as CHAMPS, a grants program that benefits local sports activities for young people; Future Olympians, a grants program that assists Olympic-caliber athletes in need of financial help to meet the costs of training, equipment, travel and medical expenses; and Indiana Evans Scholars, a scholarship program for former golf caddies who graduate in the top 25 percent of their high school class and need assistance with college expenses.

Youthlinks events take place at various area golf courses. For up-to-date schedule and ticket information, contact the Indiana Sports Corporation.

Sports Organizations

In addition to the facilities, teams and events listed in this chapter, Indianapolis is home to a number of national sports organizations. While these organizations primarily represent the interests of coaches and athletes in specific sports, they're also good sources of information for spectators interested in learning more about individual sports.

Indiana Amateur Athletic Union (AAU)
3400 W. 86th St. • 872-8680

The AAU's Indiana affiliate promotes and develops amateur sports throughout the state. A nonprofit, volunteer-driven organization, it represents some 25,000 athletes, coaches, volunteers and officials.

National Governing Bodies (NGBs)

The following organizations regulate and sanction national competitions within their respective Olympic sports and represent those sports and their athletes in the international arena.

U.S. Canoe/Kayak Team, 201 S. Capitol Avenue, Suite 610, 237-5690

USA Gymnastics, 201 S. Capitol Avenue, Suite 300, 237-5050

USA Track & Field, 200 S. Capitol Avenue, Suite 140, 261-0500

United States Diving Inc., 201 S. Capitol Avenue, Suite 430, 237-5252

United States Rowing Association, 201 S. Capitol Avenue, Suite H 400, 237-5656

United States Synchronized Swimming, 201 S. Capitol Avenue, Suite 510, 237-5700

United States Water Polo Inc., 201 S. Capitol Avenue, Suite 520, 237-5599

The Man Who Put the Hinkle in Hinkle Fieldhouse

Paul Daniel "Tony" Hinkle (1898-1992) is an Indianapolis sports legend. A native of Logansport, Indiana, Hinkle earned All-American honors while playing basketball and football at the University of Chicago (1916-1920). After graduating from college, he pitched for a semipro baseball team in Chicago.

In 1921, Hinkle moved to Indianapolis, joining the Butler University coaching staff as an assistant football coach. Five years later, he was promoted to head coach. Over the next 44 years, Hinkle's Butler Bulldogs won nine Indiana Collegiate Conference titles, compiling a 171-100-12 record.

In addition to football, Hinkle also coached Butler's baseball and basketball teams. Under his direction, both teams did well. In both sports, he could boast a 44-year win-loss record exceeding 50 percent. And in basketball, Hinkle invented the "Hinkle System," a system that emphasized movement on the floor and the use of passes, picks and screens. The Hinkle System became a model for other coaches, including Indiana University's Bob Knight who adapted and modified it in the course of creating his own offensive strategies.

In 1928, Hinkle helped inaugurate the new Butler Fieldhouse, which for more than two decades was the largest gymnasium in the country. At various times over the years, Hinkle ran the fieldhouse concession stand and buffed its floor, all while continuing his coaching duties.

In honor of Hinkle's many contributions to the university, Butler officials named him athletic director in 1932. And in 1965, they renamed the fieldhouse — it officially became Hinkle Fieldhouse, which, in a manner of speaking, it always had been. That same year, he was elected to the James Naismith Basketball Hall of Fame.

Hinkle was widely respected throughout the country. He served for two terms

Photo: The Indianapolis Star and The Indianapolis News

Paul D. "Tony" Hinkle was the legendary coach and athletic director at Butler University.

(1937-1938 and 1942-1950) on the NCAA Basketball Rules Committee; he chaired the committee from 1948 to 1950. He was also the president of the National Association of Basketball Coaches (NABC), 1954-1955. In 1962, Hinkle was awarded the National Collegiate Basketball Coaches Association Award, and in 1986 the NABC gave him its Golden Anniversary Award.

Though he retired from Butler in 1970, Hinkle remained active in both university and community affairs. When he died in 1992, he left behind a legacy that included his belief in honorable competition, sportsmanship and dedication as well as an insistence on respect for opponents, authorities and the rules of the game.

Sports-Related Attractions

When you're in the mood for sports spectating of a different sort, drop by the following.

The National Track and Field Hall of Fame
One RCA Dome, 200 S. Capitol Ave.
• 261-0483

From Jim Thorpe and Jesse Owens to Wilma Rudolph and Babe Didrickson, the achievements of 150 of track and field's greatest athletes are chronicled here. It's open daily except on special event days and holidays. Admission is $3 for adults, $2 for children 5 to 17 and free for children 4 and younger.

The Indianapolis Motor Speedway Hall of Fame Museum
4790 W. 16th St. • 484-6747

This facility inside the Motor Speedway contains the world's largest, most varied collections of racing, classic and antique cars, including more than 30 Indianapolis 500 winners. It's open every day but Christmas from 9 AM to 5 PM. Admission is $2 for adults; children younger than 16 are admitted free. (For more information, see our Auto Racing chapter.)

National Art Museum of Sport (NAMS)
University Place Conference Center,
850 W. Michigan St. • 274-2339

If you think Leroy Nieman is the last (and only) word in art depicting athletes in action, stop by NAMS. Home to what's reputed to be the largest collection of sports-related art in the nation, this museum has works ranging from 19th-century wood engravings by Winslow Homer to a silkscreen by Mr. Floats-like-a-butterfly-stings-like-a-bee himself, Muhammed Ali. Situated inside the hotel-conference center on the campus of Indiana University-Purdue University at Indianapolis (IUPUI), the museum is open during regular business hours. Admission is free.

The Indiana Basketball Hall of Fame
One Hall of Fame Court, New Castle • 529-1891

Well, OK, it's not in Indianapolis, but given the deep and meaningful relationship people all over Indiana have with basketball, this place is part of every community in the state. Videos and artifacts depict famous players and great moments in Indiana basketball history. Interactive exhibits put visitors into the locker room and on the court. This is Hoosier Hysteria at its best.

The museum is open Tuesday through Saturday 10 AM to 5 PM and Sunday noon to 5 PM. It's closed on Mondays. Admission is $3 for adults, $1 for children.

It's clear that racing
is more than just a part
of the city's history.
It's also a factor in
its future.

Auto Racing

Indianapolis is synonymous with auto racing. Since 1909, when automotive entrepreneur Carl Graham Fisher joined forces with three other local businessmen to develop the Indianapolis Motor Speedway, the city and the sport of auto racing have been inextricably linked.

Today, Indianapolis is not only the site of the internationally renowned Indianapolis 500, but it's also home to two more of racing's most significant events — the Brickyard 400 stock car race and the International Hot Rod Association's U.S. Nationals. In addition, area tracks also host a variety of other national and regional racing events. What's more, the presence of high-quality venues and high-visibility events has led to the creation (or relocation) of some 250 racing-related businesses in Indianapolis. The city is home to businesses ranging from race-car engineering and design firms to racing organizations and equipment manufacturers.

Indianapolis is a major beneficiary of this auto-racing business. For example, a recent study revealed that the 1994 Brickyard 400 resulted in $31.5 million of direct spending by 350,000 fans and another $30 million in roll-over spending. That's an economic impact of more than $61 million from a single (and admittedly large) racing event.

Add to that the international attention that hosting large-scale racing events focuses on Indianapolis, and it's clear that racing is more than just a part of the city's history. It's also a factor in its future.

Indianapolis Motor Speedway

Getting to the Indianapolis Motor Speedway
4790 W. 16th St. • offices, 481-8500 • tickets, 484-6700
From downtown: Take 16th Street west for about 4.5 miles to the front entrance, or 30th Street west for about 4.5 miles to the back entrance.
From I-465: Follow the Speedway signs to Exit 16A, then go east on Crawfordsville Road to the track.

This is it, the granddaddy of oval track racing, a mecca for serious race fans and drivers alike. This is the place that, in a manner of speaking, put Indianapolis on the map, and it's still the city's most internationally recognized landmark. Even if they don't know ex-

---

INSIDERS' TIP

The Indianapolis Motor Speedway not only hosts two of the world's major auto races, it also broadcasts those races on its own radio and television outlets. The Indianapolis Motor Speedway Radio Network consists of 600 stations in the United States and Canada, plus several hundred other stations worldwide that pick up the race broadcast via Armed Forces Radio. WNDY (INDY-TV), Channel 23, is the Speedway's official television station. Due to that status, WNDY has unparalleled access to a variety of track events and personalities. Its track-related programming is beamed out to other stations and cable channels around the country, including ESPN.

Photo: S.G. Aniskiewicz

Dale Jarret's crew works on his car during a pit stop in the Brickyard 400.

actly where the city is, people all over the world know about the Indianapolis Motor Speedway, home of the Indianapolis 500.

It began with one man's idea. The man was Carl Graham Fisher, a racing pioneer and wealthy businessman (see our close-up in this chapter). His idea was to develop a racetrack for testing locally made automobiles (in the early decades of the 20th century, Indianapolis was home to dozens of automakers), as well as for hosting races.

Fisher pitched that idea to three of his business acquaintances. The first was James A. Allison, co-owner (with Fisher) of the Prest-O-Lite Company, an auto headlight manufacturing firm. The others were industrialists Arthur Newby and Frank Wheeler. (For more information on each of these men, see our close-up, "The Men Who Brought the Speedway Up to Speed.")

Together these four men developed a 2.5-mile-long oval race track on a 320-acre plot of ground northwest of downtown Indianapolis. Surfaced with a combination of crushed stone and asphalt, the track opened for business on August 19, 1909.

The first race on that day was a twice-around-the-oval dash won by driver Louis Schwitzer, who guided his Stoddard-Dayton to victory despite treacherous conditions: The track's surface broke up from the heat and the

traffic, leading to an accident that killed one driver, two mechanics and two spectators. That disaster led the track's owners to decide to repave the racing surface with bricks — 3,200,000 of them to be exact. Hence the track's nickname, "The Brickyard." The first official race on the new surface took place on December 17, 1909.

Following a series of poorly attended races the following year, Fisher and his partners decided to limit the race schedule to one big event — a then-unheard-of 500-mile race — to be held in May. To lure top drivers and spark fan interest, they decided to offer a huge purse: $25,000 to be split by the first 12 finishers.

Indianapolis 500

The first Indianapolis 500-Mile Race was held on Memorial Day, 1911, with Carl Fisher driving the pace car in what is believed to have been the first rolling start of an auto race. Fisher led the 40-car pack for one lap around the track before exiting as the green flag dropped, signalling the official start of the race. That first race set the pace for all those that have followed. It was fraught with drama, steeped in controversy and marred by tragedy — all elements that have reappeared time and again throughout the 500's history.

The drama was supplied by race winner Ray Harroun who, in the absence of a ride-along mechanic (which the other 39 cars in the field had), mounted a mirror above the cowling of his Indianapolis-built Marmon Wasp to help him watch for traffic. Some auto historians claim that was the first use of the rear-view mirror. Thanks in part to his mirror, Harroun avoided accidents for 200 laps and crossed the finish line at the head of the field, having averaged 74.59 mph during the six hours and 42 minutes it had taken him to cover 500 miles.

The controversy came about when driver Ralph Mulford claimed he hadn't been credited with a lap he completed when an accident distracted officials. Throughout his life, Mulford contended he was the true winner of the first Indianapolis 500.

And the tragedy — well, death has been part of auto racing since auto racing has been part of life. On lap 13, Arthur Greiner crashed his Amplex, killing his riding mechanic Sam Dickson.

Since that first race, a lot has changed at the Speedway.

Ownership, for instance. In 1927, the original track partners sold the Speedway to a group of Michigan investors that included World War I flying ace (and former Indianapolis 500 driver) Eddie Rickenbacker. That group held on to the track until 1945 when three-time 500 winner Wilbur Shaw arranged for Terre Haute businessman Anton "Tony" Hulman to buy it.

Buying the Speedway proved an astute investment for Hulman and his heirs. The family still owns the track — and they operate it as a privately run enterprise. As such, getting certain types of information about the 500, such as attendance figures and race revenues, is impossible. The family refuses to disclose how much money the race generates, though it's obviously several million dollars, with a resulting impact on the community of hundreds of millions. Today, Hulman's grandson, Tony George, is president and CEO of the Speedway.

Another change has been in the track surface itself. While the bricks gave the track its nickname, they weren't the best racing surface since they shifted whenever the ground froze and thawed, and the slightest moisture tended to make them slippery. By the 1930s, under the Rickenbacker group's ownership, asphalt was applied to stretches of the track, a process that escalated rapidly after Hulman bought the Speedway.

By 1945, the track was in rough shape. Closed for four years during World War II, it not only needed resurfacing, but the grandstands and other facilities needed to be replaced. Hulman did that and more. By 1961, all that remained of the old brick track was a 3-foot section at the start-finish line (it's still there today); the rest had been covered with asphalt.

Over the years, the cars have become very specialized. At first, many of the cars in the 500 were slightly modified versions of street cars, but today's cars (which are officially known as Indy cars) are far-removed from anything you'll ever see on any street anywhere. The cars that compete in the 500 these days are mostly chassis, engine and transmission, over which is bolted a lightweight, aerodynamic body.

And the speeds have increased tremendously. By 1919, speeds had begun to top 100 mph; by 1937, 125 mph; by 1962, 150 mph. Tom Sneva crossed the 200 mph threshold in 1977, and in 1989, Emerson Fittipaldi did better than 225 mph. And during qualifications for the 1996 race, Arie Luyendyk turned a lap at the record-setting pace of 237.498 mph, a speed that due to engine and chassis changes that become mandatory in 1997, is unlikely to be surpassed for years to come.

Then there is the money. From the original $25,000 in prize money, the 1996 Indianapolis 500 purse had grown to a whopping $8.11 million. Add to that millions more in corporate sponsorships and endorsements, lap money and other 500-related events, and the Indianapolis 500 offers drivers, car owners and technical crews one of the richest paydays in motorsports.

In 1994, the Speedway ended a 77-year-long tradition of hosting only one major race a year when it added the Brickyard 400, a NASCAR (National Association of Stock Car Auto Racing) event, to its schedule. Now there are two reasons — the 500 in May and the 400 in August — to go to the track.

But adding the Brickyard 400 was just the beginning of changes at the Speedway. In early 1995, Tony George announced the formation of the Indy Racing League, an organization devoted to the promotion of oval track racing. To induce racing teams to take part in IRL events, George promised that 25 of the 33 starting positions in the 500 would go to IRL members, as long as their cars met minimum speed requirements.

That's all it took to set off the owners of Championship Auto Racing Teams (CART). For years, CART had dominated the 500, forcing out smaller teams and independents who increasingly were frustrated by the high cost of competing with the cash- and sponsor-rich CART teams. But the IRL guidelines dictated that to have a shot at the majority of the slots for the 500, teams had to participate in other IRL events. CART owners balked, saying there were too many conflicts between CART and IRL schedules.

In the end, with the exception of two teams, CART boycotted the 1996 Indianapolis 500. Instead, it staged its own 500-mile race in Brooklyn, Michigan, on the same day as the 500. That race had many of CART's star drivers, including Michael Andretti, Al Unser Jr. and Bobby Rahal.

Nonetheless, the 500 went on as always, with a number of new drivers. And that was the point, insisted George. To give all the deserving drivers and car owners who had been shut out of Indy a chance to race at the Speedway.

What's going to happen in the battle between the IRL and CART remains to be seen—at least at the point of this writing. But one thing's certain: the 500 is a going enterprise.

Billed as "The Greatest Spectacle in Racing," the 500 lives up to its name. While many races offer fans a few days of fun — some practice time and qualification runs, then the race — the 500 stretches throughout the month of May. And throughout May, people come to Indianapolis from throughout the world.

Race crews start showing up in late April, though practice for the 500 doesn't officially start until the first weekend in May. It doesn't take long for things to heat up, and by mid-May the action on (and sometimes off) the track is hot and heavy as crews search for the perfect setup, the optimum engine and frame

adjustment that fits both drivers and track conditions.

The second and third weekends in May are devoted to qualifications: timed laps used by track officials to determine the 33-car field for race day. The Thursday before the race is Carburetion Day, when officials from the United States Auto Club (USAC, the sanctioning organization for the 500) check each qualified car to ensure it meets USAC guidelines.

Though the high-tech engines in modern Indy cars no longer have carburetors, Carburetion Day retains its name from the time when mechanics tinkered with cars' carburetors to achieve maximum performance on race day. Now race teams adjust fuel injection setups and make other last-minute adjustments to their cars.

But as much fun as tracking track events can be, for avid people watchers it's even more fun to keep track of the characters who show up at the track. Once the Speedway opens to race crews in early May, it's also open to race fans for a nominal daily fee (depending on the day, it's usually in the $5 to $10 range). You can attend practice sessions and qualification weekends, which thousands of people do. And since practice and qualifications are all general admission, you can sit anywhere you like, except for the corporate suites, which are off-limits unless you have an invitation.

From the streets outside the Speedway to the suites overlooking the track, you're apt to see anyone from well-heeled millionaires to leather-clad bikers, from women wearing power suits to women wearing bathing suits, from mothers pushing strollers to fathers toting coolers, from young men sporting nose-rings to old men sporting straw hats.

The parking lots are filled with gleaming Mercedes and Cadillacs, rusty Plymouths and Fords, large RVs and compact pickup trucks. On the streets surrounding the track, homeowners put up hand-lettered signs: "PARKING $5 ALL DAY" or "NO PARKING," depending on their entrepreneurial bent and devotion to their lawns.

Inside the track, the air is redolent with sunscreen and sweat, beer and popcorn. If the cars aren't running, you can catch some tunes or track updates from a nearby boombox. If they are running, you can't hear yourself think, at least for those few moments when they come roaring past.

Nothing can prepare you for your first up-close-and-personal experience of an Indy car doing what it does best — going extremely fast. The decibel level is way off the scale — these cars are loud! And at full tilt, they're more of a blur than they are recognizable vehicles.

Indianapolis in the month of May is as close as this place gets to Mardi Gras, and the closer it gets to Race Day, the more like Mardi Gras it becomes.

May at the Speedway

Early in the month, you can go out to the track and watch as racing teams put their cars (and drivers) through shakedown runs, trying to figure how to eek every bit of speed possible out of their machines and how to adjust the cars for maximum handling and safety. If you go on a weekday, crowds are usually small, and you can sit virtually anywhere you want to watch the action.

As the month progresses, attendance grows, especially on weekends. By Carburetion Day, there are a lot of people around. Traffic outside the Speedway slows to a crawl sometimes. And race day — well, suffice it to say that the Indianapolis 500 is reputed to be the largest one-day sporting event in the world,

with a crowd estimated to be as large as 500,000 people (though, as we've said, the Speedway refuses to divulge actual attendance figures).

In brief, here's May at the track:

•Practice sessions: These begin on the first Saturday of the month and run daily through Carburetion Day.

•Qualifications: These timed lap sessions take place on the second and third weekends of the month.

•Carburetion Day: This is the Thursday preceding the race.

•Race Day: This is the Sunday of Memorial Day Weekend.

Tickets

Tickets for the 500 cost $15 for general admission to the track's infield or $30 to $140 (depending on location) for reserved seats. These prices are for tickets purchased through the Speedway box office, if you can get them.

The Indianapolis 500 sells out every year, seemingly within days. Here's how it works: As soon as one year's race ends, tickets for the next year's race go on sale. Mail-order ticket order forms are accepted at the Speedway box office the day after race day and within a couple of weeks all of the next year's tickets have been sold.

Photo: Meredith Goldberg

These children take the low ground approach to viewing the 40th annual 500 Festival Parade in May 1996.

Does that mean you can't get tickets? Of course not. Ticket brokers always have Indianapolis 500 tickets available. Try contacting:

TicketMaster • 239-5151
Circle City Tickets • 841-8056
Court Side Tickets • 254-9500
Front Row Tickets • 255-3220
Preferred Tickets and Tours • 636-0099
Tickets Galore • 247-8497
Tickets on Wheels • 579-6924
Tickets Together • 322-0000
Tickets Up Front • 633-6400,
(800) 860-INDY

Of course, if you'd rather get your tickets for free, listen to your radio. It seems that every radio station in the area has a May promotion that involves giving away race tickets.

Or you can get a job. Many area businesses use race tickets as employee incentives to improve sales and service, or they raffle off tickets for charity or have an office pool with tickets as the prize.

In other words, even though the race is perennially sold out, it doesn't mean you can't get in. Where there's a will, there's probably a ticket.

Brickyard 400

Rumors about the Speedway hosting a second major racing event had circulated for several years before Tony George announced in 1993 that NASCAR would add a race to its Winston Cup stock car series — a 400-mile event to be held at the Speedway. Christened the Brickyard 400, the first running of the new race was held on August 6, 1994, before a sellout crowd of some 350,000 fans.

Indiana native and 22-year-old NASCAR circuit phenom Jeff Gordon roared around the

The Men Who Brought the Speedway Up to Speed

Each of the four men who founded the Indianapolis motor Speedway — Carl Graham Fisher, James A. Allison, Arthur C. Newby and Frank Wheeler — were successful in various businesses before joining up to create the auspicious 1909 partnership that led to the development of an auto racing landmark. In fact, most of them had done business together before they formed that partnership.

Carl Graham Fisher (1874-1939), a native of Greensburg, Indiana, first tasted success when, at the age of 17, he went to work in a bicycle shop owned by his two brothers. It wasn't long before he turned his interest in cycling into a career as a championship bicycle racer and stuntman.

By nature a risk-taker, as well as a natural born promoter, Fisher turned next to automobiles, purportedly buying the first privately owned car in Indianapolis and shortly thereafter taking up auto racing. In 1902, he opened an auto showroom, selling and servicing Indianapolis-made Premiers and Wintons.

The challenges of business only stoked Graham's competitive fires, and in 1904 he set a world's record by circling a 2-mile dirt track in a car in just more than two minutes. That same year, he joined businessman James A. Allison and inventor P.C. Avery in a new business venture — the manufacture of auto headlights that operated on compressed acetylene. The resulting company, Prest-O-Lite, was a booming success.

Not only did Prest-O-Lite make Fisher wealthy, it also sparked an idea. Given the growing number of auto manufacturers in Indianapolis, he reasoned, why not build a track where they could test their products? Of course, when not in use, the track could also be used for races.

In 1908, Fisher presented his proposal for building just such a track to Allison and their mutual business acquaintances Arthur C. Newby and Frank Wheeler. It was an idea that made history — and lots of money — for each of them.

In addition to his success with Prest-O-Lite and the Indianapolis Motor Speedway, Fisher was involved in the creation of the Hoosier Motor Club, the formation of the Lincoln Highway Association and the development of Miami Beach, Florida.

James A. Allison (1872-1928) came to Indianapolis from Niles, Michigan, with his family when he was 8. Four years later, he quit school to work in his father's business, the Allison Coupon Company. When his father died in 1890, Allison and his two brothers assumed control of the company.

In addition to his partnership with Fisher in Prest-O-Lite and the Speedway, Allison set up the Allison Speedway Team Company, a machine shop, in 1913. Seven years later, he changed its name to the Allison Engineering Company — the forerunner of Allison Gas Turbine and Allison Transmission, which under the ownership of General Motors, became two of Indianapolis' major industrial operations. Allison also owned huge blocks of real estate in Indianapolis and southern Florida. Locally, he developed much of the town of Speedway as it grew up around the Motor Speedway.

By nature a perfectionist, Allison must have been either an odd match or the perfect foil for his flamboyant partner Fisher.

Arthur C. Newby (1865-1933) grew up on a farm near Monrovia, Indiana, and came to Indianapolis as a 16-year-old looking for a job. Landing at Nordyke and Marmon, manufacturers of grain milling equipment (and later, of automobiles), Newby worked his way up from the mail room to a management position, all the while pursuing his true passion — bicycling. He helped found the Zig-Zag Cycling Club, which was active in Indianapolis in the 1890s.

Newby also helped found the Indianapolis Chain and Stamping Company (the forerunner of today's Diamond Chain Company), which was producing 60 percent of the nation's American-made bicycle chains by the turn of the century. Promoting bicycle racing was a natural extension of his job for Newby, and in 1896 he became a partner with Fisher and Allison in the development of a quarter-mile wooden cycling track near the intersection of Central Avenue and 30th Street. This was a trial run, of sorts, for the other racing facility they would later develop.

Photo: The Indianapolis Star and The Indianapolis News

From left to right, Carl Fisher, Arthur Newby, Frank Wheeler and James Allison formed a partnership in 1909 to create the Indianapolis Motor Speedway.

Speedway to victory in the first Brickyard, earning more than $613,000 for his driving prowess. (The total purse for the race was $3.2 million.) In the process, Gordon became every aspiring young driver's hero and many a young female racing fan's fantasy. Handsome, friendly and tremendously talented, he was (and still is) a public relations gold mine for NASCAR.

For the 1995 Brickyard, Gordon was back, and he was the toast of the town. Posting the fastest qualifying time earned him the pole position for the race, but handling problems cost him the race, which was delayed for several hours due to torrential rains. NASCAR veteran Dale Earnhardt won with an average speed of 155.218 mph, earning more than $500,000 in cash and prizes. The total purse for the 1995 event was $4.5 million.

The 1996 race came down to lap 154 of 160 before Dale Jarrett squeezed past his friend and teammate Ernie Irvan to take the lead. When the checkered flag finally came down, Jarrett had earned a hefty $564,035 for his efforts. And 1994 and 1995 darling Gordon? He wound up 37 out of 40 when an accident on lap 40 put his car out of commission.

August at the Speedway

Given the brief history of the Brickyard 400, August at the Speedway isn't nearly as crazy as May. And the practice and qualifying rounds for the 400 are much shorter than those for the 500. Practice for the Brickyard begins just three days prior to the race, with qualifying taking place on Thursday and Friday of that week. The race is on the first Saturday of the month.

The practice and qualifying sessions are open to the public. Track admission on those days is $5 for Wednesday, $10 for Thursday and Friday.

Tickets

Like the 500, the Brickyard 400 sells out, though not as fast. And good seats aren't as hard to come by as they are for the 500. Avail-

able by mail from the Indianapolis Motor Speedway box-office, tickets are priced at $15 for general admission to the track's infield and $18 to $100 for reserved seating.

If you can't get them from the Speedway, all the major ticket brokers noted for Indy tickets have them as well.

Motor Speedway Attractions

Indianapolis Motor Speedway Hall of Fame Museum
4790 W. 16th St. • 484-6747

On the grounds of the Motor Speedway, this facility contains cars and race memorabilia that span the history of the Indianapolis 500. Including the yellow Marmon Wasp that Ray Harroun drove to victory in the first 500-mile race in 1911, paintings, photos, programs, pit passes, engines, helmets and trophies — this is the sanctum sanctorum of the 500.

FYI

Unless otherwise noted, the area code for all phone numbers in this guide is 317.

It's also a repository of products from the city's glory days as a center of automobile manufacturing. Former Indianapolis-made models such as Stutz, Cole, Marmon, National and Duesenberg are all represented in the museum's collection.

The Hall of Fame, which dates to 1952, was established to commemorate the achievements of drivers and auto makers alike who've influenced racing. From Eddie Rickenbacker and Louis Chevrolet to Tony Hulman and Mario Andretti, the Hall of Fame pays homage to the greats.

The Indianapolis Motor Speedway Hall of Fame Museum is open every day except Christmas from 9 AM to 5 PM. Admission is $2 per person; children younger than 16 get in free.

Brickyard Crossing
4790 W. 16th St. • offices, 481-8500
• tickets, 484-6700

An 18-hole championship-level golf course originally built in 1929 and redesigned by legendary course architect Pete Dye in 1991,

Brickyard Crossing is inside (holes 7 through 10) and adjacent to the Speedway. This is home to the Senior PGA Tour's Brickyard Crossing Championship tournament (for more information, see our Sports and Parks and Recreation chapters).

Track Tour
4790 W. 16th St. • offices, 481-8500 • tickets, 484-6700

Whenever the track isn't in use, you can tour it aboard a minibus that takes you all around the world's most famous oval. Ask about tour availability at the Hall of Fame Museum.

Indianapolis Raceway Park

Getting to the Indianapolis Raceway Park
10267 E. U.S. Hwy. 136 • 291-4090

Indianapolis Raceway Park is just west of Clermont on U.S. 136, about 7 miles northwest of the Indianapolis Motor Speedway and 15 miles northwest of downtown Indianapolis.

Indianapolis Raceway Park (a.k.a. IRP) has certainly earned its reputation as "America's Great Race Place." IRP's facilities include a 4,400-foot drag strip, a .686-mile oval, and a 2.5-mile road course (with 15 turns). All are asphalt-paved. From drag racing to sports cars, this multitrack venue west of the city is as much a part of auto racing history as the Indianapolis Motor Speedway.

The permanent home of the National Hot Rod Association's premier event, the U.S. Nationals, IRP also hosts the Kroger NASCAR 200, the Miller Genuine Draft "Night Before the 500" midget car race, The NASCAR Craftsman Truck Series Cummins 200, the Sports Car Club of America Nationals, the Corvette Nationals and the MOPAR Nationals. It's also the site of such events as the American Motorcycle Association's ProStar championships, the Super Chevy Show and the Goodguys Hot Rod Nationals.

In addition to its on-site crowds, IRP has attracted a national following among racing enthusiasts who tune into ESPN's *Thunder Series* and the Total Sports Network to watch telecasts of the venue's events.

What's more, race driver training programs, such as the Lyn St. James Racing School and the Skip Barber Racing School, use IRP's road course for classes ranging from the introductory to the professional level.

In the late 1950s, Frank Dicke dreamed of owning a half-mile-long dirt oval racetrack. When he approached driver Rodger Ward and USAC officials Tom Binford and Charlie Brockman, they liked what Dicke (a well-dressed businessman with plenty of experience in promoting sprint, midget and stock car races at a dirt track in his home town of New Bremen, Ohio) outlined for them. They agreed to join forces and develop Dicke's track somewhere in the Central Indiana area.

That somewhere turned out to be near Clermont, about 15 miles northwest of downtown Indianapolis. Originally envisioned as a modest $75,000 project, the track's development budget grew as the partners dreamed up additions to Dicke's simple oval. A drag strip, for instance. And a road course. By 1960, it was clear that they had a $1 million-plus project on their hands.

To raise some of the needed finances, the partners sold 50,000 shares of stock at $10 each. Indianapolis Motor Speedway owner Tony Hulman was the largest shareholder, and he continued to buy new stock as it was issued or as other shareholders sold theirs.

IRP's drag strip started hosting meets in September 1960; the 273-acre facility's other tracks followed in 1961. As the project developed, it was obvious that IRP was going to be a major racing venue, and it received a major vote of confidence when National Hot Rod Association (NHRA) officials decided to hold the prestigious U.S. Nationals at IRP in September 1961.

That was also the year that IRP's road course was the site of a 200-mile sports car race that attracted such well-known drivers as Lloyd Ruby, Ken Miles and IRP partner (and road course designer) Rodger Ward. Another sports car event in 1961 included drivers Roger Penske and Jim Hall, both of whom are now owners of successful Indy car teams.

The same oval track, which had been increased in distance from Dicke's half-mile concept to five-eighths of a mile, hosted stock and sprint car events in which Indianapolis 500 drivers Parnelli Jones and A. J. Foyt took part. In retrospect, 1961 was an auspicious beginning for IRP.

In the years since, IRP has earned a reputation as one of the country's premier racing venues. During that time it has hosted such historically significant events as the Yankee 300 (later the Yankee 250) stock car race from 1963 to 1972; the first road course race ever sanctioned by USAC in 1965; and several American Motorcycle Association races in 1962 and from 1967 to '69. One event that got away at the last minute was the 1965 Formula One Grand Prix of the United States. Behind-

Racing Festivals

In Indianapolis, an auto race isn't necessarily a stand-alone event — at least two of the major races aren't. They come complete with festivals.

The 500 Festival
201 S. Capitol Ave., Ste. 201 • 636-4556

From the first running of the Indianapolis 500 in 1911, community leaders started promoting the idea of a citywide celebration to mark the event. But it took 46 years before the first 500 Festival became a reality. Since then, it has become as much a part of May as the race itself.

In fact, the month-long 500 Festival is May in Indianapolis.

Among its many events are:

•The Mini-Marathon: The Festival literally hits the ground running with the annual mini-marathon on the first Friday in May. The 13.1-mile event attracts runners from around the world.

•The Mayor's Breakfast: This gathering of mayors from towns and cities statewide epitomizes the term "power breakfast." In addition to politicians, it attracts a variety of Indiana's movers and shakers as well as ordinary folks willing to ante up $35 for a ticket. This event culminates with each ticketholder getting the chance to drive his/her car around the Speedway's 2.5-mile track.

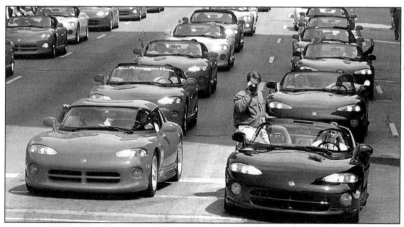

Photo: Frank Espich

In 1996, Dodge Vipers — all 575 of them — started out the 500 Festival Parade in downtown Indianapolis.

•500 Festival Kids Day: Held on Monument Circle, this is the city's largest outdoor festival for children. It regularly attracts more than 30,000 youngsters and their families to such activities as Big Wheel races, arts and crafts, sports clinics, science demonstrations and hands-on music-making.

•The 500 Ball: A black-tie gala held at the Indiana Convention Center on the Friday before the race, this event brings out 2,500 of the area's well-heeled. It also attracts many of the celebrities who are in town for the race.

•The 500 Festival Parade: Held the day before the race, this huge parade is the Festival's pièce de résistance. It includes elaborate floats and marching bands, celebrities and all 33 of the race's drivers, clowns and giant helium balloons — all moving past several thousand spectators lining downtown streets. How big of a deal is the parade? If you want to sit in the bleachers that line the parade route, you'll need a ticket, which you can get for $10 from 500 Festival Inc. Call 636-4556 for information. Otherwise, bring a lawn chair or be prepared to stand for the duration (which thousands of parade-goers do). Not only is it telecast locally but nationally on cable TV's Nashville Network.

The 400 Festival
201 S. Capitol Ave., Ste. 201 • 237-3407

Not only did the Brickyard 400 make its debut in 1994, but its companion festival did too. At present, it's a much smaller affair than the 500 Festival: The 1995 400 Festival consisted of five events (not counting track activities).

•Do Run Run: Sponsored by WRTV 6, this fun run isn't nearly as serious as the 500 Festival's mini-marathon. Held on the Saturday prior to the Brickyard 400, Do Run Run events (a 5K competitive walk, a 5K family fitness walk and a 10K run) follow a circuit from the IUPUI campus around the Indianapolis Zoo to Military Park.

•Circle Fest: A daylong downtown festival, Circle Fest brings thousands of people to the Circle for live music and food from noon to midnight on the Saturday before the race.

•Welcome NASCAR Rally: Held at Pan Am Plaza from noon to 5 PM on the Tuesday prior to the race, this event welcomes NASCAR competitors to town.

•400 Festival Kids' Day: Hosted by the Major Taylor Velodrome and the Lake Sullivan Sports Complex, this event for kids between ages 6 and 12 is on the Thursday before the race from 10 AM to 3 PM. It includes a foot race, sack races, dancing and games.

•Miller Genuine Draft Race Fest: Combining a huge picnic/barbecue with a rock concert, this event is held on the Thursday prior to the race from 3 PM to midnight at the Indiana State Fairgrounds.

---

the-scenes politics led the American Competition Committee of the United States to yank the Grand Prix away from IRP, leaving everyone involved to speculate "What if?'

Not that there was a lot to lament. So pleased was the NHRA and its drivers with IRP that the U.S. Nationals became a permanent fixture there. And in 1979, the NHRA bought IRP outright.

Since then, IRP has become one of the best-known racing venues in the United States.

The U.S. Nationals

With a handshake under a tree outside Detroit Dragway's pit area, IRP cofounder Tom Binford and NHRA president Wally Parks agreed in 1960 to develop a national championships drag racing event in Indianapolis. On that basis, Parks and other NHRA officials decided to hold the U.S. Nationals at IRP in 1961. Fan response was so great (in its short existence, IRP had never had such large crowds) that the U.S. Nationals have been a permanent fixture at IRP ever since.

The U.S. Nationals are the longest-running (six days), richest-paying (the 1995 purse was $2 million), most well-attended (more than 150,000 fans) event in drag racing history. More than 1,000 racing teams, including those of such superstars as John Force, Indiana's own Bob Glidden, Don "Snake" Prudhomme and former NFL coach Joe Gibbs make for exciting events.

The Nationals consist of a series of races, including elimination rounds, in four categories: Top Fuel Dragster, Pro Stock, Funny Car and Sportsman Class. Depending on the day, qualifications and competitions start as early as 8 AM and run into the evening.

General admission, one-day tickets for the U.S. Nationals range from $5 to $45 for adults and from $5 to $10 for children 6 to 15; children 5 and younger are admitted free. Advance tickets are $5 off. Six-day passes are $130 in advance, $168 at the gate. All advance tickets include pit passes. Tickets are available from IRP or through area TicketMaster locations.

For information on dates and times, contact Indianapolis Raceway Park.

The Race Cars

The Speedway's two races utilize different types of cars. Those in the Indianapolis 500 are specially built Indy cars, low to the ground and very high-tech in terms of their mechanical and frame components. An Indy car is 78.5 inches wide, 195 inches long, 32 inches high and has a wheelbase of between 109 and 112 inches. It weighs 1,550 pounds and runs on methanol racing fuel.

The machines racing in the Brickyard 400 are stock cars, essentially modified (very modified) versions of street cars, such as the Chevy Monte Carlos, Ford Thunderbirds and Pontiac Grand Prixes.

They're 60 inches wide, 194 inches long, 51 inches high and have a wheelbase of 110 inches. A stock car weighs 3,400 pounds and runs on ordinary gasoline — some on leaded, others unleaded.

The one thing the two types of cars have in common is noise.

They both make lots of it.

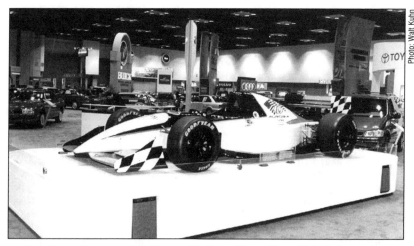

Photo: Walt Kuhn

An Indianapolis race car is built — and looks — like no other vehicle. It also reaches speeds other autos will never match.

Other Events at IRP

In addition to the U.S. Nationals, IRP hosts a variety of other racing events during its March-to-October season. What follows are highlights form the track's calendar.

Because dates and admission costs vary, contact the IRP's box office, 293-RACE, for current schedules and ticket information.

The Kroger NASCAR 200

Since its inaugural running in 1982, the Kroger NASCAR 200 has become the largest, most prestigious short-track stock car race in the Midwest. Attracting more than 30,000 fans annually, this event is credited with proving the appeal of a NASCAR event in Central Indiana, paving the way for the creation of the Brickyard 400 at the Indianapolis Motor Speedway.

The Kroger NASCAR 200 has attracted such well-known drivers as Dale Earnhardt, Darrell Waltrip, Brett Bodine and Jeff Gordon. In fact, Gordon, a graduate of nearby Tri-West High School, learned many of his racing skills at IRP.

Miller Genuine Draft "Night Before the 500"

As is evident from its title, this event is held the night before the Indianapolis 500. It includes a USAC-sanctioned midget car race, as well as a Formula Ford 2000 series race. Current NASCAR wunderkind Jeff Gordon won a "Night Before the 500" midget car event while still in high school.

Corvette Nationals

This annual May event pulls in Corvette owners and fans from around the country who come to IRP for a weekend-long car show and drag race competition. At this event you'll see everything from classic "Route 66"-era 'vettes to thunderous track-ready reminders that Corvettes really are high-performance machines designed for speed. It's a chance to see hundreds of examples of an American car that is poetry in motion and at ease.

Super Chevy Show

For Chevy enthusiasts, this July event is heaven on earth.

It's an all-Chevrolet combination of a drag race, car show and swap meet. You can gape as souped-up Camaros roar off the line, gawk at lovingly restored Bel-Airs and Malibus and shop for a new hood ornament for your '65 Impala ragtop. If it's a Chevy, it's here — or at least someone who knows how to get it is.

MOPAR Nationals

Held each August, this is the largest Chrysler-only car show, drag race and swap meet in the nation. Like its Chevy counterpart, the MOPAR Nationals offer Chrysler, Dodge and Plymouth fans a chance to watch their favorites in action on the track and off as well as buy, sell and trade MOPAR parts and vehicles.

Other Venues

Indianapolis Speedrome
802 S. Kitley Ave. • 353-8206

From April to September, this place is the home of rough-and-tumble racing, the down-home home of stock car and Figure 8 races. On a banked, fifth-mile course, drivers jockey and bump, careen and clip, rocket and smash — in short, this is where race fans go to escape the glitz and glitter that, at the Speedway and IRP, sometimes interfere with the sheer pleasure of watching drivers match speed, guts and driving abilities. Over the years, such soon-to-be-stars as A.J. Foyt, Johnny Rutherford and Darrell Waltrip have honed their skills at the Speedrome. For most events, tickets are $8 to $10 for adults and $3 for children. Contact the Speedrome for a schedule and specific ticket information.

Indiana State Fairgrounds
1202 E. 38th St. • 927-7500

The Fairgrounds contain a 1-mile dirt track that hosts a variety of auto and motorcycle races every year, including the Hulman Hundred, a 100-mile dirt car event held the Friday before the Indianapolis 500; and the Hoosier Hundred, another 100-miler on Labor Day weekend. This is where you can catch future Indy Car and NASCAR kings honing their skills.

Putnam Park Road Course
470 E. Northfield Dr., Brownsburg • 852-7007

Built in 1991, Putnam Park was designed for club racing, testing and driver schools. The long course is 1.8 miles in length and includes 10 turns and a main straightaway that's 2,275 feet long. The short course is just over a half-mile long and includes four turns. Both courses are paved with a special asphalt mix that minimizes tire wear while maximizing tire adhesion.

Putnam Park hosts a variety of races sanctioned by the Sports Car Club of America, Enduro Kart (go-carts) and the Western-Eastern Roadracers Association (motorcycles). It's also used for time trials and driver training by Corvette, BMW, Ferrari, Miata and Porsche clubs as well as by many car and tire manufacturers. Additionally, professional racing teams use Putnam Park to test their vehicles.

For a schedule of public events, contact Putnam Park.

Racing Schools and Organizations

Fast Company
15 B. W. Franklin St., Greencastle
• 653-2532

For motorsports fans whose need for speed has them yearning to get behind the wheel, Fast Company offers the opportunity. As Central Indiana's only racing school and as the official racing school of Indianapolis Raceway Park, Fast Company provides hands-on driving instruction to aspiring race drivers and racing buffs who want to see what it's like to sit behind the wheel.

Speedway Speak

You'll hear a lot of Speedway-related terms bandied about in Indianapolis. Here's a primer on a few:

•The Brickyard: That's the Speedway's nickname, derived from the early days when the track was actually made of paving bricks.

•Gasoline Alley: This is the garage area inside the Speedway. Visitors are free to wander through this area, peeking inside garages where mechanics and technicians fiddle with team cars. Asking for driver autographs is OK in Gasoline Alley; pestering busy drivers or race crews is not.

•Yellow Shirts: These are the Speedway's security volunteers. You'll see them everywhere throughout the facility; they provide directions and prevent access to restricted areas.

•Pit Pass: This is the much-coveted key to getting past a Yellow Shirt into the pit area alongside the track. With a pass, you're in; without one, you're rubbernecking to see what's going on in the pits.

•Snake Pit: Not to be confused with the racing teams' pit areas, this is a portion of the track's infield that once was the domain of bikers, drunks and pickup trucks with lawn chairs in their beds. It was here you'd hear guys calling out lewd requests to women to reveal their body parts as they walked by, and it was here where some of the women complied. It was Woodstock and Altamont, Steppenwolf and Hank Williams Jr., beer bellies and big belt buckles. But now it's not.

Concerned about the infield's reputation as a rough and dangerous place, Speedway officials started policing the area more closely a few years ago. While there are still some rowdies around, it's a much tamer place than it used to be.

•Qualifications: These are the officially timed laps that racing teams use to get their cars entered into either the Indianapolis 500 or the Brickyard 400. For the 500, only 33 cars are allowed in the race; for the 400, the number is 41.

•Pole Position: At the start of the race, cars are lined up according to the qualifying times; the fastest qualifier is placed in the front row, closest to the infield. That's the pole position.

•**The Turns**: There are four turns on the Speedway's 2.5-mile oval, and track regulars have their favorites (and they'll gladly debate the merits of theirs and shortcomings of the others).

Turn One offers a view of the start/finish line and lets you gauge how smoothly (or badly) the race starts.

Turn Two provides a vantage point on the first long straightaway and lets you see the jockeying for position that often happens as drivers try to pull away for a run down that straightaway.

Turn Three allows you to see the cars coming off the straightaway and heading for the crucial fourth turn.

Turn Four is the point at which drivers try to reposition themselves for the second long straightaway, the one that leads to the finish line.

Of course, there are those fans who spurn the turns for the straightaways, especially for the impossible-to-get seats by the start/finish line.

Happy racing!

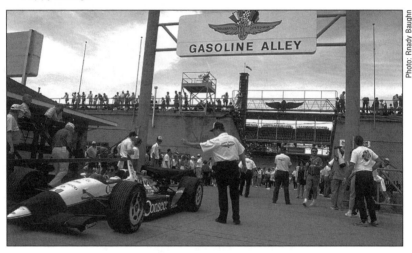

The garage area inside the Indianapolis Motor Speedway
is known as Gasoline Alley.

Using actual Sports Car Club of America Spec Racers, company instructors (all of whom have racing experience ranging from Karts to Formula One) put prospective drivers through an intensive three-day program at IRP (April through October) and at other tracks in warmer climates (January through March).

Founded by driving school veteran Hank Chapman in 1991, Fast Company has fast become a hot ticket among racing enthusiasts and corporations (several of which award Fast Company classes to top management and sales performers). What sepa-rates Fast Company training from that offered by national racing schools is its policy of allowing participants to pass one another on the track.

As this book went to press, Fast Company prepared to move its operations from Greencastle to new quarters under construction at IRP.

United States Auto Club Inc. (USAC)
4910 W. 16th St. • 247-5151

This is the nonprofit sanctioning organization that oversees and regulates more than

150 auto racing events every year, including the Indianapolis 500. In addition to its role as a regulatory body, USAC is also actively involved in safety issues. Over the years, it has been responsible for a number of improvements in the structure of racing cars, the construction of tracks and the development of protective apparel for drivers and pit crew members.

Indianapolis 500 Winners

Year	Driver
1911	Ray Harroun
1912	Jay Dawson
1913	Jules Gouz
1914	Rene Thomas
1915	Ralph DePalma
1916	Dario Resta
1917-1918 War Years: No Race	
1919	Howard Wilcox
1920	Gaston Chevrolet
1921	Tommy Milton
1922	Jimmy Murphy
1923	Tommy Milton
1924	Joe Boyer and L.L. Coru
1925	Peter DePaolo
1926	Frank Lockhart
1927	George Souders
1928	Louis Meyers
1929	Ray Keech
1930	Billy Arnold
1931	Louis Schneider
1932	Fred Frame
1933	Louis Meyer
1934	Bill Cummings
1935	Kelly Petillo
1936	Louis Meyer
1937	Wilbur Shaw
1938	Floyd Roberts
1939	Wilbur Shaw
1940	Wilbur Shaw
1941	Mauri Rose and Floyd Davis
1942-1945 War Years: No Race	
1946	George Robson
1947	Mauri Rose
1948	Mauri Rose
1949	Bill Holland
1950	Johnnie Parson
1951	Lee Lallard
1952	Troy Ruttman
1953	Bill Vukovich
1954	Bill Vukovich
1955	Bob Sweikert
1956	Pat Flaherty
1957	Sam Hanks

Photo: The Indianapolis Star and The Indianapolis News

Ray Harroun was the winner of the first Indianapolis 500-mile race in 1911.

1958	Jim Bryan
1959	Rodger Ward
1960	Jim Rathman
1961	A.J. Foyt Jr.
1962	Rodger Ward
1963	Parnelli Jones
1964	A.J. Foyt Jr.
1965	Jim Clark
1966	Graham Hill
1967	A.J. Foyt Jr.
1968	Bobby Unser
1969	Mario Andretti
1970	Al Unser Sr.
1971	Al Unser Sr.
1972	Mark Donohue
1973	Gordon Johncock
1974	Johnnie Rutherford
1975	Bobby Unser
1976	Johnny Rutherford
1977	A.J. Foyt
1978	Al Unser Sr.
1979	Rick Mears
1980	Johnny Rutherford

1981	Bobby Unser	1989	Emerson Fittipaldi
1982	Gordon Johncock	1990	Arie Luyendyk
1983	Tom Sneva	1991	Rick Mears
1984	Rick Mears	1992	Al Unser Jr.
1985	Danny Sullivan	1993	Emerson Fittipaldi
1986	Bobby Rahal	1994	Al Unser Jr.
1987	Al Unser Sr.	1995	Jacques Villeneuve
1988	Rick Mears	1996	Buddy Lazier

With four distinct
seasons Hoosiers spend
a lot of time enjoying
the outdoors.

Parks and Recreation

Part of what makes Indianapolis such a great place to live and raise a family are the top-notch recreational opportunities in and around Central Indiana. With four distinct seasons and the facilities in which to enjoy them, Hoosiers spend a lot of time enjoying the outdoors. Of course, they also play a lot of sports, and they're covered here too, in the recreation portion of this chapter. (For spectator sports see our Sports chapter.) In the parks section, we've highlighted our favorite places to commune with nature.

We have great city parks here in Indianapolis, including one of the largest municipal parks in the country, that offer programs ranging from traditional tennis and swimming classes to such offbeat possibilities as moonlight hikes, community flea markets and out-of-town adventures. Programs are designed for all ages; you'll find classes for children as young as 2, summer camps for school-age kids, ecological and art-related courses for teenagers and special options for seniors and those with disabilities. Some of the most interesting activities are open to all ages, and they're all surprisingly affordable. Pick up a free copy of the *Indy Parks and Recreation Fun Guide* at family centers or community buildings within parks; a new one comes out every few months for each new season with all the time, place and price details. Contact the parks department, 327-0000, or write 1426 W. 29th Street, Indianapolis, Indiana 46208.

Indiana also boasts an excellent state park system, and many of the parks are within easy driving distance of Indianapolis. The state also manages forests, lakes and reservoirs, fish and wildlife areas and historic sites, all of which

offer outstanding opportunities for exploring nature. The Department of Natural Resources publishes tons of brochures, guides and special updates about its many properties and programs. The annual *Indiana Recreation Guide* provides details about such options as camping, hunting and fishing at state facilities, and *Outdoor Indiana*, the DNR's bimonthly magazine, features beautiful wildlife photography and nature-related writing with a statewide focus. Contact the DNR, 232-4124 or (800) 622-4931 (in Indiana only) or write 402 W. Washington Street, Indianapolis 46204.

Parks

City Parks

You can find terrific parks all across the city, some that boast pools or aquatic centers, others that regularly draw players for pickup basketball games. Each neighborhood has its favorites, but here we've spotlighted some of the city's most popular. All parks are open from dawn to dusk, and only Eagle Creek charges admission; pools and aquatic centers within parks also have admission fees. The new aquatic centers feature such water park amenities as slides, sand play areas, diving boards and water playgrounds.

Eagle Creek Park
7840 W. 56th St. • 327-7110

The Lilly family (of Lilly pharmaceuticals) figures prominently in the history of Indianapolis, and it was J.K. Lilly who purchased this tract of land northwest of the city as a nature preserve. The 3,100 acres of park and 1,300 acres of water were given to Purdue University in the late 1950s, but the university, unable to maintain such a large hunk of land, sold it to the City of Indianapolis. For a $2 per-car fee, $3 on weekends, Eagle Creek, one of the largest municipal parks in the country, provides a wide range of recreational options and is one of the nicest things about living in Indianapolis.

Open year-round from dawn to dusk, the park includes Eagle Creek Reservoir, and the marina offers sailing, canoe, kayak and rowboat rentals, plus sailing or sailboarding lessons. It's great fun to rent a Sunfish and sail around the reservoir; little kids enjoy rowing along the shoreline with Mom and Dad. The parks department offers evening pontoon and canoe rides throughout the summer to explore wildlife along the water's edge. The park also includes a 3-acre sandy beach (with lifeguards); a 1-acre ecology pond; the 5-acre Lilly Lake, where you can rent a paddle boat or enjoy bank fishing; and several skating ponds for wintertime fun.

Off the water, Eagle Creek Park boasts more than 10 miles of trails ranging from easy to moderate in difficulty. Paths wind through open meadows, past the reservoir and into mature woods full of beech, maple, tulip, white ash and black cherry. Visitors often see deer, especially in the early morning and evening hours, but please don't feed them. You'll probably also spot Canada geese and wood ducks on the water along with plenty of smaller creatures such as rabbits and groundhogs.

The newly remodeled Nature Center Complex, which includes a 38-acre arboretum with self-guided trails, a nearly 600-year-old Douglas fir log, native wildflowers and specialty gardens offers an educational perspective on the park and its occupants.

Additional facilities include shelters and retreat houses, a world-class archery field, a shooting range and, whenever we have at least 4 inches of snow, cross-country skiing. Keep in mind that hunting, trapping, camping and ground fires are prohibited, as are snowmobiling and horseback riding.

Holliday Park
6349 Spring Mill Rd. • 327-7180

This park, incredibly popular among young families, features what's probably the best playground in the city. Its three main play areas (one for the littlest kids is enclosed) offer varying levels of climbing difficulty, with ladders, slides, tires and poles. The tallest has twisty tube slides that kids can't get enough of. They're also fascinated by "that spider web thing" (see our Kidstuff chapter), a rope climbing contraption that just about defies description. The playground also includes the more traditional swings, plus ones that accommodates wheelchairs.

Holliday Park also features great trails, many recently improved, that lead down to White River, where kids can wade, fish and poke around along the riverbank. The parks department offers a summer hike series for all ages that explores the trees, flowers, geology and wildlife of Holliday Park and a Parks After Dark program that features moonlight hikes, stargazing and a discussion of the nocturnal creatures that inhabit the park.

Though there has been talk of removing them, Holliday Park also boasts "the ruins," statues near the community center that originally graced a New York City building and columns from a local convent. The nearby wedding circle, a brick colonnade and walkway that leads up to a gazebo, offers an especially lovely spot for an outdoor wedding, if you don't mind the occasional walker or jogger in the background.

Ellenberger Park
5301 E. St. Clair St. • 327-7176

Tucked in the middle of the historic Irvington neighborhood, Ellenberger Park offers that area's many young families plenty of recreation options. It's a beautiful park, with rolling terrain that's great for winter sledding, a fitness trail, ball fields, a skating rink (ice skating in the fall and winter; roller and in-line skating in summer), playgrounds, a swimming pool, tennis and volleyball courts and lots of scenic picnic sites.

Perry Park
451 E. Stop 11 Rd. • 888-0070

This Greenwood park also offers an ice rink with an added advantage: Parents can watch their little skaters from the warmth of the snack bar area, where windows provide handy viewing. Outdoors, a small playground provides the traditional swings and a merry-go-round. A new aquatic center provides warm-weather water fun.

Broad Ripple Park
1450 Broad Ripple Ave. • 327-7161

Also popular with young families, Broad Ripple Park features a conveniently sized play area (big enough to keep the kids occupied, yet small enough for Mom or Dad to monitor), a family center where lots of classes are held, a pool and — a real plus — a library branch. On weekday mornings you'll see lots of moms and kids head from the family center to the playground to the library.

The park also offers public boat launching into White River, bank fishing, plenty of shady picnic sites, open areas (nice for kite flying) and ball fields.

Riverside Park
2420 E. Riverside Dr. • 327-7171

After considerable renovation, Riverside Park reopened with a new aquatic center, a family center with weight equipment, a community room and banquet facilities. It also features softball and baseball diamonds where various leagues from around the city play, a basketball and tennis court and two playgrounds.

The park will also be included in the new Riverside Regional Park, a sports mecca that will stretch from Bush Stadium on 16th Street to the future Penrod Art Park at the Indianapolis Museum of Art on 38th Street. It will encompass the Kuntz Memorial Soccer Stadium, the Major Taylor Velodrome, three golf courses

and the Wilbur Shaw Memorial Soap Box Derby Hill.

Southeastway Park
5624 E. County Line Rd. S. • 861-5167

Southeastway has been called one of the park system's best kept secrets, though it's sure to become more well-known as residents discover its fishing, hiking trails, picnic sites and, when there are at least 4 inches of snow, its cross-country skiing. A summer hike series that includes such programs as earth medicines, tree trivia and a "stream stomp" highlight Southeastway's natural attractions. Kids enjoy learning about creepy-crawlies during Bugfest and hiking by the light of a full moon during Moonlight Madness.

Garfield
2450 Shelby St. • 327-7220

FYI

Unless otherwise noted, the area code for all phone numbers in this guide is 317.

The city's oldest park, Garfield features formal sunken gardens, a historic conservatory, an amphitheater, topnotch horseshoe pits, ball fields, tennis courts and a pool and family center. The gardens are being restored to their former grandeur, and the conservatory has been undergoing renovation. While work did lag behind schedule, the conservancy reopened in late 1996. A wonderful place to visit on a chilly winter day (see our Kidstuff chapter), the conservatory now has a new look and an emphasis on the world's disappearing rainforests, but you can still count on such traditional favorites as the holiday poinsettia show and sale each December.

Marott Park
7300 N. College Ave.

You won't find playgrounds, swimming pools or skating rinks at Marott Park. Even though it's one of the city's largest, bigger than both Holliday and Broad Ripple parks, the emphasis here is on nature. Trails that wind through 70 acres of woods lead down to White River and offer a soothing antidote for city stress. Once you head into the woods or meadows, it's tough to remember you're still in the middle of the city, with Broad Ripple about 10 blocks south and Nora about 10 blocks north. Kids like the river access (see our Kidstuff chapter), where they can splash and explore along the bank. Throughout the summer, Marott's Saturday Morning Meanders guide visitors through the various habitats within the park, and the area offers good wildlife viewing year-round.

Krannert Park
605 S. High School Rd. • 483-3250

New amenities make Krannert even more popular with westsiders. It now features an aquatic center, a fishing pond that's a perfect place for kids to learn to wet a line, shaded picnic areas, a playground and ball fields. It also offers lots of neat classes that teach such skills as ancient methods of making fire with string, flint and steel (plan to get dirty at this one), earth and sky navigation and backyard horticulture.

Lake Sullivan Sports Complex
3601 Cold Springs Rd. • 327-VELO

This sports complex includes the Major Taylor Velodrome, a BMX track, soccer fields, a sand volleyball court and, of course, Lake Sullivan, where bank fishing yields largemouth bass, bluegill, redear sunfish, green sunfish and channel catfish.

Indy Island
8575 E. Raymond St. • 862-6867

Billed as the state's only indoor water park, Indy Island is one of the most unique recreation options in town. At the new Warren Township Middle School, this water wonderland features a lap pool and therapy pool, plus such kid-pleasing attractions as the 150-foot water slide and water playground, geysers, a meandering "lazy" river, a vortex whirlpool and a water basketball/volleyball area. Local outdoor pools operate from around Memorial Day through Labor Day, but Indy Island offers plenty of wet fun year-round.

State Parks and Facilities

Indiana's state parks and recreational facilities offer plenty of outdoor options, and many are quite convenient to Indianapolis. In fact, White River State Park, still under development downtown, will eventually offer a wide range of activities. The Indianapolis Zoo is within the park boundaries, and there is much discussion as to what sort of additional development would be appropriate. In 1995, Gov. Evan Bayh signed into law the Legislature's plans for a new state park at Ft. Benjamin Harrison, a northeast-

Photo: Jeff Hauersperger

Holliday Park is the home of "the ruins," statues that originally graced a New York City building and columns from a local convent.

side military base slated for closing (see following entry).

All state parks charged $2 per car in 1996 for Indiana residents ($3 per car for out-of-state'ers) and offer a variety of programs and service; nine employ full-time naturalists. Kids can earn Smokey's Friend patches, and older outdoor buffs can become Junior Naturalists and then participate in the Hoosier Ecologist program. The whole family can enjoy music, theater and dance performances scheduled at state parks throughout the summer.

Visitors to Indiana's parks and recreational areas should be especially vigilant about cleaning up after themselves. In 1994 the DNR initiated a carry-in/carry-out policy regarding trash. To avoid odors, scavenging animals and annoying bees that result from open trash barrels, state parks, reservoirs and recreation areas now require that visitors carry back out with them any trash they bring in. Gate attendants will provide the bags; tourists are responsible for the appropriate disposal of their own garbage. Note, however, that campgrounds still have trash receptacles for campers.

White River State Park
801 W. Washington St. • 634-4567

This expansive complex on the west side of downtown includes a variety of components — but not the typical state park pools and picnic tables. Clustered along a revitalized stretch of Washington Street are the Indianapolis Zoo, the Eiteljorg Museum of American Indians and Western Art, the National Institute for Fitness and Sport, a new IMAX 3-D theater, Victory Field baseball park and an extension of the Central Canal. For more information, stop in at the Pumphouse Visitors' Center, a facility built in 1879 that once provided water for fire protection and is now the headquarters for the White River State Park Development Commission.

Fort Harrison State Park
5753 Glenn Rd. • 591-0904

A part of Indianapolis for nearly 90 years, the Fort Benjamin Harrison Army Post was slated for closing in 1991, prompting state officials to suggest that part of the expansive northeast-side base become a state park. In 1995, the U.S. Department of the Interior approved Indiana's request to turn 1,700 acres of wooded, rolling terrain in the 2,500-acre post into a state park and nature preserve. (Much of the rest of the former base will be developed for housing.) Though as of this writing, the park offers only limited services, you'll find it a surprisingly scenic getaway in the midst of the city. Natural amenities include one of the largest tracts of unbroken hardwood forest in Central Indiana, a heron rookery, a number of small lakes and access to several miles of Fall Creek. Hiking trails wind through upland woods, ravines, bluffs and hardwood forest; a multi-use trail offers access for runners, walkers, bicyclists and in-line skaters; and a horse trail is expected to open in 1997. The Garrison restaurant, the former officers' club, offers dining and conference facilities, and lodging is available at the Harrison House and three former officers' homes. But one of the most anticipated amenities is the well-regarded Fort Harrison Golf Course, formerly available primarily to post personnel, which opened for public play in late 1996.

Brown County State Park
Ind. 46 between Columbus and Nashville
• (812) 988-4418

This is the place Indianapolis residents head to when the leaves start to turn. In one of the state's most scenic counties, it draws tons of tourists year-round. Don't expect solitude; in the middle of summer and on autumn weekends lines just to get in the park can be frustratingly long, and rental cabins are often booked two years in advance.

Still, you can't beat the amenities. Only an hour or so away from Indianapolis (via I-65 south to Ind. 46 W.), it's the state's biggest park with rolling terrain, plenty of picnic spots and scenic overlooks for picture-taking, a pool, well-maintained camping facilities and lots of wildlife. In fact, managing the ever-increasing deer population has become troublesome in recent years. Tourists who toss treats out of car windows contribute to the problem, so snap all the pictures you want, but don't feed the animals.

The park offers an abundance of hiking trails, several types of camping facilities, fishing lakes and a horsemen's campground, but no hunting. The park's Abe Martin Lodge offers pleasant accommodations for those who prefer comfort over camping.

Nashville, with its many artists and artisans, is nearby, and the town offers an abundance of top-notch arts and crafts (in addition to the standard touristy merchandise). The village itself draws thousands of tourists, so traffic into the town is quite heavy on summer and fall weekends and again during the holidays. Go midweek to avoid the crowds.

Yellowwood State Forest
722 S. Yellowwood Rd., Nashville
• (812) 988-7945

For a bit more nature and somewhat smaller crowds, try Yellowwood State Forest, a beautiful area known for its fishing and boating. Not far from Brown County State Park, Yellowwood offers fewer amenities than the popular park, but you can get a little closer to nature. The forest offers camping and hiking, but it also allows hunting, so hikers must remain alert and stay within the appropriate areas.

T.C. Steel Historic Site
4220 S. T.C. Steele Rd., Nashville
• (812) 988-2785

Close to both Brown County State Park and Yellowwood, this historic site includes the home, gardens and studio of Hoosier impressionist artist T.C. Steele, who helped establish Nashville as an artists' colony. The somewhat remote setting is beautiful in the fall, but in the spring, the rolling terrain blooms with hundreds of daffodils.

McCormick's Creek State Park
Rt. 5, Box 282, Spencer • (812) 829-2235

Some would say Owen County is even more scenic than Brown County. It's certainly less traveled and less commercial. For those who don't mind driving a bit farther, McCormick's Creek State Park, about 14 miles northwest of Bloomington, offers an alternative to Brown County.

Indiana's first state park, McCormick's Creek boasts thickly wooded areas, unique limestone formations, a waterfall and even caves. It's great for hiking and offers a variety of camping facilities. The housekeeping cab-

ins are quite popular, though, and are often booked a year in advance. The park's Canyon Inn offers comfortable accommodations and a great breakfast buffet.

Turkey Run State Park
Rt. 1, Box 164, Marshall 47859
• (765) 597-2635

This park, situated west of Indianapolis, offers lots of recreation possibilities. Rent a bike or a horse, hike the deep sandstone ravines, splash along Sugar Creek, camp or take it easy in the Turkey Run Inn, which boasts an indoor pool.

It's also fun to rent a canoe from one of the roadside liveries and paddle through the park and beneath covered bridges on Sugar Creek. Most canoe rentals will drop you off, pick you up downstream and take you back to your car.

Shades State Park
Rt. 1, Box 72, Waveland 47989
• (812) 665-2158

This is the place to go for a little peace and quiet. Fewer amenities means fewer crowds, and sometimes that can be a big plus. Still, there's camping, hiking, reservable shelters and, oddly enough, an airstrip, where you can lean against a tree and watch a few small planes land or take off. At Shades State Park, about 17 miles southwest of Crawfordsville off Ind. 47, you can hike through some spectacular scenery; its deep ravines were once known as "the shades of death." Hence, the name. Sugar Creek also runs through this park, and the views from a canoe can be even better than from the trails.

Nearby Pine Hills Nature Preserve offers even more scenery and even fewer crowds but fairly strenuous hiking.

Mounds State Park
4306 Mounds Rd., Anderson
• (765) 642-6627

Just off I-69 in Madison County (less than an hour northeast of Indianapolis), Mounds State Park offers a small campground, trails, picnic sites and a swimming pool. But the main attractions are the curious earthworks, built by prehistoric Indians around 160 B.C. Archeologists believe they were used for religious

Show your true colors at the Indianapolis 500 Parade.

ceremonies. Also of interest is the nature center, located in the Bronnenberg House, one of the oldest homes in Madison County.

Morgan-Monroe State Forest
6220 Forest Rd., Martinsville
• (765) 342-4026

About 45 minutes south of Indianapolis on Ind. 37 lies Morgan-Monroe State Forest, which has been called the gateway to southern Indiana's rolling, wooded terrain. It's certainly beautiful and includes more than 23,000 acres of virtually unspoiled forest. It offers a small campground, hiking trails, fishing and hunting. It also offers the reservable Draper's Cabin, a no-frills log cabin where you'll have a roof over your head but little else; you gather your own firewood, build your fire and carry in bedding and provisions.

Hunting is allowed in Morgan-Monroe, so hikers are advised to wear bright colors and stay within designated areas.

Lake Monroe
4850 Ind. 446 S., Bloomington
• (812) 837-9546

The water is the draw here, and Lake Monroe, not far from Bloomington and Indiana University, offers plenty of it. Its 10,750 acres offer water-skiing, beaches and fishing, while the recreational area boasts hiking trails, a nature center, picnic areas and more than 300 campsites.

Brookville Lake
P.O. Box 100, Brookville 47012
• (765) 647-2657

Very popular among the RV crowd, Brookville Lake offers loads of amenities, including a 5,260-acre lake with two beaches, room for water-skiing and more than 400 campsites. Southeast of Indianapolis, Brookville also has hiking trails, plenty of picnic sites and shelterhouses. Naturally, the lake provides excellent fishing, and hunting is allowed.

Whitewater Canal Historic Sites
P.O. Box 88, Metamora 47030
• (765) 647-6512

Not far from Brookville is the historic village of Metamora, with its Whitewater Canal and the Metamora Grist Mill. You can ride a horse-drawn boat on the canal, browse through the village's 120 antiques and crafts shops or hike or bike along the Whitewater Canal Trail.

Camping

Many state properties, including parks, forests and fish and wildlife areas, offer a variety of camping, ranging from primitive to electric; a few offer ultra-primitive backcountry camping (you hike in and hike out). Prices in 1996 ranged from $5 per night for bare-bones campsites to $13 for Class AA spots at some reservoirs. Most state parks will take reservations, usually beginning in March, for your favorite campsite; though you can call to check on availability, all reservations must be made by mail directly to the campground. The DNR's free *Indiana Recreation Guide* (see chapter introduction) spells out all the details.

Another helpful publication, *The Hoosier Camper Guide*, available free from the Recreational Vehicle Council, 247-6258, lists Indiana's privately owned campgrounds.

Recreational Activities

Are you ready to come out and play? Whether you're interested in fitness or just in fun, you'll find that Indianapolis has a lot to offer.

Enjoy yourself.

General Information

Several local organizations offer a variety of fitness and recreation programs. Among them are the following.

Indy Parks and Recreation
1426 W. 29th St. • 327-0000

Indy Parks operates an array of programs for adults and children at parks, community centers and schools throughout the city. Call and ask for a copy of the most recent *Fun Guide*, a publication that lists what's going on, where and when. Then it's a matter of making

some choices — from archery to wrestling, there's something for everyone.

Indianapolis Sports Club
Municipal Gardens, 1831 Lafayette Rd.
• 327-7190

Run by Indy Parks, this club provides developmentally disabled teens and adults (16 years an older) opportunities to take part in a variety of sports and recreational activities.

Jewish Community Center
6701 Hoover Rd. • 251-9467

With the opening of its new indoor pool and state-of-the-art fitness center in the spring of 1996, the JCC became one of the best fitness and recreational facilities in the city. There's also a new indoor tennis center. Enjoy all this in addition to an outdoor pool, tennis courts and playing fields, as well as a roster of fitness and recreation activities. You need not be Jewish to become a member of the JCC and take advantage of its programs.

YMCA Main Office
615 N. Alabama St. • 266-9622

There are 11 YMCA facilities in the greater Indianapolis region. Each one offers various programs for children and adults. Contact individual Ys for details:

Baxter Branch YMCA (south), 7900 S. Shelby Street, 881-9347; Fall Creek Parkway Branch YMCA (central), 860 W. 10th Street, 634-2478; Intercollegiate Branch YMCA, Butler University, 4600 Sunset Avenue, 283-9542; Arthur Jordan Branch YMCA (north), 8400 Westfield Boulevard, 253-3206; Ransberg Branch YMCA (east), 501 N. Shortridge Road, 357-8441; West District Branch YMCA (west), 7412 B Rockville Road, 271-5305, and in Lebanon, 482-0481; YMCA at the Athenaeum (downtown), 401 E. Michigan Street, 685-9705; Hamilton County Branch YMCA, 942 N. 10th Street, Noblesville, 776-3440; Barbara B. Jordan

---

INSIDERS' TIP

Take the lobby elevators of the City-County Building, 200 E. Market Street, to the top floor observation deck for a bird's-eye view of downtown.

Branch YMCA, 2039 E. Morgan Street, Martinsville, 342-6688; Ruth Lilly YMCA Outdoor Center, RR 1, St. Paul, 525-6730.

YWCA
4460 Guion Rd. • 299-2750

Some of the activities at this northwest-side facility are for girls and/or women only, others are for families. Individual and family memberships are available.

Boys & Girls Clubs of Indianapolis
5532 W. Raymond St. • 241-1712

This organization operates six area clubs for young people, offering a variety of sports and fitness activities such as basketball, volleyball, swimming, soccer, martial arts, etc. Contact the club nearest you for details:

Atkins Unit, 3131 W. 16th Street, 632-5766; Concord Village Unit, 3125 Concord Court, 635-1214; Gorman Unit, 1400 English Avenue, 632-2010; Keenan-Stahl Southside Unit, 1949 E. Troy Avenue, 784-4561; LeGore Unit, 5532 W. Raymond Street, 241-0557; Wheeler Unit, 2310 E. 30th Street, 926-4222.

Archery

Eagle Creek Park
7840 W. 56th St. • 327-7110

Eagle Creek Park boasts a world-class archery field; archery competition during the 1987 Pan Am Games was held here. The field is now used primarily for classes and competition. Call the parks department at 327-0000 for information.

J&J Archery
3438 Madison Ave. • 784-3632

J&J provides archery sales and service, arrow fletching and repair and a large indoor range. The staff can also set you up with an archery league.

Van's Archery Shop
5526 W. Stones Crossing Rd. • 422-9315

Here you'll find the state's largest selection of bows and accessories in addition to 22 indoor shooting ranges. You can also sign up for lessons or get involved in a league.

Ballroom Dancing

Heartland Ballroom Dancing
722 N. Howard Rd., Greenwood • 271-9319

This organization, a chapter of the United States Amateur Ballroom Dancers Association, hosts monthly dances, offers workshops, forms dance teams and promotes dancing at local festivals. It also sponsors an outreach program for youngsters, seniors and the physically challenged.

Birdwatching

Audubon Society Amos W. Butler Chapter
3650 Cold Spring Rd. • 926-9456

Contact this group for information on a variety of nature-related activities in addition to birdwatching.

Indy Parks and Recreation
1426 W. 29th St. • 327-0000

The parks department regularly schedules Saturday or Sunday morning bird hikes, often with members of the Amos Butler Audubon Society. Beginners can learn about the calls and habitats of resident and migratory birds; experienced birders can hone their skills.

Baseball and Softball

If "Take Me Out to the Ball Game" makes you yearn not for peanuts and Crackerjack, but for the thrill of snagging a grounder or hefting a bat in your hand, then here are a few options.

Indy Parks and Recreation Softball Office
1426 W. 29th St. • 327-7202

Indy Parks operates a variety of softball leagues including recreational and competitive divisions for men, women and coed play. These leagues compete at three sites, all of which are also available for rental, other softball games or tournaments: Bluff Park, 555 W.

Hanna Avenue; Chuck Klein Softball Complex, 4900 Rockville Road; Riverside Park, 2420 N. Riverside E. Drive.

Other sites around the city also offer softball league play and facility rentals. These include: Indianapolis Sports Park, 6701 S. Harding Street, 784-1447; Midwest Sports Complex, 7511 New Augusta Road, 875-8833; Mongans Sports Club, 1100 Moon Road, Plainfield, 839-4598; Stony Creek Softball Park, 1405 S. Post Road, 899-4733.

Youth Baseball and Softball

For young people, male and female, there are a number of baseball and/or softball options:

Franklin Township Girls Softball, 4151 S. Bazil Avenue, Wanamaker, 862-1557;

Franklin Township Rookie League, 6620 Shelbyville Road, 782-3161;

Indianapolis Police Athletic League, 1107 Broadway, 632-2487;

Little League Baseball Central Regional Headquarters, 9802 Little League Drive, 897-6127.

With 16 area leagues, each with some 400 players, Little League baseball is a going enterprise in the Greater Indianapolis area. For general information, contact regional headquarters, which can put you in touch with the league nearest you. Some of the leagues in the metro area are:

Beech Grove Little League, 724 S. 9th Avenue, Beech Grove 784-1348;

Bell-East Little League, 3340 N. German Church Road, Cumberland, 894-0505;

Carnine Little League, 1001 S. Belmont Street, 685-9411;

Franklin Little League, 2123 Younce Street, Franklin, 738-9974;

Garfield Little League, 300 W. Southern Avenue, 787-3622;

Indiana Central Little League, 4910 S. Keystone Avenue, 783-1066;

Irvington Little League, 6945 E. Raymond Street, 357-0620;

Lowell Little League, 5600 E. Terrace Avenue, 359-3979;

Southport Little League, 350 Anniston Drive, Southport 784-0716;

Warren Little League, 11850 Brookville Road, 862-4899;

Westlane Delaware Trail Little League, 1301 W. 73rd Street, 253-9933.

Roundtripper Baseball Academy
138 W. Carmel Dr., Carmel • 767-3013

For youngsters (and parents) who take baseball seriously and want to improve existing skills and develop new ones, Roundtripper may be the answer. Classes are offered for Pee Wees (6- to 8-year-olds) through teens in hitting, fielding, pitching, softball and conditioning.

Basketball

You're smack dab in the middle of hoops country, so you know there have to be plenty of places to play (besides your driveway). And there are. Try these.

Leagues

Indy Parks and Recreation
1502 W. 16th St. • 327-7200

Indy Parks operates a number of leagues and programs at a number of sites around town, including:

Men's "C" Basketball League: For less competitive players, 18 years old and older, who want to play for fun and exercise.

Men's 35 & Over Basketball League: The name says it all.

Men's Open Basketball League: For competitive players, 18 and older.

Men's College Basketball League: For high-energy, college-age players.

Women's Open Basketball League: For female competitive players, 18 and older.

Over 25 Half-Court Basketball: For those players who regard full-court basketball as cruel and unusual punishment.

Parent/Child Basketball: For parents and kids who want to play together for the fun of it.

Indiana Pacers Drug Free Basketball League: For youngsters 9 to 17 who want the opportunity not only to play basketball, but also to learn teamwork, cooperation and discipline in a setting that emphasizes equal play for everyone and the importance of staying drug free.

Lighted Outdoor Courts

In addition to the preceding offerings, the parks department maintains outdoor basketball courts at 40 parks throughout the area, including lighted courts at these locations:

Belmont Park, 1300 N. Belmont Street
Bethel Park, 1634 Golay Street
Bertha Ross Park, 3700 N. Clinton Street
Pride Park, 1129 S. Vandeman Street
Watkins Park, 2360 Dr. Martin Luther King Jr. Street

Jewish Community Center
6701 Hoover Rd. • 251-9467

Basketball is one of a variety of sports and fitness activities at this northwest-side complex for adults and kids.

YMCA Main Office
615 N. Alabama St. • 266-YMCA

Most of the area Ys offer a variety of basketball programs for adults and children ranging from leagues to open court time. Contact the main office above or the Y nearest you

(see list in the "Organizations" portion of this chapter) for details.

Community Leagues

Many area churches, schools and community centers host evening and weekend basketball leagues or programs. Contact the ones in your neighborhood for information.

Bicycling

Bicycling is a booming pastime in Central Indiana, both from fitness and recreational standpoints. If you're serious about cycling, or want to make contact with people who are, there are three organizations you need to know about.

Indiana Bicycle Coalition (IBC)
P.O. Box 20243, Indianapolis, Ind. 46220 • 327-8356, (800) BIKE-110

This bicycle advocacy organization acts as the hub for more than 20 cycling groups statewide, representing their concerns on is-

Photo: Randy Baughn

The Major Taylor Velodrome hosts world-class cycling events.

sues that have an impact on cyclists. IBC also serves as a resource for cyclists, state and local government officials and members of the media in need of accurate information on bicycling in Indiana. IBC is also developing a series of maps designed specifically for cyclists, indicating safe routes throughout the state.

Central Indiana Bicycling Association (CIBA)
P.O. Box 55405, Indianapolis, Ind. 46205 • 255-0559, 251-2422

With more than 1,500 members, CIBA is one of the largest bicycling organizations in the country. Members can take part in a variety of types of rides throughout the year, including the rigorous Hilly Hundred, a two-day, 100-mile ride held each October in the hills of south Central Indiana. (See separate entry in the "Bicycle Tours" section of this chapter.)

Where to Ride

While Indianapolis is noticeably deficient in bike paths, there are designated bike routes throughout the area. Look for roads and streets with bike route markers (signs bearing the symbol of a bicycle) alongside them. These routes tend to be less busy and more scenic than main arteries.

To help riders sort out where they should or should not ride, the Mayor's Bicycle Task Force developed a map indicating safe and unsafe routes. You can get one for free by joining the Central Indiana Bicycling Association (see entry above), or buy one for $2 from the Indiana Department of Natural Resources (DNR), 402 W. Washington Street, 232-4180. Some area bike shops stock them as well.

Other options include the following.

Central Canal Tow Path
One of the most popular trails in the city is the Central Canal tow path. The path, which runs south from Broad Ripple and passes through residential and nonresidential areas, attracts runners, walkers and bicyclists alike. Tree-lined and well-maintained, the path is a lovely alternative to busy streets. If you follow the path all the way from Broad Ripple to 30th

Street, which is the most scenic portion of the path, it's about 3.5 miles.

Park Routes
A number of Indianapolis parks contain bike trails and/or bike routes. These include: Brookside Park, 3500 Brookside Parkway S. Drive, 327-7179; Douglass Park, 1425 E. 25th Street, 327-7174; Eagle Creek Park, 7840 W. 56th Street, 327-7110; Ellenberger Park, 5301 E. St. Clair Street, 327-7176; Riverside Park, 2420 E. Riverside Drive, 327-7171.

Track Riding
If you're looking for a safe auto-free, dog-free, pothole-free place to ride, try the following.

Major Taylor Velodrome and Lake Sullivan BMX Track
3649 Cold Spring Rd. • 327-VELO

Named in honor of Marshall "Major" Taylor, an Indianapolis cyclist who became the first black American to win a world championship (in 1899, he won two world bicycle racing titles), the Velodrome not only hosts world-class cycling events, it also encourages public use of the facility when no events are scheduled. Open riding, group or individual, is Monday through Friday from 10 AM to 5 PM.

Bicycle Tours

Hilly Hundred
Central Indiana Bicycling Association, P.O. Box 55405, Indianapolis, Ind. 46205 • 255-0559, 251-2422

Generally held in early to mid-October, this annual two-day event covers a 100-mile route through the hills of south Central Indiana. Not for the faint-of-heart or the out-of-shape — 50 miles a day over this undulating terrain takes its toll. Due to the Hilly Hundred's popularity, CIBA now limits participation to the first 5,000 registrants. For information, contact CIBA.

Trails Unlimited
RR 4, Box 318, Nashville Ind. 47448 • (812) 988-6232

If the idea of riding through some of the wild backcountry of Brown County appeals to you, Trails Unlimited offers a 15-mile mountain bike excursion that *Bicycling Magazine* called a "high adrenaline" event. Reservations are required; rides take place on Saturday or Sunday morning.

Hoosier Bikeway System
Department of Natural Resources, 402 W. Washington St. • 232-9200

The 800-mile-long Hoosier Bikeway System is a series of 11 routes throughout the state that are considered safe for cyclists. The DNR sells guidebooks of the routes for $1 each.

Boating

Just because Indianapolis is situated smack in the middle of farming country without even a navigable river doesn't mean we don't have a lot of boating aficionados; you'll see plenty of those "I'd Rather Be Sailing" bumper stickers. And those who really want to get their feet wet will find plenty of opportunities.

Eagle Creek Park Marina
7840 W. 56th St. • 327-7130

Here you can sign up for sailing or sailboarding lessons or rent a rowboat, canoe, kayak, catamaran, sailboat or pontoon. The parks department also occasionally offers U.S. Power Squadron boating safety courses.

Geist Marina
11695 E. Fall Creek Rd. • 849-8455

Call the marina at popular Geist Reservoir for information on slip rentals or details on area fishing.

Morse Reservoir Marina
2099 Hague Rd., Noblesville • 984-3301

Morse is just about as popular as Geist, so the water here can get crowded too. Call for details about docking a boat or dropping a line.

Bowling

If bowling brings to mind visions of TV's Al Bundy (or for another generation Archie Bunker), the you haven't kept up with this rapidly growing pastime. Around here, this family-ori-

ented activity proves quite popular. Local leagues exist for kids, couples, singles — you name it. Several organizations can provide you with detailed information on leagues and competitive play: Central Indiana Tournament Bowlers Association, 784-3753; Greater Indianapolis Bowling Association, 578-1000; Indiana Youth Bowling Association, 357-2695; and Indiana Women's Bowling Association, 353-9422. Also check out one of the many alleys around town. Here are a few to get you started.

Action Duckpin Bowling
325 S. College Ave. • 632-2879
1105 S. Prospect Ave. • 686-6006

Duckpins are shorter and squattier and the bowling balls smaller (making duckpin bowling easier for the kids and novices), but the point is the same: set 'em up and knock 'em down.

All Star Bowl
726 N. Shortridge Rd. • 352-1848

Here you'll find 48 lanes, a new "accuscorer," a pro shop that offers videotaping, a lounge, snack bar and bumper bowling. The adventurous can check out "cosmic bowling," a late-night weekend special, with glow-in-the-dark balls and pins, laser lights and fog machines.

Eagle Bowl Centre
2802 Lafayette Rd. • 926-2333

Billing itself as a "new adventure in bowling," this facility offers 36 lanes, league play, open bowling and lessons. You can also take advantage of the restaurant, arcade, billiards and lounge.

Sport Bowl
3900 S. U.S. 31 • 788-0878

You can reserve one of the 32 lanes for open bowling or league play here, where you'll also find a lounge, snack bar, arcade and pro shop.

Woodland Bowl
3421 E. 91st St. • 844-4099

A big draw here is the smoke-free environment. You'll also find 80 lanes, a variety of leagues and bumper bowling.

Boxing

Sarge Johnson Boxing Club
2420 E. Riverside Dr. • 327-7222

This facility, which is operated by Indy Parks, offers beginning and experienced boxers alike a place to work on their pugilistic skills. Whether you want to take up boxing as a fitness activity or train for amateur competition, Sarge Johnson's in your corner.

Fencing

So you've always wanted to learn the fine art of swordsmanship (or you just want to put your rapier wit to good use)? Check out the following.

Indianapolis Fencing Club
401 E. Michigan St. • 685-9705

Based downtown in the Athenaeum, this organization is an affiliate of the U.S. Fencing Association. It offers classes for beginners (9 years old to adult) and participates in national competitions.

Fitness Training

Both Indy Parks and area YMCAs offer an array of fitness activities ranging from aerobics to weight training. For information, contact Indy Parks or the Y nearest you (see entries in the "Organizations" section of this chapter).

Other options include the following.

National Institute for Fitness and Sport
250 N. University Blvd. • 274-3432

This is a state-of-the-art fitness research, education and training facility. Open to professional and amateur athletes, as well as the general public, the institute contains a 200-meter indoor track, a regulation-size basketball court, a rubberized workout floor and weight- and cardiovascular-training equipment.

Memberships here are not cheap (students pay a one-time initiation fee of $75 plus $35 per month; others pay the initiation fee plus $500 per year or $140 per quarter), but they offer the added value of fitness testing done by well-trained staff members who also help tailor individual workout programs. This is the fitness facility of choice for a variety of area businesses, police and fire departments and serious athletes.

Bally's Scandinavian
5435 Pike Plaza Rd. • 293-9436
517 U.S. Route 31 N., Greenwood
• 885-0242
8831 Commerce Crossing • 844-1515

Calling itself "America's Health Club" (there are 340 clubs nationwide), Bally's three Indianapolis-area sites offer aerobics classes, StairMasters, free weights and weight machines, racquetball courts, indoor pools, indoor tracks and the much-Bally-hooed (via TV commercials) 30-minute workout program.

Family Fitness Centers
7126 N. Keystone Ave. • 255-9751
6407 E. Washington St. • 359-6938

At the two Family Fitness sites you'll find Cybex circuit training equipment, Hammer Strength equipment and free weights as well as recumbent cycles, treadmills and step aerobics classes. There's a private workout area for women and personalized instruction and nutritional guidance for all members. Both sites are open seven days a week.

Gold's Gym
8736 E. 21st St. • 897-7556
4041 Office Plaza Blvd. • 297-5238
8481 Bash St. • 598-9399

From aerobics to body-sculpting, each Gold's Gym site has the equipment and the staff to help you tone down or bulk up. At Gold's, you'll find an array of free weights and weight machines, stair climbers and treadmills, aerobics classes and trained personnel who can help you make the best use of them.

Greenbriar Athletic Club
1275 W. 86th St. • 257-3261

With 12 racquetball and handball courts, along with aerobics classes, StairMasters and Life Cycles, Greenbriar aims to get your heart pumping. For your muscles there are free

weights and Nautilus machines available, as well a staff trainer to help you make best use of them.

Livrite Fitness Centre
Geist Centre, 6220 N. Butler Ave.
• 257-1004

Each of the Livrite locations has an indoor pool and track, plus treadmills, StairMasters, rowing machines and exercise bikes. There are also tons (literally) of free weights. Enjoy Nautilus machines, aerobics and aquacize classes and racquetball and basketball courts. An exercise physiologist is available at each site to help you develop a personalized training program, and there's a massage therapist to help you work out the after effects of working out.

Racquets Four Sports Centre
4002 Southport Rd. • 783-5411

From water aerobics to indoor tennis, swimming to basketball, racquetball to aerobics, Racquets Four offers plenty of ways to get fit. There's also an indoor track — and (for those who overdo it) whirlpools, a sauna and an on-site massage therapist.

Zike's Fitness & Aerobic Co.
6450 W. 10th St. • 248-2326

Consistently rated one of the city's best health clubs by the readers of *Indianapolis Monthly* magazine, Zike's specializes in programs for people who are new to fitness training. On the club's roster are fat-burning classes, aerobics classes, StairMasters, Nautilus, other weight equipment and a world-class body building program.

Fitness Trails
Usually a half-mile to 1 mile in length, these trails include fitness stations that offer runners or walkers a chance to perform stretches and strength-enhancing exercises designed to increase personal fitness levels. You'll find trails at:

Broad Ripple Park, 1450 Broad Ripple Avenue

Christian Park, 4125 English Avenue
Garfield Park, 2450 Shelby Street
Municipal Gardens, 1831 Lafayette Road
Sahm Park, 6800 E. 91st Street

Football

If your idea of a great afternoon of football includes actually laying your hands on a ball and running like mad for the end zone, then check into the football programs offered by the following.

Indy Parks and Recreation
1502 W. 16th St. • 327-7200

Men-only and coed teams play in Indy Parks' flag football program. Additionally, the parks department can probably hook you up with some of the football teams and leagues that use park facilities for their games.

Indianapolis Sports Park
6701 S. Harding St. • 784-7447

This multisports complex on the south side of town is used by a number of teams.

Go-carts and Minigolf

Load up the family or grab a date and head to one of these recreation centers for some good clean fun.

Greatimes
5341 Elmwood Ave. • 780-0300

You can enjoy 36 holes of miniature golf plus go-carts and arcade games at this family fun park.

Post Road Recreation Center
4700 Post Rd. • 897-7908

This 15-acre facility offers four go-cart tracks that operate year round, plus a golf driving range, 18-hole miniature golf and bank shot basketball.

Putt-Putt Golf and Games
10499 E. Washington St. • 899-4536
6320 W. 34th St. • 291-7437
1936 E. Southport Rd. • 787-4852

You'll find the traditional kitschy mini golf courses plus go-carts and game rooms at these facilities; call about group rates for parties.

Rustic Gardens Golf Driving Range
1500 S. Arlington Ave. • 359-8183

This location offers a lighted driving range

and putting green as well as 27 holes of miniature golf on real grass.

Golf

Public Courses

"Golf course building is an art," Pete Dye, renowned course designer and former Indianapolis resident, said in a 1995 interview with the *Indianapolis Business Journal*. "I design (courses) with a challenge for golfers of all levels." Indianapolis has three Dye-designed public courses where you can pit your skill level against his artfulness.

Brickyard Crossing
4790 West 16th St. • 484-6572
This 18-hole, championship-caliber course on the grounds of the Indianapolis Motor Speedway includes three lakes, 72 sand traps and 650 trees. The site of the annual Brickyard Crossing Championship, a Senior PGA Tour event, it's not a course for the fainthearted.

Eagle Creek
8802 W. 56th St. • 297-3366
Golf Digest rated this 27-hole complex inside Eagle Creek Park as one of the top-50 public courses in the nation. Built in 1971 and renovated in 1988, the facilities include an amateur golf training center and driving range in addition to nine- and 18-hole courses.

William Sahm Golf Course
6880 E. 91st St. • 849-0036
This 18-hole course is one that Dye himself rates among his best local efforts; it was also one of his first. It's an open, flat course of moderate length. A creek and lake offer additional challenges and considerable scenic beauty.

Coffin
2209 W. 30th St. • 327-7845
Inside Riverside Park, this 18-hole course recently underwent major renovation. You'll find tree-lined fairways, rolling terrain and plenty of water hazards.

Douglass
2801 Dr. Andrew J. Brown Ave. • 924-0018
Relatively short with few hazards and compact, well-trapped greens, this nine-hole, par 34 course appeals to beginners and seniors.

Pleasant Run
601 N. Arlington Ave. • 357-0829
This 18-hole course comes with seven water hazards and tree-lined fairways. A winding creek makes it quite scenic.

Riverside
3600 White River Pkwy. W. Dr. N.
• 327-7300
The oldest course in the city, Riverside has small greens, mature trees, and relatively flat terrain with few hazards. This 18-hole, par 70 course appeals to a wide range of players.

Sarah Shank Golf Course
2901 S. Keystone Ave. • 784-0631
This is a beautiful 18-hole course with open fairways and two creeks. The terrain rolls slightly and includes some wooded areas.

Carl E. Smock Golf Course
3910 S. County Line Rd. E. • 888-0036
This is one of the longest courses in the city, with large greens, open fairways and multiple sand traps. You'll also find two creeks, two ponds. Hills add to the excitement of playing this 18-hole, par 72 course.

A. J. Thatcher Golf Course
4501 W. Vermont St. • 244-0713
A short nine-hole course with narrow tree-lined fairways and three water holes, this is a challenging course for the average golfer.

Whispering Hills
10751 Brookville Rd. • 862-1237
The newest municipal course in the city, Whispering Hills offers rolling hills, lakes and woods — in other words, all the obstacles you could ask for in a nine-hole round of golf.

Winding River
8400 S. Mann Rd. • 856-7257
The longest nine-hole course in the city, Winding River consists of wide fairways and rolling terrain with few hazards.

Hunting and Fishing

Unless you own a good-size stand of woods or know someone who does, it may be best to stick to state-owned lands that are managed for hunting. State forests, recreation areas and reservoirs all allow various types of hunting, but Indiana's 16 fish and wildlife areas may offer the best options; they're maintained primarily for hunting and fishing. Most allow deer, squirrel, upland game and waterfowl hunting. Indiana hunters must have a license, available from some sporting good stores, bait shops and, of course, from the DNR. Contact the Division of Fish and Wildlife, 402 W. Washington Street, Room 273, 46204, or call 232-4080 for more information. Hunter education programs are now required for all first-time hunters born after 1986 and teach youngsters about firearm safety and responsible hunting. For class schedules, contact the DNR's Division of Law Enforcement at 232-4010.

If your idea of relaxation is wetting a line and waiting for a bite, then pack the tackle box and head to one of the many fishing spots around the city. But don't forget your license; anglers between the ages of 17 and 64 must carry a current Indiana fishing license. Most fishing sites around town are either in or adjacent to city parks; pack a lunch and make a day of it.

Here are a few of our favorite fishin' holes: At **Eagle Creek Reservoir** 7840 W. 56th Street, you'll find a number of promising places to drop a line. We hear the fish are also biting at the **Waterfowl Sanctuary**; it's about a third-mile hike from the 71st Street parking area.

For other bank fishing spots, try near the **Eagle Creek Marina**, the **42nd Street boat ramp** and **Lilly Lake**, where you can pull in bluegill, largemouth bass or channel catfish. Just follow the directional signs within the park. You can also launch a boat on the reservoir itself from the 42nd Street ramp; boats are limited to 26-foot maximum length (8-foot minimum) and a 10 hp motor. Call 327-7110 for information on a season boat launching pass. During the summer, you can rent a rowboat or canoe from the park marina. You'll need a

cash deposit and picture ID. Note that no boats are allowed within 500 feet of the dam, and you can't fish from the dam or the 56th Street bridge.

Warm summer days often draw anglers to the city-owned stretch of land along the west side of **Fall Creek** from 30th to 38th streets. You can also pick out a spot along **Fall Creek Parkway** from 38th Street to Geist Reservoir. Fall Creek is stocked with largemouth bass, smallmouth bass, bluegill, crappie, gizzard shad and channel catfish.

Three city parks — **Broad Ripple**, **Marott** and **Holliday** — offer convenient bank fishing along **White River**. Broad Ripple Park boasts a boat ramp, while Holliday and Marott offer beautiful wooded hiking trails and plenty of places for kids to explore along the water (see our Kidstuff chapter).

Pick a shady spot along the bank and drop a line at **Krannert Park**, 605 High School Road, or at Lake Sullivan, 3500 N. White River Parkway. You may pull in largemouth bass, bluegill, crappie, longear sunfish or channel catfish. (Check our descriptions in the city parks section of this chapter for more info on park amenities.) At **Ruster Park Pond**, 11300 Prospect Avenue, you'll likely find a comfortable spot along the bank to angle for the stocked largemouth bass, bluegill, redear sunfish and gizzard shad.

FYI

Unless otherwise noted, the area code for all phone numbers in this guide is 317.

Ice Skating

Facilities

Carmel Ice Skadium
1040 Third Ave. SW, Carmel • 844-8888

This is a year-round ice facility open for figure skating and hockey. Open to the public, this "skadium" is also available for private rentals.

Pepsi Coliseum
1202 E. 38th St. • 927-7536

Open from October to April for public skating, this rink also offers lessons and league hockey.

Indiana/World Skating Academy
201 S. Capitol Ave. • 237-5555

Enjoy public skating year round whenever skating or hockey events or practices are not going on. This is your chance to skate in a place designed to bring out the best in world-class skaters.

Indy Parks and Recreation
1426 W. 29th St. • 327-0000

Indy Parks operates two indoor rinks that are open for ice-skating from October to April: Ellenberger Ice Rink, 5301 E. St. Clair Street, 327-7176; and Perry Ice Rink, 451 E. Stop 11 Road, Greenwood, 888-0070.

Organizations

Indianapolis Skating Club
c/o Carmel Ice Skadium, 1040 3rd Ave., SW, Carmel • 844-8888, 844-3574

This organization, which is a member club of the United States Figure Skating Association, provides its members (adults and children) opportunities to practice figure skating, free style and ice dancing. It also offers learn-to-skate classes. The club skates three nights a week, September through April, at the Carmel Ice Skadium.

Indy Speed Skating Club
c/o Indiana/World Skating Academy • 237-5555, 848-9410

If whizzing across the ice as a blur of blades, is your dream, this organization can help you realize it. The club meets twice a week at the Indiana/World Skating Academy to practice.

Sycamore Club
c/o Perry Ice Rink, 451 E. Stop 11 Rd., Greenwood • 888-0070, 888-2957

Whether you're a competitive skater or just like gliding around for fun, this group offers you a chance to do so with like-minded skaters during Perry Ice Rink's October-to-April season.

Winter Club
c/o Pepsi Coliseum, 1202 E. 38th St. • 927-7536, 888-5543

From kids to grandparents, this club provides ice time for its members at the Coliseum, October through April. The club offers individual and group lessons and helps train competition-level and recreational skaters.

In-Line Skating

While you'll see a lot of in-line skaters on streets and sidewalks in certain areas of the city — downtown, Meridian Kessler, Butler Tarkington, Broad Ripple — there are other options. Some of the parks, most notably Eagle Creek, Garfield, Krannert and Holliday, have ample roadways for skating. Or you can go to:

Ellenberger Park
5301 E. St. Clair St. • 327-7176
Perry Park
451 E. Stop 11 Rd. • 888-0070

From June to August, the skating rinks at these two parks are open for in-line skating. Learn-to-skate classes for children and adults are also available.

Major Taylor Velodrome
3649 Cold Spring Rd. • 327-VELO

As long as there are no cycling events scheduled, you can skate on the Velodrome's banked track Monday to Friday, 10 AM to 5 PM. A modest fee buys you two hours of skating time. During the summer, you can also take skating classes.

RCA Dome
100 S. Capitol Ave. • 262-3410

During the winter, the Dome's concourse is open for in-line skating. Call for a schedule and fee information.

Martial Arts

Indy Parks offers classes in various martial arts disciplines at various parks' activity centers. Call 327-0000 for information. Several YMCA branches also offer martial arts instruction. Contact your nearest Y for details.

With more than three dozen commercial martial arts studios to choose from, you're bound to find one that's right for you. Some of the choices include:

A-1 Masters Martial Arts
6957 Madison Ave. • 783-7000
5999 Crawfordsville Rd. • 244-3600
8859 Pendleton Pike • 898-0704

The focus at all three A-1 centers is on building confidence, teaching self-defense and self-discipline and enhancing fitness. A-1 instructors teach traditional Korean martial arts; classes are open to men and women.

Academy of Chung Do Kwan
1744 E. 86th St. • 571-1400
2989 W. 71st St. • 328-1400

Under the direction of grandmaster Jay Park, who has taught martial arts at DePauw and Indiana universities as well as for the United States Air Force, these two facilities have classes for adults and children. Both sites offer special rates for families.

Steve Anderson's AOK Karate Studio
2501 S. Madison Ave. • 788-7050
3820 N. High School Rd. • 299-1580
3815 N. Shadeland Ave. • 542-0025

Owned and operated by World Martial Arts Hall of Famer Steve Anderson, the three A.O.K. studios teach karate, kung fu, judo, jiu jitsu and taekwondo. Classes for men, women and children are available.

Choi Brothers' Oriental Martial Arts College & Fitness Club
5404 W. 38th St. • 297-1000
7275 N. Keystone Ave. • 257-4458

Youn Pyo Choi and Joon Pyo Choi (the latter was a U.S. Olympic coach in 1988) offer instruction in taekwondo and other martial arts, including the use of weaponry. They strive to instill confidence, patience and respect in their students while teaching self-defense and improving coordination. Classes are open to men, women and children.

Herb Johnson's KarateWorld Champion Karate USA
9423 E. Washington St. • 898-4444
5060 E. 62nd St. • 255-6872

Three-time world karate champion and trainer of 14 other world champions, Herb Johnson runs a karate program that stresses self-discipline and self-confidence. Personalized instruction for men, women and children includes group and private lessons, as well as training for women in self-defense and rape protection.

Photo: The Indianapolis News and The Indianapolis Star

A father and daughter duo take advantage of the snow at a local park.

Ray Sarkine's Martial Arts School
6324 W. Washington St. • 241-5425

With more than 20 years' experience in martial arts, Ray Sarkine teaches aikido, kick boxing and weaponry use to men and women in private and group settings. He also offers classes for kids.

Sevenish Martial Arts America
1140 N. State Rd. 135, Greenwood • 889-5425

Ranked among the top 100 martial arts schools in America, this family-oriented facility offers such trademarked programs as SuperKids, SuperTots, Street-Smart Safe, and Mind-Your-Manners.

Roller Skating

When was the last time you strapped on a pair of roller skates and wobbled out to skate the night away with your friends?

Well, here's your chance.

Ellenberger Park
5301 E. St. Clair St. • 327-7176
Perry Park
451 E. Stop 11 Rd. • 888-0070

Operated by Indy Parks, these two rinks offer both roller and in-line skating from June through August.

Melody Skateland
5101 W. Washington St. • 241-8100

One of the largest roller rinks in the country, this westside facility has provided Indianapolis residents with first-class skating for nearly 40 years. In addition to open skating, the rink is available for private parties; it also offers group rates. Novices or aspiring competitive skaters can get instruction here from regional and national champions.

United Skates of America
3902 Glen Arm Rd. • 291-6794
5001 N. Shadeland Ave. • 546-2457

These two sites are the local outlets of the largest chain of roller rinks in the Midwest. They offer state-of-the-art audio and lighting systems, clean-with-a-sheen hardwood skating floors and contemporary decor. In addition to public skating, they host private birth-day parties and other special events and offer group skating rates.

Rowing

Eagle Creek Regatta Course
Eagle Creek Park, 7350 Eagle Beach Dr. • 327-7110

The only rowing course in the United States that's sanctioned for international competition by the International Federation of Rowing Associations, the Eagle Creek regatta Course is open for use by trained and certified rowers. Instruction and certification for rowers from high school age to adult is available through Community Rowing of Indianapolis (CRI). Call 297-7185 for information.

Running and Walking

Indy Runners/Walkers Inc.
• 290-7867

For serious runners and walkers, this is the organization to belong to. An affiliate of the Roadrunners Club of America, Indy Runners/Walkers provides training information and racing opportunities for both recreational and competitive runners and walkers. It also hosts a variety of events, ranging from weekly runs and walks to races, throughout the year.

Indiana University
Track and Field Stadium, 901 W. New York St. • 274-6780

The premier outdoor running facility in the city, this Olympic-caliber stadium has a nine-lane, 400-meter rubber track that is considered one of the fastest in the world. When not in use for competitions, the stadium is open for public use. Contact the IU Natatorium, which is adjacent to the stadium and connected to it by a tunnel, about guidelines and fees.

Monon Trail
62nd St. and Guildford Ave., Broad Ripple, Information: Indianapolis Greenways • 327-7431

The newest — and one of the prettiest — places to run, walk, skate or bike is the Monon

Trail, a 3.5-mile-long trail stretching from Broad Ripple north to 86th Street. It opened in June 1996. A great example of a rails-to-trails conversion, this former Monon Railroad route is now a paved path that offers users a comfortable alternative to sidewalks and busy streets. Be forewarned however: On a nice weekend, the trail is in constant use from dawn to dark, so don't expect to have it all to yourself. But trail rules are clearly posted, and the folks who use it are largely a polite bunch.

There are plans to extend the trail north to 96th Street and south to downtown. Eventually, in fact, you may be able to follow it from downtown Indianapolis all the way north to Westfield, though that's several years away yet. In the meantime, the portion of the Monon that's open is long enough to work up a good sweat.

Other Options

There are other outdoor tracks at various schools throughout the city, most of which are available for public use. If you like to run outdoors, but not around an oval, there are a number of other good places. Try these parks: Lake Sullivan Sports Complex, 3601 Cold Springs Road; Riverside Park, 2420 E. Riverside Drive; Garfield Park, 2450 Shelby Street; and Holliday Park, 6349 Spring Mill Road.

Other good running options include the Central Canal towpath south from Broad Ripple; Fall Creek Parkway, north of 46th Street; and Washington Street west of Circle Centre, past the Indianapolis Zoo and back through the IUPUI campus.

Snow Skiing

Cross-Country

When there are at least 4 inches of snow on the ground, you can ski the trails at:

Eagle Creek Park
7840 W. 56th St. • 327-7110

Ten miles of trails wind through this park. Some trails require experience; all guarantee a good workout. You can rent equipment at the park if you don't have your own.

Southeastway Park
5624 E. County Line Rd. S. • 861-5167

With 188 acres of woods and open land, this park is a good place to practice your skills. You can rent skis, boots and poles here, but you'll have to bring your own motor control.

Downhill

OK, Aspen this isn't. And slopes there aren't — at least not in the immediate metropolitan area. But if you don't mind driving an hour or two, you can get to some Indiana hills that are tall enough to allow you to gather a little speed before reaching the bottom.

Ski Paoli Peaks
U.S. 150 W., Paoli • (812) 723-4696

Whether you're a beginning skier or a flashy snowboarder, this facility 100 miles south of Indianapolis has something for you. Giant snow-making machines keep the 15 slopes and trails ski-ready even when Mother Nature hasn't any snow to spare. The longest run here is 3,300 feet; the vertical drop is 300 feet. There are package deals available ranging from learn-to-ski excursions to midnight madness and holiday specials.

Ski World
2887 W. S.R. 46, Nashville • (812) 988-6638

This downhill complex in Brown County, about 45 miles southwest of Indianapolis, has a vertical drop of 310 feet. The longest run is 2,500 feet, but if you're a beginner you can practice your moves on the bunny slope. Chair lifts and rope tows get you up the slopes, and a lodge awaits you once you've come back down. You can rent your equipment or buy it from the on-site ski shop.

Soccer

Both Indy Parks and YMCA branches offer soccer instruction and team play. Contact Indy Parks, 327-0000, or the Y nearest you for information.

Another good way to find out what's going on locally is to contact the largest soccer equipment supplier in the area.

Soccer Unlimited
622 S. Range Line Rd., Carmel • 848-4797
916 E. Main St., Greenwood • 888-0640
6907 Lake Plaza • 845-5466

At any of these locations, you can locate teams and leagues throughout Central Indiana. One organization you're likely to hear about is the Metropolitan Soccer Club, which represents a number of soccer teams around the state. For information, call 253-8816 or 786-3557.

Organizations
Other area soccer organizations are:

Central Indiana Youth Soccer League, 5954 N. College Avenue, 726-0009;

Indiana Youth Soccer Association, 5954 N. College Avenue, 255-0499;

Northeast Youth Soccer League, 7045 Hampstead Lane, 842-6975.

Fields
There are several good soccer fields in the area, including:

William Kuntz Memorial Soccer Stadium, 1502 W. 16th Street, 327-7194;

German Park, 8600 S. Meridian Street, Greenwood, 881-0053;

Juan Soloman Park, 64th Street and Grand View Drive, no phone;

Zionsville Soccer Park, 1100 Bloor Lane, 873-3491.

Indy Indoor Soccer & Sports
6382 W. 34th St. • 291-2729

Despite its name, this is a soccer-only facility. During the winter, it hosts amateur teams (kids' teams and adult teams) from throughout Central Indiana; in the summer, it organizes in-house teams and holds kids' soccer camps.

Indy Sports & Fitness Inc.
4002 N. Franklin Rd. • 898-2285

The wind may be howling outside, but inside this northeast-side facility soccer balls are flying. In addition to indoor soccer leagues for kids and adults, Indy Sports also offers arena football (flag only, no tackle), basketball and volleyball. In the spring, play moves outdoors where there are five softball diamonds and two sandpit volleyball courts.

Swimming

Indiana University Natatorium
901 W. New York St. • 274-3518

On a daily basis, except when a major event is scheduled, the natatorium's main pool is open for lap swimming. There are also learn-to-swim classes, scuba-diving classes, and water safety classes available.

If you're looking for more than a place to swim, the natatorium has Polaris weight machines, aerobic classes and other fitness activities available.

Indy Parks and Recreation
1426 W. 29th St. • 327-0000

In addition to the Indiana University Natatorium, other public swimming facilities include the following park pools. Unless otherwise noted, these are all outdoor pools, open between Memorial Day weekend and Labor Day weekend. Those with adult lap swimming schedules or lap pools are noted. Call individual sites for specific information.

Bethel Pool, 1634 Golay Street, 327-7324;

Broad Ripple Pool, 1450 E. Broad Ripple Avenue, 327-7333;

Brookside Aquatic Center, 3500 Brookside Parkway S. Drive, 327-7331;

Douglass Pool, 2759 Dr. Andrew J. Brown Avenue, 327-7325;

Ellenberger Pool, (offers separate adult lap swimming times), 5301 E. St. Clair Street, 327-7326;

Garfield Pool, 2450 Shelby Street, 327-7327;

Gustafson Pool, 3110 Moller Road, 327-7334;

Indy Island Aquatic Center, (indoor water park, including a separate lap pool), 8575 E. Raymond Street, 862-6867;

Krannert Aquatic Center, (has a separate lap pool) 605 S. High School Road, 862-6867;

Martin Luther King Pool, 1701 Broadway Avenue, 327-7332;

Perry Aquatic Center, 451 E. Stop 11 Road, 889-0825;

Rhodius Pool, 1001 S. Belmont Avenue, 327-7328

Riverside Aquatic Center, 2420 E. Riverside Drive, 327-7272

Photo: Randy Baughn

The Eagle Creek Regatta Course is the lone rowing course
sanctioned for international competition.

Sahm Aquatic Center, 6800 E. 91st Street, Fishers, 849-2227

Thatcher Pool (indoor), 4649 W. Vermont Street, 327-7390

Wes Montgomery Pool, 3501 N. Hawthorne Lane, 327-7329

Willard Pool, 1700 E. Washington Street, 327-7330.

Public Beaches

Absent both a large lake front and sea shore, Indianapolis is lacking in large public beach facilities. Still, there is:

Eagle Creek Beach
7602 Eagle Beach Dr. • 327-7132

Part of Eagle Creek Park, the beach abuts Eagle Creek Reservoir, and offers a wide stretch of sand, shade trees and picnic sites. Swimming is permitted. Lifeguards are on duty during the Memorial Day to Labor Day beach season.

Tennis

Indianapolis Tennis Center
755 University Blvd. • 278-2100

As the site of the annual RCA Championships, one of the favorite tournaments for players on the Men's Professional Tennis tour, the Tennis Center is the crown jewel of the local tennis scene. There are 18 outdoor courts and six in the companion indoor facility. When not in use for competitions, the courts are available to tennis center members and nonmembers alike. Membership entitles you to court reservations, lessons and other amenities not available to nonmembers.

Indy Parks and Recreation
1426 W. 29th St. • 327-0000

In addition to maintaining public tennis facilities, Indy Parks also provides court time to two significant tennis programs — the National Junior Tennis League, which provides young people ages 7 to 18 with tennis instruction, and the Indiana Recreational Tennis Foundation, which offers adult lessons, clinics and league play. Indy Parks maintains public tennis facilities at a number of sites, including:

Broad Ripple Park, 1450 Broad Ripple Avenue, 327-7161, six lighted courts;

Christian Park, 4200 English Avenue, 327-7163, three courts;

Douglass Park, 1425 E. 25th Street, 327-7174, four lighted courts;

Ellenberger Park, 5301 E. St. Clair Street, 327-7176, 12 lighted courts;

Garfield Park, 2450 Shelby Street, 327-7220, six lighted courts;

Fall Creek & 16th Park, Fall Creek Parkway and 16th Street, 267-0532, 10 courts;

Oxford Terrace Park, Rural Avenue and 30th Street, 267-0532, 10 courts;

Perry Park, 451 E. Stop 11 Road, 888-0070, four courts;

Rhodius Park, 1001 S. Belmont Street, 327-7165;

Riverside Park, 2420 E. Riverside Drive, 327-7171, 12 lighted courts;

Sahm Tennis Center, 6801 E. 91st Street, Fishers, 849-8655, five lighted courts;

Tarkington Tennis Center, 45 W. 40th Street, 327-7178, eight lighted courts;

Watkins Park, 2360 Dr. Martin Luther King Jr., 327-7175, four lighted courts.

Indianapolis Racquet Club
8249 Dean Rd. • 849-2531

This facility has indoor and outdoor tennis courts available for use by members and non-members.

Volleyball

Indy Parks maintains sand volleyball courts at the following sites:

Ellenberger Park, 5301 E. St. Clair Street, 327-7176;

Lake Sullivan Sports Complex, 3601 Cold Springs Road, 327-VELO;

Post Road Community Building, 1313 S. Post Road, 327-7214;

Thatcher Park, 4649 W. Vermont Street, 327-7390.

Additionally, a number of the YMCA branches offer indoor volleyball. Contact the branch nearest you for details.

Situated as it is in the center of the state, Indianapolis offers easy access to places of interest throughout Indiana.

Daytrips and Weekend Getaways

While Indianapolis and surrounding environs offer ample recreational, cultural and historical sites and activities, sometimes it's nice to get away for awhile. Thanks to the foresight of Indiana's forefathers, that's easy to do.

Situated as it is in the center of the state, Indianapolis offers easy access to places of interest throughout Indiana. Whether for a day or a weekend, you owe it to yourself to explore what the state has to offer. Here are some suggestions.

Daytrips

U.S. Highway 40 E. Corridor

The Old National Road, which was the first to link Indianapolis with the East Coast, is now U.S. Highway 40. Its eastern segment between Indianapolis and Richmond is rich with things to do, especially for history buffs and antique lovers.

Greenfield

Just a 35-mile jaunt east of Indianapolis, Greenfield was the boyhood home of famed Hoosier poet **James Whitcomb Riley**, author of such enduring schoolroom classics as "Little Orphant Annie" and "When the Frost Is on the Punkin'." His family home at 250 W. Main Street (U.S. Highway 40), 462-8539, has been preserved and is open to visitors.

To see the swimming hole where Riley and his childhood chums passed many a hot sum-mer afternoon, stop by **Riley Memorial Park** at the intersection of U.S. 40 and Apple Street. You'll also find the **Old Log Jail Museum** in this park, a testimony to the ingenuity of pioneer jailers who embedded nails in the log walls to prevent prisoners from sawing their way out.

Woodworking of another sort provides the historical backdrop for **BarnaBe's Cafe, Sodas, & Spirits**, 210 Center Street, 462-2883, in downtown Greenfield. Once a lumber mill, this old-fashioned soda fountain is an inviting stop, complete with stained-glass windows, a tin ceiling and antiques.

Knightstown

This town, just minutes east of Greenfield, is one of several antique centers along U.S. 40. The Knightstown Antique Mall, which houses 75 dealers, is a treasure trove of furniture and collectibles. For information about this mall and other area dealers, call (800) 676-4302.

There are more than 700 antique dealers positioned on or near U.S. 40 between Knightstown and Richmond, which has led to the highway's designation as **"Antique Alley."** (For more details, see our Shopping chapter.)

Also in Knightstown, at 112 W. Carey Street, you'll find the **Carthage, Knightstown & Shirley Railroad**, (800) 676-4302, which offers an excursion train trip through the surrounding countryside. The 10-mile route crosses the Big Blue River, recapturing the scenic pleasures of rail travel. (See our Kidstuff chapter for more information.)

New Castle

Let's start with the obvious: You're in the heart of basketball country. Hoosier Hysteria, that affliction that hits fans on every level from high school hoops to the NBA playoffs, isn't hyperbole. It's a fact of life in Indiana, and nowhere will you find its history chronicled better than in the **Indiana Basketball Hall of Fame**, 408 Trojan Lane, New Castle, (765) 529-1891.

Utilizing multimedia and computers, artifacts and interactive displays (try hitting the winning shot as the clock ticks off the final five seconds of a game), the Hall of Fame celebrates the role that basketball has played in Indiana over the past century. Appropriately enough, right next door is New Castle High School, home of the world's largest high school gymnasium.

To get to the Indiana Basketball Hall of Fame, take U.S. 40 E. to the Ind. Highway 3 Exit. Follow Ind. Highway 3 into New Castle.

Cambridge City

At one time, **Overbeck Pottery** was one of this country's best-known producers of stoneware, and Cambridge City's own Overbeck sisters (there were six of them) were responsible for the artistry of that pottery. The **Museum of Overbeck Pottery**, 33 W. Main Street, (765)478-3335, chronicles the Overbecks' achievements and their contributions to American art history.

Indiana history is the focus of the Huddleston Farmhouse Inn Museum, U.S. 40 W., (765)478-3172. This restored farm focuses on life as it was lived by a 19th-century family and the pioneers who stopped here on their way west along the National Road.

Richmond

In 1966, a gas main explosion ripped through downtown Richmond, killing and injuring scores of people. But out of that tragedy, the city created something special: a nationally acclaimed pedestrians-only district that combines historic buildings, brick walkways, green spaces and flowing fountains. The result, which is known as the **Promenade**, is a wonderful place to while away a couple of hours shopping or merely sitting under a shade tree.

If you time your visit correctly (spring or summer), you can also catch the splendor of the **E.G. Hill Memorial Rose Garden** and the **All American Rose Garden**, both in Glen Miller Park, 2500 National Road E. (U.S. 40), (765)962-1511. The former is a memorial garden planted in honor of Richmond's famed rose specialist, Gurney Hill, who developed a number of popular roses; the latter is an award-winning garden containing 1,600 roses as well as hundreds of other flowers.

At the **Indiana Football Hall of Fame**, 815 N. A Street, (765)966-2235, you'll find displays of football history from Indiana high school, college and professional players. For pigskin lovers, this place makes clear the fact that there's more to sports in Indiana than hoops.

For more information about the Richmond area, contact the **Richmond-Wayne County Convention and Tourism Bureau**, 600 Promenade, (765)935-8687 or (800) 828-8414.

The I-65 S. Corridor

I-65 S. connects Indianapolis with Louisville, Kentucky. However, you don't have to take that two-hour trip to find something to do. In fact, all it takes is a 40-mile drive down to the Edinburgh-Columbus area. That's a daytrip worth taking.

Edinburgh

At the intersection of I-65 and U.S. 31, on the outskirts of this small farming community, you'll find the **Horizon Outlet Center**, (812) 526-9764, home of 65 factory outlet stores, including Eddie Bauer, Spiegel, Levi Strauss and Corning/Revere.

Columbus

Without a doubt, one of the most architecturally significant communities in the world, this town of some 31,000 people contains buildings and sculptures by some of the 20th century's most renowned architects and artists, including such luminaries as I.M. Pei and Henry Moore. The best way to get oriented and educated is to drop by the **Columbus Visitors Center**, 506 Fifth Street, (812) 372-1954. There you'll find maps and audio tapes you can use for self-guided tours of the town's architectural landmarks; you can also call ahead and reserve a place on a guided tour. For advance information, contact Columbus Area Visitor Information, (812) 378-2622.

If wandering around town makes you hungry, drop by **Zaharako's Confectionery**, 329 Washington Street, (812) 379-9329. In this turn-of-the-century landmark, you'll find onyx soda fountains, a genuine Tiffany lamp and a 1908 German pipe organ. And don't forget the homemade ice cream, candy and sandwiches.

Also in the turn-of-the-century vein is the **Columbus Inn**, 445 Fifth Street, (812) 378-4289. Formerly the town's city hall, it's now one of the Midwest's most elegant bed and breakfasts. It contains 30 rooms and five suites, all with cherry furniture (including custom-made beds from France). There are also three daily tea times: morning, afternoon and high.

If you're a mall aficionado, make sure you check out **The Commons** on Washington Street in downtown Columbus. Designed by famed architect Cesar Pelli, The Commons not only contains a variety of stores, but it also houses a wonderful play area for children and a fascinating scrap metal, kinetic sculpture by Jean Tinguely called Chaos I.

Brown County

For rugged, natural beauty, you can't beat Brown County. Less than an hour's drive south of Indianapolis (I-65 south to State Road 46 west), this is hill country. Like a herd of shaggy humped prehistoric creatures, the heavily wooded hills of Brown County spread across the landscape for miles, a feast for the eyes and the heart. It's easy to fall in love with this place.

A lot of people have. And some of them have stayed. Professionals, mostly, from Indianapolis, Columbus and Bloomington. People who can afford to build or buy the lovely log houses in or near Nashville commute to their jobs, but there's not enough of them to make much of a crowd. Brown County is still sparsely populated. There's no real industry here, and the land rolls too much to support

large farms. Tourism is the largest single source of income for many of the county's residents who are painters, potters, silversmiths, antique dealers and restaurant and hotel employees. People live here because they love it, not because they expect to get rich off what amounts to seasonal work. Summer and fall are the busy times, but that doesn't mean that the pace escalates too much. Brown County isn't the fast track, and the folks here like it that way. It's somewhere you can go to slow down, take a walk in the woods, browse through art galleries or sit and contemplate your place in the universe.

On weekends in October, at the height of leaf season, the hills are ablaze in gorgeous colors and people pour in from around the state (and from surrounding states). On peak color weekends expect crowds standing in line at restaurants, jostling through the Nashville streets and jamming the entrance to Brown County State Park.

But even then, if you venture off the main byways onto lesser-traveled county roads, you can enjoy the splendor of the landscape far from the madding crowds. Brown County is a place you owe it to yourself to discover and explore.

Some favorite Brown County spots are:

Nashville: Fifteen miles west of Columbus on State Road 46, you'll find Nashville, home of some 700 residents and 250 restaurants, art galleries and craft and antique shops. The county seat, it's also the surrounding county's cultural and tourism center.

Brown County's reputation as a haven for artists and craftspeople is well-deserved and evident in the fact that throughout Nashville you'll find galleries and shops selling pottery, jewelry, quilts, wood carvings, hand-blown glassware, handmade musical instruments and metal sculptures. In fact, many such shops are housed in a downtown facility known as the **Artists Colony Shops**, 125 S. Van Buren, (812) 988-0600.

If you're wandering the streets looking for a change of pace, stop by the **John Dillinger Historical Museum**, 90 W. Washington Street, (812) 988-1933. Inside you'll find about 95 percent of all the known artifacts from Indiana bad boy Dillinger's life and reign as one of America's most wanted criminals.

For a museum of another sort, try the **Brown County International Blacksmith Museum**, 98 W. Washington Street, (812) 988-8811. The only museum in the world dedicated to the history of blacksmithing, it contains examples of items made by blacksmiths in 20 countries over the past 4,400 years.

If you're hungry, the **Nashville House** at the corner of Main and Van Buren streets, (812) 988-4554, is in order. Here you'll find baked ham and roast turkey, fried chicken and barbecue ribs, sassafras tea and fried biscuits with baked apple butter — food guaranteed to make you clean your plate, all served up in a room filled with antiques. It's country cookin' at its finest.

The **Brown County Playhouse** on S. Van Buren Street, (812) 988-2123, is the state's longest-running professional stock theater. It produces comedies, musicals and mysteries during the summer and fall, using performers from Indiana University's theater and drama department.

Other theaters in the area include the **Nashville Follies Theatre**, 63 E. Washington Street, (812) 988-9007 or (800) 449-SHOW; the **Pine Box Theater**, 168 Jefferson Street, (812) 988-6827; and the **Melchior Marionette Theatre** on the west side of S. Van Buren Street, 535-4853.

Like its larger namesake in Tennessee, Nashville is home to a popular Country music venue. The **Little Nashville Opry**, a mile west on S.R. 46, plays host to a variety of local, regional and national musicians during a season that runs from March through November. For information, call (812) 988-2235.

Brown County State Park, Indiana's largest, is right outside of Nashville on Ind. 46. With 15,000 acres, this park is a splendid place to spend a day hiking (there are 27 miles of roads, hiking and horse trails) and picnicking — unless you're trying to do it in October, during the height of leaf season. The wooded hills ignite in glorious color in the fall, and that attracts throngs of sightseers; estimates range up to 100,000 visitors on some autumn weekends. If you go during that time, expect to wait to get through the gate to the park. But the rest of the year, this area is a wonderful place to visit.

When the snow flies in Brown County, skiers head for **Ski World** on S.R. 46 southwest of Nashville, (812) 988-6638. With eight slopes and trails, a ski shop and a lodge, this place is as close as you can get to Aspen in Indiana. It's also the site of the annual **Brown County Winter Festival** in February. Open year round, Ski World's warm-weather activities include water slides, bumper boats, go-carts, and batting cages.

One of the earliest and best-known artists to live and work in Brown County was T.C. Steele (1847-1926) whose landscapes and other paintings earned him an international reputation. You can visit his home, gardens and studio at the **T.C. Steele State Historical Site**, 1.5 miles south of S.R. 46, near Belmont.

Bean Blossom: This tiny community north of Nashville on S.R. 135 has long been the home of the annual **Bean Blossom Festival**, a summer celebration of bluegrass music organized and hosted by the father of bluegrass, Bill Monroe. You'll also find the **Bill Monroe Bluegrass Hall of Fame** right on S.R. 135. For more information, call (812) 988-6422.

Gnaw Bone: If you've got a taste for the sweeter things in life, stop by this burg 4 miles east of Nashville on S.R. 46 in the fall. That's when sugarcane from area fields is turned into molasses at the **Brown County Sorghum Mill**, which uses a process involving a horse-powered press. Not only does this place sell sorghum but also other Brown County specialities such as persimmon pudding, apple butter and black walnut fudge. The only caveat is that the mill is only open September through November.

For more information on the preceding and other Brown County attractions, contact the **Brown County Convention & Visitors Bureau** at the corner of Main and Van Buren streets in Nashville, (800) 753-3255 or (812) 988-7303.

FYI

Unless otherwise noted, the area code for all phone numbers in this guide is 317.

Bloomington

Less than an hour south of Indianapolis via S.R. 37 (or if you're in Brown County, a few minutes west of Nashville on S.R. 46), you'll

Photo: Jim Mellow

Visitors to Pokagon State Park in northeastern Indiana enjoy the toboggan run.

find Bloomington. As the home of Indiana University, Bloomington is the cultural heart of south Central Indiana. The setting for the movie *Breaking Away*, it's a place where the arts, sciences, sports and humanities intermingle in the classrooms and on the streets. It's a town of blue-collar laborers and white-collar academics. It's busy and bustling yet comfortable and unpretentious. It's a place where pedestrians and bicyclists are as prevalent as drivers.

The place to start, if you're new to town, is the university campus, which was rated one of the five most beautiful in the country by author Thomas Gaines in his book, *The Campus as a Work of Art*. Set amidst 1,860 acres of rolling, wooded land, the university includes numerous buildings constructed from Indiana limestone mined from area quarries. Among the campus' many attractions are the I.M. Pei-designed **Indiana University Art Museum** on E. Seventh Street, (812) 855-5445, which is home to some 30,000 artifacts and works of art, including examples from Greek and Roman, African and Pre-Columbian, Native American and Asian cultures.

Murals by Thomas Hart Benton grace the lobby of the **I.U. Auditorium**, across from the Art Museum on E. Seventh Street, (812) 855-1103. The auditorium plays host to concerts, Broadway shows, dance performances and theatrical productions during its fall-to-spring season.

Also on E. Seventh Street, next to the Auditorium, is the **Lilly Library**, internationally acclaimed for its collection of rare books, manuscripts and musical composition sheets. On permanent display are such rarities as a Gutenberg Bible (printed before 1456), the Coverdale Bible (the first in English, c. 1535) and the original printing plates for John James Audubon's *Birds of America* series. For information about the library's hours and services, call (812) 855-2452.

If you're on campus some Friday night during the school year and suddenly have a ringing sensation in your ears, don't fret. It's just the bells in the **Metz Carillon Tower**, at the intersection of 17th Street and Jordan Avenue, that you're hearing. There are regular Friday evening carillon concerts.

Speaking of music, the **I.U. School of Music** consistently ranks with Julliard in terms of quality and prestige. The importance that the university places on its music program is evident in the **Musical Arts Center** on Jordan Avenue, (812) 855-7433. Inside is a 1,460-seat opera theater, home of the longest opera production season in the western hemisphere. In front of the building, you'll find one of Alexander Calder's sculptures.

Art of another sort — the fine art of basketball — is evident every fall and winter in **Assembly Hall** on 17th Street, (800) 447-4648. Home of the Hoosiers basketball team coached by Bob Knight, Assembly Hall also houses the university's department of intercollegiate athletics and its Athletic Hall of Fame. Next door to Assembly Hall is **Memorial Stadium** where I.U.'s football team does battle every season.

But the I.U. campus isn't all there is to Bloomington. In the downtown district alone you'll find a variety of art galleries, crafts and collectibles shops, bookstores, clothing stores and restaurants. In the center of the 11-block downtown district, surrounded by shady trees and well-kept lawns, is the limestone courthouse, c. 1908. The courthouse grounds are often the site of community events, including lunchtime concerts by local performers.

Just south of the courthouse is **Fountain Square**, an enclosed mall that houses a number of art galleries and speciality shops. Two blocks north, you'll find the **Antique Mall**, a renovated grocery store that is now home to some 100 antique dealers.

But there's more to life than sightseeing and shopping — like food, for instance. And in Bloomington, which attracts students and instructors from around the world, there's something to please every palate.

Feel like Greek food? Try the **Trojan Horse**, 100 E. Kirkwood, (812) 332-1101, for great gyros. Prefer Yugoslavian? Then head for **Janko's Little Zagreb**, 223 W. Sixth Street, (812) 332-0694. How about some sushi? You'll find it at **Ekimae Japanese Restaurant**, 12th and Walnut streets, (812) 334-1661. For fresh fish, oysters and lobster, **Fisherman's Dock,** (812) 336-3474, at 4501 E. Third Street is the place. If it's wood-fired oven pizza you're craving, the only place to go is the **Malibu Grill**, 106 N. Walnut Street, (812) 332-4334.

But without a doubt, the most unexpected restaurant in town is the **Snow Lion**, 113 S. Grant Street, (812) 336-0835. It's one of the only restaurants in the country to specialize in Tibetan food. Owned by Jigme K. Norbu, the nephew of the Dali Lama, the Snow Lion serves up dishes that make use of traditional Tibetan spices and herbs while playing down the Tibetan preference for dishes that utilize such things as liver and fat.

The restaurant is not Bloomington's only link to Tibet. The city is also home to the **Tibetan Cultural Center**, Indiana University Memorial Hall, (mailing address: P.O. Box 2581, Bloomington 47402), (812) 855-8222. The TCC owns 20 acres south of town, on which you'll find the only Tibetan chorten in this country. The chorten is a 35-foot-tall concrete monument that pays tribute to the thousands of Tibetans who have died during the decades of Chinese control of Tibet. The chorten is at 3655 Snoddy Road, and visitors can stop by free of charge.

If you're ready for a break, there's plenty of outdoor recreational opportunities in the area. For swimming, fishing and sailing in a beautiful setting, head for Lake Monroe, a 10,750-acre man-made lake about 10 miles south of Bloomington. While there are fancy resorts offering tennis, golf and accommodations, you don't have to be a guest at one of them to enjoy the lake. Take S.R. 37 to the Harrodsburg Exit, then take Strain Ridge Road east and follow the signs.

If you prefer staying closer to town, check out **Griffy Lake**, a 109-acre, man-made lake that's open only to non-motorized boats. Fishing (with the proper Indiana license) is permitted: Griffy contains largemouth bass, bluegill, redear sunfish and channel catfish. Two hiking trails and a nature trail wind through the 1,200-acre nature preserve that surround the lake. To get to Griffy Lake, take the 45/46 Bypass to Matlock Road, then turn north and follow the road to the lake.

If your idea of a day in the country includes wine, a trip to the **Oliver Winery**, 7 miles north of Bloomington on S.R. 37 (the address is 8024 N. State Road 37), is in order. Indiana's oldest and largest winery, this place is as friendly as it is successful. Tours are free, as is wine tasting. Since its founding in 1971, Oliver Winery has created several award-winning wines and made many friends by holding free concerts and hosting an annual summer festival on its lovely, rolling acres. To learn more, call (812) 876-5800.

If you prefer grain to grapes, drop by the **Brewpub in Lennie's**, 1795 E. Tenth Street, (812) 323-2112, home of The Bloomington Brewing Company, for a taste of hometown brews. Tours are free every Saturday.

Anyone familiar with the resorts in Bloomington will want to turn their daytrip into a weekend getaway. The Point Golf and Tennis Resort, 2250 E. Pointe Road, (800) 824-4040, is a private 400-acre resort that includes golf, tennis, watersports and luxurious condominiums. The PGA Championship golf course, five tennis courts, an Olympic-size pool, a playground and bike rentals offer plenty of recreational possibilities.

FourWinds Resort and Marina, 9301 Fairfax Road, (800) 538-1187, on the shores of Lake Monroe provides a peaceful retreat amid beautiful scenery. You can sail, swim, enjoy PGA Championship golf, tennis, fitness trails and planned activities for kids.

For more information about Bloomington and surrounding Monroe County, contact the **Monroe County Convention & Visitors Bureau**, 2855 N. Walnut Street, (800) 800-0037.

The I-69 Corridor

I-69 starts (or ends, depending on your perspective) at Indianapolis and extends north to Lansing, Michigan. But for daytrip purposes, we'll venture no more than an hour's drive up the road, starting at Anderson.

Anderson

About 30 miles north of Indianapolis, this town is home to several interesting attractions, starting with Mound State Park, 4306 Mounds Road, (765)642-6627. This park offers a glimpse into Indiana's distant past through a number of earthen mounds built by the prehistoric Adena-Hopewell Indians. The largest mound, the Great Mound, is thought to date from 160 B.C. There's also an on-site nature center as well as hiking trails.

History of another kind is evident at the **Historical Military Armor Museum**, 2330 N. Crystal Street, (765)649-8265. This facility is home to the most complete collection of light tanks (from WWI to the present) in the country, all of which have been restored to fully operational condition. (And you were ready to settle for a Hummer!)

Speaking of armored vehicles, Anderson is also the site of the **Indianapolis Colts Training Camp**, on the campus of Anderson University, every July and August. For a modest admission fee, you can watch NFL players up close as they prepare for a new season. For information, call (765)643-5633 or (800) 533-6569.

Also on the university's campus is the **Reardon Auditorium**, 1100 E. Fifth Street, (765)641-4140, home of the **Anderson Symphony Orchestra**. The performance hall is known for its excellent acoustics as well as for its marvelous architecture.

For knockout performance halls, check out the **Paramount Theatre Center**, 1124 Meridian Street, (765)642-1234. Harkening back to the glories of big movie houses, this c. 1920 facility contains both a theater for classic movies and stage productions and a lavish ballroom for special events.

For centuries, Bavarian artisans have handcrafted wax art figures and ornaments. Now, at **Alpine Acres**, 5080 W. S.R. 32, (765)649-4342, you can watch the craft being done and buy the end results. This is one of the few places in the United States where traditional wax art techniques are in use.

Hoosier Park, 4500 Dan Patch Circle,(765) 642-RACE, is Indiana's first pari-mutuel harness and thoroughbred racing track. Even if you're not the wagering type, it's fun to watch the horses run and hard not to get caught up in the excitement.

For more information about the Anderson area, contact the **Anderson/Madison County Visitors & Convention Bureau**, 6335 Scatterfield Road, 643-5633 or (800) 53-ENJOY.

Fairmount

By dying young and becoming a legend, rebel without a cause James Dean put this small farming community, his hometown, on the map. It's the site both of his grave, which is in Park cemetery on County Road 150E,

Source: Jim Davis

Jim Davis, creator of famous comic strip feline Garfield, is a native Hoosier who lives in Muncie.

948-4040, and of the **James Dean Gallery and Gift Shop**, 425 W. Main Street, (800) 748-3326, which contains the world's largest collection of Dean memorabilia. Fairmount, which incidentally was also the childhood home of cartoonist Jim Davis, the creator of "Garfield" who now lives and works in nearby Muncie, is also the site of an annual James Dean festival every September. For information, contact the Fairmount Historical Museum, 203 E. Washington Street, (765)948-4555. To get to Fairmount, take I-69 N. to S.R. 26.

Muncie

Central Indiana isn't a place you'd expect to find tropical splendor, but find it you will in Ball State University's greenhouse, home of the **Wheeler Orchid Collection**. With 7,000 plants, this collection contains more varieties of orchids than any other in the world. You'll find the greenhouse amid a 17-acre botanical wonderland known as **Christy Woods**, which houses an arboretum, gardens and a nature center. For information, contact the university's biology department, (765)285-8820.

As the home of the Ball Corporation, internationally known for its glass canning jars and other containers, Muncie is a glass lover's gold mine. The **Ball Corporation's Glass Collection**, which is on exhibit in the company's headquarters, 345 S. High Street, (765)747-6100, features examples of glass work from canning jars to aerospace items. And **Indiana Glass Outlet**, 1300 Batavia at S.R. 32, (765)284-7046, is a warehouse-size outlet for all sorts of glassware.

The **Minnetrista Cultural Center**, 1200 N. Minnetrista Parkway, (765)282-4848, is a multifaceted facility in which galleries showcase exhibitions devoted to history, art, science and industry. It also hosts concerts and various theme festivals.

For more information on the Muncie area, contact the **Muncie Visitors Bureau**, 425 N. High Street, (765)284-2700 or (800) 568-6862.

Weekend Getaways

While our Daytrips suggestions will get you started exploring Central Indiana, if you've got a whole weekend, you can wander farther afield. The state abounds with historic, scenic and intriguing destinations. Some require a two- or three-hour drive, but if you have a couple of days, even in the middle of the week, gas up the car, throw in an overnight bag and set out to see the state.

Of course, you can always head to Chicago, St. Louis or Cincinnati, three traditional out-of-state getaways, but here we'll direct you to some of our best in-state destinations. We do suggest, of course, that you always call ahead or make reservations; after a day of shopping or sightseeing, no one wants to face a no-vacancy sign. If you decide to check out Cincinnati, be sure to pick up a copy of *The Insiders' Guide® to Cincinnati*.

We've tried to spread out across the state, and if you manage to get away to all eight of our weekend wonders, then you really will have "wandered Indiana." (Wander Indiana was a license plate slogan and state tourism theme some years back.) And while you're wandering, don't hesitate to stop along the way and check out some of our previously mentioned Daytrip destinations.

P.S. Send us a postcard.

Amish Country

One of the country's largest Amish settlements is in northern Indiana. Concentrated in Elkhart and LaGrange counties, this area, called the Crystal Valley, is home to a thriving, growing Amish community that eschews many of today's modern conveniences in favor of a simple life built around God, family and community.

The Amish came to the area in the 1800s, and settlements grew around the towns of Napanee, Middlebury and Shipshewana. The small towns and cities in the area have become well-known for shops that showcase the many Amish-made products: fine furniture, quilts, woven rugs and, perhaps most tempting, delicious food items. In the rural areas, you'll drive past farms still plowed with draft horses; notice how many houses aren't connected to electric lines or telephone poles.

You'll also soon notice the many horse-drawn buggies that travel the roads of Elkhart and LaGrange counties. The LaGrange courthouse still boasts operational hitching posts, and you'll even see buggies hitched outside fast food restaurants. Snap a photo of the buggy if you're so inclined, but don't photograph the Amish people; being photographed violates their religious code and can make them very uncomfortable.

To learn about the Amish lifestyle and see the countryside at the same time, plan to begin in Elkhart (be sure to allow several hours to get there). For the most direct route from Indianapolis, take U.S. Highway 31 north to U.S. 6, then take U.S. 6 about 15 miles to Napanee; travel north on Ind. 19 into Elkhart. At the Elkhart County Visitors Center, just off Ind. 19 near I-80/90, you can pick up the Heritage Trail, a tour route that extends 90 miles through northern Indiana's Amish country.

At the visitors center, a refundable deposit gets you a guidebook, map and cassette tape that lead you off the beaten path and into the countryside via the Heritage Trail. Though the trail can be driven without stops in just more than two hours, you'll want to poke along at your own pace, stopping here and there to browse, shop and dine at some of the finest establishments in the Midwest (keep in mind that some shops and establishments close on Sunday). You'll discover the historic Bonneyville Mill, the oldest continuously operating grist mill in Indiana, where daily from May through October water power still grinds corn, wheat, buckwheat and rye; flours and meals are available for purchase. The grist mill is in Bonneyville Mill County Park, 2.5 miles southeast of Bristol on County Road 131, south of Ind. 120.

In Middlebury, you can park the car and explore the town on foot, stopping in at quilt shops and antique stores before driving out to **Das Dutchman Essenhaus**, 240 U.S. Highway 20, (219) 825-9471. This huge operation serves up some of the area's best food in its warm, comfortable Country Kitchen. Served family style or a la carte, the hearty country fare proves excellent — comfort food at its best. Essenhaus offers delicious roasted chicken, roast beef, homemade noodles, real mashed potatoes. And for goodness' sake, don't forget the pies. Before or after dinner, browse through the nearby shops surrounding the Country Kitchen and the adjacent Country Inn, where you'll find baked goods, homemade candies, housewares, crafts and clothing.

The Heritage Trail continues farther east to Shipshewana, where you can easily spend a whole day. The small town, called Ship-she by the locals, offers shops full of antiques, gifts and handmade crafts as well as inviting restaurants and cafes. But on Tuesdays and Wednesdays from May through October, the town hosts thousands of visitors at the **Shipshewana Auction and Flea Market**. More than 1,000 outdoor vendors sell everything from antique china to designer sunglasses. At the **Antique and Miscellaneous Auction Barn**, visitors bid on one-of-a-kind treasures, and at the livestock auction next door, you can watch as dealers from across the country buy and sell cattle, hogs and the highly regarded Amish draft horses. Across the street from the flea market, the **Menno-Hof Visitors Center**, (219) 768-4117, presents an in-depth look at Amish and Mennonite cultures. The **Morton Street Bed and Breakfast Homes**, (800) 447-6475, three stately homes in the middle of Shipshewana, offer charming accommodations and breakfast at the well-known **Buggy Wheel Restaurant**, which serves up tasty soups and sandwiches. Call (800) 447-6475 for more information.

Back on the Heritage Trail, you'll hit **Goshen**, which offers excellent shopping. The **Old Bag Factory**, a restored 1890s manufacturing complex, includes 17 shops showcasing local artists and artisans. Then in Napanee, known for top-quality cabinetry, you'll find **Amish Acres**, 1600 W. Market Street, Napanee, (800) 800-4942, an 80-acre farm listed on the National Register of Historic Places. Interpreters explain the Amish way of life, and craft demonstrations showcase such traditional skills as quilting, weaving, broom making and baking with an outdoor brick oven. But the place is likely most famous for its threshers' dinners in the **Restaurant Barn**, meals that begin with thick, hearty bean soup and end with fresh shoo-fly pie; the 650-seat restaurant earns high ratings. Visitors can also watch a performance of the Broadway musical *Plain and Fancy*, a comedy about Amish life and love, in the Round Barn Theatre from late April through mid-November. Lodging is available at the adjacent Inn at Amish Acres.

From Napanee, the Heritage Trail heads back north to Wakarusa, host of the annual Maple Syrup Festival in early spring, before leading travelers back to Elkhart.

Lodging is available all across Elkhart and LaGrange counties, and you'll find everything from cozy bed and breakfasts to modern motel chains. Some of the most well-known inns include the **Checkerberry Inn**, (219) 642-4445, whose award-winning restaurant was featured in *Gourmet* magazine; **Coneygar Bed and Breakfast**, (219) 825-5707, a 40-acre horse farm with beautiful views and rolling countryside; the Patchwork Quilt Country Inn, (219) 825-2417, situated on a quiet farm outside Middlebury very close to the Michigan state line; and the **Victorian Guest House**, (219) 773-4383, an elegant 1887 historic home in Napanee.

For more information on Northern Indiana's Amish country, contact the **Elkhart County Convention and Visitors Bureau**, 219 Caravan Drive, Elkhart, 46514, or call (800) 262-8161.

Fort Wayne

While Indiana's Amish country offers excellent shopping, browsing and antiquing, in nearby Fort Wayne visitors will find loads of family-related activities. A two-hour drive up I-69 from Indianapolis brings you to Fort Wayne, Indiana's second-largest city and home to more than 190,000 residents.

Here you'll find plenty of activities to build a weekend around. Arrive early on a Saturday and head to Fort Wayne's **Children's Zoo**, 3411 Sherman Boulevard, (219) 427-6800, a facility ranked among the top 10 in the country and host to more than a half-million visitors each year. Of special note is the world's only endangered species carousel, the African Veldt, the Australian Adventure and the new Indonesian Rain Forest Exhibit and Orangutan Valley. The well-maintained zoo features easily accessible, paved walkways, beautiful landscaping and enough variety to keep youngsters tugging Mom and Dad along to the next exhibit. The zoo opens from late April through mid-October.

Kids will also dig **Science Central**, 1950 N. Clinton Street, (219) 424-2413, a brand-new hands-on interactive science center that opened in the fall of 1995. Designed to make math, science and technology enjoyable and accessible for everyone, Science Central allows kids of all ages the opportunity to create their own earthquake, bend a rainbow, dance across a giant keyboard, walk like an astronaut across a moonscape and peer out from inside a giant bubble. And Kids Central is a special exhibit area designed for youngsters ages 2 through 7.

INSIDERS' TIP

For a real change of scenery, look into local airline American Trans Air's one-day trips. You could be on the beach in the Bahamas before noon but back home in time for the 11 o'clock news.

Another Fort Wayne attraction is the **Lincoln Museum**, 200 E. Berry Street, (219) 455-3864, which houses the world's largest private Lincoln collection. The new 30,000-square-foot downtown facility, which opened in late 1995, includes 11 galleries, four theaters and computerized and hands-on exhibits for all age groups. Call for details.

Sports fans can cheer on the **Class A Wizards** baseball team, the Fury CBA basketball team or the **Komets IHL** hockey team. Call (219) 483-1111 for sports schedules and ticket information.

Those who want to strap on some skates themselves should head out to **Glenbrook Square Mall**, which in addition to more than 170 stores features an indoor ice skating rink. For a more pastoral afternoon, check out the **Lakeside Rose Garden**, 1400 Lake Avenue, (219) 427-6000, where visitors can enjoy more than 2,000 rose bushes representing more than 150 varieties in one of the country's largest rose gardens. Explore a tropical paradise as well as a desert environment at the **Foellinger-Freimann Botanical Conservatory**, 1100 S. Calhoun Street, (219) 427-1267. The **Allen County Public Library**, 900 Webster Street, (219) 424-7241, offers the country's second-largest genealogy department with professional on-site counselors to help you begin or continue a search for your family's roots.

If you visit Fort Wayne in mid-July, plan to attend the **Three Rivers Festival**, a nine-day extravaganza of music, art, sports and entertainment. Call (219) 745-5556 or (219) 424-3900 for details.

But if you're in the area in the winter, you owe it to the kids to head north to **Pokagon State Park**, (219) 833-2012; it's in Steuben County near Angola off I-69. The beautiful area is a natural for outdoor activities year round, but the most exciting attraction is the quarter-mile toboggan track. Yes, you have to tote your rented toboggan uphill, but the trip down on the well-maintained track is one thrilling ride. Pile on the toboggan with the kids, and let it take your breath away. The park and its newly renovated Potawatomi Inn (which features an indoor pool, sauna and whirlpool — tempting after all that tobogganing) is open year round, but the toboggan track only operates from Thanksgiving through February.

On the way to or from Pokagon, stop in Auburn, the DeKalb County seat, and visit the **Auburn Cord Duesenberg Museum**, 1600 S. Wayne Street, (219) 925-1444. Listed on the National Register of Historic Places, the art-deco building, once the 1930s factory headquarters of the Auburn Automobile Company, now houses more than 100 vehicles, from the early "horseless carriage" to luxurious Duesenbergs of the 1930s to sports cars of today. The museum opens every day except Thanksgiving, Christmas and New Year's Day; call for admission fees and group and family rates.

You'll find all the major motel chains in the Fort Wayne area as well as charming bed and breakfast inns. Popular restaurants include the more than a dozen Don Hall's restaurants; try the prime rib at **Don Hall's Factory**, 5811 Coldwater Road, (219) 484-8693, or the steaks, seafood and Cajun cooking at **Don Hall's Old Gas House**, 305 E. Superior Street, (219) 426-3411. Or you can splurge at the highly regarded **Cafe Johnell**, 2529 S. Calhoun Street, (219) 456-1939. Don't miss the fresh fish, duck and prime filets.

For more information, contact the Fort Wayne Convention and Visitors Bureau, 1021 S. Calhoun Street, Fort Wayne, (800) 767-7752.

French Lick

There is really no quick and easy way to reach Orange County, home of basketball legend Larry Bird, from Indianapolis. To get to **French Lick Springs Resort**, 8670 W. State Road 56, (800) 457-4042, a grand old 485-room hotel, you just have to take your time. And maybe that's part of the allure of the place that once hosted the movers and shakers (and, some say, gamblers and gangsters) of the 1920s and '30s.

The scenic route through Brown County and the Hoosier National Forest requires driving the curvy Ind. 135 south from Indianapolis to Salem, then taking Ind. 56 west to Paoli. There you'll pick up U.S. 150 for a while before getting back on 56 for a few miles to French Lick. Or you can head south from Indianapolis on Ind. 37, travel through Bloomington, Bedford, Mitchell and Orleans before hitting Paoli and continue on from there, which will likely prove quicker. Still, set aside several hours for the drive. Regardless of route, the trip through southern Indiana offers beautiful scenery, especially in the fall.

Once in the tiny town of French Lick, it's easy to find the resort. The elegant old hotel dominates the town. Once inside the lobby, it feels as if you've stepped back in time. You can easily imagine the resort in its heyday when people came to relax in the soothing mineral baths the resort was famous for. The "Pluto Water" that bubbled up from a natural spring was thought to have healing properties; you can still relax in a Pluto mineral bath in the hotel's well-known spa. Though the hotel offers a number of spa packages, the treatments, which include massages, a salt rub, a sea mud wrap, facials, manicures and pedicures, can be purchased a la carte as well. They don't come cheap, though. A 60-minute facial will set you back about $50; you can be wrapped in sea mud for about $40. But a 30-minute Pluto mineral bath only costs around $12.

If being plastered with mud isn't your idea of a good time, the resort also offers golf just about year round, and golf packages generally include 36 holes of golf (per night's stay) on the 18-hole **Valley Golf Links** or, for an extra fee, on the Donald Ross-designed Country Club Course. Tennis and ski packages are available (Paoli Peaks is only about 9 miles away), and the resort also schedules holiday weekend packages throughout the year. Prices in 1996 (based on double occupancy) vary from $79 for a basic room to golf getaways at $238 for two to a weekend spa sampler for $299 per person.

While you're in the area, check out the former **West Baden Springs Hotel** in nearby West Baden. There's been considerable interest in restoring the once-magnificent domed building that, until the Houston Astrodome was built, was the largest freestanding domed structure in the country. Historic Landmarks Foundation of Indiana plans to purchase and restore the 380,000-square-foot building. Built in 1902, the hotel featured 708 rooms; its free-standing dome stretches more than 200 feet across and soars 130 feet high.

Also nearby is the huge **Patoka Lake** and the adjacent **Tillery Hill State Recreation Area**, which offers camping, boating, hunting, fishing, a swimming beach, even a Frisbee golf course. For more information, contact the Department of Natural Resources Office of Reservoir Management, 402 W. Washington Street, Room W282, Indianapolis 46204, or call 232-4060. Contact the Patoka Lake office directly at Route 1, Box 290, Birdseye, Indiana 47513, or call (812) 685-2464.

Indiana Dunes

You don't expect surf and sand in Indiana, but just head northwest to Lake Michigan and you'll find both, though it will take you several hours to get there. The Indiana Dunes National Lakeshore stretches across Porter and LaPorte counties, and the area offers visitors from Central Indiana a definite change of scenery. Indeed, the unique area ranks fourth among the entire National Park System for plant diversity, and the land offers considerable diversity as well. Here you can explore bogs, marshes, beaches, an oak forest, the state's largest tract of ancient prairie and the park's largest living sand dune. Bring your camera or sketchbook if you want to capture a bit of the park to take home; all plants, natural and historic features are protected by law — do not disturb them.

Begin your visit at the Dorothy Buell Memorial Visitors Center, on Kemil Road at U.S. Highway 12, 3 miles from Ind. 49, (219) 926-7561; the facility was named for an early crusader who worked to save the dunes from encroaching industrialization. Here you'll find plenty of information about the area, a bookstore and an accessible trail amid wooded dunes. Pick up a map and you can head either east or west along the lake. Go for a swim or just walk along the beach. There's nothing like a beach at sunset to make you forget the road construction and rush-hour gridlock back home. (Keep in mind, however, that some areas within the park are private property; you'll see plenty of posh lakeside homes in the ritzy Beverly Shores area.)

The Mt. Baldy area on the eastern end of the National Lakeshore, which features the parks' largest living sand dune, offers climbing, on marked trails, with the payoff of beautiful vistas; other climbing dunes are located at

West Beach at the opposite end of the lakeshore. But don't be too disappointed if nearby steel mills or the Northern Indiana Public Service Company facilities mar your view. Northwest Indiana is simply an industrialized area. Still, the protected dune areas really are beautiful. Central Beach, Kemil Beach and West Beach are watched by life guards in the summer, and these popular areas hosts thousands of visitors each year.

You'll find campgrounds and picnic sites all along the **National Lakeshore**, 1100 N. Mineral Springs Road, Porter, (219) 926-7561, and in the **Indiana Dunes State Park**, 1600 N. 25 E., Chesterton, (219) 926-1952. The lakeshore area is also home to two historic farms: the Baily Homestead, a newly restored home and historic cemetery with hiking, tours and activities; and the **Chellberg Farm**, a turn-of-the-century active farm with tours, demonstrations and animals. For more information about either homestead, call (219) 926-7561.

Those who prefer shopping bags to beach bags also head to northwest Indiana, but they have Michigan City in mind, home of **Lighthouse Place Outlet Center**, 601 Wabash Street, (219) 879-6506. Shoppers come to hunt for bargains in such outlets as Bennetton, Reebok, Speigel, Florsheim, Corning Revere, Pepperidge Farms and London Fog. The many shops in this unique downtown mall are open from 9 AM to 8 PM Monday through Saturday and from 10 AM to 6 PM Sunday.

Also in Michigan City is the **Old Lighthouse Museum**, (219) 872-6133, the state's first lighthouse, built in 1858 and enlarged in 1904. Keepers lived here until 1940 when the U.S. Coast Guard assumed control of the light. Restored by the Michigan City Historical Society, the lighthouse now houses a museum that showcases the history of lighthouses as well as special exhibits and changing displays. To reach the museum, take I-94 east to U.S. 421; follow that north all the way to Ninth Street. Turn right then immediately left onto Pine Street. Follow Pine as it curves into Washington Park, and watch for signs. The museum is open Tuesday through Sunday from 1 to 4 PM; it closes on Mondays, holidays and for the month of February.

Other area attractions include the **Wizard of Oz Museum** in Chesterton, where you'll find collector dolls, accessories and memorabilia from the movie. The mid-September Wizard of Oz Festival has featured some of the original MGM munchkins as well as other Oz-related celebrities. Call (219) 926-7048 for museum and festival information.

Those who long for a bit of adventure can try the popular sport of parasailing. You take

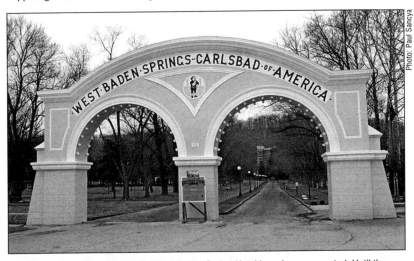

Photo: Paul Sancya

The Arches at the entrance to West Baden Spring Hotel have been renovated. Until the Houston Astrodome was built, the hotel had the world's largest dome of its type.

off and land from the boat that pulls the parachute; participants don't even get wet. Take along a camera or binoculars and enjoy the view as you rise skyward and sail above Lake Michigan. No special skills are required, and just about anyone can parasail: young, old, physically challenged (the minimum weight is 70 pounds; the maximum is 300). If it sounds appealing, contact **Up, Up & Away Parasail**, (800) 655-3880, a business based in nearby New Buffalo, Michigan. You can parasail from mid-May through September every day except Tuesday and on weekends in October — weather permitting, of course.

After a day at the beach, you'll need a rest, and you'll find major motel chains and cozy bed and breakfast inns throughout the area. Try **The Brickstone Bed and Breakfast**, 215 Sixth Street, in Michigan City, (219) 878-1819, an historic dwelling built in 1880 by the First Congregational Church as its parson's home. Or check out **The Inn at Union Pier**, 9708 Berrien Street in Union Pier. Only 200 steps from the beach, this relaxing hostel was selected as one of the area's best small inns by *Chicago Magazine*. For more information on the Dunes region, contact the Porter County Convention, Recreation and Visitor Commission, 800 Indian Boundary Road, Chesterton 46304, or call (219) 926-2255.

Lafayette/ West Lafayette

It only takes about an hour to get to Lafayette from Indianapolis, making this western Indiana city a perfect quick getaway. For a terrific Lafayette-area getaway, plan for mid-October and hit the **Feast of the Hunters' Moon**, visit **Wolf Park** and take in a **Purdue Boilermakers** football game.

One of the best festivals in the area (see the close-up in our Events and Festivals chapter) is the Feast of the Hunters' Moon, a recreation of an 18th-century gathering of French and Native Americans. Usually scheduled in mid-October at Fort Ouiatenon Historic Park, the festival features lots of costumed participants who re-create 18th-century life with everything including food, military drills and Native American dances. For more information,

contact the **Tippecanoe County Historical Association**, 909 South Street, Lafayette, 47901, or call (765)742-8411.

Wolf Park, on Jefferson Street (call 567-2265 for directions), a unique education and research wildlife park, features several packs of wolves and a herd of bison as well as coyotes and foxes. On Wolf Howl Night, held year round on Friday evenings, visitors can watch the wolves when they're most active, learn how the wolves communicate and even join in on some howling themselves. On Sunday afternoons from May through November, the wolves are allowed to interact with a small herd of healthy bison. Though the wolves are not allowed to injure the bison, visitors can watch as the wolves test their prey and as the bison protect themselves and their young against predators. The park opens daily from May through November from 1 to 5 PM; it's closed on holidays. Guided tours are offered on weekends.

A fall weekend in the Lafayette area just wouldn't be complete without Boilermaker football. For some real rivalry, plan to attend a game against Indiana University, Notre Dame or the University of Michigan. Get ready for some energetic cheering; Purdue fans take their football seriously. For ticket information and other details, call the **Purdue University Athletic Ticket Office**, (765)494-3194.

If you don't care to spend Saturday or Sunday in the bleachers, then head downtown and explore Lafayette's historic architecture: the renovated **1882 Tippecanoe County Courthouse** on the town square and the **Greater Lafayette Museum of Art**, 101 S. Ninth Street, (765)742-1128. You'll also find numerous specialty shops, antique stores and the usual bookstores and clothing shops indigenous to college towns as well as a wide variety of restaurants, including everything from pizza joints to prime rib.

Though the area abounds with chain motels, check out the **Purdue University Union Club** at the corner of State and Grant streets, (800) 320-6291, to get a real feel for the campus. **University Inn and Conference Center**, 3001 Northwestern Avenue, (800) 777-9808, is another comfortable near-campus option.

For more information on events and lodging, contact the **Greater Lafayette Convention and Visitors Bureau**, 301 Frontage Road, Lafayette 47905, or call (800) 872-6648.

Madison

This charming river town prospered in the early 1800s as the area's main river port, railway center and supply town for pioneers moving into the Old Northwest Territory. And today, thanks to plenty of preservation work, Madison offers visitors a beautiful downtown, historic architecture and an inviting atmosphere.

Except for the July 4th weekend, when the town hosts the Madison Regatta and the Governor's Cup hydroplane race, when unlimited hydroplanes zoom along the water at 200 mph, Madison is a quiet community. Visitors enjoy walking along the riverfront, prowling through antique shops and exploring the town's 133 blocks that are listed on the National Register of Historic Places.

Start at the **Visitors Center**, open daily at 301 E. Main Street, (800) 559-2956, and watch a video presentation and pick up a map of the area. On a walking tour, you can stop in at the **Early American Trades Museum**, 313 E. First Street, (812) 273-6568, and watch demonstrations by 19th-century wheelwrights, blacksmiths and carpenters. The museum opens weekends from late April through Thanksgiving and on weekdays by appointment.

Madison's downtown area features several restored homes, including the **1849 Shrewsbury-Windle House**, 301 W. First Street, (812) 265-4481, a National Historic Landmark; the **Jeremiah Sullivan House**, 304 W. Second Street, (812) 265-2484, an 1818 mansion that features the only known restored Federal serving kitchen in the country; the **Francis Costigan House**, 408 W. Third Street, (812) 265-2967, home of one of the area's famed architects; and **Dr. William D. Hutchings Office**, 120 W. Third Street, (812) 265-2967, a 19th century doctor's office preserved exactly as used by Dr. Hutchings, a local physician, until his death in 1903. Most homes open daily from April through November.

The most impressive Madison home may be that of **J.F.D. Lanier**, whose loans to the state equipped Union troops during the Civil War. His 1844 home, 511 W. First Street, (812) 265-3526, a Greek Revival mansion and National Historic Landmark, is open daily (except Mondays) year round. The mansion grounds also include a restored 1850s cutting and vegetable garden. A recently received grant will allow for extensive renovation of the historic site.

Though you'll find few chain motels in Madison, the town boasts a variety of charming bed and breakfast inns, including the well-known **Cliff House**, 122 Fairmont Street, (812) 265-5272; the antique-filled **Federal Inn**, 710 E. Main Street, (812) 265-4501; the cozy **Old Madison Bed and Breakfast**, 517 Mulberry Street, (812) 265-6874; and the comfortable **Schussler House Bed and Breakfast**, 514 Jefferson Street, (800) 392-1931. The city also offers lots of cozy cafes and restaurants to choose from clustered in the downtown historic district. You'll find delicious light fare at the **Cinnamon Tea Room**, 302 West Street, (812) 273-2367; and hearty sandwiches and dinners at the **Historic Broadway Hotel and Tavern**, 313 Broadway Street, (812) 265-2346.

For more information about Madison, contact the **Madison Area Convention and Visitors Bureau**, 301 E. Main Street, Madison 47250, or call (800) 559-2956.

FYI

Unless otherwise noted, the area code for all phone numbers in this guide is 317.

Saint Mary-of-the-Woods

Not all getaways need be focused on shopping and sightseeing. Those looking for a more spiritual experience will appreciate the serenity of Saint Mary-of-the-Woods, the mother house of the Sisters of Providence, a Roman Catholic order of women religious, and home to Saint Mary-of-the-Woods College.

To reach this spiritual oasis, take I-70 west to Terre Haute; take Exit 3, and travel north on Darwin Road. Turn right on U.S. Highway 40, left onto U.S. Highway 150, then left again onto Saint Mary's Road. Begin your visit at the

Providence Center, the welcome center for all visitors to Saint Mary-of-the-Woods that includes the National Shrine of Our Lady of Providence, a candlelit area that holds the portrait of Our Lady of Providence; the Heritage Museum and the Hall of Memories, which tells the history of the site through exhibits and photographs; and the Gift Shop, where you'll find unusual gifts, religious items and "sister-made" crafts.

More than 300 sisters live at Saint Mary-of-the-Woods, and visitors are welcome to celebrate Mass with the sisters in the Church of the Immaculate Conception on Monday through Saturday at 11:30 AM and on Sunday at 10 AM. Visitors can also explore the grounds and visit other sacred places: the Blessed Sacrament Chapel; the tiny, outdoor Saint Anne Shell Chapel; and the Our Lady of Lourdes Grotto, a replica of the Lourdes Shrine in France. Other grottoes and shrines can be discovered along wooded paths that crisscross the grounds on guided or self-guided walking tours.

Families are invited to visit the center, and events throughout the year allow parents to share a spiritual experience with their children. Among the annual events are the outdoor family Stations of the Cross during Lent; Vespers in the Church of the Immaculate Conception each Sunday during Lent at 4 PM; an environmental walk in the fall; and a special Children's Sabbath in October at the 10 AM liturgy in the Church of the Immaculate Conception that includes a special reception honoring children.

Another favorite event is the Sisters of Providence Annual Christmas Bazaar and Bake Sale held each fall in mid-November. Items sell quickly, and you'll have to arrive early to purchase the sister-made quilts, needlework, paintings, wall hangings, Christmas ornaments, candy and baked goods at this popular sale.

Breakfast, lunch and dinner are available daily in the O'Shaughnessy Dining Room; a bountiful Sunday Brunch at the Woods, including Belgian waffles, hearty entrees and an extensive dessert selection, is available on Sundays from 10:30 AM until 1:30 PM. Overnight lodging is available at Saint Mary-of-the-Woods College, (812) 535-4141, or at a number of motels located at the intersection of I-70 and U.S. Highway 41.

For more details on tours, pilgrimages and special events, contact the Providence Center, Sisters of Providence, Saint Mary-of-the-Woods, Indiana 47876, or call (812) 535-3131. For additional lodging information, contact the Terre Haute Convention and Visitor Bureau at (812) 234-5555.

Vincennes and New Harmony

Southwestern Indiana abounds with historical sights, so get ready for a history tour when you plan a getaway here. Begin at Vincennes, Indiana's oldest city. But start early, since it'll take you more than two hours to get here from Indianapolis. Though it doesn't look like a direct route, the quickest way is likely I-70 west to Terre Haute, then U.S. Highway 41 south to Vincennes; Ind. 67 also leads from Indianapolis to Vincennes, though you'll be traveling on a two-lane state road and going through lots of small towns along the way.

Vincennes, the former territorial capital was founded in 1732. Situated right on the banks of the Wabash River, it played a pivotal role in the American Revolution. The George Rogers Clark Memorial commemorates a little-known but extremely important battle that took place on February 25, 1779 — the only Revolutionary War battle fought in Indiana. Clark and a small band of men marched more than 180 miles through often-flooded plains to surprise the British Lt. Gov. Henry Hamilton and capture Fort Sackville — and gain control of the Northwest Territory.

A massive granite and marble memorial now marks the location of Fort Sackville. Inside murals depict the fort's capture; listen to the story via headphones as you look around the rotunda, which also boasts a larger-than-life statue of Clark. A bench runs along the wall of the rotunda; sit at one end of it and have a friend sit at the opposite end and whisper to you. Thanks to the room's architecture, you'll hear the whisper as though it were right in your ear.

Near the memorial, other historic sites offer a glimpse into life in the Indiana Territory. Indiana's first church, the **Old Cathedral** (St. Francis Xavier Catholic Church), boasts par-

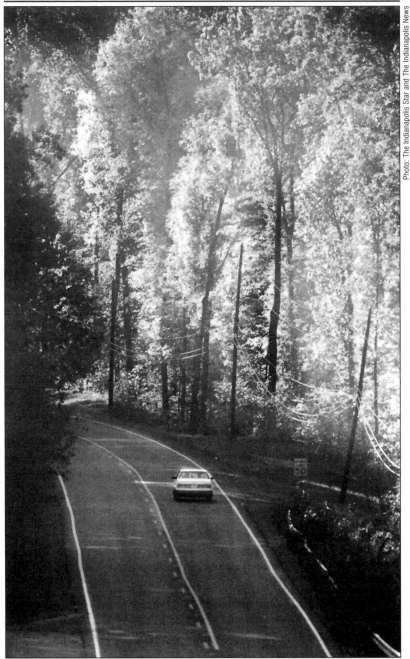

Photo: The Indianapolis Star and The Indianapolis News

Less than an hour's drive south of Indianapolis, scenic Brown County is definitely the place to be during the height of leaf season in October.

ish records dating from 1749; a cemetery includes graves of early settlers and Native Americans. Grouseland, the mansion home of Territorial Gov. William Henry Harrison, later the country's ninth president, is furnished with some period pieces. The home, at 3 W. Scott Street, can be toured daily except for Thanksgiving, Christmas and New Year's Day; an admission fee is charged. A few blocks away is **Vincennes University**, an early Indiana college, as well as the **Elihu Stout Print Shop**, a reproduction of an early print shop, and the **Old Indiana Territory Capitol** building.

For a real taste of Vincennes' historic past, plan a visit during Memorial Day weekend, when the **Spirit of Vincennes Rendezvous** takes place. Offering Revolutionary battle recreations, authentic arts and crafts of the era and plenty of Colonial-style meals to sample, the rendezvous draws more than 30,000 visitors each year. 1996 marked the 20th anniversary of the festival.

Many motels serve Vincennes, and if you arrive Friday evening, you can spend Saturday morning soaking up the history. Try the **Executive Inn Hotel and Convention Center**, a complete travel and entertainment center with a pool, bakery, gift shop and **Dillon's Country Dance Hall**, (800) 457-9154. If camping is your thing, pitch your tent at **Kimmell or Wabash Trails** parks; call (800) 886-6443 for parks information. For more information on the Rendezvous, lodging or Vincennes in general, contact the **Vincennes/Knox County Tourism Commission** at 27, N. Third Street, Vincennes, or call (800) 886-6443.

Unless you're visiting during the Rendezvous, most historic sites in Vincennes can be seen in a morning. Hit the highway after lunch and head south on U.S. 41, then take I-64 west to Ind. 68 at Poseyville. This curvy road will lead you west to **New Harmony**, one of Indiana's most unique villages.

The site of two utopian communities, the tiny town boasts a rich historic legacy. Led by George Rapp, a group of Lutheran Separat-

ists came to the area from Wurttemberg, Germany, in 1804 to create a model community while awaiting the millennium. By 1824, the group had built more than 150 structures. The village was later sold to Robert Owen, a Welsh-born industrialist who hoped to fulfill his own utopian dream of educational and social equality. Joined by a number of creative thinkers of the day, their contributions to education, trade schools and women's suffrage had far-reaching influence.

Today, many of the historic buildings are open for touring; the whole village can be easily explored on foot. Begin a visit at the **Atheneum/Visitors Center** at North and Arthur streets, (812) 682-4474, a surprisingly modern building designed by Richard Meier that includes an auditorium, exhibits and gift shop; tours begin here.

Wander through the town on your own if you prefer. Don't miss the **Roofless Church** on North Street, an interdenominational site, walled but indeed roofless, which was dedicated in 1960 to honor New Harmony's religious heritage. In the **Harmonist Cemetery**, off West Street, 230 members of George Rapp's Harmonie Society are buried in unmarked graves. Woodland Indian burial mounds dating from c. 800 A.D. are also within cemetery walls. The **Labyrinth**, a restored maze of hedges that symbolized the Harmonist's difficult journey toward perfection, can be found about eight blocks south of the stoplight on Ind. 69. See if you can find your way to the middle and back out again. (Don't worry; the hedges are only about shoulder high, and you can easily keep a friend in view.)

The downtown area of New Harmony includes plenty of interesting shops; a number are open on both Saturday and Sunday. The **New Harmony Inn**, 506 N. Street, (812) 682-4491, provides beautiful accommodations furnished with a Shaker-like style and simplicity. Eighteen of the 90 rooms feature fireplaces; many have balconies overlooking the beautiful gardens. Pleasant lodging can also

---

INSIDERS' TIP

Indy Parks sponsors daytrips and longer getaways to nature events around the area. Call 327-0000 for information.

be found at the **Old Rooming House**, 916 Church Street, (812) 682-4724; or the **Raintree Bed and Breakfast**, 503 West Street, (812) 682-5625. While in town, don't miss dinner (and the Shaker lemon pie) at the well-known **Red Geranium Restaurant**, 508 N. Street, (812) 682-4431.

Camping is available at the nearby **Harmonie State Park**. For information, write Route 1, Box 5A, New Harmony, Indiana 47631, or call (812) 682-4821.

For more information on the area contact **Historic New Harmony**, P.O. Box 579, New Harmony 47631, or call (812) 682-4488.

We have so many old, established neighborhoods, not to mention new developments, that discussing them all proves nearly impossible.

Neighborhoods

Indianapolis is often called a city of neighborhoods. On all sides of town are tree-lined streets, well-kept homes and a community spirit that keeps them that way. A renewed appreciation for our central city neighborhoods began in the late 1960s, when the first urban homesteaders started eyeing the Victorian cottages in Lockerbie Square, the mansions of Woodruff Place and the grand old homes of the Old Northside and Herron-Morton. This revitalization continued into less well-known neighborhoods, and now areas such as Cottage Home and Fletcher Place have become havens for renovators as well.

We have so many old, established neighborhoods, not to mention new developments, that discussing them all proves nearly impossible. Here we've tried to spotlight our city's most well-known neighborhoods and up-and-coming districts and to take a look at new developments and exclusive addresses. We'll start downtown and work our way out into the residential areas then move on to the suburbs for an inside look at where Indianapolis lives.

Lockerbie Square

Considered one of the best examples of Victorian renovation in the country, Lockerbie Square exudes charm. This downtown neighborhood of cobblestone streets, restored Victorians, wrought-iron fences and tiny flower gardens was once home to Hoosier poet James Whitcomb Riley; his home has been restored and is open for touring (see our Attractions chapter). Bounded by Michigan, New York, Davidson and East streets, Lockerbie Square attracts professionals who work downtown, members of the arts community and historic preservationists who belong to its active neighborhood association.

Midtown

This area is seeing considerable redevelopment and includes the Canal District, Indiana Avenue and Lockefield Gardens. As recently as the early '80s, the downtown portion of the Central Canal was little more than a weed- and trash-filled ditch. It's now a watery oasis in the middle of the city, with walkways, fountains, bridges and nearby residential and business development such as Canal Overlook and Canal Commons. However, there has been some opposition from longtime residents, some of whom were forced to move to make way for development.

Nearby Indiana Avenue, famous in its heyday for its celebrated jazz joints, has also undergone significant change in recent years. Though still dominated by the Madame Walker Urban Life Center, an excellent example of African- and Egyptian-inspired architecture and a focal point for the African-American community, much of the neighborhood housing stock has been cleared over the years to make room for the growth of IUPUI (the Indianapolis campus of Indiana and Purdue universities). Still, some of the remaining historic retail space has being converted into apartments, as has a former church building. A new apartment complex was completed in 1996, and development continues on a nearby restaurant and retail center.

Renovation is complete on Lockefield Gardens, one of the nation's first public housing complexes. Built in 1936, Lockefield Gardens was a model community of tidy brick buildings and beautiful grounds. As the inner city deteriorated after World War II, however, so did Lockefield Gardens, and it languished as a boarded-up eyesore for years. The 1980s saw renewed interest in living downtown, and

Lockefield Gardens was renovated as apartments.

Chatham Arch

Between Lockerbie and the Old Northside, Chatham Arch has seen a great deal of renovation in the past five to 10 years. Anyone who bought in the mid- to late '80s, when the neighborhood was just being rediscovered, is sitting pretty now. Downtown professionals and young families love the housing stock, which ranges from two-bedroom cottages to larger Italianate homes. The nearby Real Silk factory lofts, with East Coast-style exposed brick and wood floors, also attract professionals and empty-nesters to this popular neighborhood.

Cottage Home

East of Chatham Arch on the other side of interstates 65 and 70, lies the Cottage Home neighborhood, where renovation is less concentrated and where bargains can still be found. The late-19th-century workmen cottages, small two- or three-bedroom frame houses built for early laborers and factory workers, that make up the bulk of this neighborhood's housing stock can prove less daunting for do-it-yourselfers than the more sprawling homes of, say, Herron-Morton. Expect to see continued interest in this ethnically diverse area over the long haul. Those interested in the neighborhood should check out the Cottage Home Block Party, usually scheduled for the third Saturday of September.

Fletcher Place

Platted in 1835, Fletcher Place is one of the city's oldest neighborhoods and was home to many recent immigrants. The neighborhood still holds onto its German, Irish and Italian heritage; Holy Rosary Catholic Church, with its annual Italian Festival, has been a neighborhood mainstay over the years, and Klemm's German Sausage and Meat Market is nearby. This near-south side neighborhood achieved historic designation in the mid-1980s and began to see a corresponding rise in the number of rehabs and renovations of its 19th- and early 20th-century cottages. It's bounded by I-

70 and Lord and East streets and is near Fountain Square, another historic area.

Fountain Square

South of Fletcher Place, Fountain Square is bounded by Shelby Street, English and Keystone avenues and Pleasant Run Parkway. Drive into the neighborhood, and you'll feel like you've entered a small town. Its historic business district (see our Shopping chapter) is home to the Indianapolis Downtown Antique Mall and the Fountain Square Antique Mall, as well as G.C. Murphy, a traditional five-and-dime, and Fountain of Mystery bookstore. The neighborhood association remains concerned with historic preservation of its business district, the area's characteristic 19th-century workmen cottages and the rehabbing of some properties for low-income housing.

University Heights

The homes clustered around the University of Indianapolis, spreading out on the southside from the 1400 block of E. Hanna Avenue, boast the same appeal as Little Flower: The neighborhood is a more affordable alternative to such areas as Irvington and Broad Ripple, which are becoming increasingly more expensive. Savvy buyers can discover tidy bungalows, similar in style to those in ever-popular Broad Ripple, for much less money. The university, with its new Christel DeHaan Fine Arts Center, remains a cultural focal point for the neighborhood.

Homecroft

Originally a small town developed in the early 1920s, the southside neighborhood of Homecroft is bounded by Loretta and Maynard drives and Madison and Orinoco avenues. At the center of the area is the Homecroft Historic District, recently placed on the National Register of Historic Places. This popular and well-maintained neighborhood features a mix of housing stock, including bungalows, Cape Cods and Tudors, plus lots of trees, tidy lawns and antique-style lampposts. Residents enjoy easy highway access and a quick commute to downtown Indianapolis or the towns of

Photo: Randy Baughn

Woodruff Place, platted in 1872, was designed as an exclusive out-of-the-city getaway.

Greenwood and Southport. Perry Township schools serve the area; Southport High School is nearby.

The Old Northside

In the late 1800s, the Old Northside, just north of Downtown, was home to many prominent local residents, and the neighborhood is being renovated according to rigorous historical guidelines. Bounded by I-65, Pennsylvania, Bellfontaine and 16th streets, the area boasts a wide variety of housing stock, from Italianate and Queen Anne mansions to small carpenter cottages. Though the area has been plagued by crime in the past, an active neighborhood association and a renewed emphasis on community policing has helped curb such problems. The Old Northside has attracted a variety of residents, including Gov. Frank O'Bannon and his wife, Judy, who now make their home at the Governor's residence, situated on historic North Meridian Street. The neighborhood also includes a number of low-to middle-income apartment buildings and a string of attached townhomes and condominiums.

Herron-Morton Place

More and more young families are moving into such near-downtown neighborhoods as Herron-Morton, an area bounded by 16th, Pennsylvania and 22nd streets and by Central Avenue. Home to the John Herron School of Art (at least until it moves to the former law school building on the main IUPUI campus) and the annual Talbott Street Art Fair, the neighborhood attracts an eclectic mix of residents who enjoy its artistic atmosphere and offbeat reputation. As with the Old Northside, vigilant neighbors and an increased police presence have worked to reduce crime and prostitution in the area. Despite such realities of urban life, many people can't resist Herron-Morton's grand Victorians, Italianates and Queen Annes, and renovation continues. Check out the neighborhood at Christmastime; a number of the grand old homes are decorated in lights.

Fall Creek Proper

This newly designated neighborhood, near the Center Township government office building on Fall Creek Parkway, is seeing considerable activity. Extensive landscape work along the southern banks of Fall Creek, new home construction and the renovation of existing homes has combined to create interest in this area bordered by Central Avenue, Delaware and 25th streets and Fall Creek. Though surrounding areas need considerable improvement, this little enclave shows lots of potential.

Brendonwood

Fall Creek also borders this neighborhood. Brendonwood, however, is one of the city's most private and parklike areas and one of the most well-designed. Platted in 1917, the 350-acre area was designed with winding, wooded streets by George Kessler (namesake of Kessler Boulevard), a St. Louis city planner. Included in the neighborhood are a nine-hole golf course, a swimming pool and tennis courts. The large, traditional homes are a mix of Colonial and Tudor designs with some sprawling ranch houses scattered through the neighborhood. The area is defined by Fall Creek on the north and west, Brendon Forest Drive on the east and 56th Street to the south. Nearby Kessler Boulevard provides easy crosstown access.

Woodruff Place

Platted by James Woodruff in 1872 as an exclusive out-of-the-city getaway, this neighborhood was inspired by the residential parks of Italy and France and may be the setting for Booth Tarkington's *The Magnificent Ambersons*. The self-contained area features statuary, grassy esplanades and water fountains, which the neighborhood association has worked hard over the years to restore. Though some remain split up into apartments, many of the grand old mansions have been restored. Unfortunately, the surrounding area isn't nearly as grand. Woodruff Place is bounded by 10th, Michigan and Tecumseh streets and by West Drive; the Indiana Women's Prison is a nearby

neighbor. Still, the self-contained and well-defined neighborhood proves quite appealing to those who like the beautiful old homes coupled with the convenience of nearby Downtown attractions. Check out the annual Woodruff Place Flea Market in early June (see our Festivals and Events chapter) for plenty of antiques and other bargains.

Irvington

This historic east-side neighborhood was once home to Butler University and retains something of a literary ambiance; it's home to one of the city's oldest and most active book study groups. The expansive Ellenberger Park, with its pool, ice skating rink and sledding hills, also lies within the neighborhood. The large neighborhood boasts a wide variety of housing styles, from 1800s mansions to bungalows and farm houses. Residents count the resulting mix of socioeconomic levels and ethnic backgrounds a plus; they enjoy Irvington's diversity. Still, they wish for more new business development along the Washington Street corridor, where the artsy Irving theater is located, and wonder how the closing of Howe High School will affect the area that is bordered by 10th Street, Brookville Road and Edmondson and Kitley avenues.

Little Flower

As neighborhoods gain in popularity, naturally they go up in price. Irvington, for example, has long been seen as a more affordable alternative to Meridian-Kessler. But with Irvington's increasing popularity, those who like its style but can't afford its price tag have turned to the Little Flower area. Named for Little Flower Catholic Church and bounded by 10th and 16th streets and Emerson and Shadeland avenues, the area is a transitional neighborhood — young couples and families are buying from older residents.

Chapel Hill

On the west side, the Chapel Hill area is also home to plenty of young families. They like the traditional homes and subdivisions in this large area that centers around 10th Street and I-465. You'll find traditional suburban ranch homes, split-levels and frame homes in the older areas. Residents enjoy plenty of shopping and dining options and easy interstate access. Basketball and marching band powerhouse Ben Davis High School is nearby.

Watson Road

In the central city, just south of 38th Street on either side of College Avenue, Watson Road features a surprising array of large traditional-style stone and brick homes with well-maintained lawns and shady sidewalks. You'll find some bargains here in this eclectic, diverse neighborhood, which boasts an offbeat Grateful Dead-inspired shop, a Christian tea house and a handy Walgreens drugstore. Nearby housing stock, however, is a mixed bag: some good, some not-so-good.

Meridian-Kessler

This large and diverse neighborhood, bounded by 38th and Meridian streets, Winthrop Avenue and Kessler Boulevard, includes lavishly restored Meridian Street mansions, beautiful Tudors and Colonials and modest two-story homes in need of a lot of work. But this range in housing stock means diversity in neighbors; there's a mix of socioeconomic levels and ethnic backgrounds similar to that of Irvington and Butler-Tarkington. A small retail district at 49th and Pennsylvania offers a drugstore, a coffee shop, a hardware store, a vegetarian cafe and antique and gift shops. Young families who like Meridian-Kessler's unique shops and restaurants — but who can't afford the more established areas — are moving into the southeast section of this neighborhood and rehabbing. The active neighborhood association is putting a lot of effort into revitalizing the College Avenue corridor, and a new branch library is planned for the corner of

College and 42nd Street (see the entry on South Broad Ripple).

Butler-Tarkington

A lot of people with their hearts set on brick Tudors with leaded glass windows start here. And they often find what they're looking for. The neighborhood, bordered by 38th and Meridian streets and by Westfield Boulevard and the Central Canal, offers beautifully restored homes in the Butler University area and some in the southwest area still in need of renovation. Butler remains one of this diverse neighborhood's strongest selling points; Clowes Hall provides superb cultural entertainment within walking distance. And a small but vibrant shopping district at 56th and Illinois, with restaurants, a grocery store, meat market, ice cream shop and upscale specialty stores, adds convenience. An organization called the Quad Parish, made up of the four churches clustered around 46th and Illinois streets, serves the area with a neighborhood outreach program.

Meridian Street

Historic North Meridian Street, listed on the National Register of Historic Places, stretches from 38th to 56th street and is lined with mansions built by the local movers and shakers of the early 1900s. Federal-, colonial- and Tudor-style homes boast meticulously landscaped yards. The street is especially beautiful in the spring, and St. Margaret's Hospital Guild often chooses a Meridian Street mansion for its May Decorators' Show House. The governor's residence is here as is the former home of Pulitzer Prize-winner Booth Tarkington. Sightseers enjoy walking through the area and admiring the 1920s-era architecture. Christmas lighting displays make Meridian Street a popular holiday drive. Though it does perhaps lack privacy (one resident notes that you can't really use those beautiful front yards), Meridian Street remains one of the city's most highly prized addresses.

Broad Ripple

One of the city's favorite neighborhoods, Broad Ripple, where cars stop as the many ducks and geese waddle through traffic, is active, vibrant and probably the most interesting. The streets are lined with the much-coveted Broad Ripple bungalows, and residents tend to keep the area spiffy. That's not always an easy task when thousands of people walk through your neighborhood every weekend on their way to the many bars, restaurants, art galleries and specialty shops. Still, you can't beat the amenities: In addition to its many galleries and boutiques, Broad Ripple boasts a convenient drugstore, grocery, hardware store, natural foods store, a superb used book shop, a comedy club and enough restaurants — Italian, Greek, Indian — to please just about any taste. Plus it's got the Vogue and the Patio, primo live music venues. No wonder it's so popular.

South Broad Ripple

Actually the southeastern corner of Meridian-Kessler, this area, dubbed "SoBro" by those in the real estate biz, has become increasingly popular as prices rise in ultra-trendy Broad Ripple. The SoBro area includes Atlas Supermarket (one of the city's best gourmet groceries), the well-known Red Key and Bulldog taverns, two coffee shops, a jazz joint and Moe & Johnny's restaurant, a great family place that serves hearty home cooking. Those who want to be near the shopping and nightlife, but who can't afford Broad Ripple's prices, look here and find well-made homes with the same amenities (hardwood floors, fireplaces, nice yards with lots of trees) for considerably less. Many do, however, require considerably more work. The area, loosely bounded by 42nd and 54th streets and College and Winthrop avenues, has seen significant redevelopment along the College corridor, where a new police precinct, fire station and a planned branch library expansion have spurred residential renovation.

Meridian Hills

Situated north of Broad Ripple along Meridian Street, the separate town of Meridian Hills (an "included" town under Unigov), where a three-member town board handles neighborhood concerns, boasts more wooded terrain than you'd expect in the city plus the convenient shopping and amenities of Broad Ripple and Nora. Home to more than 1,800 residents, Meridian Hills remains very stable, with little new development — and residents like it that way.

Williams Creek

Some real estate professionals peg Williams Creek (another separate "included" town north of Meridian Hills) as one of the most prestigious addresses within the city, much more private than historic Meridian Street, for example, but with similar cachet. The large, traditional homes are situated on expansive lots with beautiful rolling, wooded terrain, and the neighborhood proves so popular that it's not unusual for homes to stay in the same family for generations.

Nora

This area along 86th Street between Meridian Street and Keystone Avenue, offers plenty of shopping and dining options. The nearby residential areas, just north and south of 86th Street between Meridian Street and Keystone Avenue, boast lots of ranch and traditional-style brick and Colonial homes as well as a few farmhouses. Washington Township's mega high school, North Central, lies within the neighborhood, as does the Jordan YMCA. Neighbors also appreciate the convenience of a branch library, and the Krispy Kreme doughnut shop sees plenty of early morning traffic.

Sunset Lane

Often referred to as the city's second Meridian Street, Sunset Lane was once home to members of the Eli Lilly family of pharmaceutical fame and so earned its nickname, "Pill Hill." A private drive that extends north and

Photo: Randy Baughn

Ducks are part of the scenery in Broad Ripple.

south of Kessler Boulevard toward White River, Sunset Lane boasts homes similar to the Meridian Street mansions with the privacy that Meridian Street lacks. But you won't see the "for sale" signs that are common along Meridian; homes here rarely change hands.

"Excluded" Towns

Many people who live in Greater Indianapolis make their home in our surrounding communities that lie geographically within the county but remain curiously separate. When Unigov consolidated Indianapolis and Marion County, four towns chose not to be included and earned the designation "excluded towns." It may be tough to tell where Indianapolis ends and Speedway, Lawrence, Southport or Beech Grove begin, but these towns are separate entities, each with its own personality. Those who live on S. Emerson Avenue will likely think of themselves as Beech Grove, rather than Indianapolis, residents; someone whose child plays basketball for the Speedway Spark Plugs may feel more involved in that west-side community than with Greater Indianapolis. In general, these communities retain a small-town look and feel, and residents prize this atmosphere.

Speedway

Speedway has the look of a small town with blocks of brick bungalows and Cape Cods, but it's only about 6 miles from downtown. It's bounded by 10th and 30th streets and by I-465 and the Indianapolis Motor Speedway. There are considerable shopping and dining possibilities nearby, but the neighborhoods remain rather quiet. Except, of course, in May when traffic becomes heavy all over the west side, and especially in Speedway. The track now hosts the Brickyard 400 in August as well, so the neighborhood sees increased traffic in late summer too.

Lawrence

Fort Benjamin Harrison once dominated the Lawrence area, but the Army base is now in the process of closing. The closure will certainly affect Lawrence, but a new state park and new housing developments will be created in the base area, which boasts an excellent golf course. Within the large community you'll find traditional well-established neighborhoods (Old Lawrence) and new subdivisions and planned developments (new Lawrence), as well as plenty of shopping and dining. The former officers' club is now The Garrison restaurant; you'll also find a number of Korean restaurants in the area. Lawrence stretches from the base on Post Road to the southern edge of the Geist Reservoir area within Lawrence Township. The well-regarded Lawrence Township school system serves the area.

Beech Grove

Southeast of downtown lies the community of Beech Grove. Dominated by the Conrail railyard, where down-at-the-heel passenger cars come to get refurbished, the town also boasts plenty of comfortable older neighborhoods full of tidy bungalows. Beech Grove is bordered by I-465 and the Conrail line and by Southern and Perkins avenues. A major facility is the Indianapolis Regional Heart Center at St. Francis Hospital.

Southport

Southport, another southside community, has seen considerable residential development in recent years. You'll find new housing subdivisions, traditional homes and bungalows in the older areas. Easy highway access makes this community popular among commuters who work downtown or in Greenwood. Situated between Indianapolis and Greenwood east of Madison Avenue along Southport Road, the town boasts plenty of nearby shopping.

Exclusive Addresses

Development continues all around Indianapolis, and some of the hottest areas lie just north of the central city. Washington Township remains so popular — but so established — that people often buy the more modest ranch-style houses scattered through the area, knock them down and build more elaborate homes. Developments such as Cedar Knolls, Old Pickwick, Williamshire and Somerset Hills, situated along or around Spring Mill and Ditch roads from 82nd to about 96th streets, offer convenience coupled with privacy — but for a price. Townships farther out, such as Pike, on the northwest side, see an incredible amount of new construction. With fewer traffic hassles than the north side and beautiful wooded terrain, Pike is attracting more and more upscale homeowners to such communities as West 86th.

Also on the northwest side, Eagle Creek Reservoir offers beautiful terrain and waterfront views. The Bay Landing community, for example, boasts high-end homes with boat docks on the reservoir. Morse Reservoir, near Noblesville, also provides enticing waterfront homes, with the accompanying price tags.

Homes at Geist Reservoir, northeast of Indianapolis, also come with hefty mortgages. Some of the most exclusive include Admiral's Point, Diamond Point and Feather Cove, beautiful developments that have many professionals longing for an address on the water.

Just north of Indianapolis, Hamilton County's Clay Township and the city of Carmel continue to expand, with much of the growth concentrated in the high-end communities west of Meridian Street along Spring Mill Road. With such names as Bridelbourne, Coppergate, Laurelwood and Winterwood, these developments have some of the highest price tags in the city.

In Boone County, northwest of Indianapolis, the Zionsville area continues to entice upscale homeowners with the wooded, rolling terrain of such communities as Austin Oaks, which includes the Wintersprings, Autumnwood and Summerglen developments. The village of Zionsville itself, with its bricked streets and abundant specialty shops and restaurants, also charms buyers with its tidy cottages, Victorians and Colonials.

Northern Johnson County also offers its share of custom housing and executive homes, especially in the Greenwood area, though prices run a bit lower than in comparable northside communities. The convenience of the south side, with its abundant shopping and easy highway access, remains a strong draw.

Par for the Course

A new twist on luxury living has been the development of golf course communities. A mainstay of Sun Belt areas, golf course housing developments have become increasingly popular across the Midwest in recent years, and Indianapolis is seeing more and more interest in these specialized communities. Some home buyers especially like the "master plan" concept, in which future growth is completely mapped out from the start. The golf course at Valle Vista in Greenwood, one of the city's oldest, was designed in the early 1970s by the late Bob Simmons, who also designed the course at Prestwick. The legendary Pete Dye created the course at Morse Reservoir's North Harbour as well as the one at Maple Creek. One of the city's newest courses (and likely the state's largest golf course development), Hamilton Proper incorporates some of Hamilton County's federally protected wetlands into the Arthur Hills-designed course.

With an increase in the number of seniors in the community has come an increase in the number and variety of senior services.

Retirement and Senior Services

As is true in other metropolitan areas throughout the country, Indianapolis has a rapidly expanding senior population. And a large percentage of those seniors are choosing to stay here after retirement rather than move to Florida or Arizona as so many retirees did in the past.

With an increase in the number of seniors in the community has come an increase in the number and variety of senior services. From retirement communities, elder-law attorneys and geriatric healthcare programs to job referral services, insurance counselors and transportation providers, area agencies and organizations are offering more (and more sophisticated) services for older adults than ever before.

Where to Start

CIOCA The Access Network
(Senior Information and Assistance Center)
4755 Kingsway Dr., Ste. 333 • 254-3660, (800) 432-2422, TTY 254-5497

Formerly known as the Central Indiana Council on Aging, CIOCA The Access Network is the central clearinghouse for information about and access to senior services. The largest of Indiana's agencies on aging, CIOCA offers services to residents of Marion, Boone, Hamilton, Hancock, Hendricks, Johnson, Morgan and Shelby counties.

The organization's network of services includes adult day care, legislative advocacy on issues affecting older adults, in-home care, benefits counseling, care management, community education, congregate and home-delivered meals, employment, health promotion, home maintenance and modification, legal assistance, personal emergency response, transportation and volunteer development and opportunities.

If you're looking for help or information, CIOCA's Senior Information and Assistance Center is the place to start. For a handy reference, ask for the organization's free resource guide *Take Care of Yourself*, which includes a thorough listing of services and programs throughout the community.

Older Adult Service and Information System (OASIS)
6101 N. Keystone Ave. • 253-1951, 895-9976

Sponsored by L.S. Ayres and Methodist Hospital, OASIS offers a variety of programs designed to give adults 55 and older opportunities to go on learning, stay active and healthy, travel and volunteer throughout the community.

United Senior Action
1211 S. Hiatt St. • 634-0872

In operation since 1979, United Senior Action (USA) is an advocacy group that focuses its efforts on legislative and non-legislative matters that affect seniors. Among USA's concerns are promoting home care rather than nursing-home care for the elderly, attaining fair utility rates for seniors, limiting prescription drug prices, combatting abuse and neglect of seniors, and protecting and expanding consumer rights in such areas as healthcare and health insurance. USA memberships cost $8 a year for one person, $10 for a couple.

For information on senior services in surrounding counties, contact:

Boone County Senior Service, 403 N. Lebanon Street, Lebanon, 852-4711;

Hamilton County Senior Services, 1051 N. 10th Street, Noblesville, 773-4322;

Hancock County Senior Services, 120 W. McKenzie Road, Ste. D, Greenfield, 462-3758;

Hendricks County Senior Services, 970 E. Main Street, Danville, 745-4303;

Johnson County Senior Services, 901 N. Main Street, Franklin, 736-7736;

Morgan County Coordinated Aging Services, 1139 E. Morgan Street, Martinsville, 342-3007;

Shelby County Senior Services, 120 W. Washington Street, Shelbyville, 398-0127.

Senior Centers

Offering a range of activities and services, senior centers provide older adults with access to educational opportunities, health and fitness programs, social and cultural events, and assistance negotiating the sometimes baffling array of senior-oriented legal, medical and financial programs and issues. With some 30 senior centers in Indianapolis proper as well as dozens of others throughout Central Indiana, providing a comprehensive list isn't feasible. What follows are profiles of a few centers. For information on others, contact CIOCA The Access Network.

Christamore House
502 N. Tremont Ave. • 635-7211

This is one of the city's oldest African-American community centers, long known for its activism and advocacy efforts on behalf of its west-side neighborhood. The senior program at Christamore is open to people 55 and older and includes a multitude of activities such as daily fitness classes, a hot lunch program,

arts and crafts, sewing and quilting classes, Bible study classes and shopping trips. There's also a seniors club that meets on a monthly basis; dues are $5 per year.

Indianapolis Senior Citizens Center
708 E. Michigan St. • 263-6272

The largest senior center in the city, the Indianapolis Senior Citizens Center (ISCC) provides its members access to such services and programs as daily meals, health education, fitness activities (swimming, yoga, walking, etc.), educational classes (nature study, Indiana history, Bible study, dance lessons, foreign language instruction, etc.), social activities (bridge, dances, concerts, holiday parties, etc.), assistance with legal, tax and insurance matters and volunteer opportunities. Membership is open to anyone older than 60; dues are $12 per year.

Jewish Senior Services
Jewish Community Center,
6701 Hoover Rd. • 251-9467

Jewish Senior Services provides an array of programs for seniors including counseling, home visits, escorted transportation, assistance with insurance matters, information about and referral to other senior service providers and a national referral network for elder caregivers. In addition, the Jewish Community Center's roster of programs is open to seniors. Seniors can enjoy fitness activities (for more on these, see our Parks and Recreation chapter), cultural and social activities and volunteer opportunities. Membership to the center is open to Jewish and non-Jewish individuals and families. Call for information.

John H. Boner Community Center
2236 E. 10th St. • 633-8230

At this near east-side center, area residents 60 and older can take part in a variety of activities including a wellness program, which offers weekly blood pressure screenings, exercise classes, a hot lunch program, regular Social Security and Medicare updates and discussions

---

INSIDERS' TIP

Museums in Indianapolis welcome and actively recruit older adult volunteers.

Photo: Randy Baughn

The state capitol was carefully planned and designed before construction began in the early 1800s.

on current events. There are also twice-monthly trips to the grocery store (transportation is provided free of charge) and monthly trips to restaurants. Recreational activities include games (bingo and euchre), ceramics classes and choral music performances by the resident troupe the Jolly Off-Notes. The center also has an on-site adult daycare program.

Lawrence Senior Activities
5301 N. Franklin Rd. • 549-4815

Operated by the Lawrence Parks Department, this program is open to Lawrence area residents 55 and older. Among the activities available are ceramics classes, exercise classes, line dancing and a wellness program. There are also occasional shopping trips and trips to community events. Dining out is also a popular group activity.

Salvation Army Senior Center
234 E. Michigan St. • 637-2764

This family-style center, which is open to anyone 60 or older, offers both hot breakfast and lunch programs daily, as well as a variety of classes including exercise, ceramics, church history, current events and poetry. There are also weekly grocery shopping trips, monthly blood pressure and cancer screenings and quarterly eye exams. Guest speakers are featured regularly, talking about issues such as crime, healthcare and Social Security.

Retirement Communities

For older adults who want to live on their own yet want the security of knowing that help is close by if they need it, a retirement community may be a good choice. Many retirement communities offer older adults three types of living options: independent, assisted and nursing care. Residents choose one option or another as their needs change.

Of course, such security comes at a price. While some retirement communities operate much like apartment communities, offering rental contracts, others require a hefty front-end payment to guarantee lifetime care. The following list of some area retirement communities offers you a place to start if you're interested in learning more, but as with any decision having legal and financial ramifications, make sure you understand all the terms and conditions before signing anything (especially a check).

The Altenheim Community
3525 E. Hanna Ave. • 788-4261

This nonprofit community offers residential and assisted-living options and an on-site, licensed healthcare facility. Living quarters include studio or one-bedroom apartments; the monthly rental fee includes utilities, laundry services, housekeeping, an emergency call system, three meals a day and transportation services.

American Village
2026 E. 54th St. • 251-5580

Set on 47 acres with a lake, this community offers independent-living cottages and apartments, assisted-living apartments and an on-site licensed healthcare center. Among the amenities are transportation services, cleaning and laundry services, meals, utilities, cable TV and garage/carports.

Atrium Village
2636 N. Mitthoeffer Rd. • 899-8050

This is an independent-living community, consisting of two-bedroom apartments. While utilities are included in the monthly rental fee, other amenities, such as cleaning, laundry, transportation and cable TV, cost extra.

Clearwater Commons
4519 E. 82nd St. • 849-2244

This north-side community offers both independent and assisted-living options in either studio or one-bedroom apartments. All utilities and meals are provided, as are cleaning, laundry, cable TV and an emergency call system.

Coventry Village
8400 Clearvista Pl. • 845-0464

The services here ranges from independent living to on-site, licensed intermediate and skilled nursing facilities.

All meals are provided, as well as utilities and cable TV. Transportation services are provided, as is an emergency call system.

Crestwood Village Apartments
North: 9191 Garrison Dr., Carmel • 844-9994
South: 8801 Madison Ave. • 888-7973
East: 1423 N. Edmondson Ave. • 356-4173
West: 215 Welcome Way Blvd. • 271-6475

These four apartment communities, which are limited to people 55 and older, offer studio, one- and two-bedroom units for active, independent seniors. The monthly rent includes all utilities, transportation services and recreational opportunities. Other services, such as laundry, housekeeping, telephone and cable TV are available for an extra fee.

The Forum at the Crossing
8505 Woodfield Crossing Blvd. • 257-7406

This upscale, north-side community offers the full range of service levels, independent and assisted living and on-site, licensed healthcare. Among the amenities are housekeeping and laundry services, restaurant-style dining and social, cultural and recreational programs.

Harrison at Eagle Valley
3060 Valley Farms Rd. • 291-1112

Primarily for individuals capable of independent living, this community does offer assisted-living services. There are studio, one- and two-bedroom apartments available on a yearly lease or a month-to-month basis, with utilities and cable TV included in the deal. Housekeeping and laundry services, 24-hour security, transportation and restaurant-style dining are among the amenities.

The Home Place Apartments
6734 Millside Dr. • 856-3295

This apartment community is independent-living only, with studio, one- or two-bedroom units available on a yearly lease basis. Utilities and cable TV are included in the monthly fee, as is an emergency call system and garage facilities.

Hoosier Village Retirement Center
5300 W. 96th St. • 873-3349

This community set on 150 wooded acres on the far north side is designed for independent living in cottages, duplexes or apartments, assisted living in apartments or on-site care in licensed healthcare facilities. Residents have the option of paying for a continuing-care contract up front or choosing a monthly payment plan. Among the services provided are all

INSIDERS' TIP

The Senior Information and Assistance Center, 254-3660, can help you find out anything you need to know about the programs and services available to older adults in Central Indiana.

meals, cleaning and laundry services, transportation and cable TV.

Indianapolis Retirement Home
1731 N. Capitol Ave. • 924-5839

This facility, which is across the street from Methodist Hospital, offers three levels of service: independent living, supportive assistance and healthcare. Studio apartments are rented on a monthly basis, and the fee includes all meals, utilities, telephone, cleaning, laundry and cable TV.

Marquette Manor
8140 Township Line Rd. • 875-9700

In this northwest-side community, residents have a choice of independent living facilities: studio, one- or two-bedroom apartments or an on-site, licensed healthcare center. The only entry option is a life contract. But once admitted, almost everything is included, meals, cleaning and laundry, utilities, cable TV, an emergency call system and transportation.

Morningside at College Park
8810 Colby Blvd. • 872-4567

At this independent-living community just west of St. Vincent Hospital, residents can choose among studio, one- or two-bedroom apartments on a yearly lease basis. Rent includes all utilities, telephone, cable TV, cleaning and laundry services, transportation and an emergency call system.

Oakleaf Village
8480 Craig St. • 842-6564

In the Castleton area, not far from Community Hospital North, this independent- and supportive-living community leases studio, one- and two-bedroom apartments on a yearly basis. Included in the monthly fee are all utilities, cleaning services and an emergency call system. A flexible meal plan and transportation services are available.

Robin Run
5354 W. 62nd St. • 293-5500

Situated on a 70-acre campus on the northwest side, this community offers garden homes and apartments on a continuing care contract basis. Primarily an independent-living community, it does have a skilled nursing center on-

site. Among the services provided are all meals, utilities, cleaning and laundry.

Roland's Retirement Club
6038 W. 25th St. • 291-5228

This independent- and assisted-living apartment community in Speedway offers studio and one-bedroom units on a monthly basis.

Included in the rental fee are all utilities, cleaning and laundry services and meals. Also on-site are a beauty and barber shop; transportation is provided for weekly shopping excursions.

Westminster Village North
11050 Presbyterian Dr. • 823-6841

Set on 57 acres on the far northeast side, this community offers both cottages and apartments for independent and assisted living. Medicare-certified intermediate and skilled nursing care are available. Payment options range from a life contract to a month-by-month plan. In addition to three meals a day and an emergency call system, residents enjoy paid utilities and telephone, cleaning and laundry services, transportation and cable TV.

Westside Retirement Village Inc.
8616 W. 10th St. • 271-1020

Offering independent- and assisted-living in studio, one- or two-bedroom apartments, this community also has a licensed healthcare facility on-site. Included in the month-to-month rental arrangement are all utilities and cleaning and laundry services. Residents' safety is protected by an emergency call system. Among the amenities are transportation and recreational activities.

Nursing Homes

For individuals in need of routine, ongoing care, an alternative to retirement-community living is a nursing home. In Indiana, anyone seeking entry to a nursing home must first undergo a pre-admission screening process to evaluate his/her physical condition and to verify the need for nursing-home care. Those who can afford to pay for all their own nursing-home care can opt not to go through the screening process, but by opting out of pre-admission screening, a person risks being declared ineligible for Medicaid coverage of their nursing-home expenses for the first year after admission.

While there is no consumer organization that currently surveys and rates nursing home facilities, the following organizations do compile lists of licensed facilities and provide guidelines for choosing a nursing home:

Indiana State Department of Health, 1330 W. Michigan Street, 383-6442;

Indiana Association of Homes for the Aging, 9011 N. Meridian Street, 581-1115;

Indiana Health Care Association, One N. Capitol Avenue, Ste. 1115, 636-6406.

With more than 125 nursing homes in the Greater Indianapolis area, space prevents a complete listing. What follows is a sampling of facilities.

Alpha Home
2640 Cold Spring Rd. • 923-1518

Situated on a wooded site on the near-west side, Alpha Home offers intermediate and skilled nursing care and a comprehensive therapies program. Residents are offered on- and off-site recreational opportunities ranging from stretching and other fitness activities to shopping trips and cultural programs.

Americana Healthcare Centers
8350 Naab Rd. (north) • 872-4051
8549 S. Madison Ave. (south) • 881-9164

Both these facilities offer inpatient and outpatient therapy programs as well as respite care. Additionally, the Naab Road facility has a subacute rehabilitation unit and a specialized Alzheimer's unit with adult daycare services. The Madison Avenue facility has a specially designed care program for terminally ill patients.

Best American Health Care Centers
Barton House (downtown), 505 N. Delaware St.
• 634-9382
Highland Manor Healthcare, 2926 N. Capitol Ave. (near-north side) • 926-0254

These two Best American facilities provide residents with skilled and intermediate care services delivered by certified staff experienced

in meeting a variety of healthcare needs and concerns. Both facilities are convenient to downtown shopping, cultural attractions and area churches. They offer full-time activity programs (from arts and crafts to dances) that are designed to meet the physical, mental and social needs of residents. Both are also on bus routes.

Heartland Health Care Center
445 S. County Rd. 525 E., Plainfield
• 745-2522

Set in the bucolic countryside west of Indianapolis, this beautiful new facility offers short-term respite stays, a homeward bound program and hospice care. Among its on-site programs are extensive physical, occupational, speech and respiratory therapies and a roster of activities designed to stimulate, improve and/or maintain residents' mental alertness and physical health.

Integrated Health Services of Indianapolis at Cambridge
8530 Township Line Rd. • 876-9955

On the northwest side near St. Vincent Hospital, this facility provides complex care for all ages. Among its programs are 24-hour registered nursing care, physician services, social services, recreational therapy and specialized dietary services.

Keystone Health Care Center
2630 S. Keystone Ave. • 787-8951

This skilled and intermediate care facility across the street from Indy Parks' Sarah Shank Golf Course offers residents a choice of private or semiprivate rooms and adult daycare services. Keystone's therapy programs include physical, speech, respiratory and occupational.

Nationwide Care Inc.
Regency Place of Castleton
5226 E. 82nd St., 842-6668 • Wildwood
7301 E. 16th St. • 353-1290
Regency Place of Greenwood
377 Westridge Blvd., Greenwood
• 888-4948

These three Nationwide Care facilities offer a continuum of healthcare services including short- and long-term care, subacute services, Alzheimer's care, and physical, occupational, speech and respiratory therapies. Each facility is close to shopping and entertainment options and churches.

Springfield Health Care Center
6130 Michigan Rd. N.W. • 253-3486

Offering skilled and intermediate care, this northwest-side facility provides both around-the-clock and short-term care.

Its programs include physical, respiratory and speech therapies and special care for Alzheimer's patients. In addition to residents' rooms, the one-story center contains a chapel and a beauty shop; outside courtyards offer residents a place to socialize.

University Heights Convalescent Center
1380 E. County Line Rd. S. • 885-7050

On the campus of Community Hospital South, this facility offers a broad range of services including skilled nursing management of intravenous and pain-control therapies, a special care unit for dementia patients, social-service counseling and state-of-the-art physical, occupational, speech and respiratory therapies. In place of the bland meals sometimes associated with healthcare facilities, University Heights offers "home-cooked" meals.

Transportation

Unfortunately, there is not currently any transportation system in place to serve seniors who need a means of going shopping, doing their banking or going out socially. For such cases, the best that's available are discounts for the Metro bus system and for taxis.

Metro Transit Half-Fare Program
Metro Customer Service Office
36 N. Delaware St. • 632-1900

Metro offers seniors 65 and older half off usual fares. To be eligible, you have to visit the downtown customer service office, show proof of your age and get an ID card.

Discount Taxi Program
Indianapolis Senior Citizens Center
708 E. Michigan St. • 263-6279

On a monthly basis, anyone 60 or older can stop by the ISCC and buy a coupon book containing $10 worth of taxi fare coupons for $5.

Medical Transportation

While transportation for ordinary trips is hard to come by, there are services available for people in need of transportation to non-emergency medical appointments. Be aware that reservations are needed and that some programs have geographic and/or income restrictions.

FYI
Unless otherwise noted, the area code for all phone numbers in this guide is 317.

American Red Cross, Indianapolis Chapter
441 E. 10th St. • 684-1441

The Red Cross provides free medical transportation from 7 AM to 2:30 PM, Monday through Friday. Call two weeks in advance.

Indianapolis Senior Citizens Center
708 E. Michigan St. • 263-6279

Members of the ISCC are eligible for free transportation to and from appointments at their physicians' offices, health clinics and hospitals. Assistance is available both to mobile individuals and to those in wheelchairs.

Jewish Senior Services
Jewish Community Center, 6701 Hoover Rd. • 251-9467

Seniors who are JCC members are eligible for escorted transportation to medical appointments.

Metro Open Door
1501 W. Washington St. • 635-2100

All Indianapolis residents who are confined to wheelchairs are eligible for transportation to and from medical appointments via Metro Bus's specially equipped vans. Call ahead to schedule; the cost is $1.50 one way.

Insurance Help

In the baffling world of insurance, it's sometimes hard to know who to turn to for straight answers. These organizations can help:

Acordia Senior Benefits: Ambassador Program, 6720 Parkdale Place, 290-2800, (800) 448-8293;

Indiana Department of Insurance: Senior Health Insurance Information Program, 311 W. Washington Street, Suite 300, 232-5299.

Legal Help

Finding an attorney who knows the ins and outs of elder law can be a daunting task. For help, contact one of the following.

Legal Services Organization of Indiana: Senior Law Project
151 N. Delaware St. • 631-9424

Long an advocate for the legally underserved, Legal Services provides free legal advice and representation for seniors through its senior law project.

Indianapolis Bar Association: Lawyer/Mediator Referral Service
10 W. Market St., Ste. 440 • 269-2222

As the representative body for Indianapolis attorneys, the IBA maintains a list of attorneys by legal specialities (including those whose expertise is in elder law) and by geographic area. The referral service is free.

Employment

Retiring from one job doesn't necessarily mean you're ready, willing or able to quit working. If that's the case, the following organizations offer job counseling, training and placement for seniors. They also act as bridges between employers seeking older workers and seniors seeking jobs. But be aware that some employment programs have age and income restrictions:

AARP Employment Program, 155 E. Market Street, Room 705, 634-6416;

CICOA The Access Network, 4755 Kingsway Drive, Suite 200, 254-5478;

Indianapolis Network for Employment

and Training (iNET), 17 W. Market Street, 684-2400;

Senior Job Referral Program: Indianapolis Senior Citizens Center, 708 E. Michigan Street, 237-6272.

Volunteer Opportunities

If you prefer not to work but still want to do something to occupy yourself, volunteerism is a good way to feel connected to your community and enjoy the company of a variety of people from teens to other retirees. The following organizations can help you locate volunteer opportunities that are right for you.

CICOA The Access Network
4755 Kingsway Dr., Ste. 200 • 254-5464

In its role as Central Indiana's center of information about senior organizations and programs, CICOA not only recruits volunteers for its day-to-day operational needs, it also refers people looking for specific volunteer opportunities to other agencies around the area.

Community Action of Greater Indianapolis: Foster Grandparent Program
2445 N. Meridian St. • 927-5713

This program gives seniors who love children an opportunity to volunteer in daycare centers, community centers and after-school programs where children will benefit from the attention and compassion of older adults.

Executive Service Corps
70 E. 91st St., Ste. 204 • 574-7272

This organization provides retired executives opportunities to serve as mentors to people running small businesses, not-for-profits and government agencies. They can also put their expertise to work by helping high school students prepare for job interviews and responsibilities.

Retired Senior Volunteer Program
1400 N. Meridian St. • 236-1558

This is a clearinghouse for information about a variety of volunteer opportunities throughout the metropolitan area, including those in social-service organizations, arts organizations, hospitals and special events.

Small Business Administration: Service Corps of Retired Executives

575 N. Pennsylvania St. • 226-7264

An ancillary operation of the SBA, the Service Corps teams up retired executives with start-up and struggling small businesses in need of expertise in areas such as finances, personnel development and marketing. Working as volunteer consultants, the Service Corps' executives help business owners and their staffs develop workable solutions to their problems, or (in the case of start-ups) create realistic business plans and implementation strategies.

Fitness and Recreation Programs

In addition to programs available through many of the senior centers listed earlier in this chapter, as well as those through the organizations and programs in the Parks and Recreation chapter, the following organizations offer senior-specific fitness and recreational opportunities:

Indy Parks & Recreation

1426 W. 29th St. • 327-0000

Among this agency's offerings are "Active Older Adult Programs 50+" and the Indy Senior Olympics.

Health & Hospital Corporation of Marion County

Bureau of Health Promotion, 3838 N. Rural St. • 541-2092

Among its many health promotional efforts, this agency has a Silver Striders program for older adults that stresses the benefits of a walking program and offers opportunities to take part in regular organized walks.

YMCA

615 N. Alabama St. • 266-9622

With nine branch facilities throughout the Greater Indianapolis area, the YMCA has a number of programs that are either geared specifically for older adults or are open to them, from the Active Older Adults program to classes in yoga and tai chi

chuan. Contact Y headquarters above for information.

Mall-walking Programs

Most of the area malls have mall walking programs, which are open to people of all ages. You can register at the mall information desks at the following sites:

Castleton Square, 6020 E. 82nd Street, 849-9993;

Glendale Shopping Center, 6101 N. Keystone Avenue, 251-9281;

Greenwood Park Mall, 1251 U.S. 31 N., Greenwood 881-6758;

Lafayette Square Mall, 3919 Lafayette Road, 291-6390;

Washington Square, 10202 E. Washington Street, 899-4567.

Associations and Support Groups

Whether you're trying to cope with a change in your own physical or mental health, or with a change in (or a loss of) a loved one, chances are you can find an association or a support group to turn to for help. While there are too many for a comprehensive list, you can contact CICOA if you're looking for a specific type of group not included among the following.

Alzheimer's Disease and Related Disorders Association, 9135 N. Meridian Street, Suite B-4, 575-9620;

Arthritis Foundation, Indiana Chapter, 8646 Guion Road, 879-0321;

Bereavement Sharing Group, Methodist Hospital of Indiana, 1701 N. Senate Boulevard, 929-8611;

Bereavement Support Group, St. Vincent Stress Center, 2142 W. 86th Street, 338-4040;

Caregivers Support Group, Heritage Place, 4550 N. Illinois Street, 283-6662;

Catholic Widowed Organization, Catholic Archdiocese of Indianapolis, 1400 N. Meridian Street, 236-1586;

Diabetes Association, East Central Regional Office, 668 E. 62nd Street, 255-5132;

Families and Friends of Aging Persons, Jewish Community Outreach Services, 6701 Hoover Road, 251-9467;

Photo: The Indianapolis Star and The Indianapolis News

U. S. Senator Richard Lugar, who sought the Republican nomination for president in 1996, is a former mayor of Indianapolis.

Heart Association, Metropolitan Region, 8645 Guion Road, 876-4850;

Kidney Foundation of Indiana, 850 N. Meridian Street, 693-6534;

Lung Association, 9410 Priority Way, W. Drive, 573-3900;

Mutual Support Groups for Friends and Family of Aging Persons, Community Hospital East, 1500 N. Ritter Avenue, 355-5941;

Self-Help for the Hard of Hearing, St. Luke's United Methodist Church, 100 W. 86th Street, 846-3404;

Senior Silent Hoosiers, Indianapolis Senior Citizens Center, 708 E. Michigan Street, 263-6272 or TTY: 263-6278;

Stroke Club, Crossroads Rehabilitation Center, 4740 Kingsway Drive, 466-2010.

Senior Publications

As the senior population grows, so do the number of publications designed specifically for older adults. Locally, these publications provide information about senior concerns, as well as about area events and opportunities for seniors.

The United Senior Advocate
United Senior Action, 1211 S. Hiatt St.
• 634-0872

The Advocate is a monthly newspaper published by United Senior Action (see separate entry in the "Where to Start" section of this chapter). It covers the legislative and non-legislative issues that USA addresses on behalf of its members. You'll read about utility rates, prescription drug prices, home care versus nursing-home care, abuse and neglect of seniors and consumer rights. *The Advocate* is available as part of a USA membership, as well as through a number of senior groups throughout Indiana.

Life Times
CICOA The Access Network, 4755 Kingsway Dr., Ste. 333 • 254-3660

A quarterly magazine available free of charge from CICOA, *Life Times* focuses on such topics as senior-friendly travel destina-tions, retirement communities, senior finances, aging and health.

Senior Beacon
Quest Communications Inc.,
8935 N. Meridian St., Ste. 106 • 571-0101

A monthly newspaper, *Senior Beacon* covers such subjects as financial concerns, legal and legislative matters, healthcare, fitness, volunteer opportunities and travel. It's available free of charge at area libraries, grocery stores and drugstores, or by subscription ($10 per year).

For home buyers, one of the local real estate market's most desirable traits is affordability.

Real Estate

If you're looking for a comfortable place to live, you've found it. According to *U.S. News & World Report*, Indianapolis ranks 12th among the top-100 most desirable housing markets in the country.

For home buyers, one of the local real estate market's most desirable traits is affordability. According to the Indiana Association of Realtors, during the first quarter of 1995, the median price for a single-family house in Indianapolis was $89,900, compared to a national median price of $107,000.

Of course, as in any metropolitan area, actual prices are all over the map. Depending on location, features and condition, local housing prices can range from the low thousands for a fixer-upper to a few million for a country estate. New homes generally start around $70,000 and escalate to some 10 times that; if money's no object, you can pay even more and get what you pay for.

For renters, there are literally thousands of choices: inexpensive efficiencies, luxurious penthouses, downtown lofts and suburban townhouses. Whether you want to live in a renovated factory, a restored Victorian or a contemporary apartment community, chances are you'll find what you want at prices that are often real values compared to rates in other regions of the country.

Because you'll find information on specific neighborhoods in our Neighborhoods chapter, this chapter concentrates on information helpful to those readers in need of housing-related services such as real estate companies, home builders, apartment finders, management services and movers.

It won't take you long to find that Hoosier hospitality isn't just a phrase — it actually exists. Welcome home.

Real Estate Companies

The following is a sampling of area real estate companies. While not comprehensive by any means, it does give a fair representation of the types of services available locally.

A.M. Relocation
12774 N. Old Meridian St., Carmel
• 848-1588

Founded in 1980, A.M. Relocation focuses its efforts on corporate relocation. The local affiliate of the international RELO network, which consists of 800 independent relocation firms, A.M. Relocation provides residential sales and rental services, including area tours for newcomers, temporary lodging and transportation and home previews.

Carpenter REALTORS/Better Homes & Gardens
8722 N. Meridian St. • 844-4400,
(800) 635-4043

Carpenter REALTORS specializes in residential brokerage, family relocation and corporate transfers. Founded in 1970, the firm has 17 branch offices and 380 licensed sales associates throughout Indianapolis and Marion County as well as surrounding counties. It's the city's exclusive representative for Better Home & Gardens' real estate subsidiary.

Century 21
8425 Woodfield Crossing Blvd. • 735-2121

With 38 independently owned and operated offices and some 660 sales associates in the metro area, Century 21 is a major force in the local real estate market. While dealing primarily in residential resales, about a third of Century 21's area offices also offer building and development services either directly or through affiliated builders and developers. Among the other products and services available through select offices are corporate transfer guides, house and apartment rentals, mortgage brokerage and title insurance.

ERA Real Advantage Referral
6338 N. College Ave. • 580-1263, (800) 886-ERA1

With more than 20 years' experience and 14 offices in Central Indiana, Electronic Realty Associates Ltd. provides buyers and sellers throughout the country with electronic access to area housing information (including pictures) via Prodigy and Internet. Its services include buyer or seller representation, home warranties and relocation assistance.

A.H.M. Graves Co. Inc.
1119 Keystone Way, Carmel • 844-4545

Founded in 1924, A.H.M. Graves has seven offices throughout the Greater Indianapolis area. Among the services that Graves offers are residential sales, relocation, mortgage qualification and financing.

Pennington-Line Realtors
941 E. 86th St., Ste. 115 • 251-1574

This small but prestigious firm specializes in high-end residential real estate such as that found in the pricier portions of the Meridan-Kessler and Butler-Tarkington neighborhoods.

RE/MAX of Indiana
8888 Keystone Crossing, Ste. 1550 • 574-3355

Since entering the marketplace in 1988, RE/MAX of Indiana has grown from four offices and 37 sales associates to its present 54 offices and 750 associates statewide. Focusing specifically on residential real estate, RE/MAX offers regional and international referrals, sales information and advertising services as well as a corporate relocation program.

RE/MAX Connection
8315 W. 10th St. • 271-4844

A full-service real estate company, RE/MAX Connection is comprised of 40 independent RE/MAX agents specializing in new and existing construction, farms, rental and local commercial properties serving the west side of Marion County and the surrounding suburban areas.

F.C. Tucker Residential Real Estate Services Division
9279 N. Meridian St. • 571-2200

With 11 residential sales offices and more than 400 sales associates, Tucker has become one of the city's leading real estate firms. Founded by the late Fred C. Tucker in 1923, the company has a full-time relocation staff to help newcomers get acquainted with the city and local real estate options. Tucker also prides itself on its up-to-date understanding of the real estate market and the trends affecting it, an understanding that's based on ongoing research efforts. A full-service company, Tucker also offers mortgage and construction services through its ancillary operations.

Home Builders

If you'd prefer to build instead of buy an existing home, the following list is a representative sampling of local builders.

Biltmore Homes Inc.
25 W. Ninth St. • 756-7777

With the tagline "Quality Homes — Affordable Prices," Biltmore focuses on making home ownership available to people who can't necessarily swing six-figure mortgages. With houses in areas around the city, Biltmore offers a variety of models in prices that start around $70,0○○.

Brenwick
12722 Hamilton Crossing Blvd., Carmel • 574-3400

Specializing in what it calls "the art of creating neighborhoods," Brenwick develops residential communities with homes ranging from $130,000 to $1 million plus.

Crossman Communities Inc.
9202 N. Meridian St., Ste. 300 • 843-9514

With more than 40 communities in and around Marion County, Crossman offers home prices that vary in range from $100,000 and up for Trimark Homes to $90,000 and up for Deluxe Homes and $70,000 and up for New American Homes.

Davis Homes
3755 E. 82nd St. • 595-2800

With more than 40 years' experience in the Indianapolis market, Davis Homes builds homes in the $90,000-to-$250,000 range in communities throughout the greater metropolitan area.

Dura-Builders
**745 Beachway Dr. • 487-1800,
(800) OWN-DURA**

Locally owned and operated since 1971, Dura-Builders offers a variety of models and styles in developments throughout Central Indiana. Prices start at $80,000.

The Estridge Companies
1041 W. Main St., Carmel • 846-7311

With housing communities throughout the area, the Estridge Group is one of several building and development operations under the Estridge Companies banner; others include custom home design and building services. Prices for Estridge homes range from the low $100,000s to $2 million.

Hansen & Horn Group Inc.
7275 N. Shadeland Ave. • 849-8136

For more than 17 years, Hansen & Horn has been building homes in and around Indianapolis; prices range from $90,000 to $130,000 plus.

M/I Homes & M/I Schottenstein Homes Inc.
7321 Shadeland Station • 594-6940

From its Horizon Series of moderately priced homes to its more expensive models, M/I offers a variety of housing options throughout the area. Prices range from around $80,000 to $160,000 plus.

Melody Homes
**P.O. Box 116, N. Front St.,
Whiteland 46184 • 535-5311**

With a focus on making home ownership affordable, Melody Homes offers homes from the $70,000-to-$95,000 range in housing developments throughout the Greater Indianapolis region.

Many suburbs around the Indianapolis metro area are exploding with the construction of new homes. The fastest growing area is Fishers to the northeast, where population has more than tripled since 1987.

C.P. Morgan Co. Inc.
301 E. Carmel Dr., Ste. E-300, Carmel • 848-4040

Specializing in the development of its own communities (marketing angle: "The only builder in the neighborhood"), C.P. Morgan offers homes from $70,000 to more than $210,000, with a heavy concentration on the northeast and northwest sides of town.

Ryland Homes
7400 N. Shadeland Ave. • 845-0674

This national builder has been constructing homes locally since 1978. Ryland homes, which range from $90,00 to more than $160,000, are available in housing developments throughout the area.

Trinity Homes Inc.
3713 Turfway Ct. • 293-3690

Touting attention to detail and commitment to quality, Trinity Homes offers a variety of homes in a number of Central Indiana communities.

Publications

For more information about the local real estate market, check the real estate section in *The Indianapolis Star* on Sunday or pick up the following free publications at area grocery stores, banks and drugstores.

New Homes Directory, Zart Publications Inc., 5612 E. Washington Street, 308-2300

Homes & Land, Holloway Publications

INSIDERS' TIP

Locals and visitors alike enjoy Sunday drives, with *The Star's* real estate section in hand, through the lavish neighborhoods of Carmel and Geist and around Eagle Creek and Morse reservoirs.

Inc., 1132 S. Range Line Road, Suite 102, 846-2898

IBJ's Executive Homes, Indianapolis Business Journal, 431 N. Pennsylvania Street, 634-6200

Indianapolis Homes Illustrated, Great Lakes Photojournal Press, 1717 W. 86th Street, Suite 480, 879-1717

Apartments

There are too many apartments in the Indianapolis area and too great a variety of prices, locations and amenities to create a useful list in this chapter. But there are some resources, such as free publications, apartment finders (including *The Indianapolis*

Star and *The Indianapolis News*) and management companies, that you can turn to for help.

Publications

As with the real estate publications listed, the following publications are available free at area grocery stores, banks, and drugstores.

Greater Indianapolis Apartment Guide

Haas Publishing Companies Inc., 6666 E. 75th St. • 849-8884

Published monthly, this guide provides information about prices, locations and features as well as photos, maps and telephone num-

Photo: Randy Baughn

Low interest rates throughout all of 1996 helped spark even more housing construction in central Indiana.

bers. It's also available at area libraries and colleges and at the airport.

Apartment Tour Guide
Linder Publishing Inc., 6866 Hillsdale Ct.
• 579-2099

Organized by geographic location, this monthly provides information about prices and features for a number of area apartment communities.

Renter's Guidebook
Zart Publications Inc., 5612 E. Washington St. • 308-2300

A bimonthly, this publication provides a breakdown of prices, lease stipulations and features for apartment complexes throughout the metropolitan area.

Apartment Finders

The following are companies that specialize in helping apartment seekers find apartments with the right amenities, in the right areas for the right prices or as close as is humanly possible.

Apartment Locator Consultants, 99 E. Carmel Drive, Suite. L, Carmel, 844-7708, (800) 637-1472

Apartment Locators, 7301 E. 90th Street, 842-0311, (800) 876-0288

Apartment Finders, 5660 Caito Drive, 542-7291; 1 W. Main Street, Greenwood 888-4807

Metro Apartment Locators, 5369 E. 82nd Street, 577-1447, (800) 999-7942

Apartment Showplace, 5858 E. 82nd Street, 685-0133

Education

Learning can be a lifelong pursuit, and Indianapolis residents will find educational opportunities for all age levels, from preschool through continuing adult education. The city is home to the state's largest school district (Indianapolis Public Schools), a strong system of religious and private schools and an impressive array of colleges and universities.

Improving our schools remains a priority, and just about everyone has an opinion on current educational issues. To really find out about individual schools, our school systems or universities, talk to parents and students, visit classrooms, ask questions and get involved. But here's a quick primer to get you started.

Public Schools

Although Unigov legislation merged many city and county services and governmental bodies in 1970, public schools were not included in the merger. There just wasn't enough support for the idea. So today there are 11 school districts in Marion County. Indianapolis Public Schools serves students within the old city boundaries, with much of its enrollment coming from Center Township. Beech Grove and Speedway, as excluded towns under the Unigov system, maintain their own districts. And the remaining townships (Franklin, Decatur, Lawrence, Perry, Pike, Warren, Washington and Wayne) serve the rest of the county.

Indianapolis Public Schools
120 E. Walnut St. • 266-4411

IPS, which serves about 50,000 students, is a system in transition. The state's largest school system has struggled in recent years to deal with such urban problems as decreasing enrollment, increasing violence and an overall dissatisfaction with court-ordered busing.

That's the big picture. But the system is full of small success stories, places where people are making a difference and working to improve our schools. Local teachers participate in National Writing Project workshops. Parents volunteer in their children's classrooms. Business leaders adopt high schools. Innovative ideas are being explored in IPS magnet options across the city. These special programs highlight a variety of educational theories and approaches stressing such varying focuses at the elementary level as traditional reading, writing and arithmetic; Montessori methods; critical thinking; arts and sciences; and language arts and communication. In fact the Key School, an elementary magnet based on the idea of multiple intelligences, such as linguistic, musical or mathematical, has gained national recognition from *The New York Times* and *Life* magazine for its innovative approach.

Middle schools expand on these areas and further develop specific skills. The Key Renaissance Middle School builds on the well-regarded elementary program. Shortridge offers a program in the arts and humanities, Harshman has developed the Center for Math/Science/Technology, and Coleman offers the Center for Foreign Language and Global Studies. John Marshall has developed a Pre-International Baccalaureate program, and Crispus Attucks offers its Academic Academy, a program designed to be especially challenging.

High school magnets offer more extensive study in such areas as the performing and visual arts at Broad Ripple, foreign language, math and science and vocational careers at Arsenal Tech, agricultural technology at Emmerich Manual and business and finance at Northwest. And the Arlington College Preparatory Academy at Arlington High School is modeled on the International Baccalaureate, a program of study similar to those required for admittance to many universities around the world.

In 1992 then-superintendent Shirl Gilbert instituted Select Schools, a program that allowed parents some choice as to what school their child attended, limited, of course, by the requirements of U.S. District Judge S. Hugh Dillin's 1971 desegregation ruling, which resulted in some African-American students being bused to predominantly white township schools.

Dropping enrollment within the system, however, has forced a number of school closings. Two high schools, George Washington on the west side and Thomas Carr Howe on the east side, closed at the end of the 1994-'95 school year, despite considerable student and neighborhood protest. Budgetary shortfalls and fewer students may mean more schools will face closing in the future.

Another current issue within IPS is the creation of middle schools — buildings that incorporate 6th, 7th and 8th grades to replace the traditional 7th- and 8th-grade junior highs. A few years ago IPS adopted a middle school approach, which emphasizes smaller classes, team teaching and tough discipline and quickly converted its junior highs. Some schools were left with little time to train staffs in the new philosophy, and progress, such as improvement in attendance and national test scores, has been slow.

These issues received a great deal of attention as the school board searched in early 1995 for a new superintendent to replace Gilbert. Hired before school ended in the spring of 1995, the 1995-'96 school year was the first for new IPS superintendent Dr. Esperanza Zendejas, who in her previous job boosted test scores, improved facilities and elevated the reputation of the troubled Brownsville, Texas, school system.

In 1995, Zendejas placed 90 percent of schools across the system on academic warning or probation and instituted accountability programs that held schools to strict standards of achievement in academics and attendance and monitored test scores, suspensions and drop-out rates.

By the summer of 1996, scores showed that most schools made progress; only 16 remained on the academic probation list. Middle schools, however, showed little improvement; none reached the "satisfactory" level, leaving all 17 on either academic warning or probation status.

Several elementary schools, however, made great progress. Though no IPS schools had achieved top "academic recognition" status in '95, three elementary schools (50, 67 and 84) received the top ranking in 1996.

The city's school system will likely see even more improvement and innovation as teachers and administrators rise to the challenge and continue to wrestle with the demands of an urban school district.

Though facing their own concerns with test scores, violence and enrollment, the township schools nonetheless enjoy perhaps a less-tarnished public image. Still, a major source of controversy remains over the township schools' role in desegregation. Since 1981, African-American students have been bused from IPS to schools in Perry, Wayne, Franklin, Decatur, Lawrence and Warren townships to maintain the mandated racial balance. However, no township students have been bused to IPS. In 1984, Judge Dillin ruled parents of children bused to townships can run and vote in township school board elections, facilitating more parental involvement.

Still, opinions as to the success of busing as a means to desegregation remain mixed. Before the 1995-'96 school year began, the IPS school board approached Judge Dillin about relaxing the strict racial-balance guidelines that require more than 5,000 African-American students to be bused from IPS out to the townships. Indianapolis Mayor Stephen Goldsmith also has made no secret of his desire to push the issue back into court in an effort to end forced busing. Many residents would like to see all students allowed to attend neighborhood schools, and locals continue to speculate as to the feasibility of a county-wide metropolitan school district. Expect to see some

FYI

Unless otherwise noted, the area code for all phone numbers in this guide is 317.

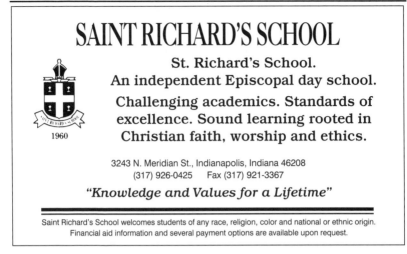

SAINT RICHARD'S SCHOOL

St. Richard's School.
An independent Episcopal day school.
Challenging academics. Standards of excellence. Sound learning rooted in Christian faith, worship and ethics.

1960

3243 N. Meridian St., Indianapolis, Indiana 46208
(317) 926-0425   Fax (317) 921-3367

"Knowledge and Values for a Lifetime"

Saint Richard's School welcomes students of any race, religion, color and national or ethnic origin.
Financial aid information and several payment options are available upon request.

changes in how IPS deals with the busing issue.

Private Schools

Those looking for an alternative to public schools will find a number of excellent options in Indianapolis. (All are day schools; interest in local boarding schools waned in the 1960s.) Some of these, however, can prove quite expensive. Tuition can run as much as $8,000 a year; still, many have waiting lists of interested students. And parents often begin gathering information on schools while Junior is still in diapers.

Most private schools maintain entrance requirements, usually a combination of exam and interview, and hold high expectations for their students. Some administer ISTEP or similar achievement tests, which allow parents to see how the schools stack up; most private schools that administer such tests surpass public school performance.

Area parochial schools remain committed to serving their parish or congregation and may accept students without the entrance exams often associated with some private schools, though these schools also expect high levels of achievement. Though generally open to all interested students, many church-affiliated schools offer reduced tuition to parishioners or church members.

Choosing the right school for your child requires plenty of research — and a lot of legwork — but the following information should get you going.

Archdiocese of Indianapolis Office of Catholic Education
1400 N. Meridian St. • 236-1430

The Catholic Church maintains the largest system of religious education in the city, with a history that extends back to 1859. Though most began as parish schools that served a distinct population, the Archdiocese of Indianapolis now administers four high schools and 33 elementary or primary (K-8) schools in the four Indianapolis deaneries, covering Marion, Hendricks and Hancock counties and parts of Morgan and Johnson counties.

A 1989 media blitz and additional advertising in 1991 to increase awareness of Catholic schools as an alternative to public education seems to have worked; enrollment jumped more than 5 percent in 1991-92. Currently, nearly 15,000 students attend Roman Catholic schools in Marion County.

But religion isn't necessarily the draw. Between 12 and 14 percent of students are not Catholic. As for curriculum and textbook selection and teacher certification, Catholic schools remain in accordance with Indiana Department of Education standards, though they outperform Indianapolis Public Schools across the board on standardized tests. In addition, more than 90 percent of students who enter Catholic high schools as freshman graduate in four years.

Tuition for the 1996-'97 school year at the inter-parochial high schools averaged about $2,600 for the first student in a Catholic family. Tuition at the 33 elementary schools, located in neighborhoods across the city, as well as in Beech Grove, Greenwood, Brownsburg, Plainfield and Greenfield, ran about $1,500 for the first Catholic child. Rates are lower for additional students in the same family. Contact your local parish or the Office of Catholic Education at the above number and see the following listings for more information.

Academy+
1717 W. 86th St. • 879-9010
1329 W. 96th St.

An increasing number of students who can benefit from smaller class sizes are enrolling in Academy+, a full-time nonprofit school for elementary and secondary students. Pupils enjoy a 1-to-10 teacher-student ratio in individual academic subjects.

Bishop Chatard High School
5885 Crittenden Ave. • 251-1451

Enrolling approximately 550 students in grades 9 through 12, Chatard, located in a Broad Ripple-area neighborhood, boasts a student-teacher ratio of 16-to-1. Like all local Catholic high schools, Chatard holds a first-class commission from the Indiana Department of Education and offers art, music, drama, sports programs and plenty of extracurricular activities. All students participate in religion class and activities.

Cardinal Ritter Jr./Sr. High School
3360 W. 30th St. • 924-4333

Ritter serves about 450 students in grades 6 through 12 at its west-side location. It boasts a student-teacher ratio of about 15-to-1, holds a first-class commission from the Indiana De-

partment of Education and offers art, music and drama, the standard academic courses, plus plenty of sports and extracurricular activities. All students participate in religion class and activities.

Brebeuf Jesuit Preparatory School
2801 W. 86th St. • 872-7050

Affiliated with the Roman Catholic Church, Brebeuf is a Jesuit school founded in 1962 by the Chicago Province of the Society of Jesus. Brebeuf serves as an interfaith high school with students from a variety of religious backgrounds. About 50 percent are Roman Catholic, and 50 percent are Protestant and other faiths. The rigorous college prep curriculum is quite well-regarded; 99 percent of graduates gain admittance to college. Brebeuf enrolls approximately 700 students in grades 9 through 12.

Bureau of Jewish Education
6711 Hoover Rd. • 255-3124

With recently expanded facilities, the Bureau of Jewish Education, or BJE, provides preschool programs for students from as young as 2 through kindergarten. Though it enrolls students from a variety of religious backgrounds, students celebrate traditional Jewish holidays and observe the Shabbat (Sabbath) on Fridays.

Cathedral High School
5225 E. 56th St. • 542-1481

Administered as a private rather than parish-affiliated school since 1973, Cathedral High School was originally downtown across from St. Peter and Paul Cathedral; hence, the name. The former all-boys school purchased the former Ladywood campus on the northeast side after the Sisters of Providence closed their girls school in 1976; Cathedral then moved from downtown and became co-ed. By the mid-'90s the school's enrollment was about 57 percent male and 43 percent female; ap-

INSIDERS' TIP

Butler University was the first college in Indiana and the third in the nation to admit women on an equal basis with men. It was the first in Indiana to allow students, with parental consent, to choose electives.

BREBEUF JESUIT

For Brebeuf <u>Jesuit</u> Preparatory School, the name is everything! The Jesuit heritage of the school represents more than 450 years of excellence in teaching, cooperation between teachers and students, service to the community and building a world filled with God.

Brebeuf Jesuit, an interfaith high school, serves the entire Indianapolis area. Faculty, staff and students are committed to the goals of a Jesuit education and the pursuit of excellence in all programs – academic, extra-curricular and athletic.

To learn more about Brebeuf Jesuit Preparatory School, about a financial assistance program available to academically qualified students and about the excellence which is a hallmark of Jesuit education, **please call 872-7050.**

proximately 75 percent of students are Roman Catholic. The school enrolls about 900 students, and at least 96 percent of them continue on to college after graduation. The school's mission is to prepare young people for careers, family responsibilities and community service based on Christian principles. The school also has a strong tradition of athletic excellence.

The Children's House
810 E. 64th St. • 253-3033

Though most local Montessori programs concentrate on preschool through about age 9, The Children's House, a nonprofit facility founded in 1972, offers an ungraded elementary school enrolling students from age 5 through 14; an all-day Montessori preschool serves children from age 2 through 4. The school offers open classrooms, a traditional curriculum, and Spanish, Latin, art and ballet classes at its new north-side address.

Colonial Christian School
8140 Union Chapel Rd. • 253-0649

Offering prekindergarten through high school, Colonial Christian provides a traditional Christian atmosphere as well as college prep courses. The school aims to provide a quality educational opportunity for families desiring to provide spiritual, academic, physical and social development for their children. Colonial Christian students have scored among the top

10 percent of schools nationwide in national Iowa testing.

Hasten Hebrew Academy
6602 Hoover Rd. • 251-1261

Since 1971, the Hebrew Academy of Indianapolis has offered a traditional Jewish education. Enrolling about 275 students in pre-K through 8th grade, the academy offers a curriculum that parallels state requirements in addition to providing students with in-depth instruction in Hebrew, and students consistently perform as well as or better than public school students on standardized tests.

Heritage Christian Schools
6401 E. 75th St. • 849-3441

An interfaith school serving children in kindergarten through 12th grade, Heritage Christian enrolls more than 1,000 students. The school offers a traditional curriculum and college prep courses and holds high academic standards.

International School of Indiana
612 W. 42nd St. • 926-1951

Currently offering preschool through 5th grade, the International School stresses academic excellence and is one of only a few in the country that features multilingual curricula. Even preschoolers experience immersion in a foreign language; the school currently offers a French-American and Spanish-American tracks. A recent addition to the Indianapolis educational scene, International School opened in September 1994 after a Lilly Endowment-funded study by the Indiana International Issues Task Force recommended the development of an international school. The school, which has received considerable support from the business community, parents and other volunteers, is near the Butler University campus and enrolls about 45 students (though the school eventually plans to expand through the 12th grade). Some financial aid and payment options are available.

Lutheran High School of Indianapolis
5555 S. Arlington Ave. • 787-5474

Indianapolis Lutheran High School began in 1976 with 17 students. By the early '90s, a growing enrollment necessitated a new school, and Lutheran High School of Indianapolis opened at its current location in September 1991. Affiliated with the Missouri Synod of the Lutheran Church, Lutheran High School holds a first-class commission from the Indiana Department of Education. It enrolls approximately 250 students in grades 9 through 12.

Meridian Academy of the Arts
1640 Fry Rd. • 885-9222

Indiana's only fine arts elementary school, Meridian Academy of the Arts enrolls approximately 100 students in kindergarten through 6th grade and hopes to expand its offerings through the 8th grade (the facility's Creative Learning Center offers preschool and prekindergarten programs too). Students participate in hands-on art-related activities in visual arts, dance, drama, music and language. Even the youngest study violin, piano, French, Spanish, braille and sign language; learn puppetry; put on plays and present their talents in monthly performances. Academic subjects are stressed as well, but within a holistic philosophy that incorporates the arts into math, science, social studies and other traditional courses.

Orchard Country Day School
615 W. 63rd St. • 251-9253

Established in 1922 when it opened in a N. Meridian Street home with an enrollment of 20 students, Orchard Country Day School has offered a progressive curriculum emphasizing individual educational goals for each child.

Photo: Randy Baughn

Butler University was the first in the state to allow students to select electives.

With an 8-to-1 student-teacher ratio, the school's enrollment now stands at just less than 600 in prekindergarten through 8th grade at its 50-acre site on the northwest side of the city. Some financial aid is available.

Park Tudor School
7200 N. College Ave. • 415-2700

Created in 1970 when Park School for boys and Tudor Hall for girls merged, Park Tudor School offers prekindergarten through 12th grade instruction in an academically challenging college prep environment. The school, which enrolls more than 850 students, is divided into the Hilbert Early Education Center (for 3s kindergarten, junior kindergarten and senior kindergarten), Lower School, Middle School and Upper School. Park Tudor stresses English composition, laboratory sciences, mathematics, foreign languages and the arts. The student-teacher ratio in the Upper School is 9:1. Seventy-six graduates in 1996 were accepted at schools across the country. An emphasis on academics, plus top-notch facilities, a beautiful 55-acre campus, a variety of athletics and extracurricular activities and a great deal of parental participation characterize this well-regarded school.

Roncalli High School
3300 Prague Rd. • 787-8277

This south-side school, a consolidation of two former Catholic high schools, enrolls about 800 students in grades 9 through 12. Like all local Catholic high schools, Roncalli holds a first-class commission from the Indiana Department of Education and offers such classes as music, art and drama in addition to academic and religion classes; it has strong sports and extracurricular activity programs as well.

Scecina Memorial High School
5000 Nowland Ave. • 356-6377

Named for Father John Scecina, the only priest from the local diocese to be killed in action in World War II, Scecina High School enrolls about 520 students in grades 9 through 12. Holding a first-class commission from the Indiana Department of Education, Scecina offers the standard academic and religion classes in addition to art, music and drama; it also boasts a strong sports program and plenty of extracurricular activities. The student-teacher ratio stands at about 17-to-1.

St. Richard's
3243 N. Meridian St. • 926-0425

Modeled on the traditional English country day school, St. Richard's is an independent Episcopal school; the parish of Trinity Episcopal Church, though located next door, has no control over the school. Stressing rigorous academics and high expectations, St. Richard's enrolls about 300 students from numerous ethnic and religious backgrounds in prekindergarten through 8th grade. The school is based on Christian ethics and requires chapel attendance; students wear uniforms. Financial aid and several payment options are available.

St. Thomas Aquinas
4600 N. Illinois St. • 255-6244

This kindergarten-through-8th-grade Catholic primary school in the Butler-Tarkington neighborhood ranked No. 1 in 1996 ISTEP test scores in the archdiocese and No. 5 in the state. The academically challenging curriculum aims to accommodate a variety of learning styles. Service projects promote an awareness of social justice issues. The school enrolls about 200 students.

Sycamore School
1750 W. 64th St. • 253-5288

Established in 1985 by parents who wanted an advanced curriculum for their children, Sycamore School offers an environment in which academically talented students can reach their potential while studying in a challenging environment. Learning is individualized, and the approximately 400 students in preschool through 8th grade explore a wide range of subjects. Limited financial aid is available.

Colleges and Universities

Butler University
4600 Sunset Ave. • 283-9255

Emphasizing the traditional arts and sciences, Butler University draws approximately 4,000 students to its 290-acre campus 4 miles north of Monument Circle. The beautiful campus is situated in a residential area along the east bank of White River and the Central Canal, a location that places it near downtown and the popular Broad Ripple area yet provides a definite campus feel. The traditional frat row features houses for some of the 14 national fraternities and sororities that serve Butler students.

The university includes five colleges from which students earn bachelor's and master's degrees in Liberal Arts and Sciences, Education, Business Administration, Pharmacy and the Jordan College of Fine Arts. The campus features 20 buildings, a formal botanical gar-

den and a nature preserve. The university's newest structure, the Residential College, opened in 1990. It houses 480 students in a learning-living center with faculty in residence. A $4 million addition to the Atherton Student Union was completed in 1993.

The acoustically perfect Clowes Memorial Hall brings a wide range of cultural programs, concerts and Broadway productions to Indianapolis. And the Hinkle Fieldhouse, named for Butler's legendary coach Paul D. "Tony" Hinkle, still packs in fans for college basketball and high school sectional, regional and semi-state games.

Concordia University
8465 Keystone Crossing, Ste. 195
• 259-5090

Concordia University's Indianapolis Center has been offering accelerated management and communication degree programs in Indianapolis since 1992. The small, seminar-like classes are taught in a one-night-a-week format that gives the student time for both school and family.

The main campus in Mequon, Wisconsin, has been offering adult degree programs for more than 10 years. The university, founded in 1881, has a current enrollment of more than 4,000. Nearly half the enrollment comes from the nine adult learning centers in Wisconsin, Indiana, Missouri and Louisiana.

Franklin College
501 E. Monroe St., Franklin • 738-800

This small school, which has ranked as one of the top-15 Midwest college values and as one of the 10-best Midwest liberal arts and science colleges, offers associate's and bachelor's degrees in 25 areas of study. It enrolls about 900 students, most of whom live on or around the handsome campus, which boasts attractive collegiate-looking red brick buildings. The college, south of Indianapolis in Franklin, the Johnson County seat, serves as a cultural focal point for the area bringing a variety of performances and lecture series to the community.

Indiana Wesleyan University
3520 Commerce Crossing • 574-3971

Though the main campus is in Marion, a

KEEPING THE PROMISE

• The Franklin College Leadership Program: Molding today's students into tomorrow's leaders.

• The Professional Development Program: Opportunities for professional growth in preparation for a changing future in the new Dietz Center for Professional Development.

• National recognition:
  Classified by the Carnegie Foundation for the Advancement of Teaching as Baccalaureate I – the nation's highest level and including only 4.5 percent of the nation's colleges and universities.
  The John Templeton Foundation 1993 Honor Roll for promotion of integrity and education.

• The presenter of national speakers through lectures by the Roger D. Branigin, Chair in History, the Maurice V. and Rose S. Johnson, Chair in the Humanities, the Edna B. Lacy Endowed, Chair in Business and Entrepreneurship, the E. Don and Joyce Tull, Chair in Business and Management and the Elmon and Lucile Williams, Chair in the Law and Public Service

• The home of the Pulliam School of Journalism and Indiana High School Press Association

Franklin College

501 East Monroe Street
Franklin, Indiana 46131-2598
317-738-8187

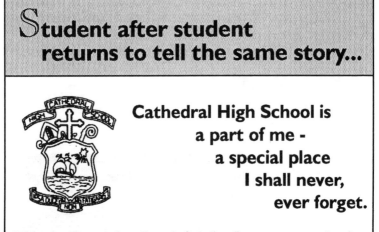

Student after student returns to tell the same story...

Cathedral High School is a part of me - a special place I shall never, ever forget.

Celebrating 79 years of excellence in Catholic college preparatory education.

community northeast of Indianapolis, Indiana Wesleyan has a presence here due to its unique LEAP program (leadership education for adult professionals) that leads to a master's degree in business administration. The 26-month MBA program is designed to fit into the schedule of a working professional. Indeed, three years work experience is required, in addition to a bachelor's degree, for admittance to the program. Concentrating on one subject at a time, students meet locally one night a week for four-hour classes.

IUPUI
425 University Blvd. • 274-4591

The bulky acronym stands for an equally lengthy name (Indiana University-Purdue University at Indianapolis), but the extra-long moniker may be appropriate for the city's largest university. Created in 1969, the campus has grown since the two universities came together to expand their regional programs and now enrolls nearly 28,000 students. Indeed, only IU-Bloomington beats IUPUI in size, dispelling the myth that this downtown campus is just a commuter college.

With more than 170 degree programs, from associate through doctoral levels, this urban campus on the west side of downtown offers the widest array of educational options in the state. It boasts Indiana's largest law school, the state's only medical and dental schools, the country's largest nursing school, its oldest

physical education school and the well-regarded John Herron School of Art.

Other innovative aspects include Learn and Shop, an award-winning program that offers college classes in shopping malls across the city, and Weekend College, the country's largest program of weekend teaching. In fact, five degree programs can be completed entirely on weekends. These programs serve IUPUI's large enrollment of nontraditional students, many of whom are returning to school or are juggling careers and family in addition to college. A program called SPAN serves academically advanced students in grades 6 through 12 who want to earn college credit while still in high school or middle school.

The IUPUI campus, which includes such top-notch facilities as the IU Natatorium, continues to expand; a $32 million state-of-the-art library was completed in 1993, a new law school building is on the agenda, and the John Herron School of Art will eventually move to the main campus from its 16th Street location into the old law school building.

Ivy Tech State College
1 W. 26th St. • 921-4800

Created by the Indiana General Assembly to provide "occupational training of a practical, technical and semi-technical nature," Ivy Tech, formerly known as Indiana Vocational Technical College (hence, the initials "I.V." through which the college came by its name

Ivy Tech) offers a wide range of courses in 13 regions throughout the state. The Central Indiana Region enrolls approximately 6,000 students in 36 areas of study. Students earn associate's degrees and technical certificates in such fields as nursing, computer informational systems, electronic technology and culinary arts. Ivy Tech is fully accredited by the North Central Association of Colleges and Schools.

Marian College
3200 Cold Spring Rd. • 929-0321

This progressive liberal arts college has been ranked by *Money* magazine as one of the best private college values based on academic performance and actual cost. Known for its "ethically sensitive" approach to education, this Catholic institution enrolls students from a wide range of religious and ethnic backgrounds. The school prides itself on its mentoring approach to education and boasts a student-teacher ratio of 13-to-1.

The college's 1,400 students earn bachelor's or associate's degrees in such programs as education, liberal arts, nursing, business and other professional studies. Approximately 15 percent of the student population is made up of minorities, and nearly 40 percent are older, nontraditional students who commute from Indianapolis or nearby areas. Still, nearly 40 percent live in residence halls on the 114-acre campus.

The park-like campus on the city's northwest side includes the Allison and Stokely mansions, two grand historic homes, which are available for public use and were built by developers of the Indianapolis Motor Speedway. The college's Kaufman Stadium serves as the city's official amateur baseball field.

Martin University
2171 Avondale Pl. • 543-3235

One of the city's most unique educational resources, Martin University was founded by a Benedictine priest, the Rev. Fr. Boniface Hardin, to serve minority and low-income college students. Only seven students attended then-Martin Center College in its first year in 1977. But by 1990, when the school achieved its university designation, it enrolled 1,100 students and boasted a 72-member faculty, of whom 45 percent held doctoral degrees.

Students earn undergraduate degrees in 26 fields of study. In 1992, the North Central Association of Colleges and Schools, this area's accrediting body, authorized Martin University to grant master's degrees. The university now offers graduate degrees in community psychology and urban ministry studies.

This private, liberal arts school, which focuses on student-centered learning, takes a multicultural, multiracial approach to education and continues its original mission of serving the nontraditional student; indeed, the average age of a Martin University student is 40. A program called Prior Learning Assessment awards college credit for life experience and skills gained on the job or in community work.

University of Indianapolis
1400 E. Hanna Ave. • 788-3216

This 60-acre south-side residential campus, which enrolls approximately 4,000 students, offers more than 65 undergraduate majors, as well as 12 graduate programs, including the state's first executive MBA program. The university is known for an emphasis on academics and boasts a highly regarded nursing school as well as the Krannert School of Physical Therapy, which ranks as one of the nation's best.

But the school, firmly grounded in the liberal arts, also places a high priority on communicating with its students. Every class is taught by a professor, not a graduate assistant, and classes are kept at a modest size to encourage student involvement and retain the emphasis on teaching.

INSIDERS' TIP

At a loss as to what to do with kids during school breaks and summer vacation? Check out Indy Parks and Recreation and YMCA day camps. They can keep youngsters occupied with a wide range of age-appropriate activities.

Preparation for Careers and Life

For 60 years, Marian College in
Indianapolis has continued its mission established
in 1851 of preparing students not only
for successful careers, but for life.

MARIAN COLLEGE
The College that Mentors

3200 Cold Spring Road
Indianapolis, Indiana
46222-1997

Toll free 1-800-772-7264

Heritage Christian School
6401 E. 75th Street
Indianapolis, Indiana   46250
317   849-3441

Educational Excellence in a Christian Environment

A nondenominational, K-12 Christian school, Heritage offers a wide-range program designed to meet the academic, spiritual, social, and physical needs of the students God has entrusted to us. Heritage works very closely with the home and the church in a constant effort to teach and reinforce the same Biblical principles necessary for success in today's world.

Accredited member of the
Association of Christian Schools International

The private institution attracts students from across the United States and from nearly 40 countries, though plenty of students come from the Indianapolis and Central Indiana area. One of the draws is the new Christel DeHaan Fine Arts Center, a $10.2 million facility that includes a two-tiered Viennese-style performance hall, practice rooms, art studios, a gallery and lecture hall.

Bible Colleges and Religious Institutions

Aenon Bible College
3939 Meadows Dr. • 547-9541

This institution, affiliated with the Pentecostal Assemblies of the World, enrolls about 100 students who earn degrees in missions, Christian education, music and religious studies.

Baptist Bible College
2305 N. Kitley Ave. • 352-8736

Offering bachelor's degrees in religious education and pastoral studies, this independent Baptist school that enrolls about 140 students also grants associate's degrees and certifications in Bible studies.

Christian Theological Seminary
1000 W. 42nd St. • 924-1331

Though affiliated with the Disciples of Christ, this seminary takes an ecumenical approach to education. The seminary's approximately 325 students come from dozens of religious backgrounds to study for the master's degrees in divinity, theology, marriage and family therapy and counseling; students can also earn a doctorate in ministry. The Edvyean Repertory Theatre at CTS concentrates on "theater with a purpose."

Heritage Baptist University
1301 W. South County Line Rd. • 882-2327

Established in 1955, this independent Baptist school enrolls approximately 100 students who earn bachelor's and master's degrees in pastoral studies and education; it also offers secretarial studies.

Indiana Bible College
3350 Carson Ave. • 784-8069

Approximately 200 students come to Indiana Bible College, affiliated with the United Pentecostal Church, to study Bible theology, music, religious education and missions.

Business and Technical Schools

ITT Technical Institute
9511 Angola Ct. • 875-8640

Offering training to nearly 1,000 students in business, technology and skilled trades, ITT

A university on the move.

The University of Indianapolis is a distinctive private university emphasizing a challenging academic environment, a flourishing campus community of international diversity, and students and faculty responsive to societal needs. For information, write the Office of the President at 1400 East Hanna Avenue, Indianapolis, IN 46227, or call 1-800-232-8634.

University of
Indianapolis

Esperanza Zendejas is superintendent of Indianapolis Public Schools.

Tech grants degrees in a variety of fields including electronics engineering technology, automated manufacturing technology, computer-aided drafting and hospitality management.

Indiana Business College
802 N. Meridian St. • 264-5656

More than 700 students enroll in the business-related courses offered at Indiana Business College and can earn associate's degrees in such areas as accounting; secretarial and office management; and hotel, fashion or travel management.

International Business College
7205 Shadeland Station • 841-6400

This school offers training or associate's degrees in such fields as accounting, computer programming, graphic design and medical and dental assisting.

Lincoln Technical Institute
1201 Stadium Dr. • 632-5553

Students at Lincoln Tech study in such fields as automotive and diesel service management and architectural drafting and can earn diplomas and associate's degrees in applied science.

Professional Careers Institute
2611 Waterfront Pkwy. E. Dr. • 299-6001, 298-4971

This school offers students training in medical and dental technology and business and computer sciences.

School Districts

Voters within most of these areas select their own school boards; the town or city councils in Beech Grove and Speedway appoint theirs. All have five members, except for IPS and Warren and Wayne townships, which have seven.

Indianapolis Public Schools
120 E. Walnut St., Indianapolis • 266-4411

Beech Grove City Schools
5334 Hornet Ave., Beech Grove • 788-4481

Metropolitan School District of Decatur Township
7523 Mooresville Rd., West Newton • 856-5263

Franklin Township Community School Corp.
6141 S. Franklin Rd., Indianapolis • 862-2411

Metropolitan School District of Lawrence Township
7601 E. 56th St., Indianapolis • 546-4921

Metropolitan School District of Perry Township
1130 Epler Ave., Indianapolis • 787-7266

Metropolitan School District of Pike Township
6901 Zionsville Rd., Indianapolis • 293-0393

Speedway City Schools
5335 W. 25th St., Speedway • 244-0236

Metropolitan School District of Warren Township
9301 W. 18th St., Indianapolis • 898-5935

Metropolitan School District of Washington Township
3801 E. 79th St., Indianapolis • 845-9400

Metropolitan School District of Wayne Township
1220 S. High School Rd., Indianapolis • 243-8251

Daycare Dilemmas

As anyone with children knows, choosing a daycare provider can prove difficult, especially if you're new to town and haven't built up that all-important list of baby-sitters. Though Indianapolis offers a variety of options (from private homes to national chains), many parents find themselves at a loss as to how to launch a search for appropriate care. Though a few employers offer on-site facilities, most notably USA Group, which

 has been lauded by *Working Mother* magazine, in most cases parents, must seek out child care without their employer's assistance. If you find yourself in this situation, here are a few places to turn for help.

Offering a computer database of child-care providers, **Parent Solutions**, 924-2312, provides members with referrals, a parenting handbook, first aid and CPR training, workshops, newsletters and telephone support.

Day Nursery sponsors **Child Care Answers**, 631-4643, which offers licensing and subsidy information, a child-care checklist and quality indicators.

Indiana Licensed Child Care Association, 925-8785, also offers information on day-care provider licensing, as does YWCA Child Care Resource and Referrals, (800) 598-5688.

Those looking for a '90s-style Mary Poppins can contact: **Indy Nannies Plus**, 842-7711; or **Nanny Connection Inc.**, 546-2669. These businesses interview clients and screen potential nannies, taking much of the hassle out of finding child care. You can expect to pay a placement fee and a retainer. Wages for a full-time live-out nanny may run from $300 to $400 a week.

Many families who have hired an au pair have enjoyed the cultural exchange. Similar to a nanny, these young Europeans, about ages 18 to 25, generally stay in this country for a year and live with a family, experiencing family life while looking after the children. For information on au pairs, contact **Au Pair America**, (800) 928-7247; **AuPairCare**, (800) 4-AU-PAIR; or the **Au Pair Homestay Program**, (815) 385-4423.

Other day-care options include **Unique "7" Academy**, 733 S. Missouri Street, 637-1529, a 24-hour, seven-day-a-week child development center. Unique "7" offers before- and after-school programs, a preschool and kindergarten and other educational programs. It accepts drop-ins, offers Saturday-night sleepovers and can accommodate infants through age 13. **Totally Kids**, 8430 Castleton Corner Drive, 849-5437, offers hourly child care seven days and evenings a week, with special toddler areas, an indoor playground, basketball, arts and crafts and themed play areas.

Sanders Diversified Home Services, 2575 E. 55th Place, Suite D, 254-1851, provides nannies as well as sick child care, a backup service for when you get caught without child care.

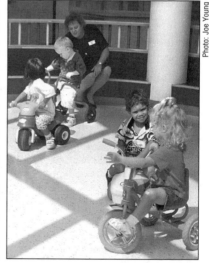

Photo: Joe Young

Two-year olds play in the solarium at the Plainfield Community Child Care Center.

There are 25 hospitals
(including those with
more than one site)
in the Greater
Indianapolis area.

Healthcare

No one likes to get sick. But it happens. And should it happen to you in Indianapolis, you're in luck. Not the getting sick part, but the being in Indianapolis part. That's because Indianapolis is home to some of the finest healthcare facilities and practitioners in the country.

For the record, there are 25 hospitals (including those with more than one site) in the Greater Indianapolis area. Among them are such renowned institutions as the Indiana University Medical Center, home not only to one the nation's most respected pediatric hospitals but also to the largest nursing school and the second-largest medical school in the United States. Methodist Hospital, the largest hospital in Indiana, operates a number of widely admired programs including an orthopaedic unit that has repaired the bones and joints of some of the world's elite athletes — professional race car drivers, NBA and NFL players. And St. Vincent Hospital's cardiac care unit attracts physicians and surgeons from around the world who come to learn new techniques. There are also numerous specialized hospitals and clinics, community health centers and immediate-care facilities. And an array of national and regional medical organizations have their headquarters here.

From a business perspective, healthcare plays a significant role in Indianapolis. In addition to a medical bag full of healthcare providers, the city counts pharmaceutical manufacturer Eli Lilly and Company, medical diagnostic equipment manufacturer Boehinger Mannheim Corporation, and The Associated Group, an insurance and health services company, among its largest employers.

So, if you're going to get sick, this isn't a bad place to do it. You'll be taken care of quite well.

Metropolitan Hospitals

Community Hospitals Indianapolis
1500 N. Ritter Ave. • 355-1411

Originating in 1956 as a single hospital on the city's east side, Community Hospitals Indianapolis has expanded to the point of operating hospitals at three sites around Indianapolis in addition to several immediate-care centers and specialized clinics.

The three Community Hospitals Indianapolis sites and their services are:

Community Hospital East
1500 N. Ritter Ave. • 355-1411

This 739-bed facility contains a full-service, 24-hour emergency room, orthopaedic and neurology services, a cardiovascular program that includes diagnostic and rehabilitation services, a cardiac catheterization lab, a maternity center, a chest-pain emergency unit, a same-day surgery center, a rehabilitation center for stroke and brain injury victims, a sleep/wake disorders center and an occupational health center.

Also on-site is the Regional Cancer Center East Pavilion.

Community Hospital North
7150 Clearvista Dr. • 849-6262

With 290 beds, this facility includes a women's unit, a single-room maternity care program, a stress-care center and comprehensive medical and surgical services (including a full-service emergency room). Also on-site are the Indiana Surgery Center and the Regional Cancer Center North Pavilion.

Community Hospital South
1402 E. County Line Rd. • 887-7000

Containing 150 beds, this facility offers complete medical and surgical services, a full-service emergency room, diagnostic imaging, a breast disease diagnosis and treatment program, fertility services, a cardiac rehabilitation program, cardiopulmonary testing, a cardiac catheterization lab and single-room maternity care.

Community Hospitals Indianapolis also operates five MedCheck Immediate Care Centers throughout the city. (See the "Immediate Care Facilities" section of this chapter.)

Indiana University Medical Center
1100 W. Michigan St. • 274-5000

On the downtown campus of Indiana University-Purdue University at Indianapolis (IUPUI), the Indiana University Medical Center consists not only of two well-respected healthcare facilities — University Hospital & Outpatient Center, a specialized adult hospital, and the James Whitcomb Riley Hospital for Children, Indiana's only comprehensive pediatric hospital — but also of the Indiana University School of Medicine (the second-largest medical school in the country), the Indiana University School of Nursing (the largest nursing school in the country), the Indiana University School of Dentistry, and the Indiana School of Allied Health.

FYI

Unless otherwise noted, the area code for all phone numbers in this guide is 317.

In fact, the I.U. Med Center's various training programs educate the majority of Indiana's healthcare workers. Approximately two-thirds of the physicians presently practicing in Indiana received all or part of their medical training at the Med Center.

In addition to training healthcare workers, the center also conducts research and testing on a wide array of fronts. In fact, given their affiliation with the Schools of Medicine and Nursing, one of the Med Center hospitals' primary focal points (aside from patient care) is research. And its drug-testing laboratory is one of only two in the United States accredited by the International Olympic Committee.

The Med Center is also a regional center for organ and tissue transplantation. It was the site for a number of Indiana firsts in that arena: the first kidney transplant, liver transplant, cornea transplant, bone marrow transplant, pancreas transplant and infant and newborn heart transplants.

In 1994, a national study of hospitals resulted in the I.U. Medical Center, which was examined as a single entity, being designated one of the nation's 100 top-performing hospitals.

The Med Center's on-site facilities include University Hospital & Outpatient Center and James Whitcomb Riley Hospital for Children.

University Hospital & Outpatient Center
550 University Blvd. • 274-4391

Since opening its doors in 1971, University Hospital has become a national leader in patient care for cardiovascular, neural and rheumatic, cancer, hypertension, and liver and endocrine diseases. The hospital is also a major center for heart, bone marrow, kidney, liver and pancreas transplantations. Its radiation therapy facility houses two of the world's most powerful pieces of radiation treatment equipment: a 40-million electron volt linear accelerator and the Scanditronix Medical Microtron.

Adjacent to University Hospital, the Robert W. Long Hospital serves as the Med Center's outpatient and family practice facility. It also houses the Elks Cancer Research Center, the Multipurpose Arthritis Center and the Specialized Center for Research into Hypertension.

James Whitcomb Riley Hospital for Children
702 Barnhill Dr. • 274-4071

Known simply as Riley Hospital, this facility specializes in pediatric care. Half the hospitals' patients are younger than two years old, a quarter are less than 2 months old. The seventh-largest hospital of its type in the country, Riley cares for children with cancer (only three other U.S. hospitals see more young cancer patients), heart problems and pulmonary disorders.

It's also home to Indiana's only hemodialysis center for children with kidney failure as well as to the state's only center for severely burned children. In addition, the hospital offers bone marrow, heart and liver transplantation programs and specialized diagnostic and care services for rare and debilitating diseases.

As this book went to press, Riley was in the process of building a multimillion dollar pediatric research center that will significantly expand the I.U. Med Center's pediatric disease research capabilities.

Methodist Hospital of Indiana
1701 N. Senate Blvd. • 929-2000

The largest single-site hospital in Indiana, Methodist, which contains 1,140 beds, was established as a ministry of the Methodist Church in 1908. It quickly became a leader in the use of medical technology, installing one of the city's first X-ray machines in 1909. Working in concert with local pharmaceutical company Eli Lilly and Company, Methodist was also one of the country's major centers of research into the use of insulin in treating diabetes (1922). More recently, it was the first hospital in the country to use an extracorporeal shock wave lithotripter to pulverize kidney stones (1984).

Today, in addition to an array of medical and surgical services (including a full-service emergency room), Methodist offers a number of specialized care services: an arthritis center, a breast health program, a cancer center, a center for geriatric medicine, a diabetes clinic, a kidney stone institute, a heart and lung institute, an eye institute and a behavioral care center. A Level 1 Trauma Care Center, Methodist also has Life Line helicopter services to airlift critically injured patients to the hospital for immediate care. Also on-site is Methodist Children's Hospital, which specializes in pediatric medicine.

In a move to decentralize delivery of services, Methodist has begun establishing healthcare complexes around the I-465 beltway that encircles Indianapolis. These complexes offer such services as family practice, immediate care, pediatrics, obstetrics and gynecology, gastroenterology, orthopaedics and sports medicine. They provide a variety of outpatient services: surgery, magnetic resonance imaging, mammography, ultrasound, x-ray, lab services and family life/public education. The complexes open presently are:

Methodist Outpatient Center East, 9670 E. Washington Street, 890-5400;

Eagle Highlands Outpatient Center, 6850 Parkdale Place, 329-7222;

Methodist Medical Plaza South, 8830 S. Meridian Street, Greenwood, 865-6800;

Methodist/Witham Medical Clinic at Zionsville, 1650 W. Oak Street, Zionsville, 873-8800;

Methodist North Medical Plaza, 151 Pennsylvania Parkway, Carmel, 817-1100.

Methodist Medical Plaza, Brownsburg, 1375 N. Green Street, 852-2251.

Clarian Health
Methodist Hospital of Indiana, 1701 N. Senate Blvd. • 929-2000

In a move to consolidate healthcare services and contain the costs of delivering those services, on January 1, 1997, I.U. Medical Center, Riley Hospital and Methodist Hospital announced the formation of Clarian Health. The announcement of the $1 billion merger was the first public step in what will likely be a long process as the three institutions sort out operations, administrative responsibilities, research, medical services and staffing issues.

Each of the Clarian partners was already among the largest and most respected medical institutions in the Midwest, so their decision to combine forces makes Clarian a formidable player in the healthcare field regionally and nationally. What this will lead to in terms of the quality and variety of patient care wasn't clear at the time of this book's publication, but what was clear was that the creation of Clarian is a sign of things to come. It seems likely that other local healthcare institutions will start looking for partners to remain competitive.

Richard L. Roudebush VA Medical Center
1481 W. 10th St. • 635-7401
2601 Cold Spring Rd. • 635-7401

Named for Richard L. Roudebush, a former Indiana congressman and veterans affairs director, the VA Medical Center is a 440-bed, two-division operation open to American military veterans. Providing primary and specialized medical, surgical, psychiatric and neurological care, the center serves as a referral hospital for Veterans Affairs medical centers throughout Indiana and central Illinois.

Among the center's specialized services and programs are cardiothoracic surgery, electrophysiology, radiation oncology, dialysis, di-

Why a medical resource especially for women?

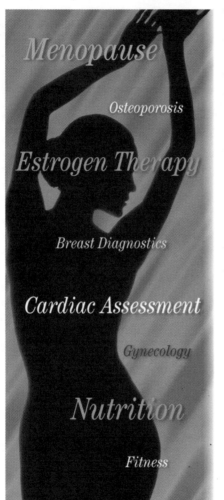

Menopause

Osteoporosis

Estrogen Therapy

Breast Diagnostics

Cardiac Assessment

Gynecology

Nutrition

Fitness

We have our reasons.

Columbia Women's Hospital of Indianapolis has joined with the Midwest Menopause Center, Nasser, Smith & Pinkerton Cardiology, and the Medical Consultants Group to form this very important medical entity – the first of its kind in the Midwest.

Our goal? To meet the special health care needs of mature women – from menopausal to general medical care.

Services include:

- Menopause Treatment & Counseling
- Hormonal Replacement and Management
- Cardiac Testing & Treatment
- Cardiovascular Risk Assessment
- Bone Density Evaluation
- Gynecological & Breast Diagnostics
- Nutritional Guidance
- General Medical Care

THE INSTITUTE FOR
Women's Health and Wellness

8081 Township Line Road, Indianapolis
317.876.7866   800.944.4741

Health care that's as unique as you are.

For more information or to make an appointment, call 1-800-944-4741.

Do it today – for the rest of your life.

We're Different. Because You Are.

As a woman, you have different needs.
Since 1983, the Columbia Women's Hospital
of Indianapolis has made fulfilling those needs
our singular focus. That's why we offer a full range
of ob/gyn services, surgical and medical services,
reconstructive and cosmetic procedures,
adult transitional care, and comprehensive
infertility treatment. No other area hospital
is totally dedicated to women's health.

We're different, because you are.

For more information call (317) 872-1800.

COLUMBIA
Women's Hospital
Indianapolis

8111 Township Line Road, Indianapolis Indiana 46260 (317) 875-5994 agnostic imaging, neuropsychiatry and treatment for chemical dependency. There is also an active research and development division with ongoing projects in diabetes, alcoholism, chronic ischemic heart disease, immunology, liver disease, cancer chemotherapy and endocrine bone diseases.

In operation since 1952, the W. 10th Street division is near the Indiana University Medical Center, and as such it serves as a teaching site for Indiana Medical School students. Its primary patient care areas are medicine, surgery and neurology.

The city's original (1932) VA hospital, the Cold Spring Road division now focuses on mental health and behavioral sciences. This division also includes a 60-bed on-site nursing home.

St. Francis Hospital & Health Centers
1600 Albany St., Beech Grove • 787-3311
8111 S. Emerson Avenue, Greenwood • 865-5000

Founded in 1912 by two members of the order Poor Sisters of St. Francis Seraph of the Perpetual Adoration, this is one of Indiana's largest Catholic healthcare organizations. In addition to its main Beech Grove campus, St. Francis opened its South Campus facilities at the intersection of S. Emerson Avenue and Stop 11 Road in late 1995.

Among the services available at the 441-bed Beech Grove site are 24-hour emergency care; cardiac testing, care and rehabilitation; radiology; a breast center; occupational and physical therapies; women's health services; a sleep disorders center; wellness programs; and inpatient and outpatient mental health services.

The South Campus contains an emergency/inpatient care center (emergency room services, maternity care, gynecology, pediatrics, diagnostics); an ambulatory care center (radiology, pharmacy, surgery and recovery rooms, lab services); a cancer care center; a family health center; and a medical office building for physician specialty groups.

St. Francis also operates PromptCare, a center for minor emergency care. (See the "Immediate Care Facilities" section of this chapter.)

St. Vincent Hospitals and Health Services
2001 W. 86th St. • 338-2345
13500 N. Meridian St., Carmel • 582-7000

St. Vincent is operated by the Daughters of Charity of St. Vincent de Paul, a Catholic order dedicated to serving those in need. Founded in 1881 by four Daughters, St. Vincent has grown both in size and in the scope of its services. Originally housed in a former seminary, St. Vincent now includes two hospitals (one in Indianapolis, one in Carmel), ancillary facilities for counseling, mental and physical therapies and cardiac care. The organization also operates three occupational health centers and five outpatient care centers.

A leader in cardiac care, St. Vincent also offers comprehensive services in orthopaedics, cancer care, pain management, obstetrics, sports medicine, stress management and alcohol and drug rehabilitation. The hospital's Institute on Aging provides specialized services to seniors, while its hospice program focuses on caring for people with limited life expectancies.

Westview Hospital
3630 Guion Rd. • 924-6661

Westview is Central Indiana's only osteopathic hospital. Osteopathic medicine is based on the concept that the body's various systems work together to maintain good health. What other healthcare providers now call "wellness," osteopathic physicians have championed for more than a century and Westview has provided to Indianapolis residents for two decades.

With 191 physicians and 95 RNs on staff, Westview is a full-service medical and surgical facility. This 120-bed hospital offers a variety of traditional medical services, such as cardiopulmonary, radiology, neurology, surgery, a 24-hour emergency room, a laboratory, intensive and extended care units and physical, speech and occupational therapies — all with an osteopathic emphasis on building good health.

Winona Memorial Hospital
3232 N. Meridian St. • 924-3392

Since 1956, this 250-bed, acute-care facility has been offering Indianapolis residents a variety of primary and specialty care services. With a medical staff of 300 physicians, Winona provides 24-hour emergency care, cardiovascular services, gynecological services, surgery (inpatient and outpatient), radiology, orthopaedic services, cosmetic surgery, neurology and neurosurgery, urology, cancer care, dermatological services and physical, occupational and speech therapies. The hospital's specialty care services include a diabetes center, foot and ankle centers, laser surgery, a sleep/wake disorders center, a bloodless surgery and medicine program, senior citizen health centers, a wound care center, a weight reduction program, and psychiatric and chemical-dependency centers.

Wishard Memorial Hospital
1001 W. 10th St. • 639-6671

The oldest hospital in Indianapolis, Wishard was originally known as Indianapolis City Hospital when it opened in 1866. From the beginning, its primary mission has been to provide healthcare to the city's poor and uninsured. Since 1975, it has functioned as an autonomous component of the Indiana University School of Medicine. Wishard was the state's first hospital to attain the status of being a Level 1 Trauma center, and it also is home to one of the state's foremost burn treatment units.

In addition, there is a special on-site tuberculosis treatment unit as well as a critical care unit that provides surgical, medical and cardiac intensive care. Wishard also houses a 40-bed inpatient mental health unit in conjunction with the Midtown Community Mental Health Center.

Wishard and the IU School of Medicine jointly operate the Regenstrief Health Center, an outpatient unit that provides primary and acute care for some 3,500 to 4,000 patients a week.

Columbia Women's Hospital of Indianapolis
8111 Township Line Rd. • 875-5994

Since its inception in 1983, The Women's Hospital-Indianapolis has specialized in providing obstetrical, gynecological and reproductive care services to women in the Greater Indianapolis area. Additionally, this facility offers women general medical and surgical ser-

vices, reconstructive and cosmetic procedures, comprehensive infertility treatment, radiology services and psychiatric services for children, adolescents and seniors.

Regional Hospitals

Hancock Memorial Hospital
801 N. State St., Greenfield • 462-5544

This 91-bed facility in Greenfield, east of Indianapolis, provides a variety of inpatient and outpatient services including emergency care, critical care, cardiology, a cardiac catheterization lab, maternity care, radiology, surgery, respiratory therapy, radiation oncology, physical rehabilitation (physical, occupational and speech therapies) and home healthcare. There's also an on-site women's health resource center and a transitional care unit.

Hendricks Community Hospital
1000 E. Main St., Danville • 745-4451

Serving the needs of Hendricks County residents, this facility offers 24-hour emergency care, same-day surgery, laser and laparoscopic surgery, mammography, sports medicine, advanced diagnostic imaging and home health services. There's also an on-site private-room birth center. Additionally, the hospital conducts a number of community programs including health screenings, safe sitter training, sign language classes and diabetes education.

Johnson Memorial Hospital
1125 W. Jefferson St., Franklin • 736-3300

In business since 1947, Johnson Memorial Hospital is a 165-bed facility providing primary-care services to the residents of Johnson County. The hospital's medical staff includes 58 primary care physicians and specialists as well as 125 consulting specialists who also practice at other Central Indiana hospitals.

Johnson Memorial's services consist of acute medical and surgical care for adults and children (including critical care), 24-hour emergency care, maternity care, rehabilitation therapies, occupational health and outpatient diagnostics, treatment and surgery. There is also a long-term care center and an on-site childcare center for children between the ages of 6 weeks and 6 years old.

Kendrick Memorial Hospital/ Kendrick Healthcare Center
1201 Hadley Rd., Mooresville • 831-1160

Established in 1881, this facility south of Indianapolis consists of a variety of specialized medical and surgical centers. On-site centers include:

Kendrick Family Physicians: This group of physicians provides families with primary healthcare such as physical exams, allergy treatments, well-baby care, children's preventative care, chronic care, lab/x-ray/diagnostic services and referrals to specialists. For information, call 831-9340.

The Regional Center for Colon and Rectal Care: This center specializes in the diagnosis and treatment of colon and rectal problems ranging from hemorrhoids to cancer. For information, call 834-2020 or (800) 601-2323.

The Kendrick Prostate Tumor Center: This center specializes in the treatment of prostate cancer through the use of radioactive seed implantation. For information, call 834-3255. Other Kendrick centers include:

The Kendrick Center for Women
1203 Hadley Rd. • 831-9345

This facility provides health screening, diagnostics and treatment for women in a variety of areas including breast health, gynecology, fertility, contraception, prenatal care, menopause management, urinary incontinence and sexually transmitted diseases.

The Center for Hip & Knee Surgery/The Sports Medicine Clinic
1199 Hadley Rd. • 831-2273

With internationally renowned orthopaedic surgeons Merrill Ritter, M.D. and E. Michael Keating, M.D. on staff, the Center for Hip & Knee Surgery is a leader in joint replacement techniques and technologies. The Sports Medicine Clinic treats physically active people of all ages, with special emphasis on high school, college and recreational athletes.

Riverview Hospital
395 Westfield Rd., Noblesville • 773-0760

Since 1909, this facility has been providing healthcare services to the residents of Hamilton County. Among its services are 24-hour emergency services, as well as surgical and rehabilitative care. Additionally, the hospital operates a seniors program, wellness and women's centers, and an occupational health program.

Acute-Care Hospitals

The following three facilities specialize in serving patients whose healthcare needs require extended hospital stays. They serve

Photo: Randy Baughn

Methodist Hospital is the largest single-site hospital in Indiana.

people with complex medical conditions who are stable but who need long-term medical care.

American Transitional Hospital-Indianapolis
3232 N. Meridian St. • 931-1676

This is a 40-bed facility on the third floor of Winona Memorial Hospital.

THC-Indianapolis
898 E. Main St., Greenwood • 888-8155

This 38-bed facility is inside CPC Valle Vista Hospital (see entry in the "Special Needs Hospitals and Programs" section of this chapter).

Vencor Hospital of Indianapolis
1700 W. 10th St. • 636-4400

This is a 59-bed facility inside a renovated factory near Indiana University Medical Center.

Rehabilitation Hospitals

Lifelines Children's Rehabilitation Hospital
1707 W. 86th St. • 872-0555

The only pediatric rehabilitation hospital in Indiana, this 35-bed facility specializes in helping infants, children and teens recover from or adjust to the effects of prematurity, head or spinal cord injuries, neuromuscular diseases, aneurysms, brain tumors, multiple bone fractures, amputations, burns or genetic or chromosomal anomalies. Patients are usually referred to Lifelines by their physicians.

In addition to working with young patients, the hospital staff provides family education training. The staff includes physicians and nurses trained in a variety of pediatric specialties, as well as therapists and social workers.

Rehabilitation Hospital of Indiana
4141 Shore Dr. • 329-2000, (800) 933-0123

A joint effort of Seton Health Corporations, a subsidiary of St. Vincent Hospitals and Health Centers, and MH Healthcare, a subsidiary of Methodist Hospital of Indiana, this 80-bed facility specializes in providing inpatient and outpatient services for adults affected by spinal cord injuries, brain injuries, strokes, amputations, orthopaedic problems, neuromuscular

disease, burns and disabilities related to any of the preceding. Patients come to Rehabilitation Hospital via referrals from physicians, nursing homes, insurance companies, families or on their own.

Among the services offered are occupational and physical therapies, respiratory therapy, psychological testing and counseling, speech therapy and social and educational assistance.

Special Needs and Services

Charter Indianapolis Behavioral Health System
5602 Caito Dr. • 545-2111
Charter Indianapolis Behavioral Health System North
11075 N. Pennsylvania St. • 575-1000, (800) 242-7837

These two facilities provide special programs for individuals dealing with drug and alcohol abuse, sexual-orientation issues, eating disorders, depression, anxiety, phobias and emotional dependency. The Caito Drive facility provides both inpatient and outpatient services to adults and young people, while the Pennsylvania Avenue facility is a residential treatment site for children and adolescents.

CPC Valle Vista Hospital
898 E. Main St., Greenwood • 887-1348

A full-service, 96-bed, private psychiatric facility, CPC Valle Vista Hospital provides a range of services to children, teens and adults with emotional, behavioral and addiction problems. Among the hospital's services are outpatient, partial hospitalization, inpatient, continuing care and residential treatment programs, along with a 24-hour mobile psychiatric assessment team, a speakers bureau, seminars and support groups.

Crossroads Rehabilitation Center Inc.
4740 Kingsway Dr. • 466-1000

This is Central Indiana's largest provider of rehabilitation services and training programs for children, adolescents and adults with mental and/or physical disabilities. Among the organization's services are child development, speech and audiology, physical and occupational therapies, training and placement, vocational evaluation and work adjustment.

Damien Center Inc.
1350 N. Pennsylvania St. • 632-0123

Established in 1987 by Christ Church Cathedral and SS. Peter and Paul Cathedral, the Damien Center provides counseling and support services to people with HIV-AIDS and their families. Among its services are medical and dental referral, financial and legal assistance, housing and transportation arrangements and counseling and education programs.

Fairbanks Hospital Inc.
8102 Clearvista Pkwy., Fairbanks
• 849-8222
Greenwood Counseling Center
1000 N. Madison Ave., Ste. W-5 • 888-2801

Founded in 1945, Fairbanks Hospital was Indiana's first full-service chemical dependency treatment facility. Today, it specializes in providing services for chemically dependent adolescents and adults and their families. Using a multidisciplinary team approach, Fairbanks' physicians, nurses, counselors, psychiatrists, psychologists, clinical social workers, family therapists and dieticians provide detoxification, inpatient, day-treatment, outpatient and aftercare services.

The Greenwood Counseling Center offers outpatient services for clients who live on the south side of Indianapolis.

Koala Hospital of Indianapolis
1404 S. State Ave. • 783-4084,
(800) 995-6252
Koala Counseling Center
532 Turtle Creek N., Ste. H-2 • 787-3190

Since 1978, Koala has been providing mental health services to adolescents and adults in the Indianapolis area. Included among those services are outpatient counseling (individual, family and group), inpatient assistance with substance abuse and emotional problems, outpatient help for chemical dependency and alcohol and drug education programs. In addition to the main hospital

site, Koala operates a counseling center on the city's south side.

Planned Parenthood of Central and Southern Indiana
3219 N. Meridian St. • 925-6747

For more than 60 years, Planned Parenthood of Central Indiana has been providing family planning and reproductive health services to Indianapolis area residents. In addition to its Meridian Street facility, the organization operates clinics at these locations: Castleton, 8121 Center Run Drive, 849-9304; South side, 4024 Madison Avenue, Ste. A, 788-0396; Northwest side, 8847 Commerce Park Place, 876-1774; East side, 9385 E. Washington Street, 899-4731; West side, 12689 W. Rockville Road, 272-2042.

Community Health Centers

In Indianapolis, community health centers (CHCs) are situated in medically underserved neighborhoods. While their fundamental mission is to provide primary healthcare to individuals and families whose circumstances (lack of insurance, poverty, homelessness) would otherwise prevent access to care, CHCs are available to anyone living in their services areas.

The services available through not-for-profit CHCs are identical to (and in some cases more extensive than) those available through for-profit clinics and private physicians' offices. From physical exams and prenatal care to pediatrics and gerontology, CHCs offer high-quality, low-cost healthcare.

Indianapolis CHCs include:

Barrington Health Center, 3401 E. Raymond Avenue, 788-4716;

Citizens Health Center, 1650 N. College Avenue, 924-6351;

Blackburn Community Health Center, 2700 Dr. Martin Luther King Jr. Street, 921-6580;

Forest Manor Community Health Center, 3840 N. Sherman Drive, 541-3400;

Fountain Square Community Health Center, 1434 Shelby Street, 685-5379;

Northeast Community Health Center, 6042 E. 21st Street, 357-2794;

Northwest Community Health Center, 7440 N. Michigan Road, 921-6580;

People's Health Center, 2340 E. 10th Street, 633-7360;

Southeast Health Center, 901 S. Shelby Street, 488-2040;

Southwest Health Center, 2202 W. Morris Street, 488-2020;

Tibbs Community Health Center, 940 N. Tibbs Avenue, 633-9560.

Immediate-care Facilities

While offering fewer and less sophisticated medical services than those available through hospital emergency rooms, immediate care facilities are convenient and less costly alternatives for treatment of minor injuries or illnesses. Area immediate-care sites include the following.

Broad Ripple MedCheck*, 1091 Broad Ripple Avenue, 355-3400;

Carmel MedCheck*, 313 E. Carmel Drive, Carmel, 575-0655;

Castleton MedCheck*, 8177 Clearvista Parkway, Fishers, 588-7800;

Doctors Immediate MedCenter, 9598 Allisonville Road, 842-7750;

Emergency Medical Care South, 532 Turtle Creek N. Drive, 788-5573;

Fast Care, (Inside Winona Memorial Hospital), 3232 N. Meridian Street, 927-2273;

First Care, 8830 S. Meridian Street, 865-2169;

Fishers Crossing Immediate Care, 11979 Fishers Crossing Drive, Fishers, 842-0202;

Immediate Care Center (west), 650 N. Girls School Road, 271-5080;

Immediate Care Center (east), 992 N. Mitthoeffer Road, 899-5546;

Immediate Care Center (north), 860 E. 86th Street, 580-3200;

Immediate Care Center (south), 1278 N. Madison Avenue, Greenwood, 888-3508.

Kids Express Clinic, 7526 E. 82nd Street, Ste. 100, 578-1313;

Lawrence MedCheck*, 10840 Pendleton Pike, 823-8121;

Library Park Family Health & Immediate Care, 1664 W. Smith Valley Road, Greenwood, 888-8112;

MedCheck East*, 1703 N. Post Road, 355-3200;

PromptCare**, 4770 S. Emerson Avenue, 782-3009;

Plainfield Medical Care, 1620 E. Main Street, Plainfield, 839-8484;

Zionsville Immediate Care, 1650 W. Oak Street, Zionsville, 873-8800.

*All MedCheck centers are operated by Community Hospitals Indianapolis.

**PromptCare is operated by St. Francis Hospital & Health Centers.

Mental Health Services

In addition to the mental health services available through the facilities listed in the "Special Needs Hospitals and Programs" section of this chapter, the following organizations provide help to people with mental and emotional problems.

For help in finding a therapist, call Indianapolis Referral Service, 844-1546.

Marion County Mental Health Associations
2506 Willowbrook Pkwy., Ste. 100
• **251-0005, (800) 901-1133**

As the local chapter of the National Mental Health Association, the Marion County Mental Health Association provides support groups for people affected by mental and emotional disorders, their families and teachers who work with them. It also provides residential services for mentally ill men and women, offers mental health education programs, serves as an advocate for the mentally ill on matters of public policy and operates telephone hotlines for crisis and suicide intervention (see separate listing below).

Suicide & Crisis Phone Line
2506 Willowbrook Pkwy., Ste. 100
• **251-7575**

Twenty-four hours a day, 365 days a year, this phone line, a service of the Marion County Mental Health Association, will put you in touch with a trained volunteer who will listen to you, talk with you and help you find the help you need to cope with depression, suicidal thoughts and other life crises (rape, child abuse, family violence, homelessness and relationship problems).

Midtown Community Mental Health Center

964 N. Pennsylvania St. • 630-7791

One of the largest providers of mental health services in the city, Midtown's Pennsylvania Street offices house its child and adolescent services, the family growth center, community and homeless mobile teams and the community support center. Midtown also operates adult outpatient clinics at these sites:

Meridian Center, 3637 N. Meridian Street, 924-7906;

People's Health Center, 2340 E. 10th Street, 685-5375;

Fountain Square Center, 1308 Prospect Street, 633-4666;

Westside Center, 5610 Crawfordsville Road, 244-2243.

Tri-County Center Inc.

N. Meridian St. and 136th St., Carmel • 587-0500

This multi-site organization provides outpatient counseling services for children, adolescents, adults, seniors and people with substance-abuse problems. In addition to its Carmel facilities, Tri-County has facilities at: 6100 N. Keystone Avenue, Suite 360, Indianapolis, 257-3903; 651 Westfield Road, Noblesville, 773-6864; and 602 Ransdell Road, Lebanon, 482-7100.

Healthcare Associations

Indianapolis is home to a number of regional and national healthcare associations, many of which can be valuable sources of information for consumers.

Alzheimer's Disease Association, 9135 N. Meridian Street, 575-9620;

American Academy of Osteopathy, 3500 DePauw Boulevard, Suite 1080, 879-1881;

American Cancer Society, (Central Indiana Area Office), 8730 Commerce Park Place, 879-4100;

American College of Sports Medicine, 401 W. Michigan Street, 634-7817;

American Diabetes Association, 7363 E. 21st Street, 352-9226;

American Heart Association of Indiana, 8645 Guion Road, 876-4850;

American Lung Association of Indiana, 9410 Priority Way W. Drive, 573-3900;

Arthritis Foundation, 8646 Guion Road, 879-0321;

Central Indiana Regional Blood Center, 3450 N. Meridian Street, 926-2381;

United Cerebral Palsy of Greater Indiana, 615 N. Alabama Street, 632-3561;

Physician Referral Services

When you're trying to find the right physician, referral services are indispensable. In the Indianapolis area, you can get help in finding a physician or specialist by contacting:

Ask-a-Nurse, 351-7800, (800) 777-7775
Community Hospitals Indianapolis, 338-2273
Hendricks Community Hospital, Danville, 745-3759
Indianapolis Medical Society, 639-3406
Johnson Memorial Hospital, Franklin, 736-3425
Methodist Hospital of Indiana, 929-2222
Riley Hospital for Children, 274-4862
Riverview Hospital, 776-7450
Speciality Physician Access Network, 816-7726
St. Francis Hospitals & Health Centers, 782-6699
St. Vincent Hospitals & Health Services, 338-2273
University Hospital & Outpatient Center, 274-4862
Westview Hospital, 920-7384
Winona Memorial Hospital, 927-2727
Wishard Memorial Hospital, 634-2273
Columbia Women's Hospital of Indianapolis, 872-1804

Indiana Academy of Family Physicians, 4847 S. High School Road, 856-3757;

Indiana Association of Osteopathic Physicians & Surgeons, 3520 Guion Road, Ste. 202, 926-3009

Indiana Dental Association, 401 W. Michigan Street, 634-2610;

Indiana Department of Mental Health, 402 W. Washington Street, 232-7800;

Indiana Easter Seal Society, 4740 Kingsway Drive, 254-8382;

Indiana Health Care Association, One North Capitol Street, Suite 1115, 636-6406;

Indiana Hospital Association, One American Square, Ste. 1100, 633-4870;

Indiana Lupus Foundation, 2701 E. Southport Road, 783-6033;

Indiana Optometric Association, 201 N. Illinois Street, 237-3560;

Indiana Pharmacists Association, 729 N. Pennsylvania Street, 634-4968;

Indiana Podiatric Medical Association, 201 N. Illinois Street, 237-3569;

Indiana Primary Health Care Association, 1006 E. Washington Street, Ste. 200, 630-0845;

Indiana State Medical Association, 322 Canal Walk, 261-2060;

Indiana State Nurses Association, 2915 N. High School Road, 299-4575;

Leukemia Society of America — Indiana Chapter, 921 E. 86th Street, Suite 205, 726-2270;

Marion County Association for Retarded Citizens, 2400 N. Tibbs Avenue, 264-1422;

Multiple Sclerosis Society, 615 N. Alabama Street, 634-8796;

Muscular Dystrophy Association, 9102 N. Meridian Street, 571-0275;

Myasthenia Gravis Foundation, 2511 E. 46th Street, 547-5291;

National Kidney Foundation of Indiana Inc., 850 N. Meridian Street, 693-6534;

Parkinson Awareness Association of Central Indiana Inc., 4755 Kingsway Drive, 255-1993;

Prevent Blindness Indiana, 911 E. 86th Street, 257-2020;

Sickle Cell Program, 3549 N. College Avenue, 927-5158;

Spina Bifida Association of Central Indiana, 4648 Bluffwood Drive N., 293-3664.

Emergency Numbers and Support Groups

For all emergencies dial 911.

For groups that deal with retirement and older adults' health issue, please see our Retirement chapter.

Alcohol/Drugs

Al-Anon/Alateen, 357-9607, 776-7235

Alcoholics Anonymous, 632-7864

St. Francis Counseling Center, 783-8983

St. Vincent Street Center Crisis Line, 338-4800

Rational Recovery Systems, 357-8905

Mothers Against Drunk Driving, 689-4118

Cancer

Family Support Group, 929-6565

The Life Center, 924-2324

Cancer Patient Support Group, 776-7325

The Wellness Community-Central Indiana, 257-1505

Debt

Consumer Credit Counseling Service of Central Indiana, 266-1300 ext. 257

INSIDERS' TIP

The Ronald McDonald House, on the IUPUI campus near Riley Hospital, provides accommodations for families of children being treated at the hospital.

Depression

Postpartum Depression Support Group, 338-4800
Depression Support Group, 251-0005
Manic Depression Group, 251-0005

Domestic Violence

Family Service Association of Indianapolis, 634-6341
Breaking Free, 923-4260
The Salvation Army Social Service Center, 637-5551

Infertility

Resolve, 329-9519

Literacy

The Greater Indianapolis Literacy League, 269-1745
Indiana Literacy Hotline, (800) 624-7585

Men's Issues

Indiana Men's Council, 283-8701

Mental Health

St. Vincent Community Stress Centers Crisis Line, 338-4800
The Alliance for the Mentally Ill of Greater Indianapolis, 638-6127
The ARC of Indiana, 632-4387

Parenting

The Family Service Assn. of Indianapolis, 634-6341
Parenting Classes, 846-3404
Indiana Parent Information Network, 257-8683
Family Support Center, 634-5050
Parents Without Partners, 547-7971, 824-4269, 388-3555

Suicide

Crisis and Suicide Intervention Service, 251-7575
National Youth Crisis Hotline, (800) HIT-HOME
Survivors of Suicide Victims, 355-4743

Veterans

Indianapolis Service Office, 226-7918
Disabled American Veterans, 632-9266

Important as they are, auto racing and agriculture are only parts of the economic scene in Indianapolis.

Business and Industry

Chicago newspaper columnist Mike Royko once dismissed Indianapolis as a racetrack in a cornfield.

To give Royko his due, there is an element of truth to that stereotype. Indianapolis is the home of not one but four racetracks, the best known of which hosts one of the world's most prestigious auto races. The Indianapolis Motor Speedway is a significant presence in the city. So are the other tracks — Indianapolis Raceway Park, home of the National Hot Rod Association's U.S. Nationals and of Sports Car Club of America races; the Indiana State Fairgrounds' track, home of such events as the Hoosier Hundred; and the Speedrome, home of numerous midget and sprint car races.

Then there are all the other racing-related businesses. More than 250 Indianapolis-area companies are involved in motorsports activities, the largest concentration of such businesses outside southern California. There are car designers, car graphics, component makers, safety equipment manufacturers, engineering firms and a number of racing teams: IndyCar teams, National Hot Rod Association teams and Sports Car Club of America TransAm teams.

Clearly, Indianapolis is a town that understands the business value of racing.

And, yes, there are cornfields all around Indianapolis. As it has been since the city's founding, farming is an important component in the local economy. According to the Indianapolis Chamber of Commerce, there are more than 600 agribusiness firms in the Indianapolis area.

Still, important as they are, auto racing and agriculture are only parts of the economic scene in Indianapolis. To see the vitality and diversity of business and industry in Indianapolis, you have to look beyond Royko's stereotype.

From Naptown to Stardom

Over the past decade and a half, Indianapolis has enjoyed tremendous growth as a business center, fueled in part by its bootstrap approach to economic development. Faced with the decline of traditional heavy industries and the subsequent loss of several major factories in the late 1970s and early '80s, local business and government leaders worked hard to develop new business initiatives and foster entrepreneurial endeavors.

The first step was the consolidation of city and county government. Known as Unigov, this 1970 state legislative act expanded the boundaries of Indianapolis, enabling it to encompass almost all of Marion County. The city's geographic area jumped from 84 to 388 square miles, and both the population and the tax base nearly doubled. This laid the groundwork for subsequent construction projects and business development efforts.

The results have been dramatic. From a long period of sluggishness that had earned the city the nickname "Naptown," Indianapolis emerged as one of the success stories of the 1980s. Focusing their development efforts on sports, city leaders forged innovative public-private partnerships to fund the renovation of existing amateur and professional sports facilities and the construction of new ones, investing more than $168 million in such projects.

It was a gamble, but one that paid off handsomely. With world-class facilities in place, the city attracted world-class events and lured a number of amateur sports organizations to relocate their headquarters here. Aggressive promotion of the city and its sports capabilities raised its profile nationally and internationally and led to the self-proclaimed title of "Amateur Sports Capital of the World."

That focus improved the Indianapolis economy. Between 1977 and 1991, sports organizations and events added more than $1 billion to local coffers.

Naptown had awakened. Dubbed the "Star of the Snow Belt" by the *Wall Street Journal*, Indianapolis suddenly became an attractive site for companies looking to relocate or for entrepreneurs looking for a friendly environment for start-up businesses.

FYI

Unless otherwise noted, the area code for all phone numbers in this guide is 317.

And what could be friendlier than a place that can claim easy access as one of its selling points?

Location, Location, Location

One of Indianapolis's oldest assets — its central geographic location — is also one of its strongest. According to a study done by the Chicago Association of Commerce and Industry, Indianapolis is the most centrally located city to the top 100 U.S. markets. More than 65 percent of the people in the United States live within a 700-mile radius of Indianapolis.

What's more, four major interstate highways and five major railway routes connect in Indianapolis. And 17 airlines provide direct and nonstop services to 90 destinations from Indianapolis International Airport. Ease of access for passenger and freight transport alike

makes Indianapolis attractive to companies looking for production and distribution sites.

Quality of Life

With an eight-county metropolitan statistical area (MSA) of 3,080 square miles and an MSA population of approximately 1.25 million people, Indianapolis is the 12th-largest U.S. city. Consistently ranked as one of the cleanest, safest places to live, it's a comfortable place to run a business and raise a family.

The authors of the 1994 edition of *The Places Rated Almanac* ranked Indianapolis eighth among 43 North America cities surveyed, citing favorable job prospects as one of the city's attractions. In fact, Indianapolis has one of the highest job growth rates in the nation. At the same time, a low cost of living coupled with an effective buying income that's higher than the national average make Indianapolis an affordable place to live.

What's more, tax rates in Indianapolis are significantly lower than those in many other metropolitan regions — though Indiana's auto excise tax, which is based on the age and value of a vehicle, is a shock to many out-of-staters accustomed to paying a flat fee for their license plates. However, the excise tax was reduced approximately $70 per car when a tax relief package passed by the state Legislature took effect in 1996.

Economic Development Alliance

In 1992, a number of local organizations banded together to attract new businesses to Indianapolis and to help existing ones maintain and expand their operations. Known as the Indianapolis Economic Development Alliance, this coalition includes representatives from the City of Indianapolis, the Indianapolis Economic Development Corporation, Indianapolis Power & Light Company, Citizens Gas & Coke Utility, Indianapolis Water Company, the Indianapolis Airport Authority, the Indianapolis Network for Employment and Training, Indianapolis Downtown Inc., and the Indianapolis Regional Small Business Development Center.

By coordinating their efforts and sharing their resources, alliance members work cooperatively rather than at cross purposes when courting new businesses to locate in Indianapolis. Members also work to help existing ones remain or expand here. In its first two years, the alliance was responsible for helping 47 new businesses open here and for helping 110 existing businesses expand.

As a result, the alliance's efforts led to Indianapolis setting three annual job-creation records: In 1992, more than 3,600 new jobs were added to the local employment ranks; in 1993, almost 3,800; in 1994, the figure was nearly 5,000.

For more information on the alliance, contact the Indianapolis Economic Development Corporation, 236-6262.

Division of Workforce Development

More jobs mean a greater need for qualified workers. To ensure that companies can find qualified employees, the Division of Workforce Development (DWD) was established in May 1994. Working in conjunction with the Office of Economic Development and the Indianapolis Network for Employment and Training, the DWD links companies in need of workers with people in need of jobs.

To learn more, contact the DWD, 232-7670.

Removing Regulatory Roadblocks

Regulatory guidelines can be both a blessing and a curse: The best of them protect consumers and businesses alike; the worst of them prevent innovation and throw up bureaucratic barriers. Enter the Regulatory Study Commission.

Formed by Mayor Stephen Goldsmith in 1992, the RSC is charged with enhancing local business productivity, encouraging entrepreneurial activities, streamlining the process of getting business permits and licenses and helping consumers get the lowest possible prices on local products and services. To achieve those aims, the commission reviews existing and proposed regulations and eliminates those that seem unnecessary or burdensome.

So far, the commission's work has led to the deregulation of taxicab licenses, a simplified process of getting construction permits, and an easing of restrictions on sidewalk vendors. Commissioners have also examined the fairness and flexibility of zoning ordinances. The RSC depends on input from local businesses to identify regulations in need of its particular brand of TLC. For more information, contact the Mayor's Action Center, 327-4622.

Global Initiatives

Though demographically not as cosmopolitan as Chicago, Indianapolis is home to some 500 companies that do business internationally. Exports of Indianapolis-produced goods and services total some $1.5 billion annually, while global investments in local manufacturing, warehousing and distribution facilities are directly responsible for 17,000 jobs.

Over the past few years, Indianapolis has developed sister-city relationships with Taipei, Taiwan; Cologne, Germany; and Monza, Italy. In addition, it shares a cultural and business exchange program with Scarborough, in the Canadian province of Ontario.

But that's just the beginning. Since 1992, efforts have been afoot to increase opportunities for local companies to do business globally. Toward that end, the Global Initiatives Task Force, which consists of local government and business leaders, has spent the past few years looking for ways to identify new international business prospects throughout Europe, Canada, Mexico, South America, Asia, Africa and the Middle East.

These efforts are bound to escalate even further as the global marketplace continues to encompass more and more goods and services. Traditionally the Crossroads of America, Indianapolis is making inroads around the world in hopes of becoming if not the Crossroads of World Trade, at least a vital way station.

Where Business Is Done

There isn't really a central business core in Indianapolis. You'll find businesses large and small spread throughout the city. However, there are key pockets of activity, most notably in the following areas:

• Downtown: In the office towers and commercial buildings throughout the Mile Square, you'll find some of the city's biggest law firms, financial institutions, stock brokerages, insurance companies and state agencies.

• North: Meridian Street, north of 82nd Street, is a hotbed of business activity with a number of commercial buildings and office parks housing large mortgage and real estate firms, banks and investment companies, data management operations, insurance companies, marketing and advertising firms and publishing companies.

• Northeast: Office parks in the Keystone Crossing, Castleton, Westfield and Fishers areas offer modern amenities to insurance and financial services companies, accounting and law firms, telecommunications and software companies and real estate and advertising agencies. This is also the area of upscale retail malls and strip centers as well as of high-volume, upscale auto dealerships.

• Northwest: Office parks in the Michigan Road and 86th Street region, as well as along West 71st Street, house a variety of small- and medium-size businesses in such diverse fields as information management, computer sales and service, cellular communications, insurance, human resources and publishing.

• West: Factories and warehouses share space with small office parks and retail strip centers. This area of town is also home to a number of the city's auto-racing enterprises.

• East: Once home to the city's industrial corridor, this area still contains some factories as well as warehouse and distribution centers. It's also home to Washington Square Mall, one of the city's largest retail centers.

• South: Manufacturing is alive and well on the south side, which is home to factories large and small in addition to machine shops, medical labs, small office parks and one of Indiana's largest shopping malls — Greenwood Park Mall.

Major Players

Indianapolis has long maintained a diverse economic base, which has helped the city as a whole weather recessions and business closings. A lively mix of manufacturing, insurance, transportation, financial operations, agriculture, communications, data processing, publishing, software development, real estate development and management, federal/state/local government agencies, legal firms and retail companies accounts for many of the 32,000-plus employers in the Indianapolis metropolitan area.

According to figures published by the Indianapolis Chamber of Commerce, the city's employment leaders are:

• Eli Lilly and Company, a multinational pharmaceutical manufacturing giant and one of the city's oldest continually operating companies: 8,750 employees

• Allison Engine Company, manufacturer of gas turbine engines: 5,700 employees

• Marsh Supermarkets Inc./Village Pantry Markets, a locally owned retail grocery chain: 5,100 employees

• Allison Transmission, manufacturer of heavy-duty transmissions: 4,700 employees

• Ameritech, the Indiana headquarters of the Chicago-based telecommunications holding company: 3,134 employees

• The Associated Group, an insurance and healthcare services company: 3,000 employees

• Thomson Consumer Electronics, a research, design and marketing center for RCA products: 2,186 employees

• USA Group Inc., a nationwide guarantor of federally sponsored student loans: 1,958 employees

• American Trans Air, the nation's largest charter airline: 1,800 employees

• Federal Express, which has a regional hub for its express mail services at Indianapolis International Airport: 1,800 employees

Eli Lilly is a multinational pharmaceutical manufacturing giant.

Photo: Randy Baughn

•Boehringer Mannheim Corp., manufacturer of medical devices and diagnostic products: 1,793 employees

•Conseco Inc., a locally founded and owned insurance holding company: 1,000 employees

Resources

If you're looking for more information about the business climate and/or employment opportunities in the Indianapolis area, contact the following agencies.

Indiana Chamber of Commerce
1 North Capitol Ave., Ste. 200 • 264-3110

Dedicated to the promotion of Indiana as a place to do business — and to the promotion of Indiana businesses domestically and internationally— the ICC is a good source of information on the state's business climate.

The Indianapolis Chamber of Commerce
320 N. Meridian St. • 464-2222

For more than a century, this nonprofit organization has been working on behalf of local businesses on such issues as infrastructure, taxes and workforce development. The Chamber provides its 3,200 member businesses (and others, upon request) with up-to-date research on area demographics and market trends as well as with networking opportunities, executive consultation services, leadership training and information on international trade concerns.

The Department of Metropolitan Development
Directors Office, 2041 City County Building • 327-4141
Mayor's Action Center • 327-4622

This city-county department, which administers the city's tax abatement and industrial revenue bond programs, is charged with helping businesses apply for assistance through these programs as well helping individuals and businesses contend with issues related to zoning, construction and development permits.

The Indianapolis Economic Development Corporation
320 N. Meridian St. • 236-6262

A nonprofit organization, the IEDC provides businesses with an array of resources, including access to information about the local business community and climate, business contacts, potential sites and financial and operational assistance.

The Indianapolis Network for Employment and Training
17 W. Market St. • 684-2400

A private, nonprofit organization, iNET provides corporate clients with information about the local labor market as well as with employee recruitment services and training funds.

The Indianapolis Regional Small Business Development Center
342 N. Senate Ave. • 261-3030

One of 14 business assistance programs in Indiana, the center provides management and technical assistance, business training, and special programming to small businesses.

The Entrepreneur Business Center
55 S. State Ave. • 236-0143

The first city-assisted small business incubator, the Center opened in 1993. Since then it has helped nearly 50 small businesses with such services as business counseling, affordable space, financing and training.

So successful has the Center been that a second city-assisted incubator is now under development.

Midwest Entrepreneurial Education Center
101 W. Ohio St., Ste. 444 • 684-3200

One of the few privately supported organizations in the country that's dedicated to entrepreneurial development, the center provides entrepreneurs and small business owners with training in the fundamentals of operating a business.

Indianapolis Downtown Inc.
201 N. Illinois St. • 237-2222

Established in 1993, IDI is a nonprofit agency focused on developing, marketing and managing the downtown district. It works with

GIFTZ

Everyone likes getting gifts, and for Indianapolis area companies, there's no better gift than having easy access to goods they've bought overseas. That's what GIFTZ gives them.

Close-up

The Greater Indianapolis Foreign Trade Zone (GIFTZ), a nonprofit subsidiary of the Indianapolis Airport Authority, provides local companies a quick, cost-effective entry point for imports. Like islands unto themselves, foreign trade zones exist outside the purview of U.S. Customs; anything that's shipped to a foreign trade zone is held there duty-free. Only upon release from the zone into a U.S. Customs territory are imports subject to duties.

But at Indianapolis International Airport, even that process is relatively painless since, in addition to the foreign trade zone facilities, there is a U.S. Customs Port of Entry on-site. When a company is ready for merchandise stored at GIFTZ, it is sent through Customs inspection, duties are assessed and the company has what it needs in a timely manner.

GIFTZ consists of a 62,000-square-foot warehouse, a 174,000-square-foot parking area and a 2,600-square-foot office complex. All that space allows the trade zone to store a variety of imported items, which it releases to area manufacturers and other businesses on an as-needed basis.

GIFTZ is one of the largest foreign trade zones in the United States, and it's poised to get bigger, at least in terms of the companies it serves. With the passage of the North American Free Trade Agreement, GIFTZ's central location proved attractive to a number of European firms looking for distribution channels to serve customers throughout the United States, Canada and Mexico.

The presence of GIFTZ is a gift that looks likely to keep on giving.

For more information, contact GIFTZ, 487-7200.

both established and new businesses on such issues as transportation, parking, space leasing, beautification and crime control; at the same time, it promotes downtown as a viable place to live and play.

Indianapolis Business Development Corporation
617 Indiana Avenue, Ste. 319 • 687-0272

This organization promotes the development of minority businesses, and provides financial and business support to help that development take place. The IBDC offers loans and lines of credit to start-up and established businesses in the retail, manufacturing, distribution, and service industries. It also provides training in the form of workshops, seminars and mentoring programs.

Hispanic Chamber of Commerce
3050 N. Meridian St. • 931-0081

Representing the interests of Hispanic-owned businesses, this organization serves as a center of information for investors and consumers interested in learning more about those businesses.

Additionally, the HCC works on attracting new Hispanic businesses — either in development or considering relocation— to the Indianapolis area.

Indiana Business Research Center
801 W. Michigan St. • 274-0892

Operated by Indiana University's school of business, the center conducts studies and compiles data on industries and individual companies, business trends, and national and international issues affecting business.

Better Business Bureau
22 E. Washington St. • 488-2222

Dedicated to the promotion of ethical business conduct, the BBB provides the public with information about its 2,300 members.

Those members are expected to regulate their business practices and to make customer service a priority.

Executive Service Corps
70 E. 91st St., Ste. 204 • 574-7272

This organization provides retired business executives opportunities to serve as mentors

to people running small businesses, not-for-profits and government agencies. They can also put their experience and skills to work by helping high school students prepare for job interviews and responsibilities.

Business Publications

Indianapolis Business Journal
431 N. Pennsylvania St. • 634-6200

This 15-year-old weekly is the best source of up-to-date information about Central Indiana businesses and industries. A lively mixture of hard news and features, the IBJ is the place where you'll find out who's who and what's what in local commerce. It's available at newsstands and in vending boxes throughout the metropolitan area, as well as by subscription.

The IBJ also publishes two annual books that offer valuable information:

BOOK OF LISTS: This magazine-style book is a compilation of lists of the largest local players in a variety of fields — construction, real estate, financial services, insurance, hospitality, marketing, etc. It retails for $35, and is available in local bookstores or directly from the IBJ offices.

BUSINESS IN INDIANAPOLIS: A comprehensive look at business in the Indianapolis area, this trade paperback book was published for the first time in 1995. Well-written and well-organized, it provides excellent, insightful coverage of more than 800 of the area's largest businesses, organizations and government agencies.

It retails for $39.95, and is available in local bookstores or directly from the IBJ offices.

Indiana Business Magazine
1200 Waterway Blvd. • 692-1200

Published monthly, this magazine focuses on business-related news throughout the state, as well as on the personalities and the companies making news. It's available on newsstands and by subscription.

Issues IN Business
911 E. 86th St. • 257-8000

As its name suggests, this monthly magazine specializes in features about business bigwigs. It also examines the trends and issues affecting local business. You can get it at area newsstands or by subscription.

Employment Weekly
202 N. Mill St. • 839-5129

Making its first appearance in early 1996, this weekly guide for job hunters grew out of a shortage of workers to fill the jobs avail-able locally. As such, its primary focus is classified ads from area employers looking for people to fill jobs in a variety of fields— computers, finance, clerical, health care, skilled trades, hospitality, telemarketing, general labor, etc.

It's available free in newspaper vending boxes around Central Indiana, at area grocery stores, banks, drugstores, and discount stores.

United We Stand

United Airlines is in the process of building one of the world's largest aircraft maintenance facilities on the grounds of Indianapolis International Airport. The $800 million project, known as the Indianapolis Maintenance Center, will cover 2.9 million square feet when completed. Phase I is done and operating now, but the final portion of the five-phase project isn't scheduled for completion until 2004.

Maintenance centers completely overhaul and repair aircraft, in effect taking an entire plane apart and reassembling it. When the United facility is fully operational, it will consist of 11 hangars and will operate 24 hours a day, seven days a week. Projected employment is at least 6,300 workers.

To land the contract for this facility, Indianapolis competed with 92 other cities around the country. In the end, it was the airport's strong infrastructure, amount of on-site land available (300 acres), quality of the city's workforce, low construction costs, central location and $297 million in incentive payments that convinced United officials Indianapolis was the right place.

Photo: The Indianapolis Star and The Indianapolis News

United Airlines is building one of the world's largest aircraft maintenance facilities at the Indianapolis Airport.

But while providing financial incentives to lure United here, city and state officials insisted on the company agreeing to repay those incentives if it reneges on promises it made regarding employment and corporate investment. This unprecedented stipulation took urban development experts around the country by surprise and led to predictions that other cities will follow suit when negotiating development deals with businesses.

Given the city's proximity to government, local papers have traditionally been strong on political coverage, a trend that continues today.

Media

Indianapolis has never been recognized as a newspaper town, unlike such regional cities as Louisville, Chicago, Detroit or Cincinnati. However, it certainly has had its share of newspapers. Six months after the city was founded it could claim its own newspaper, the *Indianapolis Gazette*, which took a politically neutral position. A year later the *Western Censor and Emigrants Guide* began publishing and took a strong partisan stand against Andrew Jackson.

Since then Indianapolis has seen an abundance of papers come and go: lots of Sentinels, Gazettes, Leaders and Heralds. Given the city's proximity to government, local papers have traditionally been strong on political coverage, a trend that continues today.

The first radio stations went on the air in the early '20s, but Indianapolis didn't secure its own permanent station until 1924 when WFBM (now WNDE) hit the airwaves. By the early 1940s, only two other stations had signed on: WIBC and WISH. But residents weren't going without radio; many local listeners tuned in to Cincinnati's WLW.

Network television began broadcasting locally in 1950. One of the longest-running local shows was Channel 13's *Kindergarten College*, which ran from 1957 to '73. Many area youngsters watched the program, wishing they, too, could go to school on TV. WFYI, the local public TV station, launched its programming in 1970 after a door-to-door fund-raising campaign by a dedicated cadre of volunteers. Following is a quick look at the major players in Indianapolis' vital media scene.

Newspapers

The Indianapolis Star
307 N. Pennsylvania St. • 633-9273

The Indianapolis News
307 N. Pennsylvania St. • 633-9070

When *The Indianapolis Star* made its debut in 1903, Indianapolis had three major morning newspapers and a couple of afternoon dailies, including the city's largest circulation paper, *The Indianapolis News*.

In four years *The Star* absorbed its morning competitors, while *The News* continued to grow in stature, becoming known as the "Great Hoosier Daily" and ranking as the state's most widely read and influential newspaper.

A series on wasteful government spending won *The News* the coveted Pulitzer Prize in 1932.

While *The News* was in its heyday, *The Star* began developing a reputation as "the businessmen's paper" and became recognized as well for its coverage of state government.

Purchased by Eugene C. Pulliam in 1944, *The Star* beefed up its sports pages, a women's section and launched a Sunday magazine in its attempt to overtake the two afternoon dailies — *The News* and *The Indianapolis Times*.

In 1948, with *The Star* having become the state's largest circulation paper, Pulliam purchased *The News* from the Fairbanks family and immediately began to consolidate and streamline business, circulation, production and advertising functions of the two newspapers. He moved *The News* into quarters adjacent to *The Star* on Pennsylvania Street (its current home) to save money.

The Times, a Scripps-Howard publication, folded in 1965, leaving the city with two major dailies.

Since 1948, *The Star's* circulation has steadily climbed to a current level of 237,367 papers sold daily (413,903 on Sunday), while the paper has received numerous honors including two Pulitzer Prize awards — one in 1975 for a series on police corruption and the other in 1991 for articles on medical malpractice.

The News, which celebrated its 125th anniversary in 1994, continues to battle declining circulation figures, reaching a low of 54,530 this year.

Despite the drop in circulation, the company has kept its pledge to publish an afternoon edition. However, the newsrooms of the two dailies are no longer separate. A merger was announced in May 1995 and was implemented four months later. In spite of the merger, the look of each newspaper is distinct, and each maintains its own separate editorial pages as well as columnists, crossword puzzles and comic strips. No layoffs resulted from the merger, and the newspaper remains a major employer in Indianapolis with 1,400 full-time workers and 500 part-timers. Also, there are 2,965 carriers.

In addition to publishing the two dailies, the newspaper prints a weekly zoned entertainment section called *US Express* that is delivered to more than a half-million households throughout the city and surrounding seven counties.

Indianapolis Business Journal
431 N. Pennsylvania St. • 634-6200

The *IBJ*, as this business weekly is called, is a must-read in offices all across town. More than 15 years old, this publication has found its niche by offering well-written, insightful business news. Owned by local businessman Michael Maurer, the tabloid-size paper can claim a circulation of approximately 17,000. The same company that publishes the IBJ also publishes two other business-related papers: the *Court*

& Commercial Record, a daily begun in 1895 as the *Indianapolis Commerical* that is devoted to detailed listings of law suits, building permits, bankruptcies and sheriff sales as well as related articles; and the *Indiana Lawyer*, a weekly tabloid focusing on the Indiana bar.

The Recorder
2901 N. Tacoma Ave. • 924-5143

The city's oldest continuously operating African-American newspaper was established in 1895 by George Pheldon Stewart and Will Porter; Stewart bought out his partner in 1899, and the paper remained in the Stewart family until the late 1980s. Local journalist Eunice Trotter bought the paper in 1988 and sold it to businessman William Mays in 1990. In the early '90s, the award-winning paper's weekly circulation stood at 15,000, and the paper continued to serve the African-American community with its news stories, issues analysis and religion section as well as arts, entertainment, sports and business coverage. Nationally syndicated columnist William Raspberry is a former *Recorder* employee.

Indiana Herald
2170 N. Illinois St. • 923-8291

One of only two African-American newspapers that continue to publish in Indianapolis, the *Herald* was established in 1949 as the *Hoosier Herald* and was known in the late '50s as the *Indiana Herald-Times*. Despite its name changes, the weekly paper continues to serve the city's African-American community. Its building received a spiffy facelift in 1996.

Topics Newspapers
9615 N. College Ave. • 844-3311

This string of 12 weeklies and one daily — including the *Noblesville Daily Ledger*, the *Fishers Sun-Herald*, the *Castleton Banner* and the *Carmel News-Tribune* — serves the northern Indianapolis suburbs.

NUVO Newsweekly
811 E. Westfield Blvd. • 254-2400

The city's only alternative newspaper, NUVO covers politics, social issues, music,

FYI
Unless otherwise noted, the area code for all phone numbers in this guide is 317.

film, arts and entertainment. Regular columns focus on visual arts, theater, jazz and dining. Launched in 1990, NUVO has developed a reputation for its investigative reporting on such topics as homelessness and police brutality. It also features comprehensive movie listings, restaurant reviews and racy "adult services" ads. It's available free every Thursday from numerous street-corner boxes, restaurants and businesses.

Magazines

Indianapolis Monthly
950 N. Meridian St. • 237-9288

An award-winning general interest magazine that spotlights local personalities, trends and issues, *Indianapolis Monthly* boasts lively writing, beautiful photos and a circulation of approximately 50,000. Readers look forward to the magazine's annual Best & Worst of Indianapolis each December as well as the People's Choice Restaurant Awards in May.

Issues IN Business
911 E. 86th St. • 257-8000

This monthly magazine, formerly called Indianpolis C.E.O, spotlights local business movers and shakers in addition to exploring business trends and issues from a feature perspective.

Indianapolis Woman
9000 Keystone Crossing • 580-0939

This publication has seen a lot of changes in its short lifespan. Originally called *Indy's Woman*, it was launched by *Indy's Child* (see specialty publications) in early 1994. It was sold a year later, and the name was changed to *Indianapolis Woman*. The monthly magazine, available free at numerous locations around town and also by subscription, covers business, health and lifestyle trends and spotlights local women in its cover stories. (Interestingly, an earlier publication called *Indianapolis Woman* — known as IW — which began publishing in September 1984 and later linked up with *City* magazine, ceased publication in August 1989 when *Indianapolis Monthly* owner Emmis Broadcasting bought and folded *City*.)

Indiana Business Magazine
1200 Waterway Blvd. • 692-1200

Established in 1957, *Indiana Business* can claim a statewide circulation of about 35,000. Though sold on the newsstand, most readers subscribe to the magazine for its focus on business features — the companies, people and issues behind the news. The magazine publishes monthly and also puts out two special issues: April's travel and meeting guide and August's corporate directory. The publishing company also puts out a visitors guide, available in hotel rooms around the city, called *WHERE Indianapolis*.

Hoosier Basketball Magazine
3750 N. Guion Rd. • 925-8200

In a state like Indiana, you've got to expect a magazine devoted to basketball. This massive annual, which began publishing more than 25 years ago, is the comprehensive guide to high school and college hoops, with an article on every high school and college team in the state, boys and girls, men and women. It also includes a page on the Indiana Pacers. The 250-plus page book comes out in November and is available on the newsstand for $4.95; by mail the hefty publication costs $7 with postage and handling.

Specialty Publications

Arts Indiana
47 S. Pennsylvania St. • 632-7894

With a circulation of about 12,000, this monthly publication covers a wide variety of arts-related news and features, spotlighting current issues and personalities in the visual, performing and literary arts throughout the state.

Indy's Child
8900 Keystone Crossing • 843-1494

This award-winning monthly parenting tabloid, established in 1984, covers issues related to children and families. It features a detailed monthly calendar as well as articles, regular columns, school and camp directories and special sections. The publication underwent a redesign and premiered its new "adult" look in May 1995. It's available free in libraries, bookstores, businesses and medical offices across town.

The Indianapolis Register
931 E. 86th St. • 253-7461

Names and faces are the focus of this monthly tabloid that recognizes people who make a difference in Indianapolis. Anybody who is anybody — especially any woman who is anybody — will likely find herself in the pages of this publication, especially if she is involved in any sort of charity or volunteer work. The Register includes a variety of special sections, including ones covering entertainment and business, and is available at libraries, bookstores and businesses around town.

The Criterion
1400 N. Meridian St. • 236-1570

Founded in 1960, *The Criterion*, a successor to the *Indiana Catholic and Record*, serves the Indiana Catholic community, focusing on events, advice and scripture with a circulation exceeding 50,000. The weekly tabloid receives no financial support from the archdiocese, but it does generally express the official Catholic position on Church issues.

Jewish Post & Opinion
2120 N. Meridian St. • 927-7800

Published weekly by the Spokesman Company, this approximately 5,000-circulation paper covers local Jewish events and organizations. *The National Jewish Post & Opinion*, published by the same company, reports on national and international events; the national paper is included with the local edition.

Senior Beacon
8935 N. Meridian St. • 571-0101

Dedicated to serving senior citizens of greater Indianapolis, the *Senior Beacon* includes a variety of short news stories, features and columns on such topics as finance, fitness and travel. The monthly tabloid is available free at locations around town.

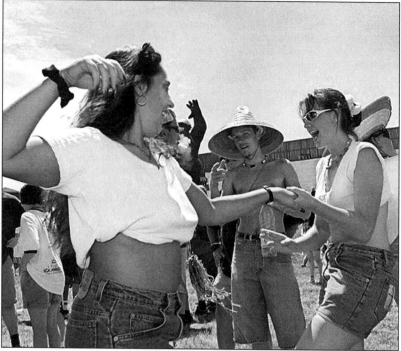

Photo: Kelly Wilkinson

Fans of Lollapalooza '96 at Deer Creek dance to the band.

Branches

P.O. Box 30348, Indianapolis 46230
• 255-5594

This bimonthly tabloid features a wide variety of articles on just about every aspect of whole-life living: spirituality, personal growth, health and the environment. The guide to services proves interesting as well; here you can find people who practice all sorts of body work, from Rolfing to acupuncture. *Branches* is available free at numerous locations, including coffeehouses and libraries.

Kids' Newsline

3409 W. Bando Ct. • 255-7466

Children and educators from around the city write and edit this monthly newspaper covering issues, ideas and activities relevant to students in grades kindergarten through 8. Distributed free to elementary and middle schoolers, the paper is also available at Indianapolis/Marion County libraries.

Teen Track

115 N. Pennsylvania St. • 638-0209

Written by local high school students, this hefty monthly tabloid focuses on issues, opinion, entertainment and sports. The not-for-profit publication, which relies on corporate, business and individual contributions, pays more than 60 teens from 32 area high schools for their work in putting out the paper.

Radio

Though radio stations are notoriously changeable, these were the call letters and formats as this book was written.

Arts and Information
WICR 88.7

Christian
WXIR 98.3 FM
WXLW 950 AM
WBRI 1500 AM
WNTS 1590 AM

Classical
WSYW 107.1 FM

Contemporary
WZPL 99.5 FM
WTLC 105.7 FM (urban)
WGGR 106.7 FM (urban)

Country
WFMS 95.5 FM
WGRL 104.5 FM

Easy Listening
WXTZ 93.9 FM
WTPI 107.9 FM

Gospel
WPZZ 95.9 FM
WTLC 1310 AM

News/Talk
WIBC 1070 AM
WNDE 1260 AM (and sports)

NPR, Jazz
WFYI 90.1 FM

Rock
WTTS 92.3 FM
WNAP 93.1 FM ('70s)
WFBQ 94.7 FM
WENS 97.1 FM (lite)
WRZX 103.3 FM

Oldies
WQFE 101.9 FM
WMYS 1430 AM

Top-40
WHHH 96.3 FM

Television

WFYI Channel 20, PBS station

1401 N. Meridian St. • 636-2020

This station went on the air in 1970 after an incredibly successful fund-raising campaign aimed at bringing public television to Indianapolis (see our feature in this chapter). Here's where you'll find such gems as *Sesame Street* and *Mr. Rogers' Neighborhood* and newer programs such as *Where in Time is Carmen San Diego*. In fact, more than 30 percent of the station's schedule is devoted to kids' programming. But this is also the place for the popular *This Old House* and *The New Yankee Workshop* as well as *The Frugal Gourmet*. And don't miss WFYI's signature program *Across Indiana*, a magazine-type show spotlighting the interesting, odd and unusual from across the state.

WISH-TV Channel 8, CBS affiliate
1950 N. Meridian St. • 923-8888

This station features the popular anchor team of Mike Ahern and Debby Knox. Ahern has been reporting locally for nearly 30 years, the longest tenure of any current newsperson. During that time, the station has won plenty of broadcasting awards, including a CASPER award (for community service) for its reporting during the blizzard of 1978. Famous alumni include former Today show co-host Jane Pauley.

WNDY Channel 23, Warner Bros. affiliate
4555 W. 16th St. • 241-2388

Formerly WMCC, this station, owned by the Hulman family (of the Indianapolis Motor Speedway), has become steadily stronger in sports programming in the last year or so; Indiana University coach Bobby Knight's basketball program now airs on Channel 23. Popular TV personality Reid Duffy, who developed the long-running segments *Duffy's World* and *Duffy's Diner* for Channel 6, signed on with Channel 23 after leaving WRTV. *The Hoosier Millionaire* lottery show also airs on this station, and there is talk that the station will develop a local newscast. Tune in the afternoon and you'll find such Warner Bros. cartoons as *The Animaniacs*.

WRTV Channel 6, ABC affiliate
1330 N. Meridian St. • 635-9788

Longtime anchor Howard Caldwell retired in 1994 after 35 years with this station; for years he epitomized local TV news. During that time, news programming at the station grew from 10-minute broadcasts to 90-minute

news shows, and it remains strong in local news. The station has earned its share of awards, including a 1989 CASPER for a documentary on police-community relations. It also produces the award-winning program *At the Zoo*, a show that goes behind the scenes at the Indianapolis Zoo.

WTHR Channel 13, NBC affiliate
1000 N. Meridian St. • 639-6397

Once deemed lackluster, this station saw considerable upgrading of its facilities and programming in the late 1970s. An increased emphasis on news resulted in numerous local awards, and former anchor Tom Cochrun won a national Emmy award for a 1982 documentary on the Ku Klux Klan. It switched network affiliates in 1979 and joined NBC (WRTV then became the local ABC affiliate). The station recently revived a former slogan and once again promotes its *Eyewitness News*.

WTTV Channel 4, Independent
3490 Bluff Rd. • 782-4444

This station first went on the air in 1949 and was located for a time in Bloomington (which made that southern Indiana city the smallest in the world to have a TV station). Though in its early days WTTV broadcast programs from all networks, it became an independent in 1957. It remains independent today, broadcasting a variety of syndicated shows and very popular college and high school sporting events, notably basketball. Its newest local program, *Hoosier Know It Alls*, has proved to be a hit as well. A whole generation of kids grew up watching its kiddie shows, and after a childhood of writing in to win its various contests, some of us still know its address by heart.

WXIN Channel 59, Fox affiliate
1440 N. Meridian St. • 632-5900

This station went on the air (as WPDS) in 1984; new owners changed the original call

INSIDERS' TIP

WFBQ's popular morning team of Bob Kevoian and Tom Griswold, known as Bob and Tom, are heard via syndication on stations across the state and throughout the country.

letters due to viewers confusing them with PBS and WTBS. In 1986, the station became the local Fox affiliate. It offers all the usual Fox favorites, plus a local 10 PM newscast that garnered notice due to its MTV-style visuals and efforts to reach a younger audience than traditional news shows. In the morning and afternoon, it's strong on kids' programming.

Public Programming

In 1970, Indianapolis ranked as the largest city in the country without a public television station. To change that and bring educational programming to Central Indiana, a group of 3,000 women hit the streets in the summer of 1970 and waged an effective door-to-door fund-raising campaign.

Led by community leader Ardath Y. Burkhart, "Ardath's Army" raised more than $300,000. On October 4 of that same year, working from a temporary studio at the Indianapolis Museum of Art, WFYI TV20 went on the air, beginning an educational and cultural mission that continues today.

October 1995 marked the station's 25th anniversary, and since going on the air with such PBS staples as *Sesame Street*, WFYI has also encouraged local programming. Its signature program, *Across Indiana*, hosted by Michael Atwood, has won regional Emmy Awards for best magazine format program for five straight years. The show, which profiles people and places across the state, was also recognized in the documentary category by the Indiana Film Society. You can see other local faces during the political panel discussions of *Indiana Week in Review* and, during the legislative session, *Indiana Lawmakers*.

In addition to television, WFYI FM 90.1 serves the listening community. A great deal of FM 90's programming is locally produced, including Sunday afternoon's *Nothin' But the Blues*.

Local support of WFYI runs strong. Though viewers and listeners long for even more local programming and complain about the telethon-like on-air fund-raising, viewer support provides a hefty percentage of WFYI's operating budget. In 1994, more than 1,000 volunteers provided more than 8,000 hours of service.

If you'd like to get involved with public television or radio in Indianapolis, call the station at 636-2020 and volunteer your services.

Photo: WFYI

Michael Atwood hosts WFYI's signature program "Across Indiana," which has won five straight regional Emmy Awards.

Religion has long played a significant role in the community life of Indianapolis and, as evidenced by the number and variety of churches and religious groups in the area, it still does.

Places
of Worship

From its earliest days, Indianapolis has been an ecumenical kind of place. As settlers made their way here, first from surrounding states, then gradually from the East Coast and Europe, they brought with them a potpourri of religious beliefs and practices. Those beliefs and practices, in turn, gave rise to discussion and debate during interdenominational meetings and revivals conducted by itinerant preachers. (One meeting spot favored by residents was a wooded knoll in the center of town, the precursor of today's Monument Circle.)

In 1823, settlers organized a Sunday school that attracted students from a variety of denominations. Two years later, the first religious group with a congregation large enough to require its own building (the Methodists) erected a log church just south of Washington Street, the tiny town's first official house of worship.

As transportation routes improved and more people made their way to Indianapolis, religious pluralism increased. Baptists, Catholics, Lutherans, Quakers, Presbyterians, Mormons, Episcopalians, Disciples of Christ, Unitarians and Jews settled here during the city's first few decades. Today, the Greater Indianapolis area is home to some 1,100 congregations spanning more than 100 denominations from African Methodist Episcopal to Zen Buddhism. While Protestantism and Catholicism predominate, there are an array of other religions and sects represented throughout Central Indiana.

This region is also home to a number of religious organizations, including the Church Federation of Indianapolis, the Islamic Society of North America and the Christian Theological Seminary. (For more on each of these groups, see the "Religious Organizations" section of this chapter.)

Religion has long played a significant role in the community life of Indianapolis and, as evidenced by the number and variety of churches and religious groups in the area, it still does. What follows is an overview of religious life and worship options in the area. By no means is it comprehensive, but we hope it will give you a sense of what's available here. Think of it as a spiritual snapshot of sorts.

Places of Worship

Bethany Lutheran Church
4702 S. East St. • 786-7854

Under the leadership of Rev. Robert C. Rohrman Jr., senior pastor, Bethany expanded its facilities in 1995, adding a new narthex and a two-story educational wing with 13 additional classrooms. In 1996 the church started its Day Care Center that is open to the public. A member of the ELCA, the church is conveniently located at the I-465 and U.S. 31 South interchange.

Bethel African Methodist Episcopal (AME) Church
414 W. Vermont St. • 634-7002

Organized in 1836, Bethel AME is the oldest continually operating African-American church in the city. And as it has been from the beginning, the church is active in social and racial issues. Once a station on the Underground Railroad, later the founding place of the Indianapolis chapter of the NAACP, Bethel today continues to serve those in need: the poor, the elderly, the young, both within and outside its congregation.

Bethel AME's downtown building, constructed in the 1870s, is the only African-American church structure in Indianapolis currently listed on the National Register of Historic Places.

Central Christian Church (Disciples of Christ)
701 N. Delaware St. • 635-6397

Since 1833, Central Christian (which calls itself "the Church of Christ in Indianapolis") has been ministering to the spiritual and social needs of city residents. Today, in addition to its Sunday morning services and church school session, it maintains an active community outreach program that serves those in need throughout the downtown area, especially the elderly and the disadvantaged. The church's motto is "Thinking, Accepting, Acting," and its congregation and pastoral staff takes those words to heart.

Christ Church Cathedral
125 Monument Cir. • 636-4577

At one time in the mid-19th century there were five churches on the Circle downtown. But by 1884, Christ Church was the only one left: The others moved to new locations as the city expanded and their congregations left downtown's Mile Square district.

Today, the lovely little Gothic church on the Circle, once the subject of a book, *The Little Church on the Circle*, by pharmaceutical magnate and benefactor Eli Lilly, is one of the city's treasures. In addition to serving as the cathedral for the local Episcopal diocese and as parish church for its 750-member congregation, Christ Church also conducts two well-respected music programs: the Christ Church Cathedral Choir of Men and Boys, which holds an annual concert series at the church; and an ongoing (though occasional) lunchtime organ music series. Christ Church Cathedral host the Annual Strawberry Festival in June, serving homemade shortcake, ice cream, straw-

berries and whip cream to raise money for charities.

The church structure is listed on the National Register of Historic Places. Weekday visitors are welcome, either on an informal drop-in basis or on a call-ahead formal tour basis. There are also tours available following Sunday services.

East 91st Street Christian Church
6049 E. 91st St. • 849-1261

This 70-plus-year-old church had been under the leadership of senior minister Dr. Russell Blowers from 1951 until his retirement in 1996. During Dr. Blowers' tenure the church has expanded: Average Sunday attendance is about 2,500, while the congregation itself numbers more than 3,000.

In addition to three Sunday morning worship services (two traditional and one contemporary) and Bible school classes for all ages, East 91st Street Christian Church offers its members a variety of other programs including home Bible study groups, a weekday preschool program and ministerial counseling. The church also hosts a number of support groups: There are groups for singles, for people recovering from divorces, for infertile couples and for battered and abused women.

Additionally, it sponsors outreach programs such as ministries for seniors and hospital-bound people as well as local missions that undertake such projects as building Habitat for Humanity houses. The church's growth and success have spawned nine daughter churches throughout the Indianapolis area.

Englewood Christian Church
57 N. Rural Ave. • 639-1541

This east-side church focuses on service both to God and to humankind. Through their Englewood Neighborhood Christian Ministries program, the church's staff and congregation operate food and clothing pantries that benefit needy individuals and families in the surrounding low-income neighborhood. They also operate an outreach program for area children, providing them a safe alternative to the streets, positive recreational activities and compassionate adults to talk to.

First Baptist Church of Indianapolis
8600 N. College Ave. • 846-5821

Established in 1822 by 15 of Indianapolis' early settlers who met in a log schoolhouse, First Baptist Church today has a congregation of some 650 members. The church's northside complex includes a sanctuary for 600-plus, a fellowship hall and 18 classrooms. There's also an on-site gym and shelter house, as well as baseball diamonds and tennis courts, symbols of First Baptist's popular youth athletics program that serves some 2,000 youngsters.

First Lutheran Church
701 N. Pennsylvania St. • 635-9505

As its name states, this church was the first Lutheran institution established in Indianapolis. Organized in 1837 by 20 local families, First Lutheran's first pastor was Abraham Reck, an advocate of a more liberal form of Lutheranism than that practiced in Europe: He believed other denominations and religious practices had spiritual values as valid as those of Lutheranism. He also believed in himself: In addition to First Lutheran, Reck organized and led five other area congregations.

Given its origins, First Lutheran has long been associated with interdenominational efforts and social welfare concerns. From its Romanesque Revival-style (c.1887) structure downtown, the church's congregation operates programs for youth and the elderly.

Grace Apostolic Church
649 E. 22nd St. • 925-8103

Gracing the southwest corner of the 22nd Street and College Avenue intersection is the stunning white building that houses Grace Apostolic. Designed by Walter Blackburn, a local African-American architect whose work has earned him national acclaim, the contemporary structure is an intriguing combination of angles and glass, at once formal and friendly.

Grace Apostolic is home to a variety of worship opportunities, including a number of prayer meetings and Bible study sessions throughout the week, Sunday morning and evening services and church school. One Sunday service is broadcast on local FM radio station WTLC. Grace Apostolic is affiliated with the "oneness" branch of the Pentecostal Church.

Greek Orthodox Church of the Holy Trinity
4011 N. Pennsylvania St. • 283-3816

One of six Eastern Orthodox churches in the Indianapolis area, this facility is the only one serving Orthodox followers of Greek descent. With approximately 1,000 families on its membership rolls, Holy Trinity is the largest Orthodox church in the city.

While it takes part in local efforts to diminish the importance of the ethnic and political differences that separate Eastern Orthodox congregations, Holy Trinity also celebrates its Greek heritage by hosting the annual Greek Festival, a weekend-long event that brings thousands of people from throughout the city to the church's Meridian Kessler location to eat Greek food and dance to Greek music.

Indianapolis Baptist Temple
2711 S. East St. • 765-6753

Under the leadership of the Rev. Greg Dixon, this south-side church has grown from a small group of founders in 1950 to its present status as one of the city's largest congregations, numbering more than 5,000 members. Its services have been broadcast nationwide.

A controversial figure locally and nationally, Rev. Dixon has garnered a lot of press for his involvement in the Moral Majority (he was a founding member) and Right-to-Life movements. He is also a leader in the fight to achieve absolute separation of church and state; Rev. Dixon refuses to recognize or abide by any local, state or federal regulations regarding the operation of a church or any of its related operations such as schools, daycare centers, etc. As such, the Indianapolis Baptist Temple is an unincorporated entity and one of the city's best-known churches.

Indianapolis Hebrew Congregation
6501 N. Meridian St. • 255-6647

Organized in 1856, the Indianapolis Hebrew Congregation was the first Jewish congregation in Indianapolis. Since the beginning,

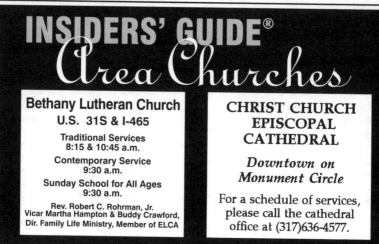

the IHC, an adherent to the liberal beliefs and practices of Reform Judaism, has been involved with community and social concerns. Through the years, the congregation has played an active role in the creation of the local Red Cross chapter and the Humane Society, opposed the Ku Klux Klan, participated in the Civil Rights movement and developed programs for both young people and the elderly.

Today, the IHC continues to be active beyond the walls of its N. Meridian Street synagogue, most recently as one of the founding members of the Interfaith Alliance, an ecumenical organization directed at establishing communication and cooperation among area denominations.

Light of the World Christian Church
5640 E. 38th St. • 547-2273

Founded in 1866 as a missionary project of an existing Christian Church (Disciples of Christ) congregation, Light of the World was originally known as Second Christian Church. Focused specifically on serving the black community, by the turn of the century the church had become one of the most prestigious in the city. In 1984, the church changed its name to Light of the World Christian Church.

Today, Light of the World has a congregation in excess of 3,000 as well as a cable television ministry with a nationwide broadcast audience of some 35 million. While it remains primarily an African-American institution, the church also joins with white churches periodically to host interracial services aimed at breaking down racial barriers and establishing common ground through worship.

Masjid al-Fajr Mosque and Islamic Center of Greater Indianapolis
2846 Cold Spring Rd. • 923-2847

This small, elegant mosque is home to one of the city's independent African-American Muslim groups. In addition to ministering to the needs of its members, al-Fajr also provides educational and informational materials to those who want to learn about Islam and takes an active role in issues and concerns affecting the black community.

Roberts Park United Methodist Church
401 N. Delaware St. • 635-1636

Named for Indiana's first Methodist bishop Robert R. Roberts, Roberts Park United Methodist Church was established in 1842. Twenty-seven years later the church moved from its original chapel to its present downtown building, a Romanesque structure based on the Temple of London. Now on the National Register of Historic Places, the church was built from Indiana limestone and black walnut, the latter milled from trees cut to make room for the church.

Throughout its history, Roberts Park has been active in civic affairs, including setting up the city's first public library, sponsoring the city's first religious radio broadcasts and using its facilities as a USO site during World War II. Though the years have taken its toll on membership (from a high of 1,700 members in the 1940s, the congregation today numbers some 425 who are mostly commuters from the suburbs), Roberts Park remains a vital presence in the religious and community life of the downtown area with programs focused on serving downtown workers, young people and the elderly.

St. John Catholic Church
126 W. Georgia St. • 637-3941

Across the street from Pan Am Plaza, in the shadow of the Indiana Convention Center and RCA Dome, St. John is the city's oldest Catholic parish. Founded in 1840 as the Church of the Holy Cross, the church was given its present name in 1850. While its congregation has dwindled over the years, attendance benefits from St. John's location as conventioneers and tourists boost daily and weekend Mass totals.

The present double-spired brick building was constructed between 1867 and 1871 and is now listed on the National Register of Historic Places.

St. Luke's United Methodist Church
100 W. 86th St. • 846-3404

United Methodists form the largest Protestant denomination in Indianapolis, a fact that St. Luke's physical layout seems to emphasize. The church and grounds spread out across acres of prime north-side real estate, a testament to the power and affluence of its congregation. But the church is also big on compassion and commitment to the multitude of needs that exist in the community. Aside from its Sunday worship services and Sunday school sessions, it hosts a variety of special interest groups for singles, widows and widowers, teens, the deaf and people with HIV-AIDS.

As evidenced by the playing fields scattered around the grounds, St. Luke's sponsors a number of youth and adult sports programs. It also provides meeting space to Boy Scout and Girl Scout troops, drama clubs and health workshops. And the church is active in outreach missionary work throughout the city and abroad.

St. Paul's Episcopal Church
10 W. 61st St. • 253-1277

On a prominent bend in Meridian Street at 61st Street, St. Paul's is hard to miss — so is the large, round stained-glass window that dominates one wall overlooking Meridian. In addition to three Sunday morning services, St. Paul's offers a Montessori-style Sunday school program for children, a youth ministry for adolescents, a health ministry (there's an R.N. on staff) and a music program complete with individualized instruction for children and adults.

SS. Peter and Paul Cathedral
1347 N. Meridian St. • 634-4519

This regal structure on the northern edge of the downtown district is center of the Indianapolis archdiocese and home of the Catholic archbishop. With a facade of Indiana limestone and an interior that includes marble statuary, mosaics and stained glass, the cathedral combines stateliness and spirituality.

In addition to serving as the parish for a small downtown congregation, the cathedral also hosts special Masses, Confirmations and Holy Order ceremonies.

Second Presbyterian Church
7700 N. Meridian St. • 253-6461

One of the oldest churches in the city, Second Presbyterian also has one of the city's largest congregations (more than 3,200 members) and one of its most prominent church buildings on one of its most prominent streets. And then there's the history.

Second Prez, as the church is informally known, was founded in 1838, and its first pastor (1839-1849) was Henry Ward Beecher who went on to a pastoral post in Brooklyn, New York, where he became one of 19th-century America's most outspoken opponents of slavery and one of its best-known orators. During his years in Indianapolis, Beecher not only introduced many of the ideas that later earned him national attention, ideas on slavery, morality and education, he also took an active role in civic affairs.

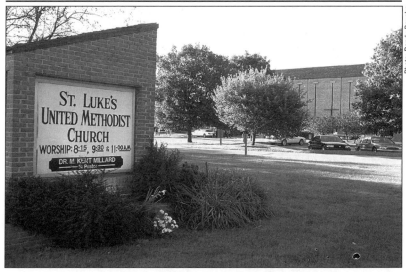

Photo: Randy Baughn

St. Luke's United Methodist Church sponsors a number of different programs
for people of all ages.

Taking a cue from Beecher, another of the church's pastors, William Hudnut III, went on to regional and national prominence on the basis of his involvement in the community. After nearly a decade (1964-1973) at the helm of Second Presbyterian, Hudnut was elected mayor of Indianapolis, a post he held for an unprecedented 16 years (1976-1992). It was Hudnut who helped guide the city out of the doldrums of the 1970s and into the spotlight as one of the country's revitalized cities in the 1980s.

The church's huge French Gothic structure is magnificent with its gorgeous stained-glass windows and its glorious pipe organ. And in its magnificence, it symbolizes the power and status that has long been associated with its congregation.

Yet for all its wealth and influence, Second Prez retains compassion, reaching out to people in need through a variety of social programs and urban ministries.

Tabernacle Presbyterian Church
418 E. 34th St. • 923-5458

Housed in a stately limestone structure at the corner of 34th Street and Central Avenue, Tabernacle calls itself "an urban, evangelical church with a metropolitan mission." That mis-

sion manifests itself in a variety of ways through programs designed to meet the spiritual, social and emotional needs of the congregation and the community-at-large. Tabernacle hosts support groups, offers counseling sessions and operates a large-scale youth sports program that provides some 1,500 young people ages 6 to 14 opportunities to participate in basketball, football, softball and soccer activities.

Tabernacle holds three Sunday morning services and two church-school sessions. There are on-site facilities to assist hearing-impaired and physically disabled individuals take part in worship services.

Trinity Episcopal Church
3243 N. Meridian • 926-1346

With a unique and diverse congregation, Trinity blends the great worship and music traditions of the Anglican Church with innovative programs, a thriving children's and youth program, and a mission that nurtures both parish members and the larger community.

Zion Evangelical United
Church of Christ
416 E. North St. • 639-5411

This downtown church has a heritage that spans more than 150 years, making it one of the oldest places of worship in the city. Originally founded by a group of German Reformed and Lutheran immigrants, Zion Evangelical now has a diverse congregation. In addition to Sunday services, the church offers programs for women, young people and seniors. It also plays an active role in its neighborhood through an outreach program (it supports four downtown homeless shelters) and takes part in missionary and relief programs throughout the world. Classes, groups and camping are offered for children and youth.

Religious Organizations

Christian Theological Seminary (CTS)
1000 W. 42nd St. • 924-1331

Formerly affiliated with the Disciples of Christ and Butler University, CTS is now an independent school of graduate studies for individuals preparing for the ministry. Calling itself an "ecumenical seminary," CTS not only offers a preordination Master of Divinity program, but also masters-level programs in church music, religious education, religious studies and pastoral counseling. See our Education chapter for more information.

The Church Federation of Greater Indianapolis
1100 W. 42nd St. • 926-5371

Since its creation in 1912, the Church Federation, which today consists of clergy and laypersons from Protestant and Catholic congregations throughout Central Indiana, has addressed not only religious concerns but also social and community issues. Included among the Federation's areas of ongoing involvement are race relations, police-community relations, religious education, youth activities and chaplaincies in hospitals and other public institutions.

Church Women United
• (800) 298-5551

Founded in 1898 as the Missionary Social Union of Indianapolis, this organization has a history of supporting a number of religious and social programs in the city. With a current membership of some 500 women from 300 churches and 15 denominations, CWU supports such local projects as Wheeler Mission Ministries (see entry in this section) and takes part in such annual events as World Day of Prayer and May Fellowship Day.

Damien Center
1350 N. Pennsylvania St. • 632-0123

A joint project of an Episcopal institution (Christ Church Cathedral) and a Roman Catholic one (SS. Peter and Paul Cathedral), the Damien Center provides education, counseling and psychosocial services to individuals with the HIV virus and to their friends and families.

Dayspring Center
1537 Central Ave. • 635-6780

Established by the Indianapolis Episcopal Metropolitan Council in 1989, the Dayspring Center provides food, temporary housing and other forms of assistance to homeless families. It's the only family shelter in Indiana that has an on-site Head Start program. With a staff of fewer than 20 people, Dayspring relies on more than 250 volunteers to help provide services and on financial aid from government agencies, churches and individuals to help underwrite its expenses.

Disciples of Christ
222 S. Downey Ave. • 353-1491

This is the international headquarters for the Disciples of Christ, a branch of the Christian Church that claims some 17,000 members in the Indianapolis area. From these offices, the Disciples organization oversees a number of operations, including domestic and overseas ministries, finances, church services, a council on Christian unity and a foundation.

Indiana Catholic Conference (ICC)
1400 N. Meridian St. • 236-1455

This is the lobbying arm of the Catholic Church in Indiana. The ICC represents the state's five archdioceses in the halls and chambers of the State Capitol, talking with legislators about the Church's stance on such legislative issues as abortion, capital punishment, school choice and private school vouchers. ICC also sends periodic updates on state and national legislative matters to Catholics throughout the state.

Indiana Interreligious Commission on Human Equality (IICHE)
1100 W. 42nd St. • 924-4226

Founded in 1968 to promote interracial and interreligious communication, the IICHE is made up of 21 members from various religious organizations. Over the course of its history, the commission has dealt with such issues as school desegregation, human rights abuses and discrimination among social service providers. It has also established interracial and interreligious discussion groups, and it sponsors the annual Dr. Martin Luther King Jr. Essay Contest, which is open to schoolchildren around the state.

Islamic Society of North America (ISNA)
Old State Rd. 267, Plainfield • 839-8157

An Orthodox Muslim organization, the ISNA provides Muslim immigrants in the United States and Canada with the support and information they need to establish themselves in their new homes. Its Plainfield compound includes a mosque and offices for the Muslim Students Association and the North American Islamic Trust. The ISNA provides educational materials to Muslims and others interested in learning about Islam.

Lighthouse Ministries
121 S. Pennsylvania St. • 636-0301

A nonprofit, nondenominational, inner-city mission for indigent men, Lighthouse was established in 1952 by Rev. Charles Oldham. The mission provides food, lodging and clothing, healthcare and job-training services to homeless males. All of Lighthouse's $1 million-plus budget comes from private donations.

Wheeler Mission Ministries
222 E. Ohio St. • 635-3575

Named in honor of its founder William V. Wheeler, who opened the Rescue Mission and Home of Indianapolis in 1893, Wheeler Mission Ministries provides a variety of services to those in need. In addition to its downtown shelter for homeless men, which includes free meals and medical care, the organization operates a camp for families and young people, a home for abused teenage girls and a mothers' club. Wheeler Mission relies primarily on contributions from individuals to meet its financial needs, though it also receives some funding from area churches and businesses.

Religious Publications

The Criterion
1400 N. Meridian St. • 236-1570

A weekly newspaper, *The Criterion* focuses on issues and concerns of interest to area Catholics. See our Media chapter for more information.

Jewish Post and Opinion
2120 N. Meridian St. • 927-7800

This weekly newspaper is actually two publications in one. The first, the *Indiana Jewish Post and Opinion*, focuses on matters of interest to members of Jewish communities around the state. The second, the *National Jewish Post and Opinion*, includes articles and columns of national interest; it's included in the Indiana edition. See our Media chapter for more information.

Religious Broadcasting Companies

WKOG TV 31
1400 N. Meridian St. • 931-0310

Operated by Kingdom of God Broadcasting, this cable TV station broadcasts Catholic religious programming 24 hours a day, though as this book went to press, none of the local cable outlets carried WKOG.

Advertisers Index

Index

Symbols

A

C

S

X

Y

Z

Going Somewhere?

Insiders' Publishing Inc. presents 40 current and upcoming titles to popular destinations all over the country (including the titles below) — and we're planning on adding many more. To order a title, go to your local bookstore or call (800) 765-2665 ext. 238 and we'll direct you to one.

Atlanta, GA

Boca Raton and the Palm Beaches, FL

Boulder, CO, and Rocky Mountain National Park

Bradenton/Sarasota, FL

Branson, MO, and the Ozark Mountains

Cape Cod, Martha's Vineyard and Nantucket, MA

Charleston, SC

Cincinnati, OH

Civil War Sites in the Eastern Theater

Denver, CO

Florida Keys and Key West

Florida's Great Northwest

Golf in the Carolinas

Indianapolis, IN

The Lake Superior Region

Lexington, KY

Louisville, KY

Maine's Mid-Coast

Minneapolis/St. Paul, MN

Mississippi

Myrtle Beach, SC

North Carolina's Central Coast and New Bern

North Carolina's Mountains

Outer Banks of North Carolina

The Pocono Mountains

Relocation

Richmond, VA

Southwestern Utah

Tampa/St. Petersburg, FL

Virginia's Blue Ridge

Virginia's Chesapeake Bay

Washington, D.C.

Wichita, KS

Williamsburg, VA

Wilmington, NC

THE INSIDERS' GUIDE ®

Insiders' Publishing Inc. • P.O. Box 2057 • Manteo, NC 27954
Phone (919) 473-6100 • Fax (919) 473-5869 • INTERNET address: http://www.insiders.com